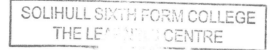
The Long Road to Peace in Northern Ireland

The Long Road to Peace in Northern Ireland

Peace Lectures from the Institute of Irish Studies at Liverpool University

Edited by
Marianne Elliott

SECOND EDITION

LIVERPOOL UNIVERSITY PRESS

First published 2002 by
Liverpool University Press
4 Cambridge Street
Liverpool, L69 7ZU

Revised second edition published 2007

British Library Cataloguing-in-Publication Data
A British Library CIP Record is available

ISBN 978-1-84631-065-2

Printed and bound in the European Union
by Bell and Bain Ltd, Glasgow

In memory of Torkel Opsahl and Eric Gallagher

Contents

Acknowledgements   *page* ix
List of Contributors   x
List of Illustrations   xiv

Introduction to Revised Edition   1
Marianne Elliott

Introduction   3
Marianne Elliott

Achieving Transformational Change   11
Sir George Quigley

The Resolution of Armed Conflict: Internationalization and its Lessons,
Particularly in Northern Ireland   25
Lord David Owen

Some Reflections on Successful Negotiation in South Africa   44
Frederik Van Zyl Slabbert

The Secrets of the Oslo Channels: Lessons from Norwegian Peace
Facilitation in the Middle East, Central America and the Balkans   54
Jan Egeland

The Awakening: Irish-America's Key Role in the Irish Peace Process   67
Niall O'Dowd

'Give Us Another MacBride Campaign': An Irish-American Contribution
to Peaceful Change in Northern Ireland   78
Kevin McNamara

Towards Peace in Northern Ireland   89
Senator George Mitchell

Neither Orange March nor Irish Jig: Finding Compromise in Northern
Ireland   96
Senator Maurice Hayes

Mountain-climbing Irish-style: The Hidden Challenges of the Peace Process 109
Martin Mansergh

The Good Friday Agreement: A Vision for a New Order in Northern
Ireland   119
Peter Mandelson

Hillsborough to Belfast: Is It the Final Lap?   124
Sir David Goodall

Defining Republicanism: Shifting Discourses of New Nationalism and
Post-republicanism   133
Kevin Bean

Conflict, Memory and Reconciliation   147
Paul Arthur

Keeping Going: Beyond Good Friday   157
Harvey Cox

Religion and Identity in Northern Ireland   175
Marianne Elliott

Getting to Know the 'Other': Inter-church Groups and Peace-building
in Northern Ireland   192
Maria Power

Enduring Problems: The Belfast Agreement and a Disagreed Belfast   207
Peter Shirlow and Colin Coulter

Appendices: Key Recommendations of:

 1. The Sunningdale Agreement (December 1973)   223

 2. The Anglo-Irish (Hillsborough) Agreement (November 1985)   228

 3. The Opsahl Commission (June 1993)   234

 4. The Downing Street Joint Declaration (December 1993)   249

 5. The Framework Document (1995)   254

 6. The Good Friday (Belfast) Agreement (April 1998)   265

 7. The Report of the Northern Ireland Victims Commission
    (Sir Kenneth Bloomfield, 1998)   276

 8. The Patten Report (1999)   280

 9. Review of the Parades Commission (Sir George Quigley,
    Sept. 2002), extracts   296

Index   306

Acknowledgements

The editor would like to thank all the contributors; Lord David Owen for conceiving the series of lectures and for his sustained support throughout the project; the Irish Independent newspaper group and the charity *Humanitas* for funding the lecture series; David McCormack of Pacemaker for the illustrations; Robin Bloxsidge, Andrew Kirk, Helen Tookey and the rest of the staff at Liverpool University Press; Paul Arthur for taking time out from a hectic schedule to read the final text; and from the Institute of Irish Studies, Harvey Cox, Linda Christiansen, Tracey Holsgrove and most of all Dorothy Lynch, for her dedication, patience and good humour throughout. I doubt it would have seen the light of day without her.

The publishers are grateful to the following for permission to reproduce copyright material: extract from 'Cease-fire' from *The Ghost Orchid* by Michael Longley published by Jonathan Cape, by permission of the Random House Group Limited; extracts from 'An Irishman in Coventry' and 'The Colony' by John Hewitt by permission of Blackstaff Press; extract from *The Cure at Troy* by Seamus Heaney by permission of Faber and Faber Limited; extract from *The Tain* translated by Thomas Kinsella by permission of the author.

List of Contributors

Professor Paul Arthur
Paul Arthur was born in Derry and educated at Queen's University, Belfast. He is Professor of Politics and Course Director of the Graduate Programme in Peace and Conflict Studies at the University of Ulster. He was Senior Fellow at the United States Institute of Peace, Washington, DC, 1997–8. He is a frequent political commentator on Northern Ireland and author of a large number of books and articles on Northern Ireland, notably *Special Relationships: Britain, Ireland and the Northern Ireland Problem* (Blackstaff Press, 2001).

Dr Kevin Bean
Lecturer in Irish Politics at the Institute of Irish Studies, University of Liverpool. He has contributed articles to a number of publications, including *Irish Studies Review*, *Fortnight* (Belfast) and the *Sunday Tribune* (Dublin), and his book, *The New Politics of Sinn Féin*, will be published by Liverpool University Press in 2007.

Dr Colin Coulter
Lectures in the Department of Sociology, the National University of Ireland, Maynooth. He is the author of *Contemporary Northern Irish Society: An Introduction* (Pluto Press, 1999) and the co-editor (with Michael Murray) of *Northern Ireland After the Troubles: A Society in Transition* (Manchester University Press, 2007).

Harvey Cox
Taught politics and Irish studies at Liverpool University and was deputy director of the Institute of Irish Studies until 2002. His publications include chapters and articles on Northern Ireland in a number of books and academic journals. He has been engaged for many years in the management of peace work of the Society of Friends in Britain and Ireland.

Dr Jan Egeland
From Norway and currently Special Advisor to the United Nations Secretary-General on matters relating to the prevention and resolution of conflict, formerly Under-Secretary-General for Humanitarian Affairs and Emergency Relief Co-ordinator with the United Nations. He has had a distinguished career in human rights and peace work, with the Norwegian Government, the Red Cross and Red Crescent

Movement, Amnesty International and a number of other non-governmental and academic institutions. He co-initiated and co-organized the Norwegian channel between Israel and the PLO in 1992, which led to the Oslo Peace Agreement of 1993, and facilitated peace talks between the Guatemalan government and the URNG guerrilla movement, which culminated in the ceasefire of 1996. In 1993 he was deputy to UN mediator, Thorvald Stoltenberg, in the former Yugoslavia peace talks, and helped facilitate the release of prisoners of war and direct talks between Serbs, Croats and Bosnian Muslims. He has published a number of articles, reports and books.

Professor Marianne Elliott FBA
Born and educated in Northern Ireland, graduate of Queen's University, Belfast and Oxford University, Director of the Institute of Irish Studies at Liverpool University, author of a number of books and articles including *Wolfe Tone: Prophet of Irish Independence*, *The Catholics of Ulster: A History*, and *Robert Emmet: The Making of a Legend*. Member of the Opsahl Commission in 1993 and joint author of its report, *A Citizens' Inquiry*; co-founder of the Conference of Irish Historians in Britain, board member of British-Irish Encounter. She was awarded an OBE in 2000 for services to Irish Studies and the Northern Ireland Peace Process.

Sir David Goodall GCMG
Former chairman of the Leonard Cheshire Foundation, the British-Irish Association and Anglo-Irish Encounter. Head of the Western European Department of the Foreign Office, 1975–9; Minister in Bonn, 1979–82; was seconded to the Cabinet Office as Deputy Secretary, 1982–4; and was British High Commissioner to India, 1987–91. During his time in the Cabinet Office and Foreign Office between 1984 and 1987 he was one of the architects of the 1985 Anglo-Irish Agreement. He is a visiting professor at Liverpool's Institute of Irish Studies.

Senator Maurice Hayes MRIA
Member of the Irish Senate, Chairman of Ireland's National Forum on Europe and Chairman of the Ireland Fund. He was previously Northern Ireland Ombudsman, assistant secretary to the power-sharing executive in 1974, adviser to the chairman of the Constitutional Convention in 1975, Permanent Secretary in the Northern Ireland Department of Health and Social Services and a member of the Patten Commission in 1999. He is a frequent contributor to various journals and newspapers and his books include his autobiographical *Minority Verdict: Experiences of a Catholic Civil Servant* (1995).

Dr Kevin McNamara
MP for Hull North 1966–2005, chairman of the all-party Irish in Britain Parliamentary Group and vice-chairman of the British-Irish Inter-Parliamentary Body 1997–2005; principal Opposition spokesman on Northern Ireland, 1987–94. In 2006 he completed a PhD thesis on the MacBride Principles at the Institute of Irish Studies, University of Liverpool.

Peter Mandelson
EU Commissioner for Trade since 2004 and Hon. Chair of Policy Network (to promote centre-left policy ideas); MP for Hartlepool 1992–2004, Secretary of State for Northern Ireland 1999–2001, Secretary of State for Trade and Industry in 1998 and Minister without Portfolio in the Cabinet Office 1997–8. He was the Labour party's election campaign manager from January 1996. He was appointed an Opposition Whip in October 1995.

Dr Martin Mansergh
Fianna Fáil TD for Tipperary South, formerly member of the Irish Senate, special adviser to the Taoiseach on Northern Ireland, Economic and Social Matters, part of the Irish delegation that negotiated the Good Friday Agreement, co-winner of the 1994 Tipperary Peace Prize for behind-the-scenes contacts with the republican movement that led to the Downing Street Declaration in 1993. He was awarded his Doctorate in French History by Oxford University in 1974 and is author of numerous published articles on the peace process and on other political and historical matters, most notably *The Legacy of History* (2003).

Senator George J. Mitchell
Chairman of the Commission which produced the Good Friday Agreement in Northern Ireland. He was senator for the state of Maine from 1980 until his retirement in 1995. Served as Senate Majority Leader from 1989 to 1995. That year, he became President Clinton's special adviser on Irish economic affairs. Among his numerous awards and honours is the Presidential Medal of Freedom, the highest civil honour bestowed by the US Government

Niall O'Dowd
Founder and publisher of *Irish America* magazine and *Irish Voice* newspaper, the two largest Irish-American publications. A graduate of University College, Dublin, he is a native of Thurles, Tipperary, Ireland, who emigrated to the United States in 1979. He was the central figure in bringing President Clinton into the peace process and in 1997 was awarded the Irish American Peace Prize for his work on behalf of the Irish peace process. He has been named one of the 100 most influential Irish people worldwide by the *Sunday Tribune* newspaper.

The Rt Hon. the Lord Owen CH
MP for Plymouth 1966–92; former Navy and Health Minister; Foreign Secretary, 1977–79; co-founder of the SDP and its leader 1983–90; EU co-chairman of the International Conference on Former Yugoslavia, 1992–95; Chancellor of the University of Liverpool, 1996–; director of the Centre for International Health and Co-operation.

Dr Maria Power
Lecturer at the Institute of Irish Studies, University of Liverpool. She is a graduate of the University of London and was formally an ESRC Post-Doctoral Fellow at the Institute of Irish Studies. Her publications include *From Ecumenism to*

Community Relations: Inter-Church Relationships in Northern Ireland 1980–2005 (Irish Academic Press, 2006) as well as other articles on the role of the churches in peace-building in Northern Ireland. She is currently researching the history of post-war mixed communities in Northern Ireland.

Sir George Quigley
Chairman of Bombardier Aerospace and Lothbury Property Trust and a director of Independent News and Media (UK). Formerly Permanent Secretary, successively, of the NI Departments of Manpower Services, Commerce, Finance, and Finance and Personnel; Chairman of the Ulster Bank, from 1989, Chairman of Shorts Brothers Ltd, Chairman of the Royal Bank of Scotland Pension Fund. He also served on the Dearing Committee on Higher Education and was President of the Economic and Social Research Institute and of the International Trade Institute of the Republic of Ireland and of the NI Economic Council. In 2001 he was appointed by Government to conduct a Review of the NI Parades Commission, which reported in Sept. 2002. In 1997 he received the Compaq Lifetime Achievement Award for promoting cross-border economic co-operation.

Dr Peter Shirlow
Senior Lecturer in Criminology at Queen's University Belfast. He is co-author of *Belfast: Segregation, Violence and the City* (Pluto Press, 2006). He has been involved in a series of intitiatives aimed at exploring intra- and inter-community-based conflict transformation. He is currently working on issues regarding the inclusion of politically motivated former prisoners.

Dr Frederik Van Zyl Slabbert
Former leader of the PFP (Progressive Federal Party). Co-founder of the IDASA (Institute for a Democratic Alternative for South Africa), and the key person bringing together a number of prominent groups in the South African conflict. Since the move away from apartheid he has chaired forums to bring about democratic transition. He is chairman of the Open Society Foundation of South Africa as well as of the Goree Institute for Democracy, Development and Culture. He runs his own investment company and is the author of numerous books and articles.

List of Illustrations

1 Garret Fitzgerald and Margaret Thatcher signing the Anglo-Irish (Hillsborough) Agreement, November 1985

2 Unionists protesting against the Anglo-Irish Agreement

3 President Clinton's visit to Northern Ireland in December 1995

4 Senator George Mitchell speaking in Liverpool

5, 6 Peace wall in West Belfast

7 Celebrations after the 'Yes' vote in the referendum on the Good Friday Agreement, 1998

8 First Minister Ian Paisley and Deputy First Minister Martin McGuinness with Irish PM Bertie Ahern, British PM Tony Blair and Peter Hain, Secretary of State for Northern Ireland, after the establishment of the Northern Ireland Assembly in May 2007

Introduction to Revised Edition

Marianne Elliott

In this new edition of *The Long Road to Peace in Northern Ireland*, former contributors have been given the opportunity to add postscripts, two new essays have been commissioned, and the appendices enlarged. I have added sections of the Opsahl Commission report and Sir George Quigley's Review of the Parades Commission (2002), which address the issues of religion, cultural identity and sectarianism, and have dedicated this edition to Torkel Opsahl and Eric Gallagher, fellow commissioner on the Opsahl Commission. Eric Gallagher was one of the four Protestant clergymen who met the IRA at Feakle in County Clare in 1974. He spent a lifetime trying to overcome the sectarianism that continues to make peace so precarious.

Despite the return of devolved government to Northern Ireland and signs of former extremes working together harmoniously, the mood is more sombre in these additions than five years ago, reflecting a recognition that the inflated expectations of what the Good Friday Agreement could deliver were unrealistic. Peter Shirlow, while recognizing the real achievements of the peace process – not least the 74 per cent decline in the murder rate – highlights the urgency of seriously tackling increasing polarization and sectarianism in Belfast (only 17.7 per cent now living in mixed areas). The Agreement over-emphasized high politics and 'merely managed polarization', while the whole 'edifice' of sectarianism was ignored. George Quigley too – drawing on his review of the Parades Commission in 2002 – reaches a similar conclusion: the Agreement 'raised the bar high, requiring enforced fraternity at the top while there was a serious lack of fraternity at the base'.

I do not entirely share Peter Shirlow's pessimism that 'the conflict cannot be resolved', although I too have argued that if sectarianism is not seriously tackled, a revival of serious communal violence is a real danger.[1] In the first edition of this collection, many argued that though the war in Northern Ireland was over, the conflict was not (Cox), and that peace-making is a lengthy, evolutionary process, rather than something confined to an initial agreement. Some of the essays (Owen, Mitchell, O'Dowd) pointed to the role of outside agencies, prepared to 'think the unthinkable and thereby progress events hitherto unimaginable'. Unfortunately, some of those agencies – notably the United States – have become more muted. The consequent internalization of the problem risks privileging traditional sectarian politics. Peter Shirlow is critical: 'At present no major political party articulates the de-segregation of society, choosing instead to represent the electorate's fears'.

There is, however, a compelling case for empowering those at the receiving end of sectarianism's consequences. At a recent conference on Protestant identities, I was struck by the way that 'polite' unionism disingenuously distanced itself from the sometimes murderous sectarianism of loyalist unionism. This kind of dishonest transfer of responsibility for sectarian violence is not confined to political unionism; it has happened in nationalism as well, not least in the widespread belief in the Republic of Ireland that only those in the North are sectarian. Sectarianism is part of Irish culture, north and south. A little bit of humility and responsibility-sharing might go some way to helping us deal with it. It has, after all, been producing conflict in Ireland for nearly five centuries.

This is why 'the heroism [of] those who don't make history', as identified by Paul Arthur, has sometimes been cynically dismissed or 'underplayed'. These are the people discussed in Maria Power's essay on inter-church groups and peace-building. She argues that while religion is part of the problem, it can also provide part of the solution. Here, ecumenical communities have been working steadily and patiently since the 1960s to dispel misunderstandings between the two main faith communities. Over years of low-key activities, often in dangerous circum-stances, they carried out a programme of 'practical' reconciliation. It was such unsung heroes who helped prevent the disintegration of civil society during the Troubles.

The conclusion of this new edition therefore is an urgent call for serious atten-tion to be devoted to the sectarianism underlying the conflict, but a reminder once more of the conclusion to the first edition. Despite the flaws in the Good Friday Agreement, we have come a very long way since the end of the Troubles, even if a 'long road' remains ahead of us as we move beyond the high politics to tackle the underlying causes. To quote Sir George Quigley, 'one has always to remain open to the possibility of being surprised by progress'.

Note

1. Ford's Lectures, Oxford University, February 2005 (*Religion and Identity in Irish History*, forthcoming from Oxford University Press, 2008).

Introduction

Marianne Elliott

The bulk of the essays in this book were delivered as part of Liverpool University's Institute of Irish Studies Peace Lecture Series, 1996–2000, and they have been left largely unchanged as reflecting opinion at the time they were given. The earlier lectures received generous sponsorship from the Irish Independent Newspaper Group and Lord David Owen's charity *Humanitas*. They are dedicated to Torkel Opsahl, the international human rights lawyer, who headed up the 1993 Opsahl Commission in Northern Ireland and died tragically early shortly afterwards, just as he was taking up his new post as head of the Bosnian War Crimes Commission in Geneva. The collection concludes with an appendix bringing together the key recommendations of the major agreements, commissions, government papers and so forth on Northern Ireland since Sunningdale. It does not pretend to be comprehensive, attempting rather to trace the long gestation of some of the key recommendations of the Good Friday Agreement.

The Institute of Irish Studies was established in 1988. As well as delivering a full degree programme, it has continued the role set out by its first Director, Professor Patrick Buckland, as a bridge between the cultures of Ireland and Britain, in particular providing a neutral forum for political debate. The Peace Lecture Series has been part of this tradition. It was initiated in 1996 by Sir George Quigley's 'Achieving Transformational Change', which, at a time when the idea was belatedly being accepted in Northern Ireland, looked at the role of a 'third party' or external agency in areas of conflict. What if this had happened earlier, he asks, and Sinn Féin's 1993–94 claim to a new commitment to democratic politics been taken at face value and the third party had brought them into talks then? He looks at other areas of conflict to show the difficulties experienced by all movements turning from violence to exclusively democratic means, particularly that of urging implacable enemies towards compromise. The idea of peacemaking as a lengthy, evolutionary process, rather than something confined to the making of the initial agreement, is a theme which was to reappear in most of the other lectures. Certainly, by the close of 2000 when Sir George added a postscript to his lecture of four years earlier, although the euphoria of the early reception of the Good Friday Agreement had disappeared in Northern Ireland, he found 'the quiet miracle of normal life' beginning to be experienced as the institutions set up under the Agreement started to deliver.

Liverpool University's Chancellor, Lord David Owen, took up the 'third party' idea and facilitated the lectures by international peacemakers Frederik Van Zyl

3

Slabbert and Jan Egeland in October–November 1997. These were delivered in Liverpool, Dublin and Belfast, and, at a time when the talks which would lead to the Good Friday Agreement five months later were still at a critical stage, they drew huge audiences, including many members of the political parties involved in the talks. I remember a particularly lively discussion in Belfast concerning the lessons which could be learnt from South Africa about the fate of former militants, their armaments, and their recruitment into the new policing system there. Frederik Van Zyl Slabbert tells of how the peace process got under way in South Africa. He does not see trust as part of the initial formula. Indeed most of the contributors to this book agree that if trust existed, no negotiations would be necessary. Rather he sees adversaries negotiating because they perceive their conflict to be unresolvable by any other means; they have arrived at 'a commonly perceived sense of deadlock'. He then traces the steps by which opposing groups arrive at a middling democratic solution. He cautions against the assumption that there is a magic formula to peacemaking. But he singles out three factors: internal recognition of the lack of moral legitimacy of one's cause; the extraordinary qualities of the leadership – in the case of South Africa, most notably that of Nelson Mandela; and, once again, the importance of external forces, in this case the rapprochement between the United States and Russia and the ending of the Cold War.

Jan Egeland, who was part of the Norwegian team which helped start the Middle East peace negotiations of 1992–95, gives an insider's view of the effectiveness of 'third-party' intercession in conflict situations. Norway, with its long-standing reputation for neutrality and expertise in international human rights issues, was well placed to win the trust of the opposing parties. Even so, it took endless meetings at secret locations in Norway and desperate efforts to prevent media discovery, which would have forced the participants to 'play to the gallery' with damaging political rhetoric. As extreme difficulties have continued, Jan Egeland reflects on the lessons to be learned. These include secrecy in the early stages and continuity of personnel; a willingness on the part of the leaders and their public to reach often painful compromises; the acceptance that the process will take time and will only endure when ordinary people experience its benefits; and the importance of adequate mediation machinery and international diplomacy to supply appropriate tools and support.

David Owen takes the idea of external diplomacy in conflict situations further and he identifies the UK's rejection of such diplomacy until 1994 as a major contributing factor to the excessively long-drawn-out nature of the 'Troubles' in Northern Ireland. He examines a number of cases of external interventions in conflict zones, notably in the former Yugoslavia, and suggests some ground rules for such outside involvement. In essence he believes that any conflict involving 'ethnic cleansing' calls for early intervention, without waiting for a perfect solution. 'In ethnic wars realities are created on the ground that are very much harder to reverse with the passage of time.' Engaging surrounding countries can help achieve peace, while negotiating with paramilitaries/freedom fighters/terrorists can benefit from the support of other powers, not only in bringing international pressures to bear, but also to overcome domestic criticism. He tells of his own experience as Britain's navy minister, 1968–70, and later as foreign secretary, 1977–79, in the handling of the Rhodesian crisis, when he recognized that Britain's sanctions were failing because it was not involving other powers. The same mistake was being made with Northern Ireland, until Margaret Thatcher involved the Irish government with the Anglo-Irish Agreement of 1985, and John Major took the courageous step of involving the United States of America. He sees this belated involvement of the United States as the crucial factor in the peace process.

The person Lord Owen credits most with the involvement of President Clinton in the process is Niall O'Dowd, who here gives his own account of how it came about. O'Dowd, as editor of the main Irish-American newspaper, *The Irish Voice*, was dismayed at attitudes this side of the Atlantic (in Ireland as well as Britain) which dismissed all Irish-Americans as too 'green' or too 'republican', and excluded those with real influence who were genuinely seeking to assist the peace process in Northern Ireland. He cites the cases of the Birmingham Six, the Guildford Four and the MacBride Principles (seeking to establish fair employment practices in Northern Ireland) as issues where Ireland simply followed British advice and froze out Irish-America. The thaw between Ireland and Irish-America started with Charles Haughey's second term as Taoiseach in 1982. But Irish-Americans remained powerless under both Ronald Reagan and George Bush Senior because of the strength of the 'special relationship' with Britain. In 1991 some began to tip Bill Clinton as their best hope, and now it is difficult to believe that but a decade ago they could muster barely 30 people for a fundraising dinner on his behalf. Nevertheless, by 1992, with Clinton at the White House, the Irish-American lobby was in a position to act legitimately as the 'third party' and Niall O'Dowd describes how, in 1993, they became convinced that republican and loyalist leaders sought to move away from violence. It was the same year as the Hume-Adams statement and the report of the Opsahl Commission – all independently saying the same thing, and all equally denounced for doing so. All very well in hindsight, of course, and until the IRA ceasefire of 1994 I remember having much the same feeling about our recommendations from the Opsahl Commission as that expressed by Senator Moynihan to Senator Kennedy, after the hullabaloo over the grant of a US visa to Gerry Adams was followed by IRA mortar attacks on Heathrow airport: 'Have we been had?'

The tendency to tar all of Irish-America with the same brush was exemplified in the MacBride campaign (here described in detail by Kevin McNamara). It was denounced by the Irish and British governments as the product of Noraid and Provo supporters, as a means of embarrassing the British government and destabilizing the Northern Irish economy. In fact it was an appeal to 'middle' Irish-America, was initially opposed by Noraid and only taken up by republicans when the propaganda value was appreciated. 'The British government had misread the situation. There were two different Americas', writes McNamara. Britain's hostility simply drove these together and put its Irish policy literally 'in the dock' as hearings on the MacBride Principles were conducted in states and cities across the USA, thus circumventing Washington and its long-standing policy of non-intervention in internal British matters. In retrospect David Owen finds it surprising that British politicians should have failed to accept that a country with 44 million people claiming Irish or Scots-Irish descent might have a legitimate interest in Northern Ireland.

Senator George Mitchell is one of those 44 million. Here was the 'third party' – with Senator Mitchell's 1996 appointment to chair peace negotiations – being finally given the central role in the Northern Ireland peace process. I have been struck by the way that, as these essays show, key people or organizations were prepared to think the unthinkable and thereby progress events in ways hitherto unimaginable. Only three years after the Opsahl Commission was denounced for stating that no peace deal could be lasting or stable without the involvement of Sinn Féin and the representatives of the loyalist paramilitaries, here was George Mitchell chairing an initiative which would bring them into face-to-face discussions with the constitutional parties. Although it was himself, Tony Blair, Bertie Ahern and President Clinton who were the key people pulling the parties to the Good Friday Agreement in the final stages, in his Liverpool address Senator Mitchell paid tribute to those who had laid the groundwork, particularly Albert Reynolds and John Major. David Owen does likewise, in particular pointing out how Major kept the unionists on board. George Mitchell admits that the Northern Ireland negotiations 'were the longest and most difficult' that he had ever been involved in, and there were times when even his legendary patience gave way. But he saw the 'peace wall', fifteen feet high and topped with barbed wire, which separates, by their own requests, the Protestant and Catholic communities of west Belfast – one of the legacies of the terrible suffering caused in Northern Ireland by the failure of its people to find a way of living together – and he continued in his effort to gain agreement. He notes something all too familiar to those of us who know and love Northern Ireland: a warmth in its people, but a touchiness and defensiveness and at times a fatalism that nothing can be done. It was this attitude which led to the 'acceptable level of violence' syndrome and more than anything underscores the most consistent theme in these essays: the need to involve external agencies in conflict situations which are generating their own momentum and when those at the heart of them have given up on a solution. Senator Mitchell believes that there is no conflict which cannot be ended. He warns against letting the 'men of violence' destroy such efforts by saying in advance that negotiations will end if acts of violence occur, and, above all, he points to the abomination of the Omagh bombing of 15 August 1998 to show that there is no alternative to the peace process. As a seasoned negotiator, he emphasizes the need for patience, for peacemaking is a process. The Good Friday Agreement is just one element.

Most of the remaining essays endorse that conclusion. Maurice Hayes, in a lecture delivered just after he started his work on the Patten Commission, examines the legendary stubbornness of the Ulsterman. He traces the entire history of attempts at settlements in Northern Ireland over the past thirty years, concluding that Sunningdale may have been an idea whose time had not yet come and that it failed not simply because of loyalist and republican violence, but because unionists were not prepared to share power with Catholics. Even so, he shares the view of many of us seeking to understand the conflict in Northern Ireland that the 3000 deaths since Sunningdale were unnecessary tragedies, for the 'power-sharing' of Sunningdale has remained the ideal, and the Good Friday Agreement is 'not that far removed from the template' developed then. But he is hopeful. Unionists no longer object to sharing power with nationalists. He too sees the Good Friday

Agreement as only a beginning: but the 'public mood is for peace, and the process, although it might falter and stutter, shows signs of being irreversible'.

Martin Mansergh has been special adviser on Northern Ireland to successive Fianna Fáil Taoiseachs, with particular responsibility for 'behind-the-scene' contacts with the republican movement in the lead-up to the Downing Street Declaration and subsequent IRA ceasefires. He too sees the Good Friday Agreement as even-handed to all traditions and as repairing the many flaws in the 1920–21 Anglo-Irish settlement. He traces the changing attitudes of Irish governments to the IRA over the past century, showing how the early months of the Troubles and the arms trials of 1970 knocked off course the developing Lemass/Lynch/Whittaker pragmatic approach to North–South relations and effectively removed the South's ability to exercise a restraining influence on the developing violence. It also made it wary of covert communications with republicans and initiated its policy of bolstering constitutional nationalism in the North. Even so he is much more critical of Britain's handling of channels of communication with republicans than most other contributors to the book, particularly denouncing the use of unaccountable 'intelligence' rather than political channels and suggesting that it was not until Britain abandoned this approach in 1992 that the negotiations which would lead to the 1993 Declaration and ultimately the Good Friday Agreement could begin. He, like others, is realistic about the difficulties which remain to be overcome, but he sees the good working relationship which now exists between Irish Taoiseach and British Prime Minister as underpinning the survival of the process.

Peter Mandelson spoke at the Institute in February 2000, in the week before he temporarily suspended the institutions set up under the Agreement. Like others, he acknowledged the similarities between the Good Friday Agreement and Sunningdale. But he challenged those who pessimistically thought that the former might go the same way as the latter. The lessons of Sunningdale's collapse had been learnt. The Good Friday Agreement is 'a broader, deeper, fairer Agreement … It recognizes that everyone who has been a party to the conflict must be a party to its resolution.' Mandelson outlined the part that every grouping was playing in its implementation, welcoming too the DUP's participation in the executive, despite its opposition to the process itself. He spelt out the alternative: another generation of bloodshed, ending up with an agreement which would not be much different. Although decommissioning was one of the stumbling blocks, he appealed to the paramilitaries, particularly the republicans:

> There are many, I know, in the republican movement who are passing from one era of strategy and organization to the next but have not yet reached the logical conclusion of their actions. I know the passions that an attempt to force decommissioning arouses. I am not naive. Surrendering long-fought and hard-line political ground is one thing. Appearing to be forced to surrender all together is quite another. That's why decommissioning is a voluntary contribution to the process of building trust. But it is also necessary in order to move forward.

The Good Friday Agreement, he concluded, was a compromise. Every word, every provision was carefully weighed and had a purpose:

Any unilateral change of detail or emphasis, no matter how small, would throw it out of balance. Everyone who brokered the Agreement understood this. Unless someone is proposing to re-negotiate it, it is this deal that has to be implemented, this deal and all of it.

A number of contributors have referred to the Anglo-Irish (Hillsborough) Agreement of 1985 as a crucial stage, whatever its flaws, on the road to Good Friday. David Goodall was one of the key architects of the 1985 Agreement. He spoke at the Institute just after the secretary of state, Peter Mandelson, had suspended the institutions set up under the Good Friday Agreement. Despite the gloom of that period, he took the long-term view. He showed how, from each stage in the long road to peace, lessons were taken. The Anglo-Irish Agreement had not delivered everything its initiator, Dr Garret Fitzgerald, had hoped. It was nevertheless an important step towards a more comprehensive agreement, for it allowed the idea of an 'Irish dimension' to bed down and it provided the two governments with the structure – the Intergovernmental Conference – to continue talking. Goodall also traces a number of other areas enshrined in the Good Friday Agreement which were embryonic in Hillsborough. Where Good Friday goes far beyond the Anglo-Irish Agreement, he thinks, is in the still under-developed British-Irish Council, which 'accords formal political recognition, for the first time since the Republic of Ireland left the Commonwealth in 1949, to the dense network of ties ... which makes the relationship between Britain and Ireland uniquely close as well as uniquely neuralgic'. While Goodall sees the implications of this as lying very much in the future, he thinks that a proper settlement of the 'Irish–British Question' will not be achieved until we have found a way of 'formulating and institutionalizing the relationship between the two sister islands in terms which reflect its unique character, without infringing the national self-respect of all concerned'.

One of the key motivations behind Garret Fitzgerald's 1985 initiative was to halt the rapid rise of Sinn Féin at the expense of the SDLP and David Goodall is not alone in commenting that exactly the opposite has been the outcome of the Good Friday Agreement. Whether that is an acceptable price to pay for peace remains to be seen. Kevin Bean sees the development not in terms of Sinn Féin replacing the SDLP as the main nationalist party so much as the former having stolen the latter's clothes. It is not, in other words, a case of Northern nationalism having become more extreme, but one of Sinn Féin having become more like the SDLP, part of 'republicanism's apparent transformation from revolutionary armed movement to semi-constitutional party'. It is a transformation doubted by unionists, denounced by extreme republicans, but one which Bean and other commentators nevertheless see as taking place. It is rooted in a re-evaluation of Britain's role in Ireland and an acceptance of the 'no selfish interest' claim first put forward by Peter Brooke. In the 1990s the language of such 'post-republicanism', Kevin Bean argues, became that of 'Hume-speak ... one of dialogue, engagement, debate, movement, process, transition, reconciliation and conflict resolution'. The most important outcome of this move away from a 'colonial', 'Brits-out' reading was a refocusing on the need to win unionist consent. Bean argues that a major reconfiguration of nationalism is taking place on the ground which, while it cannot simply be seen in terms of Sinn

Féin eclipsing the SDLP, does point towards the eventual emergence of Sinn Féin as a constitutional nationalist party. I might add the question: what's wrong with a constitutional republican party in the context of Northern Ireland? Worldwide, 'nationalism' is a less inclusive concept than 'republicanism'. Perhaps when some of the current difficulties are surmounted Sinn Féin (and indeed others) might see the space to rescue 'republicanism' from the obscenities which so tarnished (and indeed misrepresented) it in the recent past.

Kevin Bean identifies a new constituency opening up for Sinn Féin, a middle-class one. It is indeed instructive to find how little 'middle class' as an insult is now used in Sinn Féin terminology, though in common usage in the early 1990s. Harvey Cox sees the 'middle range' leaders – those not involved in the highest level of constitutional negotiation – as 'vital to the prospect of a transition from the politics of continuous confrontation to one of non-violent contest and adjustment'. Like other contributors, he views the Good Friday Agreement as just a beginning. Having started out with an analysis of what still seems such an intractable issue – Portadown and the Garvaghy Road Orange parade – he reminds us that we should not get this out of proportion. Very often the identities that we expend so much time agonizing about are local (even neighbourhood) identities, which would still be contested whatever the overarching agreement. This is a 'conflict', not a 'war', he urges. It cannot be ended with a one-off 'Peace', but resolution can be – and largely is being – pursued by non-military means. This is why, he suggests, post-Agreement politics seem dominated by disputes over symbols and traditions, the name and insignia of the police, the routing of Orange parades. If the war is over, the conflict is not. But if unionism has its constituency to which 'no surrender' means more than pragmatic modern politics, so too has Sinn Féin in the 'martyr dead', the Bobby Sands in every republican village, the unanswerable question: 'is this what they died for?' Arguably the claim of Sinn Féin that giving up weapons was no part of Irish tradition equates to the 'not an inch' argument in unionist and Orange traditions. But then the 'astonishingly radical' Good Friday Agreement was a major departure from both traditions, and Harvey Cox sees it as laying the basis for more such departures. He recalls Seamus Heaney's remarks on the 1994 ceasefire: 'We've passed from the atrocious to the messy, but the messy is a perfectly OK place to live.'

This is the 'here' of Paul Arthur's paper and he too invokes Seamus Heaney's legendary ability to draw universal messages from the small things that make up human experience. In his Nobel lecture Heaney told of one of those gestures of friendship which often cross the rigid sectarian lines in Northern Ireland. Ordered out of their van in 1976 by unidentifiable paramilitaries, the eleven workmen at Kingsmill were asked to identify the Catholics among them. A comrade's hand grasped that of the only Catholic in the group, urging him silently 'stay, we won't tell'. But these were IRA men, not loyalists – as was thought – and as the Catholic moved forward, all the rest were murdered. Recovering from (even recognizing) the horrors that we have created will take time. But such 'unnoticed acts of heroism by those who don't make history', Paul Arthur argues, will assume greater import-ance as the peace process unfolds. He thinks the role of the average person in conflict transformation has been underplayed and that a Northern Ireland public invited – by the Good Friday Agreement – to shed its 'historic fatalism' will play a major role in the peace process: 'Unquestioningly political leadership has a primary role to play in transforming a conflict … but at the end of the day there has to be a sense of ownership.' He recalls the day in April 1998 when the Irish public, North and South, went to the polls to register their verdict on Good Friday and the sense of real exhilaration among those casting their vote in this, the most mundane of democratic activities. I too remember that day and it was like nothing I have ever experienced at polling booths in England. The numbers were greater, for a start, and they walked with a sense of having finally achieved control of their destinies. There have indeed been many setbacks since then, but Paul Arthur sees the Good Friday Agreement as having opened up politics to a wider public, the 'ordinary' becoming that 'external factor' pushing things forward. I am reminded of the Belfast cabby, talking at the time of the 1998 referendum about the Troubles in which he and his colleagues figured disproportionately among the casualties, who commented to me, '*We* let it happen, we must never do so again.' Taking responsibility for the past is fundamental to escaping from its clutches.

The book concludes with my analysis of some of those issues of identity which other contributors think will require generations to resolve. These issues are the stuff of Maurice Hayes's 'race-memory', which causes each side to revert to confrontation when the other seems to behave as they had always behaved in the past. In a paper written before the Good Friday Agreement, I looked at Protestant and Catholic stereotypes of each other and how they continued to inform their politics. The paper also highlighted mutual areas of incomprehension which the long-standing religious, social, educational and political polarization in the province had encouraged. But it noted that there were glimmerings of recognition that people in Northern Ireland were more like each other than either the 'Irish' elsewhere or the 'British' with whom they chose to identify, and concluded that the problems of Northern Ireland would only ever be resolved 'by its people learning to live and work together, prior to any decision about long-term constitutional structures'. This in many ways is what the Good Friday Agreement is starting to deliver. In 1993 the Commission which Torkel Opsahl headed, and which inspired my contribution to this book, recommended 'a new government of Northern Ireland, based on the principle that each community should have an equal voice in making and executing laws or vetoing them and an equal share in the administrative authority', the core of the 'parity of esteem' agenda which informs the current peace process. It will take a generation or more to work through the implications of the Good Friday Agreement; but a start has been made and few of those involved in the various peace initiatives of a decade ago would have expected things to have progressed so far so quickly. Whatever the gravity of the problems remaining, I would urge those dispirited by the frequent crises which threaten the process to consider how far we have already come since June 1993 when opinion polls found that only 6% of Northern Ireland voters believed that political talks could succeed.

Achieving Transformational Change[1]

Sir George Quigley

The creation of the Institute of Irish Studies at Liverpool University in 1988 was an inspired initiative. Never was it so important that we in Ireland should understand *each other* and that both islands should reach out to each other in *mutual* understanding. I do not speak consciously from the standpoint of any political party or community. It is my aim to try to achieve a broad empathy – something which is sadly lacking in the situation. Parties tend to be what in business terms would be described as producer- rather than market-orientated. They appeal to their existing customer base but rarely enlarge it. The market remains heavily segmented. I hope that I shall be perceived as analytical rather than critical or censorious. We are already oversupplied with recrimination and denunciation. More problem-solving, rather than partisanship, is needed.

Let me start by indulging in a little counterfactual history. Where would we have been today if, in the midst of the relief and euphoria flowing from the cease-fires, Sinn Féin's proclamation of its commitment to exclusively peaceful means had been taken at face value and inclusive talks had been announced? No doubt much effort would have been spent in trying to get all parties to the table and it might have proved impossible. But it would have signalled strongly that the key to success lies, not in the attitudes or actions of the two governments, but in each community in Northern Ireland being able to gain the confidence and trust of the other. Could a third party, introduced at that stage, have succeeded in getting all the parties round the table?

To speculate around such a scenario is not to deny a role to the governments or to question their commitment. London has a clear responsibility for the good government of Northern Ireland as part of the United Kingdom and it must obviously be involved in working out the relationship between that part and the rest of Ireland. Dublin sees itself as trustee of the fortunes of nationalists in the North and is inevitably involved in helping to shape relationships between the two parts of the island.

However, a scenario such as I describe would have taken pressure off the governments and perhaps reduced the intensity of hostility between Sinn Féin and the UK government. It would have avoided the long delays which punctuated the process as the governments tried to align their own approaches to the meaning of the IRA ceasefire, the importance of decommissioning, the circumstances in which all-party talks could commence, and so on.

Would republican frustration over unionists' refusal to *participate* in all-party talks (if such had been the case) have been greater or less than their frustration over the delay in *calling* such talks? Would the abandonment of the ceasefire have been more, or less, likely? Is it conceivable that republicans would have been obliged to think more innovatively about ways of gaining the confidence of unionists?

But suppose that unionists *had* decided to participate to see whether, in genuine negotiation, it was possible to do business with nationalism, including Sinn Féin. There would have been one of three outcomes: success, in the shape of sufficient consensus (including support from Sinn Féin), would have been achieved; or there would have been sufficient consensus, but with Sinn Féin in dissent; or the talks would have collapsed. Given either of the latter two outcomes, Sinn Féin's commitment to the democratic process would then have been put to the test. Would they have been prepared to accept failure, which is the hallmark of the democrat, while continuing to mobilize politically in pursuit of their objectives? Or would they have failed the test and stood unequivocally revealed to the world as no more than diehard campaigners for their own cause? The current difficulties arise from the attempt to devise an alternative to that test – a means of establishing once and for all that the possibility of military action is not a jeopardy chip which can be moved forward or backward as expediency dictates.

Perhaps such a scenario for the past two years is wildly unrealistic. Many in Northern Ireland found it difficult to come to terms with the proposition that those who had been 'the enemy' and whose *bona fides* were still suspect could the next day be bargaining with them across the table. There was a rather inarticulate cry for some act of psychic catharsis, similar to that which arose in post-war France to cleanse it of the collaborationist intrigues and betrayals – the need for justice for martyred people. Likewise the Nuremberg trials were an attempt to round off a terrible war and initiate the peace with a legal act. The integrity of the moral architecture had to be restored. The same issues have arisen in Central and Eastern Europe and in South Africa, which has sought to meet the need through its Truth and Reconciliation Commission.

The need seems to be felt more deeply by the Protestant than by the Catholic population. For example, in a survey in Northern Ireland in 1996, 49 per cent of Catholics said yes to an amnesty or immunity as part of a peace settlement, whereas only 10 per cent of Protestants did so. Perhaps Protestants are more conditioned to interpret the world in terms of good and evil, as is also evident in their vocabulary of politics. This issue needs to be addressed. An Israeli author, in an open letter to a Palestinian friend, said: 'The purpose of peace is not to erase all past sufferings but to prevent further suffering.' But how does one accommodate within a peace process those who, by the drawing of a thick line through history, feel cheated of any historical justice? It can be instructive to examine how other peace processes have worked. The breakthrough in the Middle East came with the initialling of an Israeli-Palestinian Declaration of Principles. Immediately before the formal signing of the Declaration there was an exchange of correspondence between the two sides. Yasser Arafat's letter included the following statement:

> The PLO considers that the signing of the Declaration of Principles constitutes a historic event, inaugurating a new epoch of peaceful coexistence, free from violence and all other

acts which endanger peace and stability. Accordingly, the PLO renounces the use of terrorism and other acts of violence and will assume responsibility over all PLO elements and personnel in order to assure their compliance, prevent violations and discipline violators.

The letter also declared inoperative and no longer valid those provisions of the Palestinian Covenant which were inconsistent with the commitments in the letter and undertook to submit the necessary changes to the Palestinian Council for formal approval. That was successfully accomplished two and a half years later.

Yasser Arafat also wrote to the foreign minister of Norway, who had played a key role in brokering the breakthrough. The letter indicated that he would include the following positions in his public statements:

> The PLO encourages and calls upon the Palestinian people in the West Bank and Gaza Strip to take part in the steps leading to the normalisation of life, rejecting violence and terrorism, contributing to peace and stability and participating actively in shaping reconstruction, economic development and co-operation.

The Israeli government, for its part, formally confirmed its decision to recognize the PLO as the representative of the Palestinian people and commence negotiations with them within the Middle East peace process.

In his account of events, significantly called *Battling for Peace*, Shimon Peres makes some telling points. He was determined, he writes, to achieve a balanced accord, beneficial to both sides. 'I fully understood,' he says, 'the tremendous political and emotional significance for the PLO' of the return by Arafat and the leadership to Gaza and Jericho as Palestinian self-governing enclaves. Significantly, he then goes on:

> My strategic goal was to obtain, in return for 'the return', an undertaking from the PLO to recognize Israel, to forswear terrorism finally and irrevocably and to abrogate [certain] provisions of its charter ... Tactically, my purpose was to defer this aspect of the negotiations until as late as possible, knowing how important it was to the other side.

At key points, Peres saw the need to inject urgency into the negotiations, warning against letting the negotiating track become 'like chewing gum', as he put it. Or again: 'The limits of manoeuvrability have been tested. Now, the time is ripe for decision ... the biggest risk of all is the inability to take any risks.' His constant fear was that the PLO might 'opt to aspire for a too-perfect solution'. In another telling phrase, Peres writes, quoting Churchill's line about not crossing a chasm in two steps: 'With the Palestinians, the choice had been to make a great leap forward or to remain bogged down.' And a not irrelevant footnote: on the day after the Principles were agreed, seven Israeli soldiers were killed by a roadside bomb in south Lebanon.

A review of a recent book by Jeremy Ginifer (*Managing Arms in Peace Processes*), with particular reference to Rhodesia/Zimbabwe, contains the following passage which prompts my curiosity:

> Excluding the United Nations from the peace process, Whitehall ... unilaterally designed and successfully implemented a plan to demobilise the contending armies and hold a

national election ... British military professionalism, a decision not to attempt disarmament or integration of forces prior to the election, reliance on confidence-building through diplomacy rather than force, and a bit of luck combined to bring the demobilisation process to a rapid and low-cost conclusion.

There are other examples of conflict resolution which illustrate the lessons to be learnt from experience elsewhere. They underline the importance of creativity and leadership in the management of change in political as much as in business contexts. The evolution of American foreign policy in the Nixon/Kissinger era, as described in Kissinger's *Diplomacy*, is a beautiful example of the power of transformational leadership to break the mould. First of all there was the leap into fresh insight. In October 1967, Richard Nixon, still a year away from his successful bid for the presidency in 1968, and before he had even received the presidential nomination, wrote as follows in the prestigious periodical *Foreign Affairs*:

> Taking the long view, we simply cannot afford to leave China forever outside the family of nations, there to nurture its fantasies, cherish its hates and threaten its neighbours. There is no place on this small planet for a billion of its potentially most able people to live in angry isolation.

I can think of no other example of a power-hungry politician, at a critical point in his career, adopting a public position so exposed or so at variance with his stereotype – in Nixon's case, that of a hardened cold-war warrior. Substitute the IRA for China and put the words into the mouth of a unionist politician fifteen or twenty years ago and you will get some measure of how far Nixon had stepped 'outside the box'.

According to Kissinger's account, Nixon did not see the world in essentially theological terms. To persist with that view meant making the transformation of Soviet society – or disarmament – a precondition for negotiations. Nixon believed that foreign policy should be strategy, not crusade, and that the aim should be to discipline a rival power, not to chastise evil. He did not see relations with the Soviet Union in all-or-nothing terms but as a mixed bag of issues with varying degrees of solubility. Out of this thinking there emerged a highly nuanced strategy, which was a subtle mixture of confrontation and conciliation – emphasizing the areas in which co-operation was possible and using it as leverage in the areas where the powers were at loggerheads.

The Nixon/Kissinger approach drew vehement criticism from both conservatives and liberals. The critics savaged the concessions which were made. But, as Kissinger said, a negotiation is about trading concessions. Only those who eschew negotiation and its ebb and flow can afford the fantasy of a negotiation in which all the concessions are made by the other side. It is tempting to draw analogies with the Irish situation. The Nixon/Kissinger mindset had no utopian vision of some grand final outcome, some terminal point at which all problems are solved. For them, the new world is made up of the patient accumulation of partial successes. Disastrous though it otherwise was, in foreign policy the Nixon regime reflected the president as an educator, whose vision provided the framework for the debate. He shows the leader as the balance wheel, acting as moderator and integrator in the midst of contending groups which push their points to extremes. The key, I believe, was the powerful analytical skills of the major players, not least Nixon, and their geopolitical intuition (or, as we might say in other contexts, their strategic sense). But it also takes tremendous courage to act on a concept, change direction radically, face down the opposition on all sides and retain the confidence which fuels persistence. The courage is grounded in and reinforced by the cogency of the analysis. We should not underestimate the power of intelligence to prompt change and generate the courage to change.

Let me move to a different scene altogether – to Jean Monnet and the creation of what is now the European Union – in order to illustrate some other facets of leadership. It shows how leaders make things happen by the neat splicing of principle and pragmatism. Immediately after the Second World War, France as much as Britain resisted attempts to become involved in anything approaching a grand plan for a common market in Western Europe. However, a recurrent concern for France was its ability to maintain the steel production targets in the plan for the modernization of France, of which Monnet was the principal architect. These targets were threatened by the speed of German recovery and its absorption of the coke produced in the Ruhr. Monnet had a vision of a United States of Europe but he also had an acute feel for French national interest. The establishment in 1951 of the European Coal and Steel Community happily guaranteed France's continued recovery but it also laid the foundations for what became the common market, then the single market and, ultimately, economic and monetary union.

Monnet referred frequently to a United States of Europe, to federation, to integration and to concepts which were even more vague, such as the need to organize the West. As ever, though, he was the pragmatist, intent on creating first of all among Europeans the broadest common interest. 'I have never doubted,' he said, 'that one day this … will lead us to the United States of Europe, but I see no point in trying to imagine today what political form it will take. Today, no-one can say, for the changes born of change are unpredictable.' How reluctant we often are to accept that insight. We are prone to believe that everything can – and must – be mapped far ahead.

Noble causes need practical people – people who never forget the far horizon but who recognize that it will never be reached if they do not cultivate the near ground. Monnet fitted that prescription (which is also a requirement of all leadership) perfectly. His method and approach, very fully set out in his *Memoirs*, repay study in any context which entails managing a radical change agenda. He believed that practical problems are never insoluble if they are approached from the starting point of a great idea but that the way forward lies in strategic progress rather than in the grand plan. He was careful about forcing the hand of history. Progress is driven by necessity.

Monnet eschewed the term 'negotiation', believing that in such contexts each side tends to measure its own advantage in terms of the loss inflicted on the other. For progress, all the players had to realize that the essential was for everyone to win together. He believed that major change can be achieved if people's minds can be directed towards the point where their interests converge. That point always exists, but it takes trouble to find it. As it has been neatly put, people on opposite sides of the table must be put on the same side of the table, with the problems on the other side. Monnet was always ready to advance along the line of least resistance provided it led in approximately the right direction – to tear (as it were) along the perforation that is already there. Dare I again draw analogies with the situation in Ireland?

There are those who would say that such analogies are irrelevant because in Northern Ireland it is a domestic matter of law and order, to which the rules for international conflict resolution, a term often used by the republican movement, do not apply. The differences here are much more than semantic and reflect a fundamental difference of perception and approach. However, the Middle East situation clearly diverged from our own in one crucial respect. In the PLO, the Israeli government was negotiating with the militant group which discharged both political and military functions. The fact that, in Ireland, militancy is – or is perceived to be – pursued through a bimodal strategy introduces a significant element of additional difficulty.

I suspect that many people have underestimated the difficulties which face any organization seeking to abandon violence as an instrument of policy, particularly where not all its members are convinced of the wisdom of doing so. In business terms, it is tantamount to a massive programme of change management, where mission, values and a pervasive culture of 'struggle' are at issue. For republicanism, the very shape of history, its dialectic, its tendency, has traditionally presented itself as 'struggle'. A political approach implies give and take, even compromise, an unthinkable construct in a group organized exclusively around the principle of implacable resistance. 'Struggle' becomes a sacred abstraction, absolutist and sacrificial. On the unionist side, the battlefield analogy is the defence of the besieged fortress, always at risk from walls breached or undermined. This, too, makes acceptance of change and compromise difficult. Peacemaking is therefore a messy business with few neat and tidy solutions. And there are no 'perfect' solutions. In democracies, outcomes are judged by their acceptability and workability, not by their 'correctness'. Turnkey solutions are a rarity and progress is never linear.

One of the major obstacles to progress is our inability to come to terms with the past. As William Faulkner put it in the context of the American South, 'It's all now, you see. Yesterday won't be over until tomorrow and tomorrow began 10,000 years ago … We are fighting, as always, the long battalioned ghosts of old wrongs and shames that each generation of us both inherits and creates.' The risk is that we too readily suppose that there is an inevitability about what happens and so close off a whole range of possibilities for our society. To borrow and adapt some words used in a very different context the other day, we need a new history – one that is not rooted in past conflicts and failures but is anchored in the success achieved by both communities working together. No community, of course, can check its ideological baggage into the left luggage department and throw away the key, because memory is the spine of identity. Without it, our lives would be paralysed. To live in the present may be a widely held ideal but to live *fully* in the present means not simply to experience but also to assess and evaluate that experience – and that requires reference to the past. However, as Benjamin Jowett put it, 'a man should make a compact with his memory not to remember everything. Great memories are apt to disable judgement.'

Another stumbling block is that the political process with which we are familiar abstracts only one segment of life, which passes, as it were, for the molecular code of the community. Politics becomes an object in itself rather than a programmatic activity – an instrument of human life on the political plane within a generally recognized order of means and ends. Healthy politics, as Va´clav Havel, the Czech president, said, needs to draw energy and inspiration from what should be the fertile soil and multi-layered environment of civil society. This has been described as a complex welter of intermediate institutions, including businesses, voluntary associations, the arts, educational institutions, clubs, unions, media, charities and churches. It is this mosaic of often overlapping institutions and interests which constitutes a society's charter of association, reflecting a high degree of trust between individuals. This in turn supports a strong political base.

There is considerable evidence for the view that successful countries and regions have benefited from having large stocks of social capital invested in dense networks of vertical and horizontal channels of representation and communication, with the state being essentially a source of leadership and integration. The principal bonding mechanism, however, is a single, pervasive *cultural* characteristic, which is the level of trust inherent in the society.

There are grounds for believing that Northern Ireland is ripe for such an approach. We have a very strong voluntary and community sector which is seeking to practise and promote the idea of partnership. In the Northern Ireland Growth Challenge we have a business-driven initiative dedicated to creating strong industrial clusters which exemplify the truth that the enterprise capsule is no longer the individual firm but a network of interacting influences and interests. In one of those almost impenetrable pronouncements so beloved of economists, clusters have been described as setting in motion 'a process of autocentric growth based on the accumulation of place-bound external economies of association'.

A significant advance in linking civil society and the political process was taken in July 1996 when seven of the major bodies representative of business, labour and economic development interests (later joined by an eighth) came together as a group. I am involved as chairman of one of the participating bodies, the Northern Ireland Economic Council, which advises government on economic policy. All the bodies have distinct roles, personalities and agendas and their autonomy remains intact. However, they were concerned lest there was inadequate recognition that vigorous economies require a strong political base and that economic considerations therefore need to be constantly factored into the political process.

On 5 August the group issued a statement warning that only in the absence of violence and turmoil could the enormous potential of the Northern Ireland economy be realized. We also invited all nine parties engaged in the talks process to meet us. We felt that it was vital that we engage in dialogue with the parties collectively, not with each party on its own or even with groupings of like-minded parties. The meeting took place on 7 October. It was a unique occasion. Although not all parties were represented, never before had so disparate a group of business and other interests united to meet such a broad range of political opinion, including the Ulster Unionists, the SDLP and the loyalist parties. Discussion was open and extremely friendly and it was agreed unanimously to meet again when each of us had had opportunity to reflect on what had been said. Our Group of Seven was concerned to stress how important it was that the talks should succeed, since their collapse would be tantamount to the liquidation of the political process – and where, we asked, would one go from there? We invited the parties to seek fresh solutions to problems that had hitherto proved intractable and to tackle areas where agreement might be easier, if only to encourage people to have trust that the talks process could deliver results.

I have already implied some of the desiderata for success, whether the talks (with a new cease-fire in place) are inclusive of Sinn Féin or are confined to the nine existing participants. The challenge for republicans is whether to continue to espouse dreams that are whole (as dreams *can* be) or to risk having to accept what is inevitably *incomplete* reality. Let me mention a few more, broad considerations. First, it perhaps needs to be recognized that there is what it might not be going too far to call a quasi-moral imperative on any society to create institutions for its good government and through which it can pursue its collective purposes. In that sense, abdication or failure is not an option. Political institutions are of course inevitably imperfect, being merely the products of human insight and human capacity. Edmund Burke proclaimed that all government is founded on compromise and barter: 'We balance inconveniences, we give and take, we choose rather to be happy citizens than subtle disputants.' And it was an American jurist who said that 'no good society can be *unprincipled* and no viable society can be *principle-ridden*.' The great Protestant theologian Karl Barth took a realistic view of the political process. 'All it can do,' he said, 'is to grope around and experiment with the convictions which it derives from "natural law" … always making vigorous use, openly or secretly, of a more or less refined positivism.' 'Positivism' is, I think you will agree, a nice euphemism! The results, he concluded, were 'just what might be expected'. Elsewhere he asserted: 'Right itself becomes wrong … when it is allowed to rule as an abstract form, instead of serving the limitation and hence the preservation of man.'

Second, success will depend on the existence of superb negotiating skills on *all* sides of the debate. Unlike in a courtroom trial, it is the parties themselves, not a judge objectively deciding the merits of the case, who decide the outcome. It is the other party which has the power to determine how much of what I want I get. In negotiation, if there is a chance for an agreement with joint gains and the parties fail to reach it, *both lose*. If they succeed, *both win*. Since the aim is to arrive at a *mutually* beneficial solution, not to create winners and losers, each side has to make an effort in good faith to analyse its opponent's interests. In the course of a successful negotiation, the parties move towards what is really *joint* problem-solving and *collaborative* decision-making. At the end, each party has to leave the table with sufficient credibility to sell the outcome (which will reflect some but by no means all of what each party wants) back to their constituency. I suppose that what we are talking about here is what those versed in game theory would call non-zero-sum games. The most famous example, of course, is the prisoner's dilemma which illustrates the mutual gains to be derived through co-operation based on mutual trust. The theory also has interesting things to say about how (sometimes painfully) such trust can evolve.

The third broad consideration is neatly encapsulated in the remark, in relation to a business issue the other day, that concluding negotiations is about 'creating midnights', situations in which failure to agree would confront all the parties with wholly unpalatable alternatives. Those unpalatable alternatives do undoubtedly exist in Northern Ireland in the shape of further loss of life and tragically wasted economic and other opportunities but we have become too adept at adapting to adversity. Perhaps this is where the civil society, to which I referred earlier, can usefully make its voice heard. Perhaps also, in the absence of early movement, a term needs to be set to the talks process in order to inject greater urgency. The argument that talking is good per se is superficially attractive but not if it simply produces reiteration of positions and proves incapable of generating mutual trust. The risk then is that the talks become a *destabilizing* force, giving rise to fears on one side that all is up for grabs and may be lost and, on the other side, to frustration that little if anything is being achieved.

My fourth and final point concerns the need to delete much from the political debate which is vague and abstract (and therefore intimidating) and to start talking in the nuts-and-bolts terms with which the ordinary citizen is more comfortable. Terms like 'consent', 'identity', 'parity of esteem' and 'Irish dimension' go over his head. What do they mean, he wants to know, in terms of arrangements, institutions and day-to-day living? Do they, if I am a unionist, threaten the integrity of the Union? Do they, if I am a nationalist, give me enough space in which to express the Irishness to which I attach importance? Much of today's political debate presents itself as assertions and counter-assertions about 'rights'. Once upon a time, rights were very solemn moral/legal claims, ensconced in constitutional law and treated with much reverence. But new rights – and not just in Northern Ireland – are being minted at a quite inflationary rate. This is *not*, I suggest, helpful to problem-solving. People tend to treat rights-based arguments as trump cards that neutralize all other arguments. Such rights, one jurist has said, 'can be conclusions masquerading as reasons'.

Clarity will be needed above all in relation to what is likely to be the most difficult aspect of the talks process – namely the future relationship between the two parts of the island. I have long argued, in strictly non-political terms, for maximum interaction, constrained by only one consideration – namely that, overall, it should be to mutual benefit. I cannot envisage *either* part finding satisfactory a relationship based on any other premise. Any such relationship will in my view work only if it is based on the concept of an equal partnership in whatever form of activity is undertaken. Many unionists have interpreted the proposals in the Framework Document of February 1995 to mean that the South would acquire power to administer significant aspects of life in Northern Ireland. I express here no view on the proposals themselves but I certainly took them to mean that action under the proposed arrangements would apply as much to the South as to the North and that each side would have equal say in what happened. Working from what is mutually beneficial to the arrangements needed to reap the benefits would seem to be a businesslike way of proceeding. I have heard politicians of all hues acknowledge that there are numerous areas where such benefits exist.

It is only sensible to envisage that the talks *may* fail. If so, it would be better to recognize that reality sooner rather than later and to act neither as if everything were lost nor as if nothing had happened and it was simply a matter of introducing a pause and starting all over again. Reality is fact, not artifact, and, in the event of failure, it may be realistic to acknowledge that the foundations do not exist for a comprehensive top-down settlement. It *may* be necessary to have a period during which we focus on building up the civil society to which I referred earlier, as a preliminary to creating a strong political base. There are networks and partnerships, many of them cross-community, which can be strengthened. Impetus should be given to the ambitious plans for economic growth which I believe the private sector can now deliver. Local authorities which are prepared to operate on a genuinely community basis should be given greater responsibility. Existing initiatives to promote trade, investment and other links which are of mutual benefit to both parts of the island should be reinforced, as should measures which help to remove mutual misunderstanding.

To be clear, this would not be a matter of abandoning the political process. Politicians of all parties should be involved in the planning and overseeing of what would in effect be preparations for a future attempt at achieving political consensus. Working together in this way could well promote the trust which is currently so sadly lacking. It would be for the politicians themselves to indicate when there was a sufficient consensus among them to make the starting up of a formal talks process worthwhile. *Managed* disengagement of this kind from the current process would represent – and, I believe, would be seen worldwide – as a substantial achievement and could bring considerable stability in its train. The alternative to agreement and a solution is not necessarily collapse and conflict. It *is* possible to establish a plateau and to make it stable through confidence-building measures, until the time for renewing the attempted ascent is more propitious.

There will undoubtedly be a great deal of debate within Northern Ireland in the coming months and some elements may overindulge in a diet high in political cholesterol. But let us not forget that what is happening there is in fact the invention of a new and far better future. Whatever the twists and turns of political fortune may be, business will continue to build up the economic base in ways which enhance the prospects for an improved standard of living and a higher quality of life since this is a vital part of whatever new future we invent for ourselves. Bankers are in the business of measuring and evaluating risk. I would sum it up quite simply by saying that Northern Ireland is a very bankable risk.

Postscript

Writing in January 2001, I am satisfied that Northern Ireland has indeed proved to be a bankable risk and I firmly believe that, provided we do not fall back into political uncertainty and instability, Northern Ireland's enormous economic potential can now be unleashed. To make a fair and realistic assessment of the economy of the North, one has to judge it in the context of the monetary union of which it forms part – namely the United Kingdom. Viewed in that perspective, it has done remarkably well, with growth in output, exports and jobs all well ahead of the UK average.

There has been a string of heavyweight job announcements in recent months from Shorts, Nortel, FG Wilson and others. The Province has a strong line-up of high-performing companies which, through thick and thin these past 30 years, have refused to be deterred. There have been notable inward investment successes.

Of course there are challenges. Those no longer needed in security-related occupations will have to be absorbed elsewhere. While the prospects for agriculture are a little brighter, the industry needs to be helped to put itself on a far sounder long-term footing. Within the textile and clothing industry, the move up the value chain which the most enterprising companies have been making needs to be accelerated and there will be job losses which will have to be made up by growth in other sectors. We need to shift the emphasis from compensating disadvantaged areas and, instead, move them from the margins into the mainstream and empower them to shape their own destiny.

Northern Ireland can deploy a formidable array of incentives for investors. But we need to learn from the South that an exceptionally favourable corporate tax rate is in the 'winner takes all' category in the inward investment stakes. When you can tell a prospective foreign investor – as the Republic can – that the return on investment for US manufacturing affiliates in Ireland is typically 24–28 per cent, 3–4 times the European average, you are talking real money. What an arousal factor!

Now is the time for entrepreneurship in policy-making in Northern Ireland. There will never be a better opportunity to break through the economic sound barrier. Bearing in mind what has been achieved in the Republic, I would like to see the North also growing fast and faced with the dilemma of how on earth to conjure up the labour to feed a hungry *Northern* tiger. We need to think ourselves into a higher economic destiny and go hell for leather to make it happen. I suspect that, when we look back, we shall be surprised at the paucity of our expectations and the modesty of our reach. There is already encouraging evidence of what the new political institutions in Northern Ireland can deliver.

The stronger *both* parts of the island, the more mutually beneficial the economic and business links between them can be. The smooth lift-off of the new cross-border institutions augurs well for greater momentum towards the situation where the island, in economic terms, becomes in effect an integrated island-wide production platform. In September 2000 I headed a team from Shorts which was in Dublin to present to companies in the South the huge procurement opportunities offered by that expanding business. Companies in the North are plugging into those opportunities and there is now a nicely growing aerospace cluster in Northern Ireland. I would like to see Northern companies increasingly seeking out – and being offered – similar opportunities in the South. North and South can – and should – reinforce each other's efforts and grow together.

The difficulties constraining political movement after the cease-fires in 1994 were surmounted in the negotiations leading to the Good Friday Agreement in April 1998 but progress towards full implementation has been sluggish. I confess to dismay and disappointment that, two and a half years on from the Agreement, there should again be talk of it and of the institutions which flowed from it being at risk. I do not see how the Agreement can be regarded as other than a solemn and binding convenant between the main traditions on the island, enabling them to work out their destiny together, whatever the difficulties along the way. I – and I suspect many others – see the political representatives of those traditions as trustees of the covenant. Nobody has suggested an alternative remedy for our ills outside the context of the Agreement and of the institutions (and not least the Executive) which, although set up with so much difficulty, are now showing real promise of being able to live up to the high expectations so many of us had of them. The Group of Seven, which, since it was formed in July 1996, has achieved considerable profile as an independent voice strongly supportive of the peace process, said in a public statement on 19 October 2000:

> We do not believe that the vast majority of people in Northern Ireland, however dissatisfied some of them may be with certain aspects of the Agreement, want ever again to lose the ability to govern themselves.

The challenges posed for the leadership of parties and governments are obvious. They cannot get so far ahead of the parade that their followers do not know that they are part of it. They have to strike a delicate balance between listening and persuading, but they should not underestimate people's willingness to be persuaded. Northern Ireland leaders must often feel that, for them, politics is the art not of the possible but of the impossible. But we have to keep on reaching out for the apparently unattainable if we are to avoid the unimaginable. Most people know in their hearts that, however unrealistic the project for reconciliation may at times appear, permanent enmity is an even more unrealistic scenario. Most people want what someone involved in the Middle East peace talks called 'the quiet miracle of a normal life'.

We are a long way from having any real sense of shared 'community' in Northern Ireland. Our divided history precludes us from deriving it from an emotionally shared past. It has to be derived from a shared commitment to the future. Every society needs what the gurus call a 'foundation myth' – a story that embodies a shared meaning and can claim allegiance from both communities. The Agreement was intended to provide such a story, enabling us to put some anchors down, to focus forward rather than hark back.

A casualty of the rocky road since the Agreement has been the loss of much of the 'feel-good factor' which accompanied its signing and its endorsement in the subsequent referenda – the feeling that maybe, just maybe, everything can be forgiven and anything is possible; that (in President Clinton's lyric phrase at his inauguration) one can force the spring or, as Tom Paine (radical revolutionary of two centuries ago) put it, one can start the world over again. Maybe that was always an impossible dream. It involves radical adjustment and willingness to compromise on *all* sides. Too often all of us, in all domains of our lives and not just politics, are guilty of the attitude beautifully described by Mark Twain: 'I'm all for progress but I hate change.' It is not enough to compare in isolation the benefits and costs of any particular development. The same type of cost-benefit reasoning must also be applied to the problems that would still be with us if the development had not happened. Those looking for zero risk end up with zero progress. Politicians deserve commendation for the risks they have taken and must be given the confidence – on all sides – to take the further risks that continual progress requires. This is one of the rare moments when we are being pushed forward by the heave of history – pushed even *beyond* history, where past experience has far less predictive value and it is truer than ever before that life is lived forwards but understood backwards.

Postcript 2006

In my initial essay I suggested that, if difficulties persisted in the peace process, it might be necessary to have a period during which, with the political parties fully involved, the focus was on building up civil society as a preliminary to creating a strong political base: 'The alternative to agreement and a solution is not necessarily collapse and conflict. It is possible to establish a plateau and to make it stable through confidence-building measures, until the time for renewing the attempted ascent is more propitious.'

However, the focus in recent years has been primarily on establishing and then, on its collapse, restoring the Executive. The serious lack of trust and the persistent deficiency in social capital are still only too evident. I became very conscious of the sheer depth of the fault lines, reflecting a deeply riven society, during my Review of the Parades Commission (Report published November 2002, partly reproduced in Appendix 9). In subsequent evidence to the Northern Ireland Affairs Committee of the House of Commons on the Parades issue (January 2004), I drew attention to survey material showing that, over time, the proportion of Catholics agreeing with the statement 'my cultural tradition is always the underdog' had decreased exactly in line with the increase in the proportion of Protestants who agreed with that statement. 70 per cent of Catholics were confident that their own cultural tradition is protected in Northern Ireland these days, compared with only a third of Protestants. I suggested that the declining Protestant confidence in their position post-Agreement was as worrying as it would be if the statistics were reversed. Both traditions must see themselves as having a stake in a shared future. The improving situation on the streets lulled many into a false sense of security. Too little attention was paid to the massive effort required to keep the lid on potentially explosive situations during the marching season and to the paucity of evidence that underlying animosities had diminished.

Starting from the basis of realities, we now need a massive investment in the generation of social capital – but not of the kind that bonds like with like. We have enough of that, reinforcing exclusive identities and homogeneous groups. What we need is the social capital that bridges the cleavages and generates broader identities and sympathies. It is not easy to create the social filaments in a society characterized by so much segregation in housing, work, education and sport. But the need for policies to promote integration and cohesion – which is very different from assimilation and loss of identity – is as imperative as in Great Britain, where a Commission to consider such issues in the aftermath of the July 2005 terrorist attack has been established.

As I recommended in my Parades Review Report, there may have to be more emphasis on work with single identity groups as a staging post to inter-group work, particularly when one community is experiencing the nihilism and fatalism that beset those in psychological retreat. Such work needs to be conducted with care so that (as I put it in the Report) people who are suspicious of or hostile to others are not reinforced in that tendency, with the result that cultural distinctiveness becomes even more key to self-esteem.

Some of our segregated communities share many of the characteristics of defensive ghettoes worldwide, with their own authority figures (in this case the paramilitaries). There are no quick fixes, but Northern Ireland's future stability depends on finding the means of pulling the margins into the mainstream.

My previous Postscript highlighted the need to break through the economic sound barrier and drew attention to the South's exceptionally favourable corporate tax rate as an example of the entrepreneurial policy-making that we needed to emulate. Subsequent events confirm that view. On conventional measures such as numbers employed and unemployed we score well. But this masks a serious imbalance in the economy, which can only be rectified by a step change in the size of the private sector. Otherwise we are at the mercy of the level of public sector spending, which is highly unlikely to be sustained at its recent exceptional level. To have to address the consequences of such vulnerability without adequate means would make the task of an incoming Executive even more difficult.

The Northern Ireland Peace Process has exemplified my earlier observation that turnkey solutions are a rarity and progress is never linear. The Good Friday Agreement raised the bar high, requiring enforced fraternity at the top while there was a serious lack of fraternity at the base. Stability demands that, for the future, as much attention be devoted to constructing the load-bearing beams as to erecting the superstructure. I have felt – and have been saying – that there was far too much unwarranted complacency about the state of affairs at the grass roots. We really do now need to buckle down to some significant 'region-building'.

Note

1. Except for some expansion of the passages dealing with analogues to the Northern Ireland peace process and the omission of some material dealing with the (then) current economic situation, this paper is the same as the text of my Institute of Irish Studies Lecture delivered on 24 October 1996, during the period between the breakdown of the first IRA ceasefire and the creation of the negotiating process which resulted in the Good Friday Agreement in April 1998. I have added a postscript based on a speech to a Rotary International Conference in Kilkenny on 29 September 2000.

The Resolution of Armed Conflict: Internationalization and its Lessons, Particularly in Northern Ireland[1]

Lord David Owen

Large nations do not like calling for outside intervention, whether diplomatic or military, to help in dealing with conflict within their own sphere of influence, let alone within their own sovereign boundaries. No country has demonstrated that more clearly than the UK, which until 1994 rejected internationalizing its peace effort in relation to the long-standing Irish conflict.

Many nations also guard zealously that provision in the UN Charter which ensures the 'inherent right of individual or collective self-defence', and the limitation in Article 2.7 of the UN Charter which states that 'nothing contained in the present Charter shall authorise the United Nations to intervene in matters which are essentially within the jurisdiction of any state'. Yet while this UN wording has undoubtedly inhibited international intervention in the past, it has not prevented it. In the early 1990s, after the end of the Cold War, the balance shifted subtly in the Security Council in favour of some forms of international humanitarian intervention, both diplomatic and military. But Russia, and particularly China, had deep reservations. The onus of proof for any external intervention in an internal conflict was still on those who wished to intervene.

The humanitarian duty to intervene, or, as the French say, *devoir d'ingérence*,[2] was given legitimacy under the UN Charter when on 5 April 1991 the UN Security Council passed Resolution 688, strongly advocated by the then British Prime Minister, John Major, to deal with the Kurdish refugee crisis caused by the military action of the Iraqi government. President Mitterrand said: 'for the first time, noninterference has stopped at the point where it was becoming failure to assist a people in danger'. This action, under Chapter VII establishing a 'no fly zone' in Iraq, still operates in the north, but the Kurds live uneasily under constant threat and on the Security Council Russia, China and France were by 1998 against this intervention.

In the context of Somalia, in Resolution 794, passed on 3 December 1992, the Security Council authorized intervention, again under Chapter VII, because there was a humanitarian crisis and virtually no government in the capital, Mogadishu. The US was in the lead with US commanders controlling the UN operation. Initially successful, the intervention became bogged down in a trial of strength with a local Somali warlord and in effect ended with a US Ranger's body, one of 18 killed, being dragged behind a vehicle in front of the world's TV cameras. The US quickly withdrew and Somalia was left to settle its own affairs. The lesson was drawn by some that a humanitarian intervention should not 'cross the Mogadishu line' by becoming a combatant in the power struggle within the country it is attempting to help. The damaging legacy was that the US administration blamed its own failures on the UN and in the process of denigration left the UN weakened, perhaps permanently.

The UN Security Council, faced by what was then an internal conflict or civil war in the former Yugoslavia, passed Resolution 713 on 25 September 1991, placing an embargo on the whole of Yugoslavia which later inhibited the right of new member states to purchase arms. Interventions by the UN and other bodies, with the exception of NATO in Kosovo, came after there had been international recognition of the newly emerging states. The exception was in May 1992 with the first imposition of economic and political sanctions against the Federal Republic of Yugoslavia (Serbia and Montenegro) without their agreement. For example, the deployment of a UN Protection Force in March 1992 in Croatia to uphold the Vance Plan was agreed by Croatia; the June 1992 humanitarian operation at Sarajevo airport in Bosnia-Herzegovina, the August 1992 decision to deploy UNPROFOR, headquartered in Croatia, on a humanitarian mission into Bosnia-Herzegovina, and NATO bombing in Bosnia all had the support of the UN-recognized government of Bosnia-Herzegovina.

NATO first became involved in the former Yugoslavia in 1993, enforcing a 'no fly zone' over the whole of Bosnia-Herzegovina with the agreement of its government. Then in February 1994 NATO was authorized to support UNPROFOR with air strikes and then bomb more generally in 1995. NATO only came into Bosnia-Herzegovina formally on the ground in December 1995, replacing UNPROFOR as part of the multinational implementation force, IFOR, following the Dayton Accords.

In the case of Rwanda the Security Council, as part of a new US policy of 'knowing when to say no' to outside humanitarian interventions, refused to strengthen the small UN force in Rwanda in the spring of 1994. In the judgment of the Canadian general on the ground, that decision stopped the UN from preventing the worst genocide for fifty years[3] – arguably worse than Cambodia, although not as bad as the Second World War genocide of the Jews. In Rwanda the absence of a forceful outside intervention led to the war crossing over into what was then Zaire, now renamed the Congo, and the repercussions are still being felt in Central Africa at the start of the twenty-first century.

NATO's humanitarian military intervention in Kosovo in March 1999 took place against the will of the Federal Republic of Yugoslavia after disagreement within the Security Council. As a grave humanitarian crisis threatened for the winter of 1998–99 in Kosovo, the six Contact Group countries – the US, the UK, France, Germany, Russia and Italy – were, for understandable reasons, reluctant to repeat the same UN-based humanitarian intervention that had been agreed by the Security Council in August 1992 for Bosnia. The NATO countries, not prepared to contemplate ground action, threatened President Milosevic with air strikes first in June and again in October 1998. NATO was divided over deploying ground forces even around Kosovo, in Albania and Macedonia. Milosevic exploited this reluctance to commit NATO troops with a campaign of ethnic cleansing and suppression of the Kosovo Liberation Army. Eventually, under the threat of air strikes, a compromise was forged between President Milosevic and the US emissary, Richard Holbrooke, in October 1998, which at least averted a humanitarian catastrophe in the winter of 1998–99. It involved placing OSCE unarmed 'verifiers' in Kosovo. But this did not bring about meaningful negotiations on autonomy for Kosovo. The Rambouillet Conference in early 1999 was described by Henry Kissinger as 'merely an excuse to start the bombing'. Given the significant changes between the Rambouillet demands made by the US, France and Britain and the G8 settlement of June that ended the war it is hard to disagree with that assessment. President Clinton agreed with President Yeltsin to take off the negotiating table a referendum on independence after three years which the KLA had been promised by Madeleine Albright. He also agreed to UN, not NATO, administration. In the G8 settlement, in addition, there was no longer any question of NATO forces coming in through roads, aerodromes, railways and ports from Yugoslavia to Kosovo and the new form of words made it easier for Belgrade to go on shielding its war criminals.

The legality of NATO's operation under the UN Charter was at best dubious. It depended on linking the earlier UN Security Council resolutions on the impending humanitarian crisis with the belief that an urgent humanitarian intervention was impending. It deliberately did not go back to the Security Council, knowing that it would never endorse a humanitarian military intervention. The OSCE's report 'Human Rights in Kosovo', published in December 1999, makes clear that 'summary and arbitrary killings escalated dramatically' when the OSCE verifiers withdrew from Kosovo on 20 March, four days before the bombing started, and then became 'widespread' with the bombing. The flight of an estimated 863,000 Kosovar Albanians took place during the 81 days of bombing. NATO intervention ensured that all those who survived and who wished to return could do so with NATO troops, and Kosovar Albanians were from then on safe. Sadly, it was the 200,000 Serbs who then became the victims of Kosovar Albanian retribution.

As the OSCE report makes clear, violation of human rights was 'both the cause and the consequence of the conflict in Kosovo'. Nevertheless, NATO's intervention was fundamentally a humanitarian intervention and though it did not have the specific endorsement of the Security Council, it did not run counter to the spirit of the UN Charter. To go on waiting for justification, for the human rights abuses to mount further, after what we knew about Serb action in the past, would, I believe, have been against the humanitarian imperative within the Charter. That is not to say that Russian and Chinese criticisms of NATO's approach do not have some validity. The bombing of bridges over the Danube hurt the Yugoslavs' neighbours far more than the Yugoslavs. If we had been readier than we were to concede some of the Russians' criticisms we might have been at least listened to when advocating internationalization over Chechnya.[4] Chechnya is, however, very different from Kosovo. Russia, under Yeltsin, negotiated far-reaching autonomy for Chechnya; by contrast Milosevic withdrew autonomy from Kosovo.

Looking back over US attitudes and policies in the former Yugoslavia one can see that the Bush administration in 1991–92 chose to play a limited role, but was broadly supportive of the EU, which wanted to take the lead role politically, and of the Conference on the Former Yugoslavia led by the EU and UN. The Clinton administration from January 1993 to July 1995 did not find the same self-confidence or self-discipline to accept a limited role in the former Yugoslavia. It chose instead the rhetoric of leadership for two and a half years, while frustrating the UN/EU's peace efforts by being politically unwilling to make the necessary compromises[5] and militarily unprepared to contribute to UN peacekeeping or to NATO intervention until there was an actual settlement on the ground. However, following the June 1995 massacre of Bosnian Muslims in Srebrenica, the US faced the harsh realities and at last was ready to act and assume the main leadership role involving NATO action to virtually impose a settlement. The Dayton Accords also incorporated many of the political compromises that the US had hitherto rejected in earlier EU/UN and Contact Group settlement plans. From September 1995 the US played the lead role in the former Yugoslavia, because it was ready to accept the responsibilities that go with the exercise of real power.

There have been pluses and minuses to all the external interventions in the former Yugoslavia. They helped until 2001 to prevent war spilling over into Macedonia and hopefully they will do so for Montenegro. In summary, Slovenia had only a few days of war. It escaped its past association with Yugoslavia and will be the first of the former Yugoslav states to enter the EU. Croatia in effect came out on top of all the wars in the former Yugoslavia, but sadly in the process became almost completely ethnically 'cleansed'. Croatia was also left with substantial and undue influence and control over far too large a percentage of the Muslim-Croat Federation in Bosnia-Herzegovina. Republika Srpska remains by international law in Bosnia-Herzegovina, but after the first five years it was still not integrated, though small numbers of Muslims are returning. Its leaders in Pale, if not in Banja Luka, are still waiting for an eventual linkage to Yugoslavia. Macedonia was helped by the UN preventive force deployed in late 1992, but some of its Albanian minority want independence and will watch very closely what happens over independence for Kosovo. Kosovo, as a result of the G8 settlement and because of the UN Security Council, will have to remain for some time *de jure* in Serbia; yet it has already developed *de facto* independence. A serious conflict between a largely intact Serbian Army and the Muslim-led Kosovo Liberation Army looms into the future. Meanwhile the biggest risk is of the KLA turning on NATO as the Irgun guerillas did in Palestine, blowing up British forces in the King David Hotel in Jerusalem when the UK was saddled with an unimplementable UN Palestine mandate.

It is hard to believe, even with Milosevic ousted and Tudjman dead, that real peace will come to the Balkans until Kosovo becomes independent. For this to happen Serbia must be given some compensation for its loss of territory. An overall Balkan solution needs to be encouraged. Were it to emerge over the next few years we could see, with the agreement of the Bosnian government, part of the Eastern area of Republika Srpska, still dominated by hardline Serb nationalists in the elections held in 2000, coming into Yugoslavia to compensate for Serbia's loss of Kosovo; a new less nationalistic government in power in Zagreb helping the Muslims and Croats in Bosnia-Herzegovina to work more harmoniously; and, hopefully with Serbia's encouragement, the more moderate Serb leaders in the Banja Luka area, including those in Brcko, integrating fully into Bosnia-Herzegovina.

The EU, in 2001, must do more to strengthen Macedonia economically and help the Albanian minority within that country recognize that they cannot separate and join up with Kosovo. The Montenegrin and Serb governments have become ever more uneasy partners in the Federation of Yugoslavia. While Milosevic remained in power in Belgrade, the chances of Montenegro living comfortably within the Federation were remote, but even now, under President Kostunica, some in Montenegro still insist on independence. If this happens, the Serb armed forces are unlikely to accept losing all access to the Adriatic and will insist on retaining at least their naval base in the Bay of Kotor. The essential task is to help Serbia and Montenego remain together and to build a strong economy while coming close to NATO and the EU.

Kostunica's skill has been in keeping the opposition parties together in the coalition. He was right to reject Milosevic's bogus call for a second round to the election and also to resist those governments in NATO which wanted him to fight a second round. Kostunica realized that there would be no democratic transition unless he could keep the armed forces from overthrowing the ballot box. He managed to hold both the armed forces and the police out of Milosevic's control during those critical days by making it clear throughout the election and after the election that he would not allow Serbia's military or political leaders, under arrest orders, to be sent to the Hague Criminal Court. Kostunica took a risk in allowing Milosevic's supporters to contest the December 2000 elections, but it was a calculated act which helped achieve a peaceful transition. Only after this, in the summer of 2001, was Milosevic flown out of Serbia to face trial for war crimes.

This leads me to suggest a first general guideline for the resolution of armed conflict: while outside intervention in terms of the new International Court and specific tribunals, as in the cases of former Yugoslavia and Rwanda, may help prevent and even resolve conflict, *reconciliation within countries must be encouraged and allowed to take its own individual course and should not be rigidly prescribed from outside by constricting international rules and regulations.* This is the experience from post-Franco Spain, Rhodesia (now Zimbabwe), Namibia, Chile, Argentina, South Africa and Northern Ireland. International courts and tribunals need not and in my view should not amnesty those on whom they have issued arrest orders; those people should always be open to arrest abroad even if they stay in their own country as a result of an internal compromise, with an internal amnesty protecting them from arrest. But justice cannot be an absolute. The release of prisoners convicted as terrorist criminals was an essential element in the Northern Ireland peace settlement. It was arguable whether it was necessary for there to be a wholesale release but at least this was tempered by the provision that the prisoners were only released on licence and it was essential to see Peter Mandelson start to revoke those licences when faced by obvious breaches.

A second guideline from former Yugoslavia which we must learn for the future in the prevention of ethnic conflict is that *in addition to the morality of stopping deaths, torture and hardship, wars associated with ethnic cleansing must not await a perfect solution. In ethnic wars realities are created on the ground that are very much harder to reverse with the passage of time.* In Bosnia the two-and-a-half-year delay between the Vance/Owen Peace Plan, agreed in Athens but then blocked by the Bosnian Serbs in Pale, and the Dayton Peace Accords led to the American government awarding the Bosnian Serbs 6 per cent more territory for Republika

Srpska and the Croatian army taking much the same amount by force of arms. The five wars in the former Yugoslavia will leave a massive legacy of ethnic hatred and religious fervour in the Balkans which will haunt future generations.

We see the traditional reluctance to involve other states or international bodies in internal conflict situations today, most graphically in Russia's refusal to accept any outside help over Chechnya. This region lies within the internationally recognized boundaries of the Russian Federation. It was part of the Chechen-Ingush Autonomous Republic inside Russia. This small mountainous area, which unilaterally declared its independence in November 1991 soon after the break-up of the Soviet Union, has a long history of resistance. In the nineteenth century the Chechens resisted Moscow's conquest of the Caucasus for longer than any other people in the region. Then Stalin exiled the entire Chechen people to Kazakhstan, where many died. As they returned – even in the era of the Soviet Union – they began to assert their nationhood and draw on their reputation as fearless Muslim warriors.

Initially President Yeltsin had too many other problems with the break-up of the Soviet Union to contemplate military intervention in Chechnya. He focused on establishing the Commonwealth of Independent States (CIS) and, while rejecting independence for Chechnya, he was ready to offer autonomy. Georgia was allowed to leave if it wished, and not even join the CIS, which it initially refused to do. Under a former Soviet Air Force general, Dudaev, Chechnya became, within a few years, a lawless enclave with gun running, money laundering, drug profiteering and kidnapping financing an arsenal of weapons. Viewed from Moscow this was becoming a challenge it could no longer ignore, particularly because the oil pipeline from the Caspian Sea went through Chechnya, near to Grozny, and was due within a few years to carry large quantities of oil to the Russian Black Sea port of Novorossiysk.

In December 1994 President Yeltsin ordered the military to restore constitutional order in Chechnya. This was to become the Achilles heel of his eight and a half years in power. The Russian military failure over one and a half years of an incompetently conducted war was bad enough but the political damage to Yeltsin's reformist liberal constituency during 1995 and early 1996 was considerable. Yeltsin very nearly lost the 1996 presidential election and only saved his presidency, after the first round of that election, by bringing General Lebed into the government. By bowing to popular opinion and authorizing Lebed to do a deal and achieve the central electoral promise of the Yeltsin campaign, namely a truce in Chechnya, Yeltsin bought more time.

Coming from the Urals, Yeltsin was initially very understanding of the urge for autonomy and was no Moscow centralist. One saw this in the 1993 Constitution and through his second term of office, as he shaped a decentralized Russian Federation.[6] In February 1994 Yeltsin signed a treaty with the most popular of the Russian Republics, Tatarstan – an oil-rich enclave the size of Ireland in the Volga-Urals region – which gave Tatarstan its own flag, constitution and laws, the right to collect taxes and ownership of its oil. The Chechens, instead of building on this, were fixed on independence for Chechnya or nothing. Eventually the agreement of 31 August 1996, signed between Lebed and the Chechnyan leader Maskhadov, granted political autonomy, allowed for the withdrawal of Russian forces and the final status of what the separatists call the Republic of Ichkeria to be resolved by December 2001. But the Chechens did not, as they also agreed, suspend their drive for independence. It is hard to believe that Yeltsin or anyone else in Moscow believed they would.

Three years of benign neglect of Chechnya led to a malign situation but President Yeltsin saved his reputation for a second time by bringing in Prime Minister Vladimir Putin in August 1999. Putin was able initially to channel popular feelings of outrage against the Chechens, as a result of the bombs in Moscow, into a new military onslaught. Then Yeltsin, by resigning the presidency on 31 December, allowed Putin to become acting president for an election on 26 March 2000, brought forward from the normal time in June. Putin won it overwhelmingly. In this election Putin's military confrontation with the Chechens was a vote-winner.

An important question of foreign policy is how the Western democracies help Russia and President Putin to deal with the hideously complex issues that surround the Chechnya conflict. To date there has been no readiness in Moscow to contemplate outside help with mediation and even perhaps peacekeeping. Yet in two conflicts within Britain's sovereign exercise of power, namely Rhodesia and Northern Ireland, we have seen how external involvement helped us deal with the crises.

My interest in this question of internationalizing the resolution of conflicts first came about while, as an MP from 1966 to 1976, I watched as successive British governments zealously guarded Britain's independent decision-making over Rhodesia, from the moment on 11 November 1965 when Ian Smith issued a unilateral declaration of independence. Britain pursued a series of diplomatic solutions over 10 years, all dependent on qualified franchises for the black majority of Rhodesians. Having forsworn before the Rhodesian unilateral declaration of independence the use of British forces, the UK nevertheless insisted that Rhodesia was a colony in rebellion against the Crown and took the lead internationally. The British government insisted on acting initially only under a non-mandatory resolution of the Security Council. The effect of those initial sanctions was to stop oil reaching Rhodesia along the hitherto principal route, the Umtali pipeline from Beira, but not via lorries and trains from Mozambique. UN sanctions became mandatory only in December 1966 but South Africa and the Portuguese colony Mozambique protected Rhodesia from their effects. As navy minister from 1968 to 1970 I saw at close hand the futility of Royal Navy patrols stopping oil going into Beira, while the same oil tankers were free to sail into Lourenço Marques in Mozambique, in part because some of the oil was going to South Africa and we did not wish to risk a confrontation with the South African navy. From 1975 when the Portuguese revolution triggered Mozambique's independence, oil went to Rhodesia not from Mozambique but through South Africa. The Bingham Inquiry, which as foreign secretary I established in 1977, reported in 1978 and showed that ever since 1967 it had been known in Whitehall that UK sanctions law was being breached and that oil had been illegally supplied by British oil companies to Rhodesia – prior to a cynical swap arrangement in 1968 – and was again supplied illegally after the swap arrangement had been abandoned in 1971.

The US secretary of state, Henry Kissinger, made the first attempt at international involvement in southern Africa in late 1976. His diplomatic initiative over Rhodesia then collapsed at the Geneva Conference called by Britain. When I became foreign secretary in February 1977, it was clear to me that for the Labour government, with no parliamentary majority, and with the Conservative opposition in no mood to support a one member, one vote solution, there were real advantages in involving the US in a much closer partnership and effective working relationship in helping to resolve the Rhodesian conflict. This reality was underscored for me in a very personal way when I was rebuffed that summer by the Cabinet over my wish to have a Commonwealth force go into Rhodesia to supervise a negotiated ceasefire and monitor elections. This meant that US involvement would be further needed in helping us to persuade the Soviet Union not to veto a UN peacekeeping force. The Anglo-US Rhodesian Peace Plan of September 1977 kept the parties negotiating while fighting for the next two years. In the summer of 1979 the new Conservative foreign secretary, Peter Carrington, drawing on support from the Lusaka Commonwealth Heads of Government meeting, called a Lancaster House Conference for the autumn. The new UK government, to its credit, was ready to lead a Commonwealth peacekeeping force and restore, for the transition, a British governor. It was a bold and successful policy concluding with internationally supervised elections in 1980. The US was somewhat sidelined, but the settlement was fully consistent with the Anglo-American proposals, and the US, under President Carter and Secretary of State Cyrus Vance, had been powerful enough to ensure that Prime Minister Margaret Thatcher resisted her previous instinct to recognize Bishop Muzorewa's interim government or the temptation to settle for a qualified franchise. This gave the appearance of a reassertion of British diplomatic independence and, followed by the successful military recapturing of the Falkland Islands in 1982, it meant that for a few more years Thatcher was strengthened in her reluctance to compromise UK independence over Northern Ireland. Concern grew, however, about the need for Irish help in controlling the movement of terrorists over the border with Northern Ireland.

Margaret Thatcher, an instinctive unionist, had distanced herself from the approach of her Conservative predecessor, Edward Heath, in the 1973 Sunningdale Agreement. The Sunningdale Agreement promised much, but was not sustained against the Protestant workers' strike in early 1974. Perhaps it was no longer sustainable when there was a change of government from Conservative to Labour. The fundamental problem was that the Agreement took the then Ulster Unionist leader, Brian Faulkner, too far away from his own political base, and the so-called Irish dimension with the South alienated too many Unionists for him to hold his party together. What made sense around a negotiating table in England had to be saleable to the majority of Ulstermen back home. Margaret Thatcher signed the Anglo-Irish Agreement on 15 November 1985 with the then Irish Taoiseach, Dr Garret Fitzgerald, whom she had grown to trust. She hoped that the cross-border co-operation in the Agreement between the British and Irish governments would be vastly improved, but sadly, for a variety of reasons, this did not happen. The Agreement allowed, for the first time, a consultative role to the South in the government of the North. The Unionists, who thought they could rely on her, felt betrayed to Dublin. Enoch Powell, now a Unionist MP, and someone she admired, branded her a Jezebel. Only Margaret Thatcher could have made the Conservative party accept this Agreement, and in the process her close friend and parliamentary private secretary, Ian Gow, resigned, only to be later tragically blown up by an IRA car bomb. Margaret Thatcher had, however, shifted opinion among Conservative MPs to accept that the London–Dublin axis was vital for peace. While she never contemplated fully internationalizing the issue she made the crucial realization that reducing terrorism across national borders involves co-operation between neighbouring states. It was left to Prime Minister John Major to cross the rubicon of internationalizing the Northern Ireland conflict by involving the United States of America. The story of how this was done holds important lessons for conflict resolution worldwide.

The UK government's Rhodesian and Northern Ireland experience, and also the period of confrontation with Indonesia in 1963–65 suggests a third guideline: for outside intervention to help in conflict situations, *engaging the surrounding countries in any diplomatic approach, even if not in actual police or military operations, helps achieve peace.* UN experience offers some qualification of this guideline, in that many UN secretary-generals have been wary of too great an involvement in the actual peacekeeping of surrounding states, fearing that their interests are not always those of the warring country. Too often, also, their forces have not been impartial towards the warring factions. Nevertheless, a diplomatic effort that ignores the surrounding states usually suffers. Neighbouring countries that can establish co-operative economic and trading policies are often well placed to help resolve a conflict among or within their partner states. It was for this reason that many had high hopes, which have in the main been justified, of the effect on the Northern Ireland conflict of Britain and Ireland joining the European Community in January 1973. Nevertheless it was the full internationalization by involving the US after a further 20 years which appears to have been the crucial factor.

There are three main accounts of this period of internationalization leading up to the Downing Street Declaration of 15 December 1993, which itself paved the way for the 1998 Good Friday Agreement. The first is John Major's autobiography;[7] the second is *Daring Diplomacy* by Conor O'Clery, an *Irish Times* correspondent in Washington, to whom all the major participants, except the British government, spoke extensively.[8] The third book is Senator George Mitchell's *Making Peace.*[9] I have drawn on all three of these accounts as well as newspaper reports. As one would expect, there are differences of opinion and some differences over facts, but the story of how this historic dispute was internationalized is one with profound implications for solving future conflicts.

It was to try in a modest way to promote this concept of learning from other conflicts in different parts of the world that in 1997 I helped the Institute of Irish Studies in the University of Liverpool to start a series of lectures to help focus attention on aspects of other settlements in the world that might help the people of Northern Ireland reach an agreement among themselves. Two of the lectures I chaired over a 36-hour period in Liverpool, Dublin and Belfast – one by Frederik Van Zyl Slabbert, former leader of the South African Liberal party and himself an Afrikaner, the other by Jan Egeland, a Norwegian and a participant in the

Oslo peace talks which paved the way for Yasser Arafat's historic agreement with Yitzhak Rabin.

British politicians have found the involvement in Irish affairs of the United States of America, which has 44 million citizens of Irish or Scots-Irish descent, hard to accept. To some extent this is surprising. We know the issue has run very deep within our own people and various governments in Westminster have at times had to concentrate on preventing the issue from dividing people living in major cities such as Liverpool and Glasgow. It is not surprising then that it has repercussions in the US, particularly in New York and Boston. History tells us that Irish-American dollars supported Daniel O'Connell's fight for Catholic emancipation, also Charles Stewart Parnell's campaign for Home Rule and Eamon de Valera's Irish Republican Army in the War of Independence with Britain, which led to the creation of the Irish Free State and the partition of Ireland. As part of this history, when Sinn Féin calls for a united Ireland it is seen by many Irish-Americans as worthy of their support. Successive British governments, particularly when the 'Troubles' restarted in 1969, did their best in the USA to portray Sinn Féin as part and parcel of a terrorist body (the IRA) and as defying the democratic will of the majority. Yet to many Irish-Americans this majority was only within the partitioned Northern part of Ireland. Their interest was and remains with the opinion of all those who live in the island of Ireland.

A serious Irish-American political initiative started in 1975 with four key political leaders making a public statement: Governor Carey of New York, Senators Pat Moynihan and Edward Kennedy, and the Speaker of the House of Representatives, Tip O'Neill. Hitherto US presidents, while often expressing sympathy for Irish-American hopes and aspirations, had normally not been prepared to incur the wrath of British governments, zealously guarding their responsibility under international law for Northern Ireland. President Jimmy Carter openly criticized British policy in 1977 and promised economic support for any settlement. Yet thereafter he largely stayed away from the problem while in office. I remember during the Carter administration the American ambassador in London coming to see me at the Foreign Office and implying that, as a result of Congressional pressure, America would not be able to supply a particularly accurate sniper rifle for the British Army. Yet when I said that as foreign minister of their major NATO ally I could not accept this message unless it was relayed to me personally by the secretary of state, Cyrus Vance, I heard no more.

Bill Clinton was the first American president to make a sustained commitment to peace in Northern Ireland. Some say the reason for Clinton's readiness to defy John Major's wishes over Gerry Adams's visa application was that Major's Conservative party had supported Clinton's opponent, the then sitting president George Bush. That Clinton was angry with Major even in victory is clear, but I believe there are much deeper reasons why he was prepared to risk Anglo-American relations over Ireland. Some commentators point to his mother being called Cassidy or his White House meeting at the age of 16 with John F. Kennedy to explain his involvement. A more compelling factor to me is that he was at Oxford as a Rhodes scholar in 1968 at the very time when Northern Ireland became a major civil rights issue. The scenes of violence on British TV and the newspaper reporting left, I suspect, no doubt in his mind, nor in my mind as a young Labour MP, that there was intolerable discrimination in housing, employment, economic and social policies against many of the Catholics in Northern Ireland. When the British troops went into Northern Ireland in 1969 I was minister for the navy. We were due to close the Sea Eagle naval base in Londonderry. Far from wanting to reconsider that decision I urged the Admiralty Board to get out as quickly as possible, for I felt then that the army might be in for a lot longer than people expected and I did not want to see the navy enveloped as well. For the next 20 years I supported all attempts to reduce discrimination, but I regret that our narrow parliamentary majority meant that negotiating an end to the conflict was not as high a priority as it should have been for the Labour Cabinet of 1977–79.

John Major admits that in 1990 when he became prime minister he knew little about Northern Ireland, but he takes justified pride in the fact that he altered the old cliché and put Northern Ireland onto the front burner. It was Peter Brooke, as Northern Ireland secretary, who took the first imaginative step. Aware that Gerry Adams had been talking since 1988 to John Hume, Peter Brooke, in 1990, authorized the reopening of the British intelligence link to the Provisionals. Through those contacts in February 1993 came a startling message for the British prime minister: 'The conflict is over but we need your advice on how to bring it to a close. We cannot meet the secretary of state's public renunciation of violence, but it would be given privately as long as we were sure that we were not being tricked.' John Major had already established a relationship with the Taoiseach Albert Reynolds, leader of Fianna Fáil, who took office in February 1992 and he writes simply in his memoirs, 'I liked Albert a lot'. Their relationship was further enhanced, according to Reynolds, when, in the best tradition of political 'wheeler-dealing', he gave Clinton cover, persuading the Irish-American lobby in March 1993 that it was understandable that Clinton had to shelve his election commitment to appoint a peace envoy to Northern Ireland to avoid upsetting the British who were now ready to move towards a settlement. In so doing Reynolds ensured that Major would 'owe him one'. Clinton, by appointing Senator Edward Kennedy's sister, Jean Kennedy Smith, as ambassador to Dublin, nevertheless sent a clear message to London that Ireland mattered to him politically. Yet John Major's understanding was that Clinton had dropped the envoy commitment at his request as something which would have thoroughly alienated the unionists.

As prime minister, John Major's most valuable personal contribution to the peace process was his absolute determination to carry with him the Unionist leaders, first Jim Molyneaux, then David Trimble, and also to focus his attention on John Taylor and Ken Maginnis. He knew that Edward Heath and Margaret Thatcher had alienated too many Unionists and this had stymied their progress. He saw that the Unionists, not the minority party leaders, John Hume or Gerry Adams, held the irreplaceable key to peace and this was also the key over which he, as a Conservative leader, had the most influence. He appeared never to shift from this stance; his stubbornness may have provoked the IRA to restart bombing after the first ceasefire, but by holding his nerve he held the Unionists to the peace process and for that he deserves high praise. It was also to the great credit of Tony Blair that he saw how essential this Unionist relationship was and worked on it, first as opposition Labour leader and then as prime minister, holding the trust of David Trimble right up to and after the formation of the Assembly. While this concentration on the Unionists was the crucial policy for London to pursue it was a real bonus that successive Taioseachs Reynolds, Bruton and Ahern also understood its importance in Dublin. This was a new and positive feature of the Anglo-Irish relationship. There was also a far greater measure of realism about the need for a consensus across the Northern Ireland political spectrum among some of the Irish-American leaders, of whom Niall O'Dowd and 'Chuck' Feeney appear to me pre-eminent. All of this was, however, part of a dialogue that had been moving in an inclusive direction over a number of years. The real challenge for the US was always going to be whether they could deliver first Gerry Adams, and then that part of the IRA that Gerry Adams could not himself influence, for serious negotiations.

It was in relation to Gerry Adams that the key Irish-American leaders believed that the president of the United States could have an impact that no one else could have. To do this, however, meant involving the US in the detail of any Northern Ireland peace initiative, something which no British prime minister had hitherto been prepared to contemplate. During Clinton's first year in office, John Major concentrated on Dublin, establishing a set of principles which the British and Irish governments could jointly accept and to which the Unionists could sign up. Only then would a ceasefire become the priority. Two more messages were received in London from the Provisionals in May and November 1993, in addition to that of February, and the British gave two replies on 19 March and 5 November on what sort of a formally announced exploratory dialogue would be on offer after a ceasefire. Subsequent leaks and propaganda, however, fouled the atmosphere and a House of Commons statement on 21 November closed that private channel down; but it had served a useful purpose.

On 3 December 1993, in Dublin Castle, in half an hour's completely private straight talking, Major and Reynolds ironed out some real differences. This was then followed by an hour's intense negotiation between the two governments with just one official on each side, and the Downing Street Declaration was announced on 15 December.

Historians will long argue over the significance to the peace process of Clinton's decision to admit Gerry Adams to the US early in 1994, after the Downing Street Declaration, but before it had been accepted and the IRA ceasefire put in place. It was a decision that astonished and annoyed Major at the time and even in 1999 he claimed it had shaken the confidence of the Unionists and bolstered the Provisionals against pressure to accept the Declaration. To Senator Mitchell, by contrast, also writing in 1999, Clinton's decision was a transforming step which paved the way to inclusive negotiations. Interestingly Mitchell, before he became involved in the negotiations in Northern Ireland, had been one of several senators who had signed a letter to Clinton arguing for the visa to be issued to Adams. What these differences show is either that opinions rarely change even with the benefit of five years of reflection, or that the Atlantic is still a wide ocean when it comes to judging the Irish question.

What is interesting is to analyse how Clinton took the Adams decision. Even Senator Kennedy, visiting his sister at the Dublin embassy in late December 1993, was hard to convince about the need for Adams to come to the US. Only at Tip O'Neill's funeral in Boston in early January 1994 did Kennedy, influenced by John Hume, who had also had his doubts, become convinced. Kennedy then wrote to Clinton on 14 January, the day after Ambassador Jean Kennedy Smith made her formal positive recommendation to the State Department. This was despite dissent in her own embassy, and the passionate opposition of Ray Seitz, the US ambassador in London. The secretary of state, Warren Christopher, was also against granting the visa, which had to be done in his name, and Janet Reno, the attorney-general, was very unhappy at the prospect.

At the time I was deeply involved in the former Yugoslavia and was not following the Irish situation closely. The Croat–Muslim war had intensified in Bosnia and I was negotiating with paramilitary leaders who were behaving like terrorists, trying to win support for involving the US in a Contact Group with Russia, and persuading the 15 EU nations that only three of them could be represented in that Group (it was later enlarged to include Italy as well as France, Germany and the UK). I had had my differences with the Clinton administration on Bosnia, but I knew that involving the diplomatic and military might of the US was essential and that having them footloose, supporting the Bosnian Muslims in rhetoric but not in reality, was profoundly counter-productive.

In retrospect, my own conclusion is that Gerry Adams needed to have the recognition from the US that a visa entailed if he was later to stand a chance of delivering a ceasefire. In the British Parliament John Major had only a small majority, the Unionists and many in his own party would never have supported the US granting a visa to Adams and there would have been a sizeable backlash if Major had given the go-ahead. The Labour and Liberal parties in opposition would have been tempted to equivocate, under pressure from the tabloid press, and to denounce any visa. It was for the US to act, to take the political flak and to make talking to Adams respectable. To their credit this is what they did. It was somewhat similar to the situation I faced in 1978 over holding peace talks in Malta with Robert Mugabe and Joshua Nkomo as they fought Ian Smith. Without the US presence and backing in Malta I would have been in grave danger of losing a vote of confidence tabled by the Conservatives in a House of Commons where we had lost our majority. To the right-wing UK press the forces of ZANU and ZAPU were simply terrorists, and in no way freedom fighters. In the Balkans there were few saints, yet the press recognized for the most part that all had to be talked to.

This experience suggests a fourth guideline in conflict situations for democratic governments: *negotiating with freedom fighters/terrorists or paramilitaries can be helped by having other powerful nations supporting one's diplomacy, not just by bringing to bear international diplomatic pressures but also for domestic political reasons, to help overcome the criticism that merely talking to such people who hold and use arms is condoning violence.*

The US administration did all it could to limit the outcry over the visa in Britain. It was issued only three days before Gerry Adams was due to attend the New York peace conference to which other Northern Ireland political leaders had also been invited. In reality the conference had been arranged especially as a potential vehicle for inviting Adams to the US. Adams was not allowed to raise money or to go outside a specified area in New York. Back in Britain feeling was intense, for only three months before, Adams had carried the coffin of the man responsible for the Shankhill Road bombing. His voice was still banned from British TV and the British ambassador in Washington, Sir Robin Renwick, allowed his emotion, normally held on a tight rein, to show, saying on CNN, 'When I listen to Gerry Adams, I think, as we all do, it's reminiscent of Dr Goebbels.' The *Guardian* and *Independent* felt the visit was necessary but most of the UK papers saw Clinton's decision as, in the words of the *Daily Express*, 'a coarse insult'. President Clinton tried to make amends four weeks later when John Major visited Pittsburgh and then had him stay in the Lincoln bedroom in the White House. The atmosphere publicly remained frigid, but the British and American governments were talking. The British government still refused to meet Adams until there was a ceasefire. That was from their position wise, for in March 1994 the IRA on two separate occasions fired mortar bombs at Heathrow airport. These attacks prompted Senator Moynihan to write a four-word note to Senator Kennedy: 'Have we been had?'

On Wednesday 31 August 1994 the IRA declared that from midnight there would be a complete cessation of military operations. Then Gerry Adams visited the US in late September and again on 6 December. On 9 December a team of British officials openly started to negotiate with a Sinn Féin delegation, which Major asserts was the first time in a quarter of a century, though some claimed that in previous contacts there had in effect been negotiations.

On 2 January 1995 Senator Mitchell retired as a serving member of the Senate and was sworn in seven days later as the special adviser to the president and secretary of state on economic initiatives in Ireland. The job was sold to him as involving a few days' work setting up a trade conference in Washington in the spring. The argument that the way forward for American involvement in Northern Ireland was predominantly through trade was an old one. In *Foreign Policy* in 1979 there were two articles on America and Ulster. While Conor Cruise O'Brien had written a piece called 'Hands Off', an Irish-American doctor friend of mine, Kevin Cahill, called in 'Healing Hands' for an economic effort.[10] Arguing that 'as in Rhodesia, Britain's will can be strengthened by American political pressure and by the promise of American financial aid', he enumerated seven specific funding projects. The neuralgic point between London and Washington in early March 1995 was whether Sinn Féin would be allowed to raise funds on the strength of Adams promising that every issue, including decommissioning, could be on the negotiating agenda. Once again Clinton ignored British concerns and lifted the ban on fundraising. The British government was shocked and angry. To demonstrate his contempt, Major did not answer Clinton's telephone calls of explanation for five days. But John Bruton, who as Fine Gael opposition leader had opposed the earlier visa decision in Washington and had become Taioseach in November 1994, was by then telling the president, 'I was wrong Mr President and you were right.'

There had, meanwhile, been a significant shift of Unionist opinion following the visa decision. The Ulster Unionists under Jim Molyneaux had come to recognize that they could not leave the US alone, only for Gerry Adams to mould opinion, so they had visited Vice-President Gore and Clinton's national security adviser, Tony Lake, in the White House in March 1994. Molyneaux was never anti-American and had served under the command of the American 9th Army in Normandy. The Unionists' defence spokesman Ken Maginnis had, according to John Major, also very significantly, supported international involvement. Hitherto the very concept had been anathema to Unionists. Yet Maginnis had been the first to float the idea of an international commission with the British government. John Major decided with John Bruton on 21 June 1995 to ask their key advisers, as a way of helping the IRA over the fraught issue of decommissioning, to build on the commission idea. This, the start of internationalizing the peace process, was, I believe, the historic turning point and represented a very radical move for the British. To some extent the first move towards this was the establishment of the Opsahl Commission, named after its Norwegian chairman, which reported in 1993 and won widespread acceptance for its conclusion that the source of the conflict lay inside rather than outside the province.[11] The British and Irish governments worked on a twin track of further political movement from all the parties and an international commission on decommissioning. Gerry Adams opposed this twin track approach with the Irish government, yet despite this John Bruton was planning to sign up on 6 September, but had to pull back at the last moment when he found John Hume vocally opposed to going ahead. Another Gerry Adams visit to Washington took place in mid-September, when he met Vice-President Gore and Tony Lake, the national security adviser, but it achieved little. The US position in September 1995 was still strictly neutral on decommissioning, much to the fury of the British. Throughout this time the US judged that prior decommissioning was a threshold over which Sinn Fein was unlikely to cross, even if the US pushed them hard to do so. The British, by contrast, believed it was the failure of the US to push which explained why Sinn Fein refused to move.

David Trimble, as the new Ulster Unionist leader, went to Washington at the end of October 1995 to see Tony Lake, and President Clinton astutely dropped by, creating the first meeting between an American president and an Ulster Unionist leader since Terence O'Neill met President Johnson. The Americans made a favourable impression by giving Trimble the kudos due to him as leader of the largest party in Northern Ireland even though he had opposed the Downing Street Declaration and the Framework Documents and had not fully supported Jim Molyneaux's efforts. The Americans were also welcoming to Washington all the Northern Ireland parties, including the Progressive Unionist party and the Ulster Democratic party, which had grown out of the loyalist paramilitary groups. On the way out of his meeting Trimble met John Hume who, as he had been doing for years, had been assiduously moving around the key decision-makers in the US, forging a consensus. These two were to develop a grudging respect for each other and would share the Nobel Peace Prize.

On 28 November, when he met with John Major in Downing Street, Dick Spring, John Bruton's deputy and Labour leader, appeared to be unhappy with the words on decommissioning that were before the British and Irish governments. President Clinton was due to land in London next morning for a visit to encompass Belfast, which had been agreed by the British government in the summer as part of the internationalizing agenda. The Irish coalition looked, to John Major, as if it might split, but near midnight, with Clinton already in the air, Bruton signed up for the International Body for Decommissioning to be headed up by George Mitchell. Mitchell, who had impressed some of the Ulster Unionists in his economic role, was to be assisted by General John de Chastelain, former Canadian Chief of Defence Staff, and Harri Holkerri, former prime minister of Finland.

The internationalization of the Northern Ireland dispute was now a fact of life. It suggests a fifth guideline for ending conflict: *when the parties and the governments most closely involved cannot agree then internationalization with an impartial body drawn from outside nations can sometimes break the deadlock.* This has now also become the accepted pattern in the Arab–Israeli dispute.

The British position stated by John Major to reporters was that the Americans had nothing to do with the agreement, though he conceded with Clinton standing beside him on 29 November that the president's visit had 'concentrated the mind'. The personal chemistry between the two men was now better, the long arguments over; the former Yugoslavia had been buried and the Dayton Peace Accords had been signed at the end of 1995. British and US forces, which were about to deploy for the first time into Bosnia-Herzegovina, were working very closely together.

Many senior politicians and commentators in EU countries still wring their hands over Bosnia and feel that it was a defeat for the EU's Common Foreign and Security Policy and a victory for US diplomacy. The truth is very different: neither the US nor the EU comes out well from the handling of the war, from its beginning in the spring of 1992 to its end in the autumn of 1995. But it was the US that barred any imposition of a peace settlement in early 1993 and it was the US that held the most unrealistic views of what was and was not negotiable, as the end result at Dayton demonstrates. This suggests a sixth guideline for ending conflict in the post-Cold War era: *the commitment of the world's only remaining superpower, the United States of America, to any peace process is a great help and its presence on the sidelines can be a massive hindrance.*

President Clinton flew to Belfast and became the first serving American president to visit Northern Ireland. By any standard his visit was a spectacular success. He visited the Protestants on the loyalist Shankill Road, made a powerful speech in an engineering factory to a mixed audience of Protestants and Catholics, visited the Catholic Falls Road and, as if by chance, shook hands with Gerry Adams. He saw all the political leaders for a chat, recognizing Trimble again as the leader of the largest party by including him in his car on the way to the meeting. In Dublin next day Clinton attracted large enthusiastic crowds. Some believed, in the euphoria, that things would never be the same again. Wiser heads counselled caution, but things had changed. The US was now an active player in the Irish peace process.

The International Body on Decommissioning now had to prove its worth. It is to Senator Mitchell's team's great credit that they lost no time in grappling without fear or favour with the central demand with which the British government and the Unionists had become very identified: prior decommissioning. This meant, in the words of the secretary of state, Sir Patrick Mayhew, on 7 March 1995, 'the actual decommissioning of some arms as a tangible confidence-building measure and to signal the start of the process'. At the Royal Ulster Constabulary headquarters Mitchell asked the Chief Constable, Hugh Annesley, the key question: whether Gerry Adams, if he wanted to, could persuade the IRA to decommission prior to negotiations. Annesley replied, 'No, he couldn't do it even if he wanted to. He doesn't have that much control over them.' It was a courageous and honest reply from a man who had read or listened to more supposedly private conversations with IRA leaders than anyone else. It was a difficult message for the British government to hear, especially given so publicly and clearly. The fact that it was backed by the Irish police and security officials on both sides of the border was also important. Basically it had been the American position for some years.

When Mitchell and his colleagues met John Major in 10 Downing Street prior to writing their report, he told them bluntly that if they recommended parallel decommissioning, which was really the least they could do, he would have to reject the report. Mitchell, using all his senatorial political skills, got around this warning by heeding the words of a junior British minister, Michael Ancram, who suggested privately that they might use a separate section of their report for this recommendation, a hint which Mitchell took up, separating the principles of a settlement from pragmatic compromises on decommissioning to achieve a settlement. In the report the International Body asked for total and absolute commitment from all the parties for points *a* to *f* but only in a separate section recommended the parties to consider parallel decommissioning.

This suggests a seventh guideline: *when choosing enablers or negotiators from outside the conflict it is worth remembering that the compromising and manipulative skills of the politician are often particularly useful. Whereas judges, diplomats and civil servants have their value in mediating, brokering a deal to resolve an armed conflict is a rough business and politicians are often skilled at making tough trade-offs.*

On 24 January 1996 in the House of Commons, John Major matched Mitchell in political adeptness. According to Mitchell he heaped praise on his report, but then picked out one small suggestion that an election process would contribute to the building of confidence and cleverly built that up. Major defined two routes to peace: the first, that the paramilitaries start decommissioning before all-party negotiations; the second, to secure a democratic mandate for all-party negotiations through elections separately for that purpose. The choice, he said, was for the parties. In effect the only way forward was to conduct an election for a negotiating forum in which the politicians just might compromise over decommissioning and other matters among themselves. An ingenious formula produced eight parties at the table and a way was set for a negotiation which could isolate Ian Paisley and his Democratic Unionists, who were thought bound to obstruct, and still achieve the required majority.

The IRA tried terror once again and on Friday, 9 February 1996 at 5.54 pm the *Irish News* in Belfast was telephoned. 'There's a massive bomb beside South Quay station, Marsh Wall, Isle of Dogs, London,' said the caller, 'Evacuate immediately. Codeword Kerrygold.' The ceasefire was over. A second before 7.00 pm our dog whimpered on our terrace at home, sensing the shockwave, and a loud explosion followed. A crater 32ft wide and 10ft deep had been blown in the heart of Docklands, close to my house, near the new financial centre of London, less than three years since a similar explosion in the City of London.

There had been deep cynicism about the peace strategy of Gerry Adams and Martin McGuinness among the IRA in South Armagh since the August 1994 ceasefire. Even before the ceasefire was broken in February 1996 the IRA had identified London Docklands as a suitable target.[12] A dummy run had been undertaken in the middle of January. In past times this bomb would have derailed the process for months, maybe years, but this time there was a big difference: the structure was buttressed internationally. It was now too robust to be broken. On 28 February the British and Irish governments, after a meeting in London, announced that inclusive all-party negotiations would be convened on 10 June 1996. It was up to the parties if they stood candidates. All of them did.

In May Senator Mitchell was asked by both the British and Irish governments to serve as chairman of the plenary sessions, helped by his two colleagues. The negotiations started in June 1996, despite Mitchell being disowned by the Reverend Ian Paisley and subjected to what many other negotiators would have seen as a humiliation too far. Patience was rewarded and twenty-two months later, on 10 April 1998, the Good Friday Peace Agreement had the required majority among the parties. This time the key British and Irish government leaders, who were deeply involved in the negotiations in Belfast, were Tony Blair and Bertie Ahern. The Northern Ireland secretary Mo Mowlam had also done much in the previous period to create confidence in the peace process among people with broad nationalist sympathies. When this Good Friday Agreement ran into difficulties in the summer of 1999, by common consent, the only people who could rescue the process, once again bedevilled by decommissioning, were Mitchell, de Chastelain and Holkerri. They came back and delivered, after a lot of negotiating in private, a complex interlocking form of words that allowed the Assembly to begin its work.

In reality, however, Sinn Féin did not move on decommissioning prior to the establishment of the Assembly for the first time in 1999. Decommissioning remained a contested issue and led to the Assembly being suspended. It was announced in the spring of 2000 through another international initiative involving the former Finnish president, Maarti Ahtisaari, and the ANC negotiator and former South African miners' union leader, Cyril Ramaphosa, that they would verify that the IRA had put some weapons in store and 'beyond use'. That arrangement did allow the Assembly to be re-established but the Ulster Unionists still expected to see what they call 'decommissioning' happen. This issue therefore continued to upset the peace settlement in Northern Ireland in 2001, leading to David Trimble's resignation as first minister and another temporary suspension of the Assembly.

Many people have made massive personal contributions to the bringing about of a devolved Northern Ireland government involving all the parties. Only some of them have I been able to mention. Yet without the internationalizing of the process and the pivotal role of President Clinton in that international effort there would not have been anywhere near as much progress. There are important lessons from the past for resolving internal conflict in many parts of the world and reconciliation has been an integral part of most peace settlements.[13] I hope the seven broad guidelines developed in this essay may possibly be of help in resolving some future armed conflicts.

In October 2001, the Independent International Commission on Decommissioning chaired by the Canadian general, John de Chastelain, announced that the IRA, in accordance with a method agreed in August, had put a quantity of arms completely beyond use. The British government responded to the start of decommissioning by dismantling two watchtowers and border listening posts and announcing the closure of several army bases.

A statement was issued in September 2005 by the Commission announcing that all arms had been put beyond use. The announcement was broadly welcomed but there was also scepticism and even disbelief. Probably only the passage of time will build confidence that all the arms have gone or demonstrate flaws in the process. Hopefully the Assembly will start to function again, this time with the Democratic Unionist Party playing a major role.

Many factors had contributed to this outcome over many years but the new administration of President Bush had given the whole process of decommissioning a significant boost. In unequivocal terms they had made clear from the outset that they wanted decommissioning to have the highest priority. They expressed extreme displeasure at three IRA activists being arrested in Columbia for alleged involvement with FARC guerrillas. After the terrorist attacks on New York and Washington on 11 September there was a massive change in American public opinion towards all forms of terrorist activity. It was obvious to the IRA that anyone holding out against decommissioning would get short shift from the US government, the US Congress and the American people.

Notes

1. This paper is a revised version of the Liverpool University Millennium Lecture delivered on 19 January 2000.
2. Edward Mortimer, *A Few Words on Intervention: John Stuart Mill's Principles of International Action Applied to the Post-Cold War World* (John Stuart Mill Institute, 1995).
3. Colonel Scott R. Feil, *Preventing Genocide: How the Early Use of Force Might Have Succeeded in Rwanda* (report to the Carnegie Commission on Preventing Deadly Conflict, April 1998).
4. Robert Skidelsky, 'NATO's deadly legacy from Kosovo', *The Financial Times*, 14 December 1999.
5. David Owen, *Balkan Odyssey* (London: Victor Gollancz, 1995).
6. Boris Yeltsin, *A Revolutionary Life* (London: HarperCollins, 2000), pp. 708-17.
7. John Major, *John Major: The Autobiography* (London: HarperCollins, 1999).
8. Conor O'Clery, *Daring Diplomacy: Clinton's Secret Search for Peace in Ireland* (Boulder, CO: Roberts Rinehart, 1997).
9. George Mitchell, *Making Peace: The Inside Story of the Making of the Good Friday Agreement* (London: Heinemann, 1999).
10. Conor Cruise O'Brien, 'Hands Off'; Kevin Cahill, 'Healing Hands', *Foreign Policy*, 37 (Winter 1979–80).
11. T. Opsahl, P. O'Malley, M. Elliott, R. Lister, E. Gallagher and L. Faulkner, *A Citizens' Inquiry: The Opsahl Report on Northern Ireland*, ed. A. Pollak (Dublin: Lilliput Press, 1993).
12. Toby Harnden, *Bandit Country: The IRA and South Armagh* (London: Hodder and Stoughton, 1999).
13. David Owen, 'Reconciliation: Applying Historical Lessons to Modern Conflicts', *Fordham International Journal*, 19 (December 1995).

Some Reflections on Successful Negotiation in South Africa[1]

Frederik Van Zyl Slabbert

Having spent most of my intelligent life in a country riven by conflict, inequality and domination, I have no intention of trivializing the very serious nature of the problems we had to solve, and are still attempting to solve. This I would most certainly do were I to suggest that South Africa's successfully negotiated transition could be neatly, intellectually packaged and exported to other seemingly intractable conflict areas. It is customary for commentators to pay homage to the uniqueness of every situation, and then to subtly extract and sermonize to others about how it was done in situation x and why this should also be possible for situation y, if only this or that procedure or attitude was adopted. Let me state at the outset that, even with the benefit of three years of hindsight, there are still important aspects of our transition I do not understand, and have difficulty in accounting for. Therefore, if what I have to say is of any use to you, let it be on your conscience, for I do not know enough about your conflict to even judge whether you are doing the relevant thing by applying some of my insights to your situation.

At the outset, let me make it as clear as I can that I have no desire to indulge in metaphor, or conjure up some political alchemy, such as the 'magic of trust' or the 'chemistry of negotiation partners' to explain the crucial moment in the transition. Adversaries negotiate not because they trust one another; if they did, there would be no need for negotiating. To use trust as the key explanatory variable is to seriously beg the question. It seems to me that adversaries begin to negotiate if they jointly *perceive* their conflict to be unresolvable by any other means, and, perhaps more important, because if they don't negotiate, things can become very much worse before they ever get any better. If any major party to the conflict believes it can resolve the conflict at the expense of its opponents, or that it and its supporters can endure the consequences of not negotiating, the chances of compromise are negligible. A common perception of deadlock seems to be critical, and the first phase of negotiation seems to be taken up in exploring this deadlock and developing a common mental map. In the South African case the Groote Schuur Minute, the Pretoria Minute and the Record of Understanding were key moments when the major parties to the conflict spelt out their common perception of deadlock, and how to proceed away from it.

I have used the words 'perception' and 'perceive' a number of times quite deliberately. Commentators, analysts and experts may give an 'objective account' of why negotiations are necessary, or the only way out; they can give eloquent descriptions of the nature of a deadlocked situation, and spell out convincing procedures of how to move away from it. There is a wealth of conflict-resolving literature recommending 'win-win', 'I'm OK – you're OK' solutions. I am not suggesting that all of this is of no consequence, or cannot be useful in some way. For decades this kind of intellectual advocacy and prescriptive analysis have been standard fare in the South African situation. I myself indulged in it for more than 20 years, and with great commitment and enthusiasm. However, until key individuals and opponents mutually recognized the deadlocked nature of the situation, and acted on it, nothing happened. And nobody that I am aware of predicted or anticipated that initially it would be Mandela, and/or De Klerk. In fact, there is overwhelming evidence, on both sides, that key supporting interest groups would vigorously have opposed what they did, had they known about it.

A final introductory note. The outcome of the negotiations is an exemplary liberal social democratic constitution. Having been, for all of my politically active life, a liberal social democrat, I know, from first-hand experience of 12 years in the old South African Parliament, and from regular extra-Parliamentary contact with the ANC and its support groups, once I left Parliament, that a liberal democratic constitution was the one thing the Nationalist party sought, with all its might, to prevent coming about, and about which the ANC was singularly and vociferously unenthusiastic while struggling against apartheid. To say that I am pleased with the outcome of negotiations is to put it mildly. Yet the ANC and the NP negotiated the outcome without the use of third parties, facilitators, professional negotiators or outside experts. They did it themselves, which persuades me to conclude that nothing makes a democrat of an oppressor more quickly than the prospect of his opponent coming to power, and nothing makes a democrat of a liberator more quickly than the prospect of peacefully negotiating his oppressor out of power. In this sense, democracy is not about how three wolves and a sheep vote about what's up for lunch, but, as Isaiah Berlin puts it, how the freedom of the wolves can be constrained so that it does not threaten the lives of the sheep.

The Scope of the South African Transformation

In mid-1985 Cyril Ramaphosa, subsequently to become one of the principal negotiators for the ANC, and then the secretary-general of the National Union of Mineworkers, said: 'The experience of organized labour demonstrates conclusively that there is no future for free enterprise in South Africa.' Today, he is a multi-millionaire and on the main board of Anglo-American, one of the largest mining conglomerates in the world.

Alec Erwin is currently the minister of trade and industries in the South African cabinet. A member of the South African Communist party, one of his principal tasks is to promote the government's Growth, Employment and Redistribution policy, which is based on conventional IMF and World Bank economic principles, such as abolition of exchange control, privatization, a flexible labour market and keeping the deficit before borrowing as low as possible. At a conference in Paris in October 1989, he was emphatic that when the ANC came to power, there would be democratic centralism and widespread nationalization of industry; the state would capture 'the commanding heights of the economy' and the ownership of private property would be severely circumscribed.

Mac Maharaj is currently minister of transport. At a closed conference in Dakar in 1987, he started proceedings by saying: 'Before I went to Robben Island, I killed in anger, now I can kill in cold blood.' At the same conference, Penual Maduna, currently minister of mineral and energy affairs, said that he had resigned himself to the idea that he would die in the struggle and that no negotiated outcome seemed remotely possible.

During this same period, South Africa had been in the grip of a prolonged state of emergency in which the state promoted the ideology of a 'total strategy' to fight the 'total onslaught of the enemy'. Draconian measures were the order of the day to 'hunt out and destroy the enemy' and although P.W. Botha had secret discussions with Mandela, through his representatives at the time, any public meetings with the ANC in exile were tantamount to treason for him. By the end of the 1980s, South Africa was a highly polarized society in which the dominant NP and the dominant ANC liberation movement defined the success of their respective strategies as dependent on the total destruction of the power of the other. Both sides systematically propagandized their determination *not* to look upon negotiations as a way out of the conflict. When De Klerk took over from Botha, the official NP policy was that, due to the plurality of cultural/ethnic/racial groups with fundamentally irreconcilable and conflicting interests, South Africa had no choice but to create a number of different nation states in which these groups could develop separately. De Klerk was one of the most eloquent and vigorous defenders of this faith. Within a matter of months of coming to power, he was leading negotiations, willingly and knowingly accepting that South Africa would become one single nation state for all its citizens.

I give these facts not to gloat, nor to show up the fickleness of personalities caught up in the conflict. On the contrary, it is done to give you some feel of the scope of what happened in South Africa. These were seriously committed opponents who confronted one another, and they held their beliefs with great conviction. To try to understand their own and South Africa's transformation is a highly complicated task. In my analysis, I shall try to avoid excessive voluntarism – the view that everything simply depended on great individuals, that everything was possible and nothing was necessary. At the same time, I shall try to avoid excessive determinism, such that all individual choice is eliminated, everything is necessary and nothing is possible. Instead, I shall try to identify certain general trends and conducive circumstances, situate individuals and parties against them, and speculate as to what the range of options available to them were, and why they chose some and not others.

Generally Conducive Factors that Made Negotiations Possible

1. A Clear and Unambiguous Moral Choice

In the twentieth century, it is difficult to think of another ideology, with the obvious exception of Nazism, which presented such a strong unifying force as the ideology of apartheid. Opposition to it cut across national, ideological, religious and philosophical boundaries. It lent a unity of purpose to strategies and tactics to undermine and eradicate it. Those who suffered under it and opposed it were guaranteed approval and material support. Those who implemented it and tried to sustain it had nowhere to hide or seek support, and were eventually reduced to seeking partnerships with similar pariah states to overcome some of the more serious obstacles of international isolation.

Sanctions, whether of the trade, financial or cultural variety, served as a constant and uncomfortable reminder of the force of almost universal moral rejection, and those who did not participate in them were always on the defensive as to why they did not. It was this sustained and unrelenting moral climate which increasingly began to rob the dominant white groups, and Afrikaner nationalism in particular, of any kind of legitimacy. In the end, the NP establishment had alienated their own intellectuals, poets, artists, even their business community. As the NP experienced a rapid decline in moral legitimacy, so the ANC gained it. As a liberation organization it skilfully and very effectively exploited the prevailing moral climate to its own advantage. Thus, when it entered into negotiations, there was no doubt as to where the moral base of support lay.

2. A Fundamentally Fast-Changing International Climate in the 1980s

Ronald Reagan's second term of office, beginning in 1984, saw the start of an entirely new development in USA–Soviet relations. Of particular relevance for the South African situation was a growing understanding between Reagan and Gorbachev that they would not allow what they perceived to be regional conflicts to become a source of unnecessary tension between their two countries. Furthermore, they would encourage peaceful rather than violent settlements to those conflicts. In short, exporting and supporting revolution was out, and negotiations were in. This had a dramatic impact on the conflicts in Afghanistan, Angola and Namibia. The South African government participated in the negotiated settlements of Angola and Namibia, and as these were successfully concluded, in the sense that the Cubans withdrew from Angola, and UN Resolution 435 was implemented for Namibia, the irony of the South African situation became obvious.

The fact that Africa was no longer an important area of superpower rivalry had a decisive impact on the liberation strategies of the ANC. Generally it looked towards the Soviet Union and its allies for material support in the armed struggle and for their National Democratic Revolution, while the West was mobilized for generally peaceful strategies and moral support. With the rapprochement between Reagan and Gorbachev came a decline in the support for the ANC's armed struggle and this forced a rethink on the most successful way of unseating the NP government. This came at a time when the NP government found it more and more difficult to explain why, if a negotiated settlement was good enough for Namibia and Angola (and South Africa had helped with those negotiations), it was not good enough for South Africa.

3. The Spiralling Costs of Domination

By the mid-1980s it became clear, even to the P.W. Botha regime, that apartheid and separate development, as envisaged, could not work. Whatever else could be said about P.W. Botha, and that is not inconsiderable, he, and not De Klerk, introduced reforms to apartheid. In fact, De Klerk vigorously opposed most such reforms, such as the Tri-Cameral Parliament recognizing the permanence of so-called urban Blacks, giving limited autonomy to Black local councils, and so on. However, every reform by Botha simply underlined the untenability of continued White domination, and strengthened resistance and opposition to it.

Resistance intensified in numerous ways, some by design, others inadvertently. Perhaps the greatest indirect source of resistance to the plans of the NP government was the migration of millions of Black South Africans to the metropolitan areas, cities and towns. In a sense it was a massive demonstration of unreflective civil disobedience, and the regime was powerless to stop it. The forces of urbanization and industrialization simply made a mockery of the intentions of apartheid and separate development.

From 1964 until the mid-1980s the NP government had spent billions of rand in setting up co-optive structures of government in the form of quasi-independent homelands, Coloured and Indian assemblies and urban Black councils. A vast and hopelessly ineffective bureaucracy was created to service these instruments. By the time negotiations started, it was calculated that there were approximately 150 state departments – 17 departments of education, 17 departments of health and welfare, etc. Not only was it costly to set up and maintain these structures, it was even more costly to suppress and control those who did not accept them, or actively opposed them. This, coupled with South Africa's military and security involvement in Namibia, Angola and Mozambique in the face of a declining and increasingly isolated economy, put a prohibitive strain on the South African regime's ability to maintain White minority domination.

4. The Collapse of Organized Communism

When the Berlin Wall fell at the end of 1989, it symbolized the collapse of Soviet and Eastern European communist regimes. It also meant that a well organized and sustained system of patronage evaporated for the ANC liberation movement, almost overnight. For years exiled ANC supporters had received scholarships, military training and material support from Eastern Bloc countries, and ANC envoys there enjoyed virtual ambassadorial status. For Western countries, this was always a worrying factor, should the ANC ever come to power in South Africa. However, what happened in South Africa in a post-communist world, once negotiations were successfully under way, suited Western interests down to the ground. In this respect, it is significant that the first non-African country that Mandela visited after his release was the USA, for a ticker-tape parade in New York. Now on the point of retirement, he is due to visit Moscow for the first time.

The significance of the collapse of the Berlin Wall was not lost on De Klerk. In a personal discussion, I asked him why he had made his epoch-making speech in Parliament on 2 February 1990. He replied that there were two reasons: one was that he had undergone 'a spiritual leap' in which he accepted the moral untenability of apartheid; the other was, he said: 'I would have been stupid not to take the gaps that the fall of Eastern Europe presented me.' De Klerk seriously thought that the

ANC would enter into negotiations at a major disadvantage due to the collapse of organized communism. It was an extraordinary miscalculation.

5. *The Politics of Deadlock*

I have already referred to a commonly perceived sense of deadlock as perhaps the most crucial ingredient for starting negotiations. Let me repeat that South Africa, by 1990, was substantially, objectively and subjectively deadlocked. In other words, no party had the ability to inflict defeat on the other, or to resolve the conflict on its own terms. Yet each had the capacity to inflict enormous damage to the fortunes of the other. The NP would have preferred a system of co-optive domination where White domination could be adjusted, but not sacrificed; the ANC would have preferred transition through successful attrition, without having to share power. In the end, the costs of negotiations were perceived to be far cheaper than any other alternative.

There is nothing new in saying this. Many scholars and analysts have done so repeatedly in looking at the South African situation. In 1979 I co-authored with Professor D. Welsh a book entitled *South Africa's Options: Strategies for Sharing Power* in which we identified the major options and constitutional points of departure which the ANC and the NP eventually adopted. It is a very simple exercise to read the book, and compare its contents to what happened. However, then and now, our analyses had very little if any impact. Both the ANC and the NP regarded it, if anything, as a liberal cop-out and capitulation. I stress this point not to be morally self-serving – many other academics and analysts more competent and thorough than I experienced the same fate. The point is that, at a critical moment, key individuals in the conflict, for whatever reason, accepted its deadlocked nature and decided to enter into negotiations. If Botha and Chris Hani had led the NP and the ANC at this time, it is unlikely that it would have happened. In fact, objectively, the NP could have governed well into the twenty-first century at enormous cost to the country, and there is no doubt that Hani would then have escalated the armed struggle.

This is another way of saying that generally conducive factors provide necessary but not sufficient conditions which make negotiations a compelling option. What the necessary *and* sufficient factors are which make negotiations almost inevitable is not self-evident. All I know is that individuals do make a difference, and that they have to exercise a choice without being able to calculate the risk or consequences. Both De Klerk and Mandela made that choice and therein lies South Africa's good fortune. A closer look at more specific factors against the background of the more generally conducive ones I have mentioned may provide us with some clues, but, I am afraid, not the complete answer as to why South Africa successfully negotiated its transition of power away from minority domination towards democracy.

Specific Factors that Made Negotiations Possible

1. The Loneliness of Leadership

Patti Waldmeier, in her excellent book, *Anatomy of a Miracle*, gives a detailed and compelling account of all the secret discussions between emissaries of the Botha government and different sections of the ANC – particularly Mandela in prison, and Mbeki in exile. There is no doubt that these, and other discussions, contributed to undermining the will not to negotiate, on both sides. However, these discussions in themselves were not enough. It took extraordinary leadership on the part of both De Klerk and Mandela to start the process.

Ironically, De Klerk was not privy to all the secret discussions that took place during Botha's term of office. Botha was particularly hostile towards De Klerk, and deliberately excluded him from the inner and confidential councils of his reign. Only De Klerk can shed some light on why he made that precipitating speech on 2 February 1990. Very few people knew he was going to say what he said. Certainly the vast majority of his Parliamentary caucus and virtually all the party formations were unaware of it. It is with some pride that De Klerk says that even his wife, when they were driving to Parliament on his way to make the speech, did not know what he was going to say – and she was a senior official of the NP at the time. De Klerk took the whole world by surprise and caused an instant paradigm shift on what was possible, or not possible, as far as the future of South Africa was concerned.

It is important to stress that his speech was an individual and lonely act. It gives the lie to the conventional wisdom that a leader must first prepare his party and supporters for an event such as this, before he precipitates it. In fact, had De Klerk done so, it is unlikely that he would have been able to make the speech at all. By the time De Klerk became leader of the NP the structure of decision-making in the party had become so ritualized around the role of the leader that he could enjoy *carte blanche* on any major policy initiative. (This was true for Verwoerd on the Homeland policy, Vorster on security and sports policy, Botha on the Tri-Cameral Constitution and the conditional release of Mandela, and of course De Klerk on negotiations.)

It seems that after the speech, the process of negotiations developed a kind of funnel-like logic where each step narrowed down the options to the next step, and where opting out promised the possibility of exponential catastrophe. At the same time, the general expectation, both domestically and internationally, was that at the end of the day, there had to be a transfer of power away from White minority domination. Consequently, once negotiations began, opting out held a far greater risk for De Klerk than for Mandela. The latter would most likely get all the sympathy, and the former all the blame. It was this funnel-like logic that De Klerk had precipitated that forced the party and its supporters into the process of negotiations. De Klerk received massive encouragement and support across a wide spectrum – even the Nobel Peace Prize, long before negotiations were concluded.

Mandela found himself in a similarly extraordinary leadership position. The ANC was, and still is, an alliance between itself, the South African Communist party and COSATU. During the 1980s, one could identify three distinct sources of influence on strategy and tactics: so-called prison or island leadership; internal domestic leadership, which included the UDF and COSATU; and exiled leadership, which included Tambo together with Hani, Slovo and Mbeki. To argue that among them there was unanimity of purpose as far as negotiations were concerned would simply be misleading. Mandela himself admitted as much in his autobiography *Long Walk to Freedom*, when he said that he knowingly entered into discussions with both the Botha and the De Klerk governments, aware that it did not meet with the approval of his colleagues in leadership positions within the ANC.

However, once Mandela was released, he demonstrated a quality of leadership that was simply awe-inspiring. He displayed magnanimity of spirit after 27 years in prison that overwhelmed everyone; he soothed the fears of the White minority; he calmed the expectations of his own supporters; he became an international celebrity overnight, and showed extraordinary qualities of statesmanship. Like De Klerk, Mandela managed to unite the various factions within his movement and pushed them into the process of negotiations. The major difference was that he could promise his supporters something they had struggled for all their lives: the end of White minority domination.

From the outset, it was clear that the relationship between De Klerk and Mandela was an uneasy one. To say that they trusted one another, liked one another or were friends would be a gross misrepresentation. However, they both agreed that there was no alternative possible to what they were doing, and they both said so repeatedly during negotiations. The quality of their leadership in this regard was of decisive importance for the success of negotiations.

2. The Quality of Negotiators

Mandela and De Klerk did not negotiate directly with one another, but did so at arm's length through appointed negotiators from their ranks. However, from personal discussions with negotiators from both sides, it seems that Mandela was much more hands-on in the process than De Klerk. From the outset, he was not prepared to budge on the principle of majority rule: 'As long as majority rule was not compromised, we were open for any possibility.' One sensed that Mandela would rather go back to prison than concede on this issue, and his negotiators knew this with utmost clarity. De Klerk, on the other hand, appeared more and more irresolute as the process deepened. He did not hold out for the civil service, the security forces, or cultural, language and educational rights. Compared to negotiations in Chile and Poland, the position on those issues came across more as capitulation than compromise.

The negotiations went through some difficult periods and breakdowns. It was in the build-up to the signing of the Record of Understanding between Mandela and De Klerk on 26 September 1993 that the extraordinary relationship between Roelf Meyer and Cyril Ramaphosa developed. Seven months later, on 27 April 1994, the first non-racial general elections took place in South Africa. It would be small-minded and petty not to acknowledge the role of the relationship between Meyer and Ramaphosa in the success of the negotiations. When the whole process was hanging on a thread, they kept the channel of communication between the major parties open. They both acknowledge the trust and friendship that developed between them. However, it would do an injustice to the complexity of the whole situation to explain the success of negotiations simply in terms of the trust and friendship that existed between Meyer and Ramaphosa. This trust certainly could not be generalized to any of the other players on both sides. If anything, there was deep suspicion and mistrust, and there were constant attempts at outmanoeuvring and upstaging each other.

As negotiating partners, Ramaphosa and Meyer were of uneven quality. The former had many years' experience of extremely tough negotiations, having led the miners' union in talks with the mining houses. As one of the leaders of the UDF he was used to facing up to tense and uncompromising situations. Most important of all, he entered into negotiations with Meyer with complete clarity of purpose as far as his leader and supporters were concerned. Meyer, on the other hand, was relatively inexperienced in negotiations, but intelligent enough to grasp their implications. Furthermore, unlike De Klerk to this day, he accepted the principle of majority rule and negotiated from that point of departure. To my knowledge, he never received instructions to hold out for concessions that contradicted this principle, and this obviously made negotiations much easier for the ANC. Whatever else may be said, there is no doubt that the quality of these negotiators played a critical role in the success of negotiations. Ironically, despite the role they played, they were both subsequently marginalized from the mainstreams of their respective movements. That is why Ramaphosa is now in business, and Meyer is attempting to build up a completely new political movement.

3. The Key Role of Minor Parties

One tends to forget that at one stage, up to 19 parties participated in negotiating forums. Some of them left because they felt marginalized, or because they felt it was essentially an 'NP–ANC show'. Only two had the capacity to break up negotiations or to undo their consequences. These were the Inkatha Freedom party of Mangosuthu Buthelezi and the Freedom Front of General Constand Viljoen. The one represented Zulu nationalism, the other what was left of ethnic Afrikaner nationalism.

Buthelezi abandoned the process after the signing of the Record of Understanding between De Klerk and Mandela, believing that they deliberately excluded him. He was right, of course, and Waldmeier quotes Ramaphosa as saying: 'Sufficient consensus means if the ANC and the NP agree, the rest can get stuffed.' However, there was never any doubt that Buthelezi had the capacity to seriously disrupt elections in Kwa-Zulu Natal and so undermine the success of negotiations. In the end, he participated, but it was touch and go. Many believe the outcome of the elections in Natal was contrived to placate Buthelezi. Certainly, the politicians declared the outcome of elections to be 'fair and free', long before the Independent Electoral Commission declared them to be 'substantially' fair and free.

Viljoen and the Freedom Front epitomized the disunity and fragmentation of right-wing parties. Again, there is no doubt that if the right-wing parties could have united in a common rebellion against the process of negotiations, the process would have been seriously disrupted, if not broken. At one stage, it looked to be a distinct possibility. There were sporadic incidents of bombing and continued right-wing threats. The debacle of Mmbatho in the homeland of Bophuthatswana, when President Lucas Mangope was put under pressure by De Klerk and Mandela to step down, and right-wing parties rushed to his support, persuaded Viljoen to come into the process. He decided to lead his party into the elections and won a number of seats to sit in the first ever non-racial and democratically elected Parliament of South Africa. Since he did so, the ANC and Mandela have given special attention to him, and increasingly they began to take him more seriously than De Klerk and the NP.

It is important to note that the break-up of the NP over a number of years politically split White Afrikaners along class lines. The NP represented middle- to upper-middle-class Afrikaners generally, while right-wing parties represented lower-middle-class to poorer Afrikaners. The latter would obviously feel the loss of power and its economic consequences far more quickly than the supporters of the NP. This is just another way of saying that there was no organized White working class that could check the political negotiations of the NP leadership.

The entry of the Inkatha Freedom party and the Freedom Front into the elections virtually guaranteed the successful outcome of negotiations. It is clear that now, in the post-election period in the 'new South Africa', they can both pose serious difficulties of consolidation to the fragile emerging democracy.

Conclusion

If I have achieved nothing else but to give you a sense of the complexity of the process before, during and, to a limited extent, after negotiations, I shall be content. Many other factors could have been brought into my analysis with equal validity, such as the integrating role of the economy; the conciliatory role of the churches; the facilitating role of business, and so on. However, analysis is always a process of selective abstraction in which one gives more weight to some factors than to others. To quote Churchill: the successful negotiation of the transfer of power in South Africa is but 'the end of the beginning'. When does one finally measure the success of the outcome? When a nation state has been integrated, or democracy has been consolidated, or inequality has been eradicated? South Africa is currently battling with all these problems, and the analysis of the dynamics of post-liberation politics is as fascinating and absorbing as the analysis of the negotiations which preceded it.

A short answer to the question: how did you manage it in South Africa? We had the right leaders at the right time, who understood a problem in the same way, under conducive circumstances. And we were lucky. I am afraid that such a short answer obscures more than it reveals.

Note

1. This paper was first delivered as a lecture at the Institute of Irish Studies, University of Liverpool on 21 October 1997.

The Secrets of the Oslo Channels: Lessons from Norwegian Peace Facilitation in the Middle East, Central America and the Balkans[1]

Jan Egeland

1. Secretly Signing the Oslo Accord

Sometimes real-life events are even more amazing than fiction. At least this was the feeling of the three small groups gathered in the Norwegian government guest-house in Oslo on the night of 19–20 August 1993. The main participants were four Israeli and three Palestinian peace negotiators, hosted by a Norwegian negotiating team of four. The evening of 19 August opened with an official dinner hosted by our late foreign minister Johan Jørgen Holst in honour of his Israeli counterpart, Shimon Peres, who was conveniently on an official visit to Norway on that very day. The conversation revolved around general Norwegian–Israeli ties, but those of us who knew what was to come after the dinner guests had taken their leave could think of nothing else.

Just after midnight, the Norwegian security service escorted the Palestinian and Israeli negotiating teams through the back entrance. They brought with them the final, agreed version of the Declaration of Principles, signalling peace at last between Israel and the PLO. The last points of contention had been resolved only hours before at what was the fourteenth secret round of negotiations in Norway. At one o'clock in the morning, the Israeli foreign minister, Shimon Peres, joined our small group as an observer when the heads of the two negotiating teams, Abu Ala of the PLO and Uri Savir of the Israeli Foreign Ministry, initialled the historic Declaration of Principles. A greeting from Chairman Arafat was read aloud. No more than 20 people were present, many of whom had regarded one another as enemies only a few months before.

The following day, the two parties again sat down quietly at the negotiating table in Oslo, this time to start work on an agreement that was equally revolutionary. This was the Declaration of Mutual Recognition between Israel and the PLO, which was to transform the two parties from enemies into neighbours. Further rounds of secret negotiations in Oslo and Paris followed as new, decisive elements in the peace process fell into place, ultimately leading to Foreign Minister Holst's remarkable shuttle diplomacy with the actual letters of recognition between Prime Minister Rabin and Chairman Arafat.

The five-year framework agreement on Palestinian self-government in Gaza and the West Bank was analysed and discussed throughout the world. Commentators asked whether the agreement could survive at all. Editorials wondered how Palestinians and Israelis could agree to postpone negotiations on such fundamental, controversial questions as the status of Jerusalem and the Jewish settlements in the occupied territories. And how did a country such as Norway come to be at the centre of such an international political drama?

2. The Pre-negotiations Phase

A precondition for any effective third-party involvement in conflict resolution is gaining the confidence of the parties. It was Norway's close ties with Israel that made Norway so interesting for the PLO. Conversely, our direct contact with Chairman Arafat made Israel choose us as their back channel. There were countries with closer contact with the PLO than Norway, and others that had a better relationship with Israel, but few had our trusted relationship with both.

After the Second World War Norwegians, who had seen Jewish friends and neighbours rounded up during the Nazi occupation, felt a special sympathy for the Jewish people and for the state of Israel when it was established in 1948. Our Labour governments forged close ties with their Israeli counterparts. Although the Israeli occupation of the West Bank and Gaza after the 1967 Six-Day War strained this relationship, it did not destroy it. At the same time, sympathy for the plight of the occupied Palestinian people was growing, and through the 1970s and 1980s our Labour governments began to build relations with the Palestinian Liberation Organization.

After the Gulf War in 1990–91, a weakened PLO was ready for peace and needed a third party through whom they could approach the Israelis. Norway came to be seen as an interesting candidate, recommended by, among others, the outgoing Swedish foreign minister Sten Andersson, who was close to Arafat and who had helped establish an indirect channel for communication between the PLO and the US State Department. Several PLO delegations came to Oslo in 1991–92 to ask Norway to facilitate direct contact with Israel at meetings with Foreign Minister Thorvald Stoltenberg and myself. Our contact with Israel was also renewed and intensified. A new generation of Israeli 'doves' had emerged within the Israeli Labour party, which won the elections in June 1992 with a clear peace mandate.

Together with two personal friends, the director of FAFO (the Institute for Applied Social Science), Terje Rød Larsen, and my Foreign Office assistant Mona Juul, his wife, I got the green light from Foreign Minister Thorvald Stoltenberg to approach the two parties. On 11 September 1992, addressing my new Israeli counterpart, Deputy Minister Yossi Beilin, we offered to facilitate direct or indirect lines of communication to the PLO. We were able to provide the perfect camouflage for such a channel: the extensive standard-of-living studies being carried out by FAFO in the West Bank and Gaza. These required frequent contacts and meetings with Israeli and Palestinian counterparts. The discreet late-night meeting was held at my hotel room after an official dinner in Tel Aviv that Mr Beilin had hosted for my delegation visiting Israel, as well as Syria, Lebanon and the Norwegian UNIFIL peacekeepers. The meeting had been well prepared by Larsen and Juul, with Beilin's old friend, Professor Yair Hirschfeld, the only other Israeli present. Beilin refused to see the PLO directly himself, but confirmed his interest in indirect contact, as the 'Madrid set-up was bringing the peace process nowhere'. It was by then generally recognized that the official multi-party negotiations had become too big, too media-dominated and too much of a buffer between the real leaders, those who could take the real decisions regarding war or peace in the Middle East.

It was still a criminal offence under Israeli law to meet with the 'terrorist' PLO when the two courageous Israeli academics, Yair Hirschfeld and his NGO colleague, Ron Pundak of the Economic Co-operation Foundation, confirmed their willingness to come to our first meeting in January 1993. Their counterpart was the minister of economy of the PLO, Abu Ala, a moderate force in their headquarters in Tunis whom we got to know during his visit to Oslo in February 1992. Two colleagues from the staff of Chairman Arafat and Abu Mazen respectively had joined Abu Ala. A secluded country house in Sarpsborg, 100 miles south of Oslo, was the venue for the first meetings.

The two teams were determined to break away from the tradition set by earlier Israeli–Palestinian talks and most Jewish–Arab discussions and agreed *not* to dwell on the past. I remember both sides saying during the very first meeting: 'If we are to quarrel about the historic rights to these holy lands, about who was there first, or about who betrayed whom and when, we will sit here quarrelling forever. We must agree to look to the future.'

Abu Ala and his closest adviser Hassan Asfour, as well as Yair Hirschfeld and Ron Pundak, were all experts in the field of economy and development. Their no-nonsense, pragmatic approach soon produced results. They agreed on arrangements for self-rule, infrastructure development and security and, importantly, that self-rule could start up in Gaza and gradually grow to include the West Bank. The latter was an old proposal of Shimon Peres, which previously had been totally rejected by the PLO. A draft common paper was drawn up following the second meeting in February. After the third session in the seclusion of the country house, the two teams agreed on a draft declaration of principles, which included many of the elements in the final, signed agreement.

We were amazed and elated. The academic contact point we had established proved to hold far greater potential than we had originally assumed. However, the paper had one major drawback: there was still no official backing from the Israeli side. Abu Ala had not failed to point out the asymmetric levels of the two delegations: high officials of the PLO 'government' were sitting down with two unofficial Israeli citizens. To help balance this I therefore underscored the statement in the paper that the Norwegian government was pleased to note that my counterpart Yossi Beilin had welcomed these talks as I visited each of the sessions in a Foreign Ministry limousine. We were, however, more nervous than we appeared to be in front of the Palestinians: we only had Beilin's and Hirschfeld's oral assurances that they would be in touch and in due course pass on any outcome to higher political decision-makers. But, as Ron Pundak remarked in a bilateral meeting: 'The other side will for some time have to live with uncertainty about whether they are negotiating with Rabin's Israel or with two monkeys...'

3. The Official Negotiations

It took two more months, April and May 1993, for Beilin to secure the support of Foreign Minister Shimon Peres and Prime Minister Yitzhak Rabin, who were both impressed by the constructive, businesslike and moderate 'Gaza-first' text drafted in Sarpsborg. After hundreds of telephone calls in which we kept Jerusalem and Tunis informed about each other's questions, answers, threats and propositions, Beilin could report back that Israel had agreed to upgrade the talks to an official level.

Similar discussions took place in what the Palestinians described as the 'Arafat kitchen' in Tunis. Only five Palestinian leaders participated, including Chairman Arafat, Abu Mazen and Abu Ala. For the Palestinian leadership, Israel's willingness to initiate direct talks with the PLO was a breakthrough, as it meant *de facto* recognition of the organization as the legitimate representative of the Palestinians. This recognition was also reflected in the provisions of the draft agreement, which stipulated that the PLO could start to govern at least parts of Palestinian territory immediately as Israeli forces withdrew and implementation would start.

The director-general of the Israeli Foreign Ministry, Uri Savir, was sent to Oslo in May to 'test the seriousness' of Abu Ala and his two colleagues. Secrecy became even tighter. We never used hotels or other public venues for the negotiations nor the real names of our guests. Our VIP facilities at the airport were always used to avoid our guests meeting people they might know in the arrivals lounge while they were officially on other business elsewhere in Europe. It was also important for the Palestinians to be taken swiftly through the airport as they were travelling under passports that had given them and us embarrassing problems the first time they went through immigration.

When the official negotiations started in June we used the 200-year-old Heftye House belonging to Oslo municipality, which we needed, we said, for internal 'Foreign Ministry seminars'. As I prepared to leave the Ministry and join the negotiators, our press spokesman rushed into my office with a dispatch from the Washington correspondent of Agence France Press claiming that there was a secret Norwegian channel between Israel and the PLO. 'My God, Jan, what are you up to now?' he asked. I told him to inform the Norwegian and international press that the AFP story was based on a misunderstanding, and probably referred to a multicultural meeting on Palestinian refugees in Oslo in May. This had actually taken place as part of the official US-sponsored peace process and our elaborate smokescreen.

At the house I met Savir and Hirschfeld first. They read through the AFP report, which quoted anonymous State Department sources. 'I think we can deal with this, but don't tell the Palestinians since the negotiations are in a crucial phase,' Savir told me. Ten minutes later I gave the same dispatch to Abu Ala, who calmly said he knew the story through the PLO intelligence and had already instructed Tunis on how to deal with it, 'but don't show it to the Israelis,' he said, 'the negotiations are making good progress.'

Rabin and Peres, and Arafat and Abu Mazen, were following the negotiations closely and imposed increasingly strict terms for their negotiators. Their goals were ultimate and ambitious, but not mutually exclusive: the Israelis wanted maximum security for all their citizens indefinitely; the Palestinians wanted maximum self-rule, territory and economic development immediately.

4. Breakdown and Breakthrough

In July 1993 we experienced a first breakdown in the negotiations. We had rented a large country estate through a colleague of my wife some 150 miles north of Oslo and brought in the Norwegian security police to guard a session we hoped would see the final breakthrough. As talks became official I realized that our guests, in particular the Palestinians, we thought, were running an increasing security risk from extremists who would not tolerate fraternization with the enemy. With the consent of the parties our new foreign minister, Johan Jørgen Holst, told the head of the security police the necessary minimum about the channel. A team of eight policemen was assigned to help us with security, but also with the growing logistical demands as the sessions were organized more frequently, often with only a few days' notice.

The owners of the estate were told that we would bring a group of eccentric Middle Eastern academics working round the clock to finish a book. We knew that the Israelis had received the green light from Rabin and Peres to initial there and then a text that would meet the Israeli demands. Terje Rød Larsen, Mona Juul and I spent the last night on the sofas of the farm, hoping that the final pieces of the puzzle would fit together in the next few hours. Instead, the two teams broke off their talks at 5.30 am and asked to be taken to the airport. They had spent 35 of the 44 hours at the house negotiating. When the owners of the estate awoke to prepare breakfast, we had all gone. After both teams had left Oslo to report home we did not know whether there would be any further negotiations at all.

During the official negotiations in July and August both sides engaged in brinkmanship as they realized that a historic agreement might be within reach. The leaders thus instructed their negotiators to introduce a series of new and additional demands, but gave them little flexibility to accept new language from the opposing side. In addition to Savir, Joel Singer had been appointed by Rabin to join the two original and unofficial Israeli negotiators. Singer was a successful New York-based lawyer who had played an important role at the Camp David negotiations in the 1970s. His role was to scrutinize every word and nuance of the text and put hundreds of 'clarifying' questions to Abu Ala and his two colleagues, Hassan Asfour and Mohammed Abu Koush. The reason for the first breakdown in July was that the Israelis presented the other side with a new text, redrafted by Singer and containing numerous new elements compared to the old Sarpsborg text. The Palestinians felt this was a violation of the 'Sarpsborg spirit' of always having one joint text. Only after a long break and 'walks in the woods' by Abu Ala and Savir alone did the Palestinians agree to go through the new text line by line, formulating alternative Palestinian wording along the way. When the negotiators broke up they had settled dozens of smaller points, but still differed on the wording of five fundamental issues. These included any references to UN Resolutions 242 and 338 on Israel's occupation of Gaza and the West Bank, future negotiations on the permanent status, the organizing of elections in Jerusalem and the redeployment plan for Gaza and Jericho.

This and subsequent breakdowns in the negotiations were always followed by daily contact with the parties by telephone. Larsen and Juul kept their mobile phones within reach 24 hours a day and either called or were called by Uri Savir and Abu Ala continuously to discuss developments on either side. This was an important part of our facilitation: keep up a constant momentum by urging and begging them for new positions, clarifications and talks. Having learnt in the Ministry that all phones might be tapped at all times I suggested that we used a primitive code. Thus we tried to avoid all references to names and countries. The prime ministers (Rabin and Arafat) were termed 'the grandfathers', the foreign ministers became 'the fathers' (Peres, Abu Mazen and Stoltenberg/Holst) and deputy ministers became 'the sons' (Beilin, myself etc.). A typical call could be: 'They have already briefed their grandfather and will soon have news back, have you informed yours?' 'No, but the son sees his father today as he will talk with our grandfather tomorrow morning.'

The parties agreed to a second meeting in July only a week after the first breakdown. This time the Palestinians presented the other side with a new document containing some 25 new elements. The Palestinian position paper included the establishment of a corridor between Gaza and Jericho, which the Israelis saw as effectively cutting Israel in two, and reference to 'the PLO' in all places where the text had previously referred to 'the Palestinians'. Predictably, the Israelis this time became angry and refused to negotiate 'on this basis'. The parties again broke up in frustration and the Israelis warned 'this may be the end of the channel'.

We also travelled to Israel and Tunis between the sessions. In July Foreign Minister Holst had brought Juul, who was later joined by Larsen, for a previously scheduled visit to Tunis where they had several meetings with Arafat. While attending some UN meetings in Geneva I was called by Uri Savir, who urgently wanted Juul and Larsen to come to Jerusalem since Rabin and Peres had started to doubt the intentions of Arafat and the internal clout of Abu Ala. After dozens of calls between Geneva, Oslo, Tunis and Jerusalem, Larsen and Juul flew the next day directly from Tunis to Israel, where they reported on the most recent talks with Arafat and Abu Ala. Reluctantly, Rabin agreed to continue the talks. In late July and early August steady progress demonstrated the willingness of the leadership on both sides to run the race to its end.

As in other tough negotiations, the final points of contention were lifted up to the highest levels and left for the final hours before the final deadline. Shimon Peres's official visit to the Scandinavian countries in mid-August became our perceived deadline for initialling the agreement. In the early morning of 17 August Peres called Foreign Minister Holst, who was visiting Iceland: 'Can you meet me discreetly in Stockholm tonight, it is now or never.' That night Holst sat for eight hours with a phone at the Swedish Haggai Castle and transmitted messages from Peres next door to Arafat, who sat in his office in Tunis. At five o'clock in the morning the final wording on security for Israeli settlers and on the location and authority of the future elected Palestinian Council were agreed. The negotiators embraced in Tunis as well as at the Swedish Castle. Two days later the parties formally initialled the Oslo Declaration at our late-night government guest-house ceremony.

5. The Advantages of the 'Back Channel'

Our secret meetings proved to have several advantages over traditional conference diplomacy. Firstly, the news media, which tend to focus on what divides rather than on what unites, were not involved. As a former news reporter and a strong believer in free speech and open societies, I was struck by how disruptive the constant and immediate news coverage was at public peace negotiations for the Middle East. As soon as the delegates arrived in Washington or other official venues, journalists would confront them with the more hostile comments made by the opposing side, thus leading to even more aggressive responses. This was equally evident during the six weeks I spent in 1993 as a deputy to the EU and UN mediators for the former Yugoslavia, Lord Owen and Mr Stoltenberg.

Secondly, there was no time-consuming diplomatic protocol to be followed and no speeches to the gallery. The participants in the official public sessions appeared to spend almost 100 per cent of their time blaming one another, whereas the negotiators in Norway spent at least 90 per cent of their waking hours, meals included, in real negotiations. Even the many mutual provocations and acts of violence in the field did not hamper the efforts of the secret negotiators as they did the official channel in Washington.

Thirdly, an atmosphere of mutual trust and affinity was allowed to develop among a handful of individuals who spent hundreds of hours working, eating, quarrelling and joking together in front of Norwegian fireplaces and surrounded only by peaceful countryside. With only seven negotiators at the table the dialogue was always direct, honest and effective. Since the inception of the official negotiations in June, the negotiators were, except for the change of one Palestinian midway, the same individuals throughout. This provided for continuity and an institutional memory within the small group.

Fourthly, close cooperation with FAFO, the non-governmental organization, enabled us to offer the parties 'deniability' – the opportunity, if necessary, to deny that anything official had happened. If anything leaked out we could explain the meetings as academic seminars or as Norwegian participation in the official peace process. The small size of our team also helped us to keep things quiet. We were prepared to keep our secret forever if the negotiations broke down. This was important, because both sides feared that if the news of secret negotiations in Oslo were to leak out before any agreement had been reached, it might have disastrous results at home.

6. Implementing the Oslo Accord

The process that culminated in the Oslo Agreement and the subsequent negotiations has been followed by numerous crises and setbacks, but also by historical breakthroughs. Enemies of peace on both sides have repeatedly tried to derail the process, mounting terrible terrorist attacks against civilians in Hebron, Jerusalem, Tel Aviv and elsewhere. New settlements and border closures are also examples of the obstacles the peace process has run up against, and which have prevented the two Oslo Agreements from being implemented.

The process is a long way behind the original Oslo schedule and the mutual confidence built during the Norwegian channel has become depleted. The counter-forces became stronger than we originally expected. Terrorism has taken the lives of too many civilian Israelis and Palestinians, creating a paralysing insecurity and derailing the talks. A new political leadership in Israel, hostile to the original Oslo Accords and elected midway through their implementation, halted a process that had to see gradual progress to avoid regression. Still, there is no alternative to the Oslo process. This became evident as the process took a new step towards the implementation of the agreements through a massive effort by President Clinton as mediator at the Wye plantation in Virginia in October 1998.

The Oslo Agreement or the Declaration of Principles was, as the name implies, an agreement on the principles that are to guide the relationship between Israelis and Palestinians for a five-year period from 1993 to 1998 and the milestones that are to be passed along the way. An important element of the Oslo Agreement is its gradual nature. It does not try to solve all problems at once, but rather paves the way to a given destination.

The first milestone reached was the Cairo Agreement of May 1994, which established Palestinian self-rule in Gaza and Jericho. A Palestinian Authority was set up in the space of a few months, enabling almost a million Palestinians to shape their own administration. A Palestinian police force, initially assisted and funded by an international task force headed by Norway, was set up under difficult circumstances to promote security and stability in the self-rule areas. Through agreements on early empowerment in August 1994, the Palestinians were given responsibility for education and culture, health, social welfare, taxation and tourism on the West Bank in addition to Gaza and Jericho.

The second milestone – the Interim Agreement or 'Oslo II' – was reached after marathon discussions which were concluded in September 1995 in Taba, Egypt. It paved the way for extended Palestinian self-rule on the West Bank and Palestinian elections in the spring of 1996, through the withdrawal of Israeli forces from towns and villages on the West Bank. The agreement was to a large extent negotiated by the Oslo team of Abu Ala and Uri Savir.

In February 1997 a new agreement was reached on redeployment from Hebron, the largest and most conflict-ridden town on the West Bank. Coordinated by Norway, an observer group made up of representatives of six nations is currently operating as the 'Temporary International Presence in Hebron'. In October 1998 another major effort by the United States and other third-party facilitators led to a new agreement regarding further redeployment from the West Bank, as already detailed in the Oslo II agreement. Furthermore, the Palestinian side undertook an obligation to step up their fight against terrorism.

7. International Economic Assistance

One of the main arenas for international involvement in the peace processes has been economic assistance. In order for peace to endure, it must make a difference to people's daily lives by providing better living conditions, employment opportunities and a feeling of personal security. Discussing the challenge of implementation with our US counterparts as the Oslo Accord had just been initialled, we agreed that the Palestinian self-rule areas should be treated as a special case in international development assistance.

An Ad Hoc Liaison Committee (AHLC) was thus set up at the International Donors' Conference in Washington on 1 October 1993 to mobilize international assistance to the Palestinians. The AHLC consists of the co-sponsors of the peace process, the United States and Russia, the major donors to the Palestinians, and the two parties, Israel and the Palestinian Authority. Egypt, Jordan and Tunisia are associated members. Norway has acted as chairman of the AHLC since 1993. At the Washington conference, US$ 2.4 billion was raised in grants and loans. This has, after a slow start in 1994 and 1995, been disbursed according to plan. Economic activities in Gaza and the West Bank have, however, suffered a number of serious setbacks during the many long and harsh border closures after terrorist attacks in Israel. In 1996 some US$ 5 million were lost every day the borders were closed, a loss of income greater than the value of all foreign assistance in this period. Per capita income among the Palestinians has decreased in the period since 1993.

The prolonged crisis of confidence between the actors in the Middle East peace process made it evident that the understanding and trust reached between the political leaders, Rabin and Peres and Arafat and Mazen, did not filter down to the ordinary man and woman as we, perhaps naively, believed it would in 1993. Under the Oslo II agreement a major new effort was therefore launched to promote cooperation between Israeli and Palestinian citizens in fields such as economics, cultural affairs and education. This people-to-people exercise will hopefully help to do away with some of the stereotyped images of Israelis as 'occupying soldiers' and Palestinians as 'terrorists'. Norway has been asked to facilitate the programmes. Some 100 bridge-building projects are already under way involving youth groups, business people, academics and local politicians.

8. Other Multi-party Facilitation

The Oslo Accord is the most famous of a series of Norwegian efforts to assist in peace processes in Central America, the Balkans, the Caucasus, Burundi, Sudan, Sri Lanka and elsewhere – efforts which have met with varying degrees of success. In all of these cases the Norwegian participation has been within a multi-party effort by the United Nations, other intergovernmental organizations or other countries. And in all of these cases the Norwegian government has worked with or through non-governmental organizations.

Non-governmental groups often prove to have the best access to people and networks that can be mobilized quickly. They can operate in a very flexible manner. Decisions can be decentralized, and operations can be started more quickly. To utilize these resources the Norwegian Ministry of Foreign Affairs has established the Norwegian Emergency Preparedness System (NOREPS) and the Norwegian Resource Bank for Democracy and Human Rights (NORDEM). These are flexible stand-by arrangements with a number of governmental and non-governmental organizations.

There are dozens of NGOs in Norway that receive government funding for development assistance and human rights activities in more than 100 countries. Over the years, thousands of Norwegians have acquired field experience from working with these organizations as well as with the government development cooperation agency NORAD. Around 55,000 Norwegians, a number that equals more than 1 per cent of our population, have participated in UN or UN-mandated peace-keeping operations. These people constitute a valuable resource, which Norway is utilizing in conflict prevention on a rapid deployment basis. Through the stand-by procedures of NOREPS and NORDEM, several hundred relief workers, human rights advisers, peace mediators and observers are dispatched each year to more than 30 countries at the request of UN agencies, newly born democracies and the parties to armed conflicts.

9. The Peace Process in Guatemala

The peace process in Guatemala was initiated in Norway in March 1990 when representatives of the government peace commission and the guerrilla movement URNG signed the Oslo Agreement, which established a format and an agenda for future negotiations. Almost seven years later, in December 1996, the circle was finally successfully closed as the parties signed the ceasefire agreement in Oslo, bringing a generation of civil war to an end. The good offices of the UN and of the Group of Friends (Mexico, Spain, the US, Venezuela, Colombia and Norway) made steady progress at the negotiating table possible, and the final peace accord was signed in Guatemala City on 29 December 1996.

Norway facilitated this peace process through close cooperation between the Foreign Ministry and two NGOs, the Norwegian Church Aid and the Lutheran World Federation. Since 1990, we have provided financial support to the guerrilla movement to enable its members to participate fully in the negotiations. At the same time Norwegian development assistance to Guatemala, mainly channelled through non-governmental organizations, has increased considerably. We hosted a round of negotiations in June 1994 that resulted in agreements on the repatriation of refugees and on a truth commission to investigate past atrocities and human rights abuses. Norway has also made a point of trying to influence and reform the Guatemalan armed forces, which have a long history of human rights abuses and military coups. A number of military delegations from Guatemala have visited Norway, and high-ranking Norwegian officers, led by the former chairman of the Military Committee of NATO, General Eide, have visited Guatemala. They were able to convince the military leadership that the Guatemalan military forces' only chance of taking part in modern international military co-operation was by ending their 'stone-age war'. This brutal conflict was a product of the Cold War, but it continued to exact a heavy toll on the people of Guatemala, 65 per cent of whom are Maya Indians, long after the fall of the Berlin Wall.

It is now possible to say that peace has 'broken out' in Guatemala, after 36 years of civil war. The demobilization of the 3,000 guerrilla soldiers was completed by 2 May 1997, before schedule and only five months after the signing of the ceasefire agreement in Oslo. The army is reducing its size by approximately 10,000 men, and the feared anti-guerrilla village brigades have been dissolved along with the mobile military police. Now the major challenge is to prevent the increase in criminal violence which has taken place since the peace agreement, and which may, in part, be due to unsuccessful reintegration of some of the demobilized soldiers and fighters.

There are many positive signs to show that the peace agreement in Guatemala is being successfully implemented. One of the reasons we do not hear much about Guatemala is that things are going better there than in the media-exposed crises of the Middle East and the former Yugoslavia. Nevertheless, the UN and the international community must continue to help Guatemala to take advantage of the opportunity for peace that is being offered through the international support of the peace process and the deployment of the UN human rights commission in Guatemala. It is also important that the Guatemalan people take part in the democratic elections of president and Parliament which reflect the social, economic and ethnic realities of the country.

10. The Wars of the Former Yugoslavia

Norway has also tried to provide support for UN mediation and peacekeeping measures in the former Yugoslavia. In addition to our peacekeeping forces, we have, through NOREPS and NORDEM, provided hundreds of relief workers for the UNHCR, UNICEF, the International Red Cross and other organizations. For example, the Norwegian Refugee Council organized the largest relief convoys in Bosnia on a regular basis, Norwegian People's Aid has built large refugee villages inside Bosnia and the Norwegian Red Cross has established medical facilities in the conflict areas. We also provided personnel on very short notice for the admirable peace efforts of the UN/EU co-chairmen Lord Owen and Thorvald Stoltenberg. When the authorities in Belgrade gave in to foreign pressure and decided to impose internationally monitored sanctions on the Bosnian Serbs in September 1994, Stoltenberg and Owen requested personnel to monitor the Serbian/Montenegrin borders. We were able to provide 20 observers within 48 hours. Their work was essential to the credibility of sanctions against the Bosnian Serbs, as an incentive to accept the final Dayton Agreements instead of seeking advantages on the battleground.

There are many similar examples. Technical problems often have a tendency to become political, but the presence of impartial experts can help move the parties towards a solution. In January we provided an expert on electro-power within 24 hours to help the Croats and Serbs in the Krajina to implement the socio-economic agreement they had signed in December last year concerning the joint use of a hydropower dam and the electricity grid.

The main mediator in the unsuccessful Krajina negotiations along with Mr Stoltenberg was Ambassador Kai Eide, who has been seconded to the UN by the Norwegian government as Special Representative of the secretary-general. The two of them were later responsible for the successful conclusion of a peace agreement for Eastern Slavonia. As a deputy to Stoltenberg and Owen I saw first-hand that even these most dynamic and professional mediators could not reach a comprehensive agreement pre-Dayton, because the big powers, among them the US, did not give the necessary backing to press the totally irresponsible local political and military elites to make peace.

11. Lessons Learned

What are the lessons we have learned from our experience of attempting to facilitate peace on different continents and under different circumstances? Firstly, and most fundamentally, there will be no real and lasting peace if the parties themselves – their leaders as well as their public opinion – are not willing to work towards the often painful compromises that are needed to realize peace. This has been graphically illustrated by the many failures to truly implement the Oslo Accords as they have been formally adopted and signed by the Israelis and Palestinians. There has not been less mediation or facilitation undertaken by the United States, Norway and other third parties since 1996 than there was in the years 1992–95. The main change was that a new government took over policy formulation in one of the two parties. With the Netanyahu government in office almost all multi-party efforts to further the peace process have been frustrated, because the new Israeli government is not willing to compromise as the Rabin/Peres governments were.

Secondly, even when conflicting parties are willing to make peace, an inadequate mediation machinery and the absence of secret back channels can thwart the best of intentions. Israel and the PLO were able to effect negotiations and agreements themselves as soon as we managed to establish a link between the PLO leadership and the Israeli government in secret, without time-consuming diplomatic protocol, and in an environment of trust.

Thirdly, international diplomacy is surprisingly under-prepared in terms of providing the personnel, the expertise and the material support necessary for effective facilitation of a peace process. The strength of the Norwegian model of cooperation with a number of governmental and non-governmental organizations and academic institutions has improved our ability to provide without delay the appropriate tools for a mediation process. Such tools range from experts on the separation of military forces to constitutional lawyers and from remote country houses to executive aeroplanes.

What opportunities do governments have to play a more informal 'third party' role, either as facilitators or as mediators in a conflict situation? In what way can a small country such as Norway contribute to conflict resolution and peace-making in internal conflicts? I see five fundamental preconditions for effective intervention:

1. The third country must be perceived by the parties to the conflict as having no national interests that conflict with an impartial settlement of the conflict and the promotion of human rights. The third party must have the trust and confidence of the parties.
2. A national political consensus is needed in the third country, permitting a long-term political, diplomatic and economic investment in a peace programme for the conflict in question.
3. An institutional memory must exist in the form of relevant and accessible expertise and the ability to maintain a high standard of involvement.
4. Substantial foreign economic assistance must be available, with sufficient discretionary funds ('venture capital' for peace) to finance all aspects of a negotiation and reconciliation programme.

5. The third country must have the ability to draw on and make use of the flexible networks of NGOs.

Will the Oslo process ultimately lead to peace between Israelis and Palestinians? I still firmly believe so, even though I readily admit that peace will take more time and the process will see more uphill battles than we originally and optimistically expected. The strength as well as the weakness of the Oslo process is its gradual nature. To embark on a bargaining process that attempts to settle the age-old disputes around Jerusalem and other final status issues would be the same as inviting a permanent deadlock in the talks. However, gradual implementation will unavoidably lead to countless frustrations and setbacks in an atmosphere clouded by political violence and extremism. Perhaps the biggest mistake was to see the peace process in a five-year perspective rather than over a generation. It has taken many generations to build the political, social, cultural and religious barriers in the Middle East. It will take time to break them down. Whether Norway will facilitate peace agreements between conflicting parties again is an open question. Perhaps only one in a hundred attempts will succeed. Even so it will be worth the effort.

Note

1. This paper was first delivered as a lecture at the Institute of Irish Studies, University of Liverpool on 19 November 1997.

The Awakening: Irish-America's Key Role in the Irish Peace Process

Niall O'Dowd

> Political stalemate is likely to continue … the conflict in Ireland is being managed reasonably well … the British, Irish, the unionists and the nationalists in Northern Ireland all seem to have become accustomed to the present level of violence … real change must await a new generation.[1]

It would be hard to find a more incorrect summing up of the situation in Northern Ireland, just months before the peace process began to bear fruit. Yet it is not surprising that, even at the highest levels of the US government, there was considerable cynicism about any prospects for movement in Northern Ireland. On the surface, in 1993, attitudes in Northern Ireland appeared as frozen as ever. But underneath the surface, a subtle warming process had begun.

The end of the Cold War and the collapse of communism were epoch-making events, not just for the world's superpowers, but also for citizens of smaller countries where long-term conflicts raged. It is no coincidence that great strides were made in major trouble-spots after the collapse of the Soviet Union. In South Africa, the Middle East and Northern Ireland the end of the Cold War signalled an opportunity to advance long-dormant peace plans. In Northern Ireland, in particular, one of the most important changes was that the United States was suddenly able to view the conflict in a different light. In over 200 years there had been very few major international issues that the British and the Americans disagreed on. As long as the Cold War continued, Britain's vital role as the major strategic partner of the US in Europe meant that the Northern Ireland issue would also be considered by Washington an internal affair for the British to deal with. The end of the Cold War, however, allowed a new flexibility in the relationship. Amid signs of changing times in Northern Ireland, the opportunity at last presented itself to Irish-Americans of helping to create a major new initiative on Ireland that a US president could take part in. The 'special relationship' of 200 years was at last going to be challenged.

Irish-America: The Disillusioned Decades

At the beginning of the 1990s Irish-America was uniquely positioned to help create a new dynamic. For decades it had existed in a severely fractured state when it came to Northern Ireland. The divisions meant that there was very little opportunity for significant development when it came to developing a new strategy on the Northern Ireland issue. The view of Irish-America as a monolithic structure was a deeply flawed one which nevertheless became common currency in much of the British and Irish media in the run-up to the peace process. In fact the divisions were many and deep, the major one between those who reflected a Sinn Féin consciousness and those who supported the Irish government's view that the issue was best left to them and the British government. It was only when this split was healed that Irish-America was able to progress and play an increasingly important role on the Northern Ireland issue.

Since the 1970s and after an initial flurry of republican rhetoric from leading Irish-Americans such as Senator Edward Kennedy, the Irish government had worked unceasingly to neutralize those Irish-Americans whom they saw as being 'too green' in their outlook. The then Irish ambassador Sean Donlon played the major role in ensuring that the leading Irish-American voices on Ireland were muted and always reflected Irish government opinion on the issue. Those who would not toe the line were opposed bitterly by the Irish government and Donlon himself.

After Charles Haughey became Taoiseach in 1979 and tried to move him in 1980, Donlon used the powerful friends he had made on Capitol Hill to thwart his leader's wishes – an unheard-of scenario for an Irish diplomat. Donlon accomplished his goal of creating a ring fence around the major politicians and leading community figures who supported the Irish government view. The problem was that everybody else was cast into outer darkness and perceived as being too pro-Sinn Féin. Exclusion lists were drawn up for Irish embassy and consulate events, and men such as Paul O'Dwyer, perhaps the most legendary of all Irish-Americans, were refused entry because of their perceived 'green' views. The fact that O'Dwyer, for instance, held talks with loyalist paramilitaries in New York and was hugely influential in creating a political rather than a military philosophy for loyalism was seemingly lost on successive Irish governments at the time. Many people, less well known than O'Dwyer, were similarly tarred with the Noraid brush and considered undesirables. No doubt Noraid had significant support in Irish-America, but there was an unfortunate tendency to greatly overestimate their influence. Indeed, the *Zeitgeist* thinking on Irish-Americans – that they were all naïve, idealistic about the IRA and unable properly to understand the modern Ireland – is one of the great mistaken stereotypes that exists to the present day.

In fact Irish-Americans probably had it right all along. They argued for an inclusive settlement involving all parties. They argued that Sinn Féin and the IRA would have to be part of negotiations, not outside them. They argued that an American role was crucial for the success of any peace initiative. There was a minority that supported the IRA, but never in the numbers that fevered editorial writers in Britain and elsewhere imagined. When the time came for support in an inclusive peace process, Irish-America was to play a major role in bringing about the IRA cease-fires and creating a truly historic opening to the White House. At the heart of their initiative was the view that all sides had to be included. The notion of inclusive negotiation is one that goes deep in the American psyche, regardless of the dispute. The Irish preference to exclude always puzzled Irish-Americans, who could see little merit in the persistent efforts to build only from the centre and exclude those outside. All these Irish-American points of view, however, were dismissed and opposed by successive Irish governments, even though the eventual shape of the peace process and the Good Friday Agreement reflected all those realities. A deeply revisionist line had taken hold of successive Irish governments in the 1970s and much of the 1980s. It was based on a demonization of republicanism as some sort of alien force entirely outside the Irish experience, rather than an integral part of Irish history, including the formation of the state, for better or worse.

Excluding and marginalizing were only making matters worse, as was proved when the opposite tactic was employed by Charles Haughey during his second term in power. The way to stop the IRA campaign was never going to be through condemnation alone, but by creating a political alternative to armed struggle. The tension between the Irish government and the Irish-American community, who should have been well disposed towards the former, left a deep residue of ill will. It was a short-sighted policy which suited no one better than the British government, as cases such as those of the Guildford Four, the Birmingham Six and other miscarriages of justice never received any traction on Capitol Hill because the government of Ireland opposed any such moves. In one infamous incident Ambassador Donlon wrote to Congressman Hamilton Fish pointing out that moderate political leaders opposed any intervention in the Birmingham Six case. The two leaders he cited were Lord Gerry Fitt and the Reverend Martin Smyth, then leader of the Orange Order.

The British were doubtless pleased to have such a deep and seemingly unbridgeable split between the Irish government and Irish-Americans. It certainly suited their purposes of keeping international attention away from Northern Ireland. Irish-American initiatives such as the MacBride Principles, which sought fair employment practices in Northern Ireland, were opposed tooth and nail by successive Irish governments, partly at the behest of the British government. The overall result was a toothless Irish-America. The Irish government carried the moral suasion on the Northern Ireland issue in America. A survey of leading editorial writers conducted by a newspaper which I published during this era revealed that they were much more likely to side with the Irish government view on the North than any other point of view, including that of the British government. Ironically, the Irish government was during much of this era a cipher for the British government's view.

Thus, men such as Senator Kennedy were effectively silenced, apart from ritual condemnations of violence and an anodyne statement every St Patrick's Day from the Friends of Ireland group in Congress, established by the Irish government. Without Irish government backing the Irish-American lobby was unable to present a united agenda to legislators, who often checked with the government to see whether they should support an initiative. Many Irish-Americans, most notably Kennedy, suffered in their own states as a result of their obeisance to Irish government views. Years later, when he played a leading role in securing the all-important 1994 IRA ceasefire, Kennedy proved just how valuable a card the Irish government had for all those years refused to play. The reality is that issues such as the Birmingham Six and Guildford Four would have been resolved much more quickly with American intervention, dramatically shortening the time over which such major miscarriages of justice were allowed to continue.

The Hunger Strikes: An Awakening

The 1981 hunger strikes galvanized large sections of Irish-America in a way that no armed IRA campaign could ever achieve. Right at the time when IRA influence was on the wane because of a seemingly never-ending series of atrocities, the hunger strikes were an entirely different tool which created the dynamic for a political rather than a militant approach to the problem.

It is hard to recapture the atmosphere in America during those times. Huge demonstrations occurred outside all British consulates and the British embassy. In San Francisco I saw a succession of leading businessmen with no previous history of activism on this subject carry a mock coffin up and down outside the British consulate. A range of people who had never previously been involved in Irish activism found their consciences pricked by the deaths of Bobby Sands and the others. It was the beginning of a new movement that would begin to break down the barriers between the various groups in Irish-America. Even the Irish government was deeply shocked by the failure of the British government to prevent the deaths. For many who had been just peripherally involved or repulsed by the violence the hunger strikes were a clear signal that something deeper was at work in Northern Ireland. The belief developed that 'terrorists' did not starve themselves to death unless there was also a deep injustice within the society that created such a desperate act by prisoners claiming political status. The hunger strikes radicalized moderate Irish-Americans and as a result the Irish government found it much harder to explain away its position on Northern Ireland. It found itself in an impossible position, for instance, when Michael Flannery, head of Noraid, was named Grand Marshal of the New York St Patrick's Day parade amid worldwide publicity. While the Irish government succeeded in having Cardinal Cooke suspend his usual viewing of the parade and welcoming of the Grand Marshal, it suffered an enormous loss of credibility in the activist Irish-American community. Two years later the Irish government sought to prevent the new Cardinal, John O'Connor, from reviewing the parade when Congressman Peter King was Grand Marshal. O'Connor went ahead and met King anyway.

But in Irish politics too the winds of change were blowing. For all that has been said about him in other contexts since, Charles Haughey understood Irish-America and there was a clear end to the divisiveness soon after he came into power for the second time in 1982. He sent an important signal early on when he refused to oppose the MacBride Principles; rather, he adopted a neutral position on them and ensured that there was no longer any active opposition to them from his consulates. This signal did not go unnoticed in Irish-America. What had been a combative relationship became a less confrontational one. Embassies and consulates began to be staffed by people who understood the Irish-American dimension and the need to reach out rather than to isolate the community.

The Irish government was also heavily involved at the time in gaining US support for the Anglo-Irish Agreement, signed by Taoiseach Garret Fitzgerald and Prime Minister Margaret Thatcher in November 1985. It was a dramatic step forward which for the first time recognized a role for the Irish government in the affairs of the North. Though it was probably inspired by what the governments saw as the alarming rise in support for Sinn Féin, and as an attempt to shore up moderate nationalism, the Irish initiative won Irish-American support. For the first time since the outset of the Troubles the Irish government was seen to be doing something constructive on the North, rather than just engaging in crisis management. Irish-Americans were responsive to that and an improved relationship ensued.

Illegal Immigration: The Key Catalyst

Another issue arose which also helped create the dynamic that was soon to bring Irish-America and the Irish government together. Since the early 1980s tens of thousands of illegal Irish immigrants had begun to pour into the United States, fleeing poor economic circumstances at home. Their plight was obvious, as they lacked the means to make themselves legal and were often totally at the mercy of unscrupulous employers in the US, who threatened and abused them. The Irish government at first tried to deny that the problem existed. Indeed, after I had quoted in an editorial a figure of 75,000 illegal aliens from Ireland a senior diplomatic figure questioned whether I had meant 7,500. The reason for this attitude was, obviously, that the situation reflected badly on the Irish government. In these times of the Celtic Tiger economy it is difficult to imagine just how defensive Irish government representatives were back then on the issue of the poorly performing Irish economy.

However, the illegal immigrant problem soon became so large that it was impossible to ignore. There was a severe strain on many Irish organizations in America which were trying to cope with the influx without any real help from Dublin. Once the government had accepted the scale of the problem, however, it was able to forge a partnership with Irish-America that did not involve any dissent or divisiveness. The common goal was to establish a visa programme that could take care of the young Irish.

Like any foreign government, the Irish government could make its case to powerful legislators but that case was enormously strengthened if there were actual constituents of those political figures also lobbying for change. So it proved. The partnership of Irish-America and the Irish government soon began to achieve results. The formation of the Irish Immigration Reform Movement, founded by young Irish immigrants, most of them illegal, was a watershed in this fight. The new group was composed of committed young activists, highly intelligent and motivated, who soon learned the political ropes in America and how to influence each and every politician who had any input whatever into the immigration issue. The Irish government took the lead in framing legislation and getting major players such as Senator Edward Kennedy behind it. The lobbying by both the government and the Irish Immigration Reform Movement was intense, but it ended in significant success. Within two years the Donnelly visa programme, named after the Massachusetts congressman who sponsored it, and the Morrison Visas, named after Bruce Morrison, the Connecticut congressman, legalized tens of thousands of undocumented Irish. The new partnership between the Irish government and Irish-America had become a major success. Now it was time to turn that partnership into action on Northern Ireland.

The Clinton Election, 1992

The Irish-American lobby was in the wilderness during the Reagan–Bush era. The closeness of the relationship between Ronald Reagan and Margaret Thatcher, and later between John Major and George Bush, made it impossible for the Irish-Americans to gain any leverage with the White House. It became evident to some Irish-Americans, looking at the 1992 presidential race, that the Bush option was simply not on. They decided instead to support an alternative that at the time looked a very long shot. After the Gulf War George Bush's approval ratings stood at an astronomical 90 per cent and leading Democrats were fleeing the following year's presidential race in their droves.

There has been much interest in how Bill Clinton became involved in the Irish question. Perhaps the main reason initially was that Irish-American activists pursued him aggressively. There was simply no question that whoever the Democrat candidate was in 1992, he would be friendlier on Ireland than Bush. My first inkling that Clinton, then the obscure governor of Arkansas, could be interested in Ireland came in a discussion with the Irish embassy political counsellor Brendan Scannell, now ambassador to Israel, who had developed an excellent relationship with the Irish-American lobby during the immigration battles. Scannell told me that from his own soundings he had found out that Clinton was knowledgeable on Ireland, dating back to his time at Oxford as a Rhodes scholar when the Troubles first erupted. Years later Clinton explained that interest to Conor O'Clery, then Washington correspondent of the *Irish Times*. 'I was there when the Troubles began. I was living in Oxford. It occupied the attention of the country, obviously; you know, I've been fascinated by it for twenty-five years, from the day the Troubles began.' Clinton's deputy national security adviser Nancy Soderberg, his closest adviser on Ireland in his first term, said that the Oxford experience had had a deep impact on President Clinton. 'While there, he was shocked by the violence and instinctively believed America had a role to play. A quarter century later Clinton would come to power at a unique moment in the history of the conflict and in Anglo-American relations. The international situation would offer him a chance to help change the course of history.' When governor of Arkansas he had taken one Irish initiative. At the urging of Rita Mullen, an Irish nurse then based in Arkansas and now an activist in Washington, Clinton had signed a decree on St Patrick's Day in 1978 declaring that day to be Human Rights for Ireland Day.

Towards the end of 1991, as the presidential race began to take shape, I received a call from Chris Hyland, ethnic organizer for the Clinton campaign. He had been alerted to our interest in Clinton and wanted to create an official 'Irish for Clinton' group. It was the first outreach from the man who was now in a tight race to become the Democratic candidate. Because of his Irish credentials and the lack of any alternative I readily agreed to help, and we created the group Irish-Americans for Clinton in January of 1992 at a meeting in FitzPatrick's Hotel in Manhattan. Despite our best efforts we could only muster about 30 people. Bruce Morrison, the former Connecticut congressman who was a hero to Irish-Americans because of his immigration reform efforts, agreed to become chairman of the group. Shortly afterwards there was a dinner for candidate Clinton at the Hyatt Hotel in New York. Irish-Americans for Clinton agreed to take a table, but we had great difficulty in filling it. That was ironic given later developments.

Clinton staff, of course, included Nancy Soderberg, formerly the top foreign affairs aide to Senator Kennedy, who was thoroughly briefed on Irish issues. Throughout the campaign season in 1992 we kept in close touch with her on the Irish issue. In September of that year Paul O'Dwyer, Ray Flynn, then mayor of Boston, and myself had a meeting with Clinton in New York, at which he pledged, if he was elected, to work on the Irish agenda we had drawn up with Soderbergh. What was particularly memorable about that meeting was the incisive knowledge he displayed on Irish issues. Most American politicians leave the details of the Irish question to staff and would never appear on their own to answer questions from activists. Clinton, in this case, entered the room on his own and stayed until we had asked him every question. His knowledge and grasp of detail prompted the old veteran Paul O'Dwyer to remark, 'If this man is elected he'll turn the Irish issue upside down.' Prophetic words. In October 1992 candidate Clinton put down on paper his positions on Ireland. Support for the MacBride Principles and the appointment of a special envoy, in addition to an attack on collusion between security forces and loyalist paramilitaries, were at the heart of his plan. For Irish-Americans it was quite simply the best statement ever made by an American presidential candidate. The big question was whether he would live up to it.

Clinton Elected

Writing after leaving the White House to become a US ambassador to the United Nations, Nancy Soderberg noted the following steps that the White House decided to take on the Irish question: 'The peace strategy was clear. First, find ways to address the root causes of the conflict. Second: put the enormous political, moral and economic weight of the United States behind efforts to alleviate them. Add to this a never-give-up attitude and you have the beginning of a win-win course of action.' In hindsight all of this occurred, but soon after Clinton was elected his relationship with Irish-America went through a very rocky period. Irish-Americans were particularly fearful that, once elected, Clinton would forget the groundbreaking promises he had made and become just another politician who made promises he did not keep. It was evident early on that pressure would be exerted on him, particularly by the anglophile members of Congress such as House Speaker Thomas Foley, to avoid any involvement in the Irish question.

But the British government was facing a significant handicap in its own dealings with the new president. During the election campaign the Tory government of John Major had made clear its preference for George Bush to win another term. Cooperation with Bush had extended so far that the government had undertaken a search of its own files during the campaign to determine whether Bill Clinton had ever sought British citizenship while a student at Oxford to avoid the Vietnam War draft. On the eve of the election Douglas Hurd, the British foreign secretary, had sent a message to the Bush campaign wishing them success. Little wonder, then, that in his first interview after being elected Bill Clinton told the *New York Times* that the British government's actions had angered him and that he bore a grudge against John Major.

Despite this situation Irish-Americans found it difficult to make their own case. During the ten-week transition period, members of Irish-Americans for Clinton, now called Americans for a New Irish Agenda, went to Little Rock seeking a meeting with Soderberg and other key players in the administration. In the event the only person we saw was Chris Hyland, the man who had originally contacted us. All the others were too busy. It sent a chilling signal that the Irish issue was going to be tough to put on the front burner. Worse was to follow soon after when Clinton, at the behest of the Irish government, shelved the special envoy concept. In addition, an attempt by New York mayor David Dinkins to bring Gerry Adams to his city was turned down by the US state department which refused to give him a visa. It was clear that a new tactic was needed to engage the White House on the Northern Ireland issue.

The Ceasefire

In the course of a conversation that I had with Brendan Scannell, the Irish embassy political counsellor, who was a skilled and shrewd reader of the American political scene, the idea of an offer of a symbolic ceasefire from the IRA first came up. Brendan thought it an excellent idea, believing that such a signal from the IRA would send a clear message to the Clinton administration that serious business was afoot in Ireland and that the Irish republican movement wanted the US to play a major part.

I had been in touch with a senior republican figure in America, Ciaran Staunton, who later became my brother-in-law. Ciaran had a deep knowledge of the republican movement and had been charged by them with building a new outreach in America. He urged me to take the notion of a symbolic ceasefire directly to the top of the republican movement and to lay out an American plan of action. At this time the republicans were unable to engage figures of major political stature in the US in their case. The British tactic of ghettoizing republicans and making them untouchable worldwide had succeeded very well. I remember a conversation I had with two congressmen in Belfast not a stone's throw from the Falls Road. I asked them to accompany me up the Falls Road to meet with Sinn Féin politicians and listen to their side of things. Both refused for fear of news getting out that they were talking to terrorists.

Another influential meeting at the time was with Jim Reilly, formerly a top executive with IBM, who put forward the 'outside the box' theory for American involvement. According to Reilly, all the parties in Northern Ireland were frozen inside the same box, and any move was immediately countered by a checkmating move on the other side. The introduction of an 'outside the box' player, such as the US, which Sinn Féin could respond to, would completely change the dynamic inside the box. And so it proved. Reilly's theory was one I was to hear repeated on numerous occasions over the following years, often in mangled form, but the essential truth of it underpins the US involvement in the Irish peace process.

A few weeks later, around April 1994, I was sitting in a Dublin hotel talking to a leading republican about 'outside the box' theory and the notion of an IRA gesture to stir American interest in the situation in Ireland. Prior to my visit I had canvassed four leading Irish-Americans and asked them if they would be part of an ongoing delegation that would try to play a role in a new peace process in Northern Ireland. All said yes unquestioningly. They were former congressman Bruce Morrison, businessman and billionaire philanthropist Charles Feeney, leading New York businessman and chief executive of Mutual America, Bill Flynn, and the Labor movement leader, Joe Jamison. I explained the nature of the initiative, that it would involve some risk, that the US government was unlikely to acknowledge anything we were doing, but that I had reason to believe that events were moving in Northern Ireland.

One other crucial link had been established through Brendan Scannell with Trina Vargo, foreign affairs adviser to Senator Edward Kennedy, who would become a key player in the American initiative. Vargo was my contact both with Kennedy and with the new Clinton administration. A shrewd and skilful aide, she had a knowledge of Ireland unsurpassed on Capitol Hill. She also gave the administration a 'cut-out' since they would not be speaking directly to me, but through an intermediary, and could deny knowledge at any time of what we were doing.

With all that in place I set off for Ireland. My meeting with the senior republican contact in a Dublin hotel was difficult to read. As I later learned, he was a man of very few words but very incisive thinking, who preferred at all times to stay in the background. I put to him the scenario of an IRA gesture, a prearranged ceasefire for a specified period during a visit by our delegation, to be followed by a major American initiative. He said he would give it full consideration.

A few weeks later, back in the US, I received confirmation that the republicans had agreed to go ahead. An IRA ceasefire would take place as a signal to the White House during a visit by our delegation. It was an exciting moment. Finally, on 6 September 1993, the delegation went to Ireland and an unannounced IRA ceasefire prevailed during our ten-day visit. During the visit we also met with delegations from other parties. Most impressive were the Ulster Volunteer Force personnel, including Gusty Spence and David Ervine. For the first time we heard the passionate voices of working-class unionists and we realized that they too desperately needed outside help to accomplish progress in their community. One of our most symbolic moments was meeting an Ulster Unionist delegation, including future leader David Trimble. By meeting them and Sinn Féin on the same visit we broke an international taboo of many years' standing which precluded Unionists' meeting with any group that also included Sinn Féin on its itinerary.

The signal that was sent to the White House by this ceasefire was profound. Here was one of the leading paramilitary organizations in the world giving tangible proof that it was open to exploring a new political accommodation and showing its willingness to do business with Irish-America, and through them the White House. It was an exciting moment for our delegation because we knew that, back at the White House, the trip was being watched very closely.

The Visa Wars

The IRA having delivered, it was now the turn of Irish-America to do so. The White House was clearly intrigued about what had happened and we needed to act quickly. The internal debate in Irish-America was whether to pursue the special envoy concept or go for a rerun of the visa battle to get Gerry Adams into the country. A key figure was William Flynn, chairman of the prestigious National Committee on American Foreign Policy, which counted Henry Kissinger, among others, as a patron. After a meeting between Flynn, Sinn Féin's Ciaran Staunton and myself, the decision was made to pursue the visa option rather than the special envoy idea.

It had to be a perfectly calibrated campaign. The British would be exploring every conceivable avenue to prevent Adams coming into the country. On the other hand we had the element of surprise, since they clearly did not expect any visa proposal to succeed. We had to convince a number of key players – none more so than Senator Edward Kennedy – that a visa for Adams was a vital step in the burgeoning peace process. Kennedy was the king on Irish issues on Capitol Hill and every president would seek his counsel on the issue. In the case of Clinton it was inconceivable that he would act on an Irish issue without checking with Kennedy first. Fortunately for us, Kennedy and his adviser Trina Vargo were ready to take the gamble, having been convinced by what had happened when we were in Belfast, and by John Hume, among others, that Sinn Féin was now serious about a peace initiative. The Irish government would obviously play a key role also, and the Taoiseach Albert Reynolds made clear to us during our visit in September that he was fully committed to an American dimension to the new initiative that he was planning on Northern Ireland.

Having lined up congressional and Irish government support we announced the Northern Ireland conference, inviting all the party leaders, including Adams, in a series of advertisements in the *New York Times* and elsewhere. Then we commenced a large-scale grassroots lobbying effort from Irish organizations across the US. We got the direct telephone numbers of key White House personnel and made sure that calls supportive of the visa came flooding in. The British reacted tardily, believing to the last that their 200-year-old 'special relationship' would not be disturbed for something so outlandish as a visa for a Sinn Féin leader. They knew that the state department, the FBI, the justice department and the permanent bureaucracy of the US government were solidly behind them. What we had, however, was the political arm of the White House, most notably the national security council and possibly, we believed, the president himself. They understood that a gesture on the visa could bring about dramatic progress and, more importantly, would establish the US as a major player in the peace process.

Throughout this period I was acting as intermediary between Adams and the White House, via Senator Kennedy's office. Eventually Nancy Soderberg began talking to me directly as the countdown to the visa decision began. The major issue on both sides was trust. Adams was worried at times that he was being sucked into making ever more compromising statements which could cause him internal difficulties, while the White House was afraid that, once in America, Adams would use the occasion as a pulpit to press for support for the armed struggle.

During this period I received a call from the White House asking for the percentage of Irish-Americans in each state of the Union. I took this as a very positive sign that Clinton, the *über*-politician, was calculating the political odds, and I knew that there were no votes whatever in the British position. So it proved. After a tortuous series of negotiations, which dragged on until the small hours on many nights, the White House eventually took the historic step of approving a 48-hour visa for Gerry Adams to come to America.

In a flash, the international isolation and ghettoization of Sinn Féin was ended forever. The British were no longer able to justify their broadcast ban on Sinn Féin when Adams was speaking freely on American television and being beamed around the world. The president took enormous heat for the visa decision, including a vitriolic campaign against him in the British media. However, a leading Sinn Féin source told me that it moved the peace process forward by at least a year. Adams's visit was received ecstatically by his Irish-American supporters, condemned by the British government and unionists. But something fundamental had changed. The 'outside the box' theory had been proved to work. Within a few months there was a historic ceasefire; later there were two visits by President Clinton to Northern Ireland, the first in history by a US president. There was also a trade and investment conference in Washington and the appointment of a special economic envoy, later chairman of the peace talks, Senator George Mitchell.

Throughout each crisis President Clinton played a vital role in steadying not just republicans but all the parties in Northern Ireland. He struck up an excellent relationship with Unionist leader David Trimble and ensured an even-handed approach that allowed him to play honest broker. For Irish-America the visa was also the culmination of the refocused energy and commitment which the community had brought to the issue. In tandem with the Irish government, it succeeded in achieving the Holy Grail of successive Irish-American generations: involving the US in helping to resolve Ireland's problems. Irish-America had helped to supply the missing ingredient in the resolution of the Irish conflict: the presence of the US as a full participant in seeking a peaceful solution. As former deputy national security adviser, now ambassador, Nancy Soderberg stated in a recent speech: 'At the beginning of the last decade US foreign policy towards Ireland was as stagnant as the peace process itself. Events then started to break in such a way that US foreign policy-makers decided to take a second look at our involvement in Northern Ireland. Intervention by a US president and a willingness to take risks for peace can make a real difference.' With those words she confirmed that what Irish-Americans had believed all along had finally come true.

Note

1. 1993 Research Service Report on Northern Ireland, published for members of the US Congress.

'Give Us Another MacBride Campaign':[1]
An Irish-American Contribution to Peaceful Change in Northern Ireland

Kevin McNamara

Since the early nineteenth century Irish-Americans have sought to persuade the White House and Congress to intervene in the politics of Ireland and, after Partition, Northern Ireland. On all occasions they were singularly unsuccessful. There were three reasons for this failure. First, the White House claimed not to intervene in the internal affairs of another sovereign country, a principle of international relations often honoured more in the breach than in the observance by successive US governments. In the case of the United Kingdom, however, it was invariably honoured. In the nineteenth century and until the outbreak of the Second World War, the British Empire was the largest in the world and, following the Second World War, Britain with its 'special relationship' was the United States' most important NATO ally. When questioned about Northern Ireland, the White House religiously echoed the refrain of 'non-interference in the internal affairs in another country' and generally supported British policy in Ireland and, later, in Northern Ireland.

The second reason was that initiatives taken in Congress, mainly in the House of Representatives, were unsuccessful. In the early 1980s several attempts at legislative action were made by members of the Ad Hoc Congressional Committee for Irish Affairs, supported by the Irish National Caucus. They failed because successive speakers of the House and leaders of the Senate controlled the business on the floor of each House and they saw to it that no progress was made on the bills.[2] Particularly in the period following the Northern Ireland civil rights agitation, initiatives on the Hill were blocked as a result of extensive lobbying by the British and Irish embassies and pressure from the White House. John Hume, the leader of the SDLP, who was hostile to the MacBride campaign, decisively influenced Speakers Tip O'Neill and Tom Foley.[3] It was not until 1995 that the affairs of Northern Ireland were subject to an official hearing in the House of Representatives before the Committee on International Relations.[4] It was paradoxical that the hearings were held when the Republicans were in control of the House and not the Democrats, the traditional supporters of the Irish cause. The chairman of the committee, the Republican congressman Benjamin Gillman, was a long-standing member of the Ad Hoc Committee.

The third reason for failure was the almost incestuous relationship that existed between the US state department and the British Foreign Office. This was true at all levels of the bureaucracy.[5] There was an unwillingness by the state department to upset the United Kingdom because of its often uncritical support of US foreign and defence policy. This cosiness was upset for the first time by the granting of a visa to Gerry Adams by the White House against the advice of Secretary of State Warren Christopher and the state department.[6]

The tactic devised by the MacBride campaigners in New York was to appeal over the head of the US political establishment in Washington to the American people living outside the 'Beltway', and to galvanize for the first time on a nation-wide basis Irish-American political opinion. Thus the three historical obstacles would be overcome. The Irish National Caucus would vigorously continue the fight on the Hill. By using the federal system of state and local government in the USA, together with their power of the purse, a new front was opened to challenge British policy in Northern Ireland.

The MacBride[7] Principles, published in 1984 and amended in 1986, were a set of nine affirmative employment action proposals to be implemented by US companies in Northern Ireland to end anti-Catholic discrimination in the recruitment and retention of labour. They were modelled on the Sullivan Principles, a similar code for US companies operating in apartheid South Africa, but with one major difference. The Sullivan Principles called for courses of action which were illegal and known to be illegal under South African law and were aimed at breaking apartheid.[8] The MacBride Principles claimed to be legal within the terms of the Fair Employment (Northern Ireland) Act 1976, and were only seeking to encourage American firms to carry out the letter and spirit of the legislation. The original driving force behind the campaign for fair employment policies for Northern Ireland to be enacted in legislation in the United States was the Irish National Caucus. Based in Washington, it was founded in December 1978 by Father Sean McManus, brother of Frank McManus, the former Independent Unity MP for Fermanagh and South Tyrone. His brother Patrick had been killed in 1958 during the 1956–62 IRA border campaign. The Irish National Caucus lobbied for justice and peace in Northern Ireland but Father McManus had hit upon the Achilles' heel of the British position in the North that would appeal to all Americans: discrimination in employment.

Father McManus sought to campaign on fair employment policies on the Hill using the good offices of the Ad Hoc Congressional Committee on Irish Affairs – roughly the equivalent of a British all-party backbench committee. On 22 July 1981 the Ad Hoc Committee held a hearing at which a paper was presented by the late Father Brian Brady, head of the religion department at St Joseph's College, Belfast. The paper was entitled 'Anti-Catholic Discrimination in Manufacturing Industry in Northern Ireland – the American Dimension'.[9] This was the first serious documented examination of religious discrimination in employment in private industry in Northern Ireland.[10] Following Father Brady's presentation several pieces of legislation, for example the Ottinger Bill, were introduced into the House of Representatives. They embodied many of the ideas to be formalized later into the MacBride Principles, but they failed to be adopted for the reasons already stated.[11]

The important twist in policy came with the involvement in the campaign of Harrison J. Goldin, the comptroller of New York. Influenced by the success of the Sullivan campaign, Goldin instructed his office to examine whether a similar campaign could be waged against anti-Catholic employment discrimination in Northern Ireland. The task fell upon Patrick Doherty, who had just joined the comptroller's staff. Doherty became active in the formulation of the nine principles and their later amendments. He drew extensively on British legislation, codes of practice published but not fully implemented by the Department of Economic Development in Northern Ireland and, where relevant, the Sullivan Code. Father McManus claims that the Principles were conceived in August 1979, born in June 1983 and baptized in November 1984.[12]

Goldin's contribution to the campaign was the idea of using shareholders' resolutions tabled by New York City Pension Funds, of which he was the principal trustee, at meetings of US corporations that had subsidiaries in Northern Ireland. These resolutions would instruct the corporations to implement the MacBride Principles. The notion of influencing the corporations was not completely new. Following the publication of the Brady paper, Sister Regina Murphy, president of the Inter-Faith Centre on Corporate Responsibility, had sought to influence companies in a similar manner.[13] She had suggested the same to Father McManus, still busy on the Hill, but he ignored or was not aware of her suggestion.[14]

The religious orders had limited shareholdings and little financial clout. Their protestations could be easily ignored. The comptroller of New York, an elected official, was the trustee of four large pension funds of the employees of New York City.[15] The many millions of dollars invested by the funds made them prime institutional investors, movers and shakers on Wall Street. The comptroller could not be ignored. Given the experiences of the Sullivan campaign there was an implied threat of disinvestment from any company not accepting a MacBride resolution. Such an intention was vehemently denied by the MacBride campaigners. They claimed that it was the threat of bad publicity of which the US corporations were afraid and that they had continuously emphasized that they were calling for a change in working practices among the corporations, not for disinvestment in Northern Ireland. They looked for *more* investment in Northern Ireland.[16] This was a nice distinction which was not always appreciated by the companies involved, their Northern Ireland employees and the British government.

The publication of the MacBride Principles was an immediate success. The AFL-CIO was the first public body of national and international repute to endorse the proposals, on 19 February 1985.[17] The idea spread like wildfire. It had recast the nationalist case in terms of American democratic experience, civil rights, affirmative action and anti-apartheid solidarity. Following the death of the hunger strikers, it gave Irish-Americans, who did not wish to be associated with the support of paramilitary activities or Noraid, the opportunity to 'do something' for Ireland. It never strayed beyond constitutional nationalism and its deeper implications, although the Fine Gael–Labour coalition government of Garret Fitzgerald and Dick Spring together with John Hume were unable to see it in that light.[18] It also appealed to the little man against the big man, the states and the cities of the United States against control by central government, Democratic Massachusetts against Republican Washington and the tweaking of the British lion's tail.[19]

The British, American and Irish governments sought to disparage the MacBride campaign; nevertheless they treated it as a real threat. At a White House ceremony welcoming the signing of the Anglo-Irish Agreement in October 1985 President Reagan found it necessary to praise the constructive role played by US corporations in Northern Ireland and earlier that year Dick Spring attacked the campaign at an SDLP conference on 25 January. The campaigners were delighted as they had obviously touched a raw nerve. The attitude of the Irish coalition government was at first equivocal and then hostile to the MacBride Principles. It was seen by the Irish embassy in Washington as an irresponsible irritant, as it was continuing its careful policy of wooing the White House and US administration towards a more evenhanded approach to the Northern Ireland problem. The Irish government saw it as a distraction from its careful negotiations of what was to be the Anglo-Irish Agreement of 1985, which, if completed successfully, would give the Irish government the opportunity to raise all matters concerning Northern nationalists, including employment discrimination, with the British government. The then Taoiseach said quite bluntly, 'If John Hume was against it, so were we.'[20]

The original attitude of the British Information Service in New York was to produce a carefully argued five-page document blessing the MacBride Principles as being merely an extension of the existing Northern Ireland fair employment legislation. They were in the spirit of the existing Fair Employment (NI) Act and codes of practice in Northern Ireland. 'They were killing us with kisses', said Patrick Doherty.[21] But suddenly there was a volte-face. A new smaller document of only two pages was produced claiming that at least three of the Principles were illegal, two were marginal, and the rest were already in operation or impractical.[22] This led to the first trial of strength. The British government decided to campaign vigorously against the MacBride Principles on the grounds that they were illegal in Northern Ireland law and were aimed at disinvestment in Northern Ireland, where, because of terrorist activity, the economy was already very fragile. The British government further complained that the MacBride campaign was inspired by the Provisional IRA to encourage employment quotas and reverse discrimination. It said it was a smoke-screen for all those people who sought to attack the British government on other grounds.[23] Writing retrospectively in 1995, Professor John Edwards argued that '[the] real reason for the Government's need to reject the MacBride Principles was their provenance. They came with the support of the Irish National Caucus and Noraid (among others) both having links with Provisional IRA. In the light of … the imperative of presenting non-partisan legislation (and content), it is clear that no matter what the MacBride Principles had contained, the Government could not be seen to be doing business with the authors and promoters.'[24]

Initially Provisional Sinn Féin and Noraid were hostile both to the concept of the MacBride Principles and to Father McManus and the Irish National Caucus.[25] Father McManus's insistence on the independence of the Caucus and his distancing it from organizations associating themselves with violent republicanism gained the hostility of Noraid. McManus's policy was to seek the financial support of 'Irish Middle America'. The funds raised by Noraid were used for the benefit of widows and orphans of the Northern war, thus presumably releasing the IRA's own money for purchase of weapons. The argument that there was only a single Irish-American well from which Noraid and the Irish National Caucus could draw money was mistaken, since they appealed to different groupings. Noraid's original hostility was only overcome by the urging of Martin Galvin[26] and the change in the attitude of Provisional Sinn Féin. Galvin persuaded Noraid and Provisional Sinn Féin of the propaganda value of the MacBride Principles.

At earlier discussions with Danny Morrison of Provisional Sinn Féin in Belfast before the formal launching of the MacBride Principles, hostility was expressed to the campaign as being 'reformist in an unreformable state'.[27] After the launch of the campaign Danny Morrison told Pat Doherty that 'with a car at the front and a colour television it is hard to maintain a revolutionary movement'.[28] Members of Provisional Sinn Féin found it difficult to complain about unfair employment practices when they were engaged in a campaign of destruction of the economic infrastructure of many of the towns and cities of Northern Ireland. Hypocritical though it appeared, this did not stop Provisional Sinn Féin from supporting the MacBride Principles. Because of Martin Galvin's contacts with Provisional Sinn Féin, those elements within Noraid who saw the MacBride campaign as a distraction from the 'armed struggle' were sidelined. On the publication of the Principles a rumour[29] was spread that the launch was a precursor of the creation of a new republican party in the North of Ireland to be led by the ex-MP Frank McManus, Father Sean McManus's brother. Father McManus vehemently denies that this was the case and suggests that it was a rumour put about by Ruarí O Brádaigh and Dáithí O Conaill as a means of discrediting the Principles.[30]

Had the British government realized it, the 'killing with kisses' reaction was the correct one. It would have stopped the MacBride campaign in its tracks. The change of approach by the British government was to prove to be a major tactical and strategic error. The result was a bitter and bruising series of confrontations between MacBride campaigners and their opponents, fought in the State Houses and city halls across the United States. British embassy officials were embarrassed, sometimes humiliated, as their government's enemies were given frequent opportunities for a constant rehearsal of the failure of British government policy in Ireland over the centuries and, in particular, in Northern Ireland since Partition.[31] The British government had misread the situation. There were two different Americas, inside the Beltway and outside the Beltway, inside Washington DC and beyond Capitol Hill.

The first serious confrontation with a major corporation came when a resolution supporting MacBride was tabled for the annual meeting of General Motors in November 1985. Comptroller Goldin presented the case. Although the resolution was defeated, enough votes had been garnered to give a similar resolution, if tabled, an automatic place for discussion at the next general meeting of the corporation. The attitude of the British government led to the first legal trial of strength in 1986 when Goldin sought to put down a shareholders' resolution on behalf of the New York City Employees Retirement System for the general meeting of American Brands. American Brands had a major subsidiary in Northern Ireland, Gallagher's Tobacco Company. Very few Catholics were employed by the company either in its large factory in the Protestant stronghold of Ballymena or in its Belfast factory. The company refused to accept the resolution on the grounds that to table such a motion instructing it to carry out an allegedly illegal operation in a third country was contrary to the rules of the United States Securities and Exchange

Commission.[32] A preliminary hearing took place on 12 May 1986, in the US District Court in the Southern District of New York, before Robert L. Carter, a black United States district judge with a history of working for civil rights. The issue was whether the MacBride Principles, as amended, were illegal in Northern Ireland and whether, therefore, the SEC rules applied.

The British government was not represented at the trial but it closely advised the company. The pension fund case was based upon an affidavit made by Dr C. McCrudden, Fellow at Lincoln College, Oxford, supported by a statement issued by Peter Archer QC, MP.[33] Against the advice of many Irish-Americans who had bitter memories of the period when Roy Mason[34] was secretary of state for Northern Ireland in the Callaghan government, Doherty was determined to try to build relations with the British Labour party. Peter Archer and his deputy, Stuart Bell MP, from the Labour party front bench, had endorsed the MacBride Principles, although they had never been subject to a Labour party conference resolution. That support was to prove of immense importance to the MacBride campaigners when confronted with the accusation that the only party in the British Isles that supported MacBride was Sinn Féin.[35]

Although acting in his professional capacity in proffering his opinion on the Brands case, Archer had been a Labour solicitor-general and was then opposition spokesman on Northern Ireland. Archer's opinion was a professional one but it mattered that he was solicitor-general when the 1976 Fair Employment Act was passed.[36] McCrudden's affidavit, while containing fresh material, amplified many of the arguments contained in the original British Information Service's 'killing us with kisses' document. Robert L. Carter found for the Pension Fund and therefore for the MacBride campaign. No appeal was made. As far as US law was concerned the MacBride Principles were legal in Northern Ireland. The ground had been cut from beneath the British government's feet. The legality of the MacBride Principles was never challenged in the United Kingdom, not even by judicial review.

The MacBride campaign now spread rapidly throughout the United States. It did suffer one serious setback. The American Presbyterian Church, originally a champion of the MacBride Principles, withdrew its support in September 1987. This followed representations from the Presbyterian Church in Ireland and the return of a fact-finding mission of members of the Church to Northern Ireland.[37] The British embassy never knew from which city or state a fresh set of resolutions supporting MacBride was likely to appear. 'It flew under the radar.'[38] By November 1985 the Massachusetts governor, George Dukakis, had signed the first act incorporating the MacBride Principles. Dukakis was to become the Democratic nominee for the presidency in 1988. In 1986 Massachusetts was followed by Connecticut, New Jersey and Rhode Island. States and cities passed resolutions supporting the Principles or enacted legislation containing them. Gradually the MacBride campaign gained the political initiative and, particularly important in politics, it became fashionable. Not every state and city presented with the resolutions passed them. The British government had some pyrrhic victories: where they won one year, they often lost the next. The legislation might be passed by a state legislature only to be vetoed by the state governor.[39] Nevertheless the continuing political damage undermining the British position in Northern Ireland was damning.

The British government organized teams from Northern Ireland to appear as witnesses to present the anti-MacBride case at hearings in cities and states considering the implementation of the MacBride Principles. These teams of four or five people would often have a majority of Northern Ireland Catholics on them, including a trade unionist, layman or official, a Catholic member of the Alliance Party and a Catholic employer. Significantly there was never a member of the SDLP on these delegations. Although the British government itself did not formally present evidence at these hearings, an embassy official travelled with the delegations, attending all the hearings, making the necessary domestic arrangements for the delegation and standing ready to entertain local legislators and councillors. The fact that Catholics were appearing to speak on behalf of the British government was scorned by the MacBride campaigners. 'Castle Catholics' were phenomena with which they were familiar; another description was 'Catholic Uncle Toms'. As for non-Catholic witnesses, the comment was: 'They would say that, wouldn't they?'

The American Brands case was a major victory for the MacBride campaign; for the British government it was a disaster. It had to change its anti-MacBride arguments. It could no longer say that the MacBride Principles were illegal in Northern Ireland and that they called for disinvestment without appearing to challenge the federal court's decision, against which American Brands did not appeal. Officially the government's line now became that the Principles were 'a disincentive to invest'.[40] This did not stop the earlier arguments continuing to be used both in the United States and in the United Kingdom. The MacBride bush fires springing up across the United States could not be contained. This was a revolution by fax[41] and telephone, requiring few (but dedicated) people and little money. In an attempt to dampen down the fires an additional political officer was appointed to the British Information Services in New York with a specific remit to organize the anti-MacBride campaign. The British government, despite all its efforts, could not win because it and its Irish policy were continuously in the dock. The federal nature of the US constitution allowed the MacBride campaign to circumvent the domination the British government had in Washington. Now the British government had to pay attention to the Irish-American grass roots. There was a fear that the campaign would spread from Northern Ireland to Great Britain. It was never mentioned aloud but MacBride himself hinted at it in an interview some time before he died.[42]

By opposing the campaign, the British government helped to unify Irish-American opinion across the United States for the first time. Americans, not just Irish-Americans, could not understand British opposition to anti-discriminatory workplace policies which they took for granted. The campaigning in towns and states outside Washington snowballed. Irish-American opinion was being mobilized for the first time. Its strength and potential were seen and appreciated by Bill Clinton,[43] then governor of Arkansas and presidential hopeful, who in his 1992 presidential campaign supported the MacBride Principles. The political campaigning of Irish-Americans had rarely, if ever, been engaged above city or state level. Now it was to show its strength in the 'visa for Gerry Adams' campaign after the declaration of the first IRA ceasefire.[44] For the first time an American president intervened directly in the internal affairs of Northern Ireland against the wishes of the United Kingdom, his country's most important ally. President Clinton was later to honour the two other undertakings he had given to Irish-Americans. Following the first IRA ceasefire he gave specific responsibility for encouraging US industrial investment in Northern Ireland to the then secretary of state for trade, Ron Brown. This led to the appointment of Senator George Mitchell[45] as his representative in the tortuous negotiations leading up to and then implementing the Good Friday Agreement. Congressional legislation in 1998 embodied the MacBride Principles in the Appropriations Act.[46]

Having circumvented the traditional US-based obstacles to grassroots Irish-America affecting British policy in Northern Ireland, the first major success of the MacBride campaign abroad was the powerful influence it had on the passage of the Fair Employment (Northern Ireland) Act 1988, barely four years after the Principles were baptized and two years after the American Brands case. It acted as a Greek chorus commenting on the action in the United Kingdom Parliament as the Fair Employment Bill made its tortuous way to the statute book. The pressure of the MacBride campaign persuaded the British government to accept many of the Labour opposition's proposals for amendments to the Bill. The new Act contained many changes from the original Bill, the most notable being the appearance of goals and targets for reducing employment imbalances in private firms. MacBride Principle 3, the banning of provocative religious or political emblems from the workplace, was to be subject to separate legislation.[47] However, the changes were not enough to satisfy either the MacBride campaigners or the Labour opposition.[48]

The importance of the campaign lay in breaching the cosy relationship between the British and American establishments and preparing the ground for the future President Clinton's active interference in Northern Ireland affairs. Nevertheless it threatened to hit Britain where it hurt – financially, threatening future investment in Northern Ireland. It enabled Irish-Americans to mobilize their own economic strength, and that of the organizations to which they belonged and industries of which they were part, to force a change in policy by the British government. The campaigning fervour of Father McManus, the cool deliberation of Doherty, the influence of Comptroller Goldin and his successors were all essential but the campaign only succeeded because it went with the grain of American experience, democratic ideals and practice.

Postscript

By the end of the century a majority of US states, together with those sympathetic cities possessing assets totalling over half of non-federal public pension investments, had signed up to the MacBride Principles.[49] However, the enactment of the MacBride Principles into US legislation as 'principles of economic justice', the 1989 British Fair Employment (Northern Ireland) Act, and legislation following from the Good Friday Agreement[50] do not disguise the fact that the implementation of the legislation, both in letter and spirit, is far more difficult. The Agreement at St Andrews recognized the continuing problem: 'The Government will continue to actively promote the advancement of human rights, equality and mutual respect'.[51] In its recent survey on the current situation, the Campaign for the Administration of Justice (CAJ) acknowledged the degree of progress made since the 1989 Act, but nevertheless concluded that 'significant differentials across the private sector still exist'.[52] The MacBride campaigners in the United States could draw some consolation from an IRRC report to the California Public Employees Retirement System, which provided a snapshot of what was happening.[53] It had examined 51 companies in which the pension systems held investments and noted that 'Catholics were better represented at U.S. firms in Northern Ireland than at non-U.S. firms'.[54] The CAJ considered that this merited further investigation.[55] Nevertheless, what the CAJ survey revealed was that bridging the gap between reforming legislation and its effective implementation is often far more difficult than putting the legislation on the statute book in the first place.

Notes

1. A frequent saying of Gerry Adams in conversation with Irish-Americans. This paper was first delivered at the Institute of Irish Studies, University of Liverpool on 11 March 2000.

2. Werner Brandt, a member of Speaker Foley's staff and his organizer for the Friends of Ireland, said in conversation with Pat Doherty in late 1984: 'The Friends of Ireland was formed to prevent Northern Ireland from becoming an irritant in Anglo-Irish relations.' Interview with Doherty, 26 July 1999.

3. For early and differing discussions of the struggle for the MacBride Principles see A. Wilson, *Irish America and the Ulster Conflict* (Belfast: The Blackstaff Press, 1995), pp. 269-77, and Father S. McManus, *The MacBride Principles: Genesis and History and the Story to Date* (Irish National Caucus, 1993), pp. 1–30. The only successful Congressional initiative was in 1987 by Congressman Joe Kennedy, a member of the House Sub-Committee on Defence Investment, who exacted fair employment concessions from Short's Ltd, the Belfast air company which was bidding to sell planes to the American National Guard.

4. 'US Economic Role in the Peace Process in Northern Ireland'. Throughout the hearing committee members and witnesses made constant reference to the MacBride Principles. *Congressional Record, Committee on International Relations, House of Representatives, 15 March 1995.*

5. Pat Doherty puts this down to the 'East Coast elite' in the state department 'aspiring to be British'! Conversation with the author, 25 July 2000.

6. See Conor O'Cleary, *The Greening of the White House* (New York: Gill & McMillan, 1996) for how this relationship broke down.

7. Sean MacBride, Nobel and Lenin prize winner, former minister of external affairs for the Republic of Ireland and founder of Amnesty International, was the chairman of the Irish National Caucus Liaison Group in Dublin. MacBride was the principal signatory to the Principles. There were three others: Father Sean Brady (d. 1986), Ms Inez McCormack, currently president of the Irish Congress of Trade Unions, and Dr J. Robb.

8. Interview with Doherty, 25 July 2000; see B. MacCormack and J. O'Hara, *Enduring Inequality: Religious Discrimination in Employment in Northern Ireland* (NCCL, 1990).

9. Doherty papers, uncatalogued collection, City Hall, New York.

10. Discrimination in the public sector, particularly local government, had been well documented at the outset of the civil rights movement by the Campaign for Social Justice and the Cameron Commission Report, 1969, CMD 532 HMSO.

11. See Wilson, *Irish America*.
12. See McManus, *The MacBride Principles*.
13. Doherty interviews, 6 July 1999 and 26 July 2000, and Doherty papers, New York.
14. McManus interview, Washington, 18 November 1999.
15. New York City pension funds' holdings in US corporations with subsidiaries in Northern Ireland amounted in January 1985 to $310,767,740.25; report of the Northern Ireland Investment Office, Office of the Comptroller of New York, 4 February 1986. Doherty papers, City Hall, New York.
16. Doherty interviews, 6 July 1999 and 25 July 2000.
17. Following a visit of its leaders to Ireland in 1983, it had already issued a statement expressing its concern at employment discrimination in Northern Ireland.
18. This summary is mostly drawn from the undated appendix to a letter to Gerry Adams, written by Joe Jamison, explaining the success of the MacBride campaign.
19. McManus interview, 18 November 1999.
20. Conversation with the former Taoiseach, Garret Fitzgerald, 13 November 1996.
21. Doherty interviews, 6 July 1999 and 25 July 2000.
22. The reason for this volte-face has never properly been explained. Doherty puts it down to the prospect of a visit to the United States by the prime minister, Margaret Thatcher. A partial explanation was given in a letter of 11 February 1986 from Howard Beattie of the British Information Services, in which he wrote: 'I had indicated when we first spoke, the five-page document on the MacBride Principles sent by me to Comptroller Goldin's office on 31 January last year was prepared as a general discussion paper. The Government's view is more accurately reflected in the two-page commentary on each of the nine MacBride principles which, I understand, you have received separately from the New York office of the Industrial Development Board for Northern Ireland.'
23. Interview with British officials stationed in New York at the time, 6 December 1999.
24. John Edwards, *Affirmative Action in a Sectarian Society* (Avebury: Ashgate, 1995).
25. See interviews with McManus, 18 November 1999, and Doherty, 6 July 1999 and 25 July 2000.
26. Editor of the *Irish People*, leading New York Republican lawyer, supporter of Noraid and close to the Belfast leadership of Provisional Sinn Féin.
27. Interviews with McManus, 18 November 1999, and Doherty, 6 July 1999.
28. Interview with Doherty, 25 July 2000.
29. Doherty says he first heard it from Father Des Wilson; interview, 25 July 2000.
30. Ruarí O Brádaigh, then president of Provisional Sinn Féin. Dáithí O Connail, then chief of staff of the Provisional IRA.
31. See the many publicized hearings before the committees of state and city legislatures, e.g. New Jersey, 4 March 1987; Chicago City Council, 24 March 1992.
32. In a letter to the Securities and Exchange Commission on behalf of American Brands (27 December 1985), Chadbourne and Parke claim that Rule 14a-8(c)(2) implementation requiring the violation of any law of a foreign jurisdiction to which the user is subject was the basis for their opposition.
33. Now Lord Archer of Sandwell.
34. Now Lord Mason of Barnsley, secretary of state for Northern Ireland 1976–79.
35. Interview with Doherty, 25 July 2000.
36. Under Direct Rule the solicitor-general for England and Wales is also the solicitor-general for Northern Ireland.
37. For further discussion see D. Keogh and M. Haltzel, *Northern Ireland and the Politics of Reconciliation* (Woodrow Wilson Center Press; Cambridge: Cambridge University Press, 1993).

38. A phrase frequently repeated by Joe Jamison in interview in New York, 11 March 1999, to demonstrate how the British embassy was continuously outflanked and ambushed.
39. E.g. in California, where the governor justified his veto by referring to the opposition of John Hume, leader of the SDLP, and John Freeman, secretary of the ATGWU, 15 October 1991.
40. Policy change explained by former British officials in New York (interview, 6 December 1999), but in the UK ministers continued to refer to the Principles as being illegal.
41. Doherty claims that the advent of fax technology was of the utmost importance. Previously, articles written in the British Isles or America would take almost a week to cross the Atlantic and be distributed. Now they could be sent almost before the ink was dry from the printing press and instant rebuttal, if necessary, could be made. A policy of 'instant rebuttal' was later adopted by the Labour party in the 1997 general election campaign.
42. In 1995 Ken Livingstone MP raised the matter of religious discrimination at the Ballylumford power station at the general meeting of British Gas plc, which had bought the station following the privatization of the Northern Ireland Electricity Service.
43. For a blow-by-blow account of the growth of Irish-American influence on the White House see O'Clery, *The Greening of the White House.*
44. See O'Clery, *The Greening of the White House*, and interview with Jamison, 11 March 1999.
45. O'Cleary, *The Greening of the White House.*
46. Interview with McManus, 18 November 1999.
47. See the Public (Northern Ireland) Order 1987 repealing the Flags and Emblems (Display) Act (Northern Ireland) 1954; various Fair Employment Agency cases e.g. case 465/85, 1987; the Guide to Effective Practice, Religious Equality of Opportunity in Employment, September 1987; and the Code of Practice on Fair Employment, December 1989.
48. MacCormack and O'Hara, *Enduring Inequality*, pp. 72–73.
49. Interview with Doherty, 19 May 2006.
50. The Fair Employment and Treatment Order, 1998.
51. Agreement at St Andrews, Annex B, 12 October 2006.
52. *Equality in Northern Ireland: The Rhetoric and the Reality* (September, 2006), p. 158.
53. *Equality in Northern Ireland*, pp. 48–49 for an account of the IRRC report.
54. *Equality in Northern Ireland*, p. 48.
55. *Equality in Northern Ireland*, p. 49.

Towards Peace in Northern Ireland[1]

Senator George Mitchell

Lord Chancellor, Lord Mayor, distinguished guests, members and friends of the University of Liverpool, it is a great honour for me to be recognized for my work in Northern Ireland. It's a special pleasure to have that recognition come from an institution as renowned as this one. The University of Liverpool has rightly achieved a reputation for excellence within the United Kingdom and beyond. I have been asked to speak about my experience in Northern Ireland. Before doing so, I would like to say a few words about my experience in the United States. First, I should warn you that I am a product of the United States Senate, an institution that is known for long speeches. There is a rule in the Senate which permits unlimited debate: any senator may speak at any time on any subject for any length. Many frequently do, and I myself have done so, usually possessing no knowledge and conveying none, but taking up a lot of time, which, if you have paid attention in recent weeks, you will know is one of the major functions of the Senate. But I am also a product of the State of Maine, which those of you familiar with the United States will know has a tradition of few words. Fortunately for you I am no longer in the Senate but I am still from Maine, and so I shall try to get across my thoughts and my gratitude briefly.

I had the pleasure of spending nearly four years in the United Kingdom and in the Republic of Ireland. During that time I have come to know both countries and the people there, countries with which my own, the United States, is bound by ties of blood and history and values. Of course, Americans have not always used such flattering words to describe their Mother Country. Two hundred and twenty-two years ago a small group of them gathered in Philadelphia in a constitutional convention. Their objective was independence and self-government and they achieved it. They were eager to shake off British rule but they had no hesitation in accepting British law, tradition and customs. As a lawyer and a judge I spent much of my career reading the decisions of long-dead British judges in the search for answers to live American problems. I give one recent example: for the past several months the United States has been debating impeachment. The decision turned in part on what ancient British jurists and parliamentarians meant when they first used the words 'high crimes and misdemeanours'. Those are just a few of the many words in the American Constitution which were taken directly from prior British experience.

For most of our history, fortunately, our relationship has been unique and almost entirely positive; that is surely the case in this century and especially at this time. We cooperate in many areas to our mutual benefit. One such area is Northern Ireland. Of course, our roles and responsibilities there are not equivalent. Primary responsibility rests with the British government. The American role was, and is, secondary: to be helpful and supportive but not the ultimate decision-maker.

A product of the Philadelphia Convention of 1787 was the American Constitution, to me an act of political and literary genius. The part of it that we call the Bill of Rights is the most concise and eloquent statement ever written by humans of the right of the individual to be free from oppression by government. That is one side of the coin of liberty. The other is the need for everyone to have a fair chance to enjoy the blessings of liberty.

A man without a job, a woman who cannot get good care or education for her child, the young people who lack the skills needed to compete in a world of technology – they do not think much about abstract concepts of liberty and justice; they worry about coping from day to day. The same is true of people living in a society torn by violence. Without civil order, without physical security, freedom and individual liberty are mere concepts unrelated to the daily task of survival. So it was for many years in Northern Ireland. Violence and fear settled over that beautiful land like a heavy, unyielding fog. The events of recent years in Northern Ireland can be understood only in the larger context of the British domination of Ireland over many centuries. I have neither the knowledge nor the time this evening to inform this audience of that history. Indeed, I expect that if each of you were now called upon to recite that history, there would be many very different versions and many interesting interpretations. So I will go back just a decade to the 1980s when, after a half-century of no cooperation, the British and Irish governments concluded that if there was to be any hope of bringing the conflict in Northern Ireland to an end, they would have to cooperate in a sustained effort to lay the foundation for peace. The Good Friday Agreement of 1998 traces its lineage directly to the Anglo-Irish Agreement of 1985 and the Downing Street Declaration of 1993. Despite much difficulty and over many setbacks the governments persevered. For that, they deserve more credit than they have got. I have been disappointed that their contributions have not been properly recognized, especially in the United States. Tony Blair and Bertie Ahern were brilliant in bringing the process to a conclusion but they would be the first to acknowledge that it was their predecessors who set the stage and made a conclusion possible. To those predecessors, British and Irish, who kept the process going, in often exceptionally difficult circumstances, I say 'well done!'

In June 1996, after years of effort, the governments were finally able to get negotiations under way. The prime ministers invited me to serve as chairman. I had been involved in Northern Ireland long enough to know what a daunting task it was. In making my decision I reflected on my own life. My father was the orphan son of Irish immigrants. He worked as a janitor. My mother was an immigrant who worked in a textile mill. Neither of them had any education whatsoever. My mother could not read or write English. But because of their efforts, because of the openness of American society and because many people gave me a helping hand along the way, I was able to become Majority Leader of the United States Senate. So when I, who had been helped by so many, was asked to help others, I could not refuse.

That the people I was asked to help are in the land of my father's heritage was just a coincidence. That I could help was what mattered. The negotiations were the longest, most difficult I have ever been involved with. Often, indeed for most of the time, no progress seemed possible, but somehow we kept going. There was an especially bleak and dangerous time in the Christmas season of 1997 and the early months of 1998. There was a determined effort by men of violence on both sides to destroy the process. In early December 1997 we had tried to get an agreement on a statement of key issues to be resolved and on a process for resolving them. Despite intense effort, over a period of several weeks in December of 1997, no agreement was possible. So when we adjourned for the Christmas holiday the prospects were bleak. If they could not even agree on a definition of the issues, I thought, how will they ever agree on solutions to those issues? Two days after Christmas Billy Wright, a prominent loyalist, was murdered while in prison. That touched off a sharp increase in sectarian killings as a vicious cycle of revenge took hold. The negotiations were moved to London in January and Dublin in February in an effort to encourage progress, but the opposite occurred. The London meeting was largely taken up by the temporary expulsion of the Ulster Democratic party. The Dublin meeting was taken up by the temporary expulsion of Sinn Féin. The process was moving backwards. It was in mid-February on the flight from Dublin back to the United States that I first began to devise a plan to establish an early, unbreakable deadline for the talks. I was convinced that the absence of such a deadline guaranteed failure. The existence of a deadline could not guarantee success but it made it possible. It took me a month to put a plan together and to persuade all of the participants to support it. By late March they were ready. I recommended a final deadline of midnight, Thursday 9 April. They all agreed. They wanted to reach an agreement. They recognized that there had to be a deadline to force a decision. As we neared the deadline there were non-stop negotiations. Blair and Ahern came to Belfast and showed true leadership. There would not have been an agreement without their personal involvement.

When Tony Blair took office in May 1997 his first trip outside London was to Belfast. There he demonstrated keen knowledge of the situation and the courage to take risks for peace. In April 1998, in the final stages of the negotiations, he and Ahern took a huge political risk when they came to Belfast. There was no assurance of success and I suspect that most political consultants would have told them to stay away. But they came and they had a decisive impact. The delegates were particularly impressed that Bertie Ahern came to Belfast twice on the day of his mother's funeral, returning to Dublin at midday for her burial. I spent much of that night with him and I do not recall ever seeing a man as exhausted or as determined. Blair and Ahern did not just supervise the negotiations, they conducted them. Word by word, line by line, they put together a compromise that attracted support from a broad spectrum of Northern Ireland's political parties. It was a dangerous high-wire act. A single missed step meant failure, but slowly and steadily, with great skill and assurance, they got safely across the divide.

President Clinton made an important contribution as well. He stayed up all that last night at the White House, telephoning the prime ministers and me and several of the delegates at critical times in the final hours. So in a tight time frame a powerful focus was brought to bear and it produced the right result. But the very fact that getting an agreement took such extraordinary effort was a warning signal of the difficulties that would follow as an effort was made to implement the Agreement. Finally, in the late afternoon of Good Friday, an agreement was reached.

It is important for everyone to recognize that the Agreement does not, by itself, provide or guarantee peace, political stability or reconciliation. It makes them possible, but there will have to be a lot of effort in good faith for a long time to achieve those results. I hope the Agreement will endure because it is fair and balanced. It requires the use of exclusively democratic and peaceful means to resolve political differences and it commits all of the parties to the total disarmament of all paramilitary organizations. It stresses the need for mutual respect and tolerance between communities. It is based on the principle that the future of Northern Ireland should be decided by the people of Northern Ireland. It includes constitutional change in the Republic of Ireland and in the United Kingdom. It creates new democratic institutions to provide self-governance in Northern Ireland and to encourage cooperation between the North and South to their mutual benefit. It explicitly repudiates the use of force or the threat of violence for any political purpose. Most importantly for its survival the Agreement was overwhelmingly endorsed by the people of Ireland, North and South, in a free and democratic election. That was a strong statement by the people. It sends a powerful message to the political leaders that the people want peace and that they support the Agreement as the way to get it.

In the past few months, since I returned to the United States following the referendum, I have often been asked what lessons Northern Ireland holds for other conflicts. I shall try to answer that question briefly now, but I begin with caution. Each human being is unique, as is each society. It follows logically then that no two conflicts are, or ever will be, exactly the same. Much as we would like it, there is no magic formula which, once discovered, can be used to end all conflicts. But there are certain principles in which I have come to believe which arise out of my experience in Northern Ireland and I would like to mention some of them to you here now. First, I believe there is no such thing as a conflict that cannot be ended. Conflicts are created and sustained by human beings. They can be ended by human beings. No matter how ancient, no matter how hateful, no matter how hurtful, peace can prevail if there is determination and a will for peace. When I arrived in Northern Ireland four years ago this month, I found to my dismay a widespread feeling of pessimism among the public and the political leaders. It is a small, well-informed society where I quickly became well known. Every day that I was there people in the dozens would stop me on the street, in the airport, in a restaurant. They always began with kind words: 'Thank you, Senator', 'God bless you', 'We appreciate what you are trying to do.' They always ended in despair. 'But you are wasting your time. This conflict cannot be ended. We have been killing each other for centuries and we are doomed to go on killing each other for ever.' As best I could I worked to reverse such attitudes, but that is the special responsibility of political leaders from whom many in the public take their cue. Leaders must lead and one way is to create an attitude of success, the belief that problems can be solved, that things can be better – not in a foolish or unrealistic way but in a way that creates hope and confidence among the people.

The second need is for a clear and determined policy not to yield to violence. Over and over again, men of violence in Northern Ireland, on both sides, tried to destroy the process, and several times they nearly succeeded. Last July three young boys were burned to death as they slept. In August, that devastating bomb in Omagh killed 29 people and injured more than 300. These were acts of appalling ignorance and hatred. They must be totally condemned. But to succumb to the temptation to retaliate would give the criminals what they want: escalating sectarian violence and an end to the peace process. The only way to respond is to swiftly bring those who committed these crimes to justice and to go forward in peace. That means there must be an endless supply of patience and perseverance. Sometimes the mountain seems so high and the river so wide that it is hard to continue the journey, but no matter how bleak the outlook, the search for peace can never end. Seeking an end to conflict is not for the timid or for the tentative. It takes courage, perseverance and steady nerves in the face of violence. I believe it a mistake to say *in advance* that if acts of violence occur, negotiations will end. That is an invitation to those willing to use violence to destroy the peace process and it transfers control of the agenda from the peaceful majority to the violent minority.

The third need is a willingness to compromise. Peace and political stability cannot be achieved in sharply divided societies unless there is a genuine willingness to understand the other point of view and enter into principled compromise. That is easy to say, very hard to do because it requires of political leaders that they take risks for peace. Most political leaders dislike risk-taking of any kind. Most get to be leaders by avoiding and minimizing risk. To ask them in the most difficult and dangerous circumstances to be bold is asking much, but it must be asked and they must respond if there is to be any hope for peace. I know it can be done because I saw it first-hand in Northern Ireland. Men and women, some of whom had never before met, never before spoken, who had spent their entire lives in conflict and hostility, came together and reached an agreement for peace. Admittedly it was a long and difficult process and the Agreement is not yet implemented. But it did happen, and if it happened there it can happen elsewhere.

A fourth principle is to recognize that the implementation of agreements is as difficult and as important as reaching them. That should be self-evident, but often just getting an agreement is so difficult that the natural tendency is to celebrate and then to go home and turn to other issues. But as we are now seeing in Northern Ireland, in the Middle East, in the Balkans, getting it done is often harder than agreeing to do it.

There is a final point that to me is so important that it extends beyond open conflict. I recall clearly my first day in Northern Ireland. I saw for the first time the huge wall which physically separates the communities in Belfast. Thirty feet high, topped in places with barbed wire, it is an ugly reminder of the intensity and the duration of the conflict. It is one of the most depressing man-made structures that I have ever seen. Ironically, it is called the peace line. On that first day, I met in the morning with nationalists on their side of the wall, in the afternoon with unionists on their side. Their messages had not been coordinated but they told me, separately, the same thing, that there is a high correlation between unemployment and violence in the urban areas of Northern Ireland. They said that where men and women have no hope, no opportunity, they are more likely to take the path of violence. As I sat and listened to them I thought that I could just as easily be in Chicago or Detroit or Johannesburg or Calcutta or any big city in the world. Despair is the fuel for instability and for conflict, and hope is essential for peace and stability. Men and women everywhere need income to support their families and they need the satisfaction of doing something worthwhile and meaningful in their lives. The conflict in Northern Ireland is, however, obviously not exclusively or even primarily economic. It involves religion and national identity. The majority identify with and want to remain part of the United Kingdom. The minority identify with and want to become part of a united Ireland. The Good Friday Agreement acknowledges the legitimacy of both aspirations and it creates the possibility that economic prosperity will flow from and contribute to a lasting peace.

My most fervent hope is that history will record that the Troubles ended on 15 August 1998, at Omagh; that the bomb which shattered the calm of that warm summer afternoon was the last spasm of a long and violent conflict. Amidst the death and destruction there was laid bare for all to see the utter senselessness of trying to resolve the political problems of Northern Ireland by violence. It will not work. It will only make things worse.

Two weeks later I accompanied Prime Minister Blair and President Clinton to Omagh to meet with the survivors and the relatives of the dead. There were hundreds of people present; among them were two with whom I spoke whom I will never forget. Claire Gallagher is fifteen years old, tall and lovely, an aspiring pianist. She lost both of her eyes in that bombing. As we spoke, she sat with two large patches where her eyes used to be, an exemplar of grace and courage. Michael Monaghan is 33 years old. He lost his wife, who was pregnant, their 18-month-old daughter and his wife's mother. Three generations wiped out in a single, senseless moment. Michael was left with three children under the age of five. One of them, Patrick, two years old, asks his father every day, 'When is mummy coming home?' Despite their terrible and irreparable loss, both Claire and Michael urged that the peace process go forward. Their courage gave me hope and their determination gave me resolve. I pray that they will also give hope and resolve to the political leaders of Northern Ireland, for it is they who must make this process work.

When he came to Belfast for the final phase of the negotiations, Tony Blair said that he felt the hand of history on his shoulders. It is still there, and it is also on the shoulders of David Trimble, John Hume, Seamus Mallon, Gerry Adams, David Ervine, John Taylor, Séan Neeson, Monica McWilliams, Gary McMichael and all of the other political leaders of Northern Ireland. The decision taken this week by the Assembly to approve the structure of the new Executive is an important step in the right direction. It leaves unresolved the issue of decommissioning and the functioning of the Executive. That difficult, important and emotional issue must be resolved. In dealing with this and with the other problems they will surely encounter, the political leaders of Northern Ireland must have the courage and the determination of Claire Gallagher and Michael Monaghan. They must rise above adversity, they must defy a long history of conflict. They must not and they cannot let this process fail. The alternative is unacceptable. It should be unthinkable, unspeakable. The people of Northern Ireland have come too far down the path of peace to go back now. They want to go forward and their political leaders must show the way. I am not objective, I am deeply biased in favour of the people of Northern Ireland. Having spent four years among them, I have come to like and admire them. They can be quarrelsome, very quick to take offence, but they are warm and generous, energetic and productive. They have made mistakes but they are learning from them. They are learning that violence will not solve their problems, that unionists and nationalists have more in common than they have differences, that knowledge of history is a good thing, but being chained to the past is not. There will be setbacks along the way but I hope that the direction for Northern Ireland was firmly set when the people approved the Agreement in referendum. The people there are sick of war, they are sick of so many funerals, especially those involving the small white coffins of children prematurely laid into the rolling green fields of their beautiful countryside. They want peace and I hope that they can keep it.

During the two years of the negotiations, I was asked almost every day by the media whether I would leave in disgust and frustration at the failure to make progress. I only seriously considered leaving once. It was a low point for me personally but I made a decision to stay, in the fall of 1997, when my wife gave birth to our son. A few nights after his birth I was up with him in the middle of the night and I began to think about what his life would be like, lived as it will be almost entirely in the twenty-first century. I then began to wonder what his life would be like had he been born in Northern Ireland. I called my staff in Belfast and found that on that same day, 16 October 1997, 61 babies were born in Northern Ireland, and I began to wonder what their life would be like had they been born Americans. The aspirations of parents everywhere are the same. My wife and I want for our son a good, healthy start in life, physical safety, a good education, a chance to go as high and as far as his talent and willingness to work will take him. Surely the parents of those 61 children in Northern Ireland want the same for their young sons and daughters.

It was on the flight back to Belfast just a few days after my son's birth, sad at the knowledge that I would see little of him in the first several months of his life but determined that for those 61 friends of his in Northern Ireland, people he might never know but who shared with him a fate, that I resolved that I would not leave the talks no matter what and that I would do everything within my power to bring them to a successful conclusion. And my hope and prayer is that the 61 children of Northern Ireland born on 16 October 1997 and the many thousands of others who followed them will never know war and will for all of their days know peace, political stability and reconciliation.

Note

1. Institute of Irish Studies Peace Lecture, delivered 18 February 1999 on the occasion of the conferment of an honorary Doctorate of Laws by the University of Liverpool on Senator George Mitchell.

Neither Orange March nor Irish Jig:
Finding Compromise in Northern Ireland[1]

Senator Maurice Hayes

The title of this lecture is intended to suggest the underlying rationale of the Northern Ireland Agreement – that no one tradition should be allowed to dominate the other, but that both should have equal respect. It should be read as plural and inclusivist rather than narrow and exclusivist: both march and jig should continue, but not in competition and not at each other's expense. A slightly sobering footnote to the cultural nuances of continuing division is the failure to secure a common name in popular usage for the Agreement itself. For nationalists it is the Good Friday Agreement. Unionists, particularly those who do not like it, refer more prosaically to the Belfast Agreement.

The extent of the progress achieved in the last six months may be measured against the fact that two years ago, and even later, it was still possible to describe the state of political negotiations in Northern Ireland in terms of a late Beckett play. There was a bleak landscape, an empty stage, a bunch of nondescript and dispirited characters, a lack of dramatic movement, and meaningful dialogue reduced to a monosyllabic minimum. I entitled an earlier version of this talk by reference to a classic book on negotiation by Roger Fisher of the Harvard Law School. He called it *Getting to Yes*. Given the tortuous, tortoise-like and entirely tentative progress of the Northern Ireland peace process, and a lack of clear definition of where it was going, I thought that a description of these procedures might only merit the title *Creeping to Maybe*. Then, as movement on the ground became apparent, a more upright stance seemed justified, and a more optimistic title: *Staggering to Perhaps*.

For a long time people in Northern Ireland (at least those who accepted that there was a problem) took the view that there was indeed an answer out there but that it was somebody else's job to find it. This has deep roots. The literary figure for this phenomenon appears in *The Táin*. Thomas Kinsella's translation presents perhaps the stereotype of the dour, uncommunicative, bloody-minded Ulsterman, unable to compromise and unwilling to admit that he will not do so. Cúchulainn has been killing the Connaught men and they send representatives to sue for peace.

> MacRoth came to Cúchulainn again and said they would give him the noblest women and all the milkless cattle out of their plunder if he would stop using his sling against them at night – he might kill as he chose by day.
> 'I can't agree to that,' Cúchulainn said, 'for if you take away the bondwomen our free-women will have to take to the grinding-stones, and if you take away our milch cows, we would have to go without milk.'

MacRoth came to Cúchulainn again, and said they would leave him instead the bond women and the milch cows.

'I can't agree to that either,' Cúchulainn said, 'for the men of Ulster would sleep with the bondwomen and beget slavish sons, and they would use the milch cows for meat in the winter.'

'Is there anything that will do?' the messenger said.

'There is,' Cúchulainn said, 'but I won't say what it is. If you can find anyone who knows what I mean, I'll agree to it.'

The implication was that there was a person out there with the answer if only he could be found.

There was indeed a guru out there, and the answer he gave, twenty years ago, was, 'The problem is, there's no solution.' This was the considered judgment of an American political scientist, Richard Rose, who had written one of the best books on Northern Ireland, *Governing without Consensus*, and a couple that were not so good, before he moved on, as conflict analysts do, to another conflict. His declaration of the problem as insoluble was based on the analysis that since the conflict was about the great issues of identity and allegiance, the 'great unbargainables' as he called them, and since the parties were seeking diametrically opposed goals, no resolution was possible.

Put in this way, of course, he was right. But the essence of politics is to find ways of managing conflicts which are non-resolvable in absolute terms, to help people to live with them until other times and other circumstances do allow the problem to be reformulated in terms in which it might possibly be resolvable. It is no surprise that in the wider world the trend of academic studies and of practice has shifted from conflict resolution to conflict management. This is a recognition that the best one can do, often for long periods, is to ameliorate the more damaging effects of conflict. In doing so it might be possible to arrive at a situation in which resolution becomes possible. The metaphor I sometimes use is that of a bone fracture, where it is necessary first to deal with the pain and reduce the swelling before the bones can be brought together and healing effected.

Another version of the external expert syndrome is to find someone outside to blame and to require them to fix it. In our circumstances, for far too long, the British have filled this role. This was the de Valera view, as John Horgan has so clearly illustrated in his recent fine study of Sean Lemass. The British had engineered Partition and could be persuaded to re-engineer it – a policy which, as Horgan remarks, had the benefit of simplicity and the drawback of failure. Another version of the same theory is to blame the unionists for being unionist, who would move if they were kicked enough; to blame the British government for not kicking, and the Irish government for not prevailing on them to do so; and, in the final analysis, getting the Americans to put pressure on the Brits to put the boot into the unionists. It is only in recent years that the issue has been faced that the problem is in Northern Ireland and must be confronted there, that it is a problem of persuading differing groups to live together in some modicum of harmony and mutual respect. There might even now be an opportunity to achieve this, one of those rare combinations of people and circumstances which allow for a change of gear. In 'An Irishman in Coventry', in the context of the legend of the Children of Lir, John Hewitt wrote:

> This is our fate: eight hundred years' disaster,
> crazily tangled as the Book of Kells;
> the dream's distortion and the land's division
> the midnight raiders and the prison cells.
> Yet, like Lir's children banished to the waters,
>
> our hearts still listen for the landward bells.[3]

We might just now be hearing them.

One model of the Northern Ireland conflict is of two opposed groups each looking outside for support, the nationalists to Dublin and the unionists to London, but having more in common with each other, perversely, than either has with its outside sponsor. Northern Catholics have less and less in common with the young, modernizing, pluralistic, Euro-focused population which is now riding the Celtic Tiger, just as the unionists have little in common with the general state of a materialistic, post-Christian, multiracial Britain. Both display the characteristics of what are known as fragment societies – detached pieces of a parent culture, fossilized, held in aspic, protected by the need to survive from the influences which have changed the parent, promoting a culture of victimhood and defensiveness, a nostalgia for old values and a fear to move or to change in case all should be lost. The fact of there having been a separate sub-state for 75 years has created its own sense of difference; created, almost against the will of those involved, new affinities, both uniting and dividing, throwing unionist and nationalist on top of each other, even in their antipathy, and creating a distance from the different experiences of their co-religionists elsewhere. Northern Ireland has become, as Dervla Murphy expressed it, a place apart. In 'The Colony', John Hewitt describes it in terms of the Roman withdrawal from Britain in the fifth century:

> the use, the pace, the patient years of labour,
> the rain against the lips, the changing light,
> the heavy clay-sucked stride, have altered us;
> we would be strangers in the Capitol;
> this is our country also, nowhere else;
> and we shall not be outcast on the world.[4]

The fact that unionists and nationalists were thrown in on top of each other leaves them too close together, yet too far apart – in John Montague's words, 'Chained together in hate on a narrow bed of suffering'.

Another model is of the double minority. This was developed by Harold Jackson in the late 1960s and still holds good. Whereas the conventional view of Northern Ireland is of a 60 per cent unionist/Protestant majority and a 40 per cent Catholic/nationalist minority, this view sees two minorities. There is the unionist group, a local majority within Northern Ireland, but potentially a minority in a united Ireland. The Catholics, a minority in Northern Ireland, see themselves as part of a potential majority on the island. Thus both groups display at the same time the worst features of each category: the arrogance of a majority and the insecurity of a minority. This is the original end-game. There is no way to solve the problem of one minority without creating an equal and opposite problem, replacing a truculent Catholic minority of 40 per cent in the North with an even more disgruntled, disaffected and aggressive 20 per cent Protestant minority in the South. What they have in common in their present position is memories of a troubled past, anxiety about an uncertain future, unwillingness to give up prepared defensive positions, and fear of change.

Another way of looking at the problem is to see it as the overlap of nationality. This view was advanced by Keith Kyle in the early 1970s. On this model, Northern Ireland is the place where Britishness overlaps with Irishness, a transitional border area, the sort of thing that goes unnoticed on a continental land-mass, as in Alsace-Lorraine or Schleswig-Holstein, but which is made more difficult in Ireland by the North Channel. On this model, Northern Ireland is where Irish and British reside together, and the problem of containing the mix is the problem of accommodating different national allegiances within the same nation state.

There is also a slightly zany theory based on demographics which claims that, left to themselves, the Catholics will out-breed the Protestants and produce a majority for unity. Apart from the fact that this would be replacing one problem with another, the facts are that Catholic and Protestant fertility rates are converging rapidly, and there is a fairly consistent poll finding that 25–30 per cent of Catholics would not necessarily vote for a united Ireland. This approach to conflict resolution amounts to saying: if we can't out-fox or out-fight them, we can surely out-breed them.

After 50 years of uneasy peace, or at least non-war, Northern Ireland blew up in the late 1960s. The presenting problem was systematic discrimination in electoral practices, in housing allocation and in appointments to public authority jobs, the sort of patronage available to regional and local government. Underlying this was the effect of one particular time bomb, the 1947 Education Act, which, by providing free access to secondary and tertiary education for all, had produced a generation of able young Catholics who were educated beyond the capacity or the willingness of the society to find suitable work for them.

The civil rights movement which emerged was suitably non-sectarian and nonpolitical in the constitutional sense. Gerry Fitt's contribution was to say in Parliament, 'Here I am, a British subject, what are you going to do about it?' It began to go wrong when the naivety of marching students uncorked the wells of sectarian hatred latent in the society, when the majority community reacted with violence, and when the armed republican tradition began to use it as a front. It is an unanswered question how far the IRA saw the civil rights movement as a new departure or as a means of getting back to the old game. There is no doubt, as Lord Scarman diagnosed, that the unionists saw it as an insurrection, and the Catholics saw the violent response as a pogrom. Both sides were overstating, but the impressions remained, deeply etched in the race-memory on both sides. When the Catholics were attacked, as in Bombay Street, the Marxist IRA found that the little red book was a very poor defence against an armed mob of arsonists.

The civil rights movement, the collapse into violence, the IRA campaign and its aftermath, Bloody Sunday and its aftermath, all led to the prorogation of Stormont and the imposition of Direct Rule. Since then the story has been of the British state trying to extricate itself from Direct Rule while keeping the place going, and attempting to keep the lid on violence and prevent it from spreading to the larger island and to the City of London. The Irish government too has been similarly engaged, primarily at first to prevent unofficial action and to ensure state control of what was done, and increasingly, as British and Irish interests converged within Europe, in building a partnership of varying degrees of stability and cordiality (depending on emotions and on the personalities concerned on both sides) to manage the Northern Ireland conflict, to prevent it from spreading or from damaging the wider relationship, and to bring it to some sort of reasonable conclusion. Apart from Europe, this has been the biggest policy issue in Irish foreign policy for two decades and has absorbed more of the time of successive foreign ministers and Taoisigh than any other.

The first attempt to put things together again was Sunningdale, and it is the benchmark against which subsequent attempts are measured. This recognized two main elements: the need to counter Catholic alienation by providing for participation in government, and the need to recognize the desire of the nationalist minority for links with the rest of the island which would recognize their Irishness. The shorthand label for this was 'power-sharing and the Irish dimension'. Power-sharing was to be achieved by an Executive capable of attracting cross-community support, and the Irish dimension by a Council of Ireland, made up of ministers in the Executive and the Oireachtas with some executive powers. As well as that there were provisions requiring non-discrimination by public bodies and a Human Rights Commission. This was taken in a wider context of police reform, of the introduction of proportional representation, the appointment of an Ombudsman and a Fair Employment Commission.

In fact Sunningdale was but a convenient label – the main agreement had been hammered out in talks chaired by William Whitelaw involving the parties of the centre, excluding the men of violence on both sides and the DUP. The Sunningdale gathering involved the Irish government in the process for the first time, which was to provide the institutional underpinning for the expression of the Irish dimension. There is some evidence that the Irish overbid their hand, supported by the SDLP, while Brian Faulkner (unsupported by Edward Heath) overestimated his ability to sell the outcome to the unionist grass roots. In the event, he claimed that the Agreement 'copper-fastened the union', while an enthusiastic SDLP backbencher declared that it was 'the vehicle which will trundle us into a United Ireland'. The irony is that the nationalists believed Faulkner and the unionists believed the SDLP man, increasing fear and insecurity on both sides.

In the event, the Executive lasted for five months. It worked well. It was, at the time, quite inspiring to see people of ability such as John Hume and Brian Faulkner, who had been sworn enemies, sit down together and gain respect for each other as they worked on common problems of social and economic development. It was brought down by growing opposition within the Unionist party and by the militant action of Protestant industrial workers. Opposition was ostensibly to the Council of Ireland (not to power-sharing), which was regarded as a bridge too far. Conventional wisdom has it that unionists would have accepted power-sharing on its own, but not with the supercargo of the Council of Ireland. I do not agree. I think that there was a deep-seated aversion to giving any power to nationalists, but it was not politically correct to say so, and in any case, the Council was a better stick to beat the proposal with. A key factor was the change of government in London which cost the Executive its main sponsor, after an election in which 11 anti-Sunningdale Unionist MPs were returned, and only one, Gerry Fitt, in favour. Crucially, too, the IRA stepped up its campaign. If the Agreement had brought peace, the unionist majority might just have bought it; in the event they did not get that either.

For months Faulkner was progressively weakened as his back-benchers were picked off in turn by the bullying of the anti-Agreement parties and by grassroots pressure. The Executive was finally brought down by a strike inspired and backed by the loyalists, which a supine Labour government allowed to close down the power stations and to bring commercial and economic life to a standstill, while the police and the army stood, literally this time, idly by.

This again was the end-game, the double bind. Nationalists had proved that they could bring down Stormont by withdrawing their consent to be governed. Unionists had proved that they could stop any alternative by withholding theirs. So it was back to Direct Rule, which remained in force for a quarter of a century. One thing that was saved from the wreckage was the requirement, to which successive British governments have adhered, that any proposed arrangement must be able to command widespread support in both parts of the community. The elected Constitutional Convention of the mid-1970s, dominated by unionism in a supremacist mood, was thus stopped in its tracks when the government declined to accept its report on the grounds that it could not command such support. This did not stop the unionists trotting it out as the essence of pluralistic democracy right through the 1980s and into the 1990s.

In the succeeding years, talks went on sporadically against a background of sustained violence as governments tried and failed to get agreement out of the local politicians – the Atkins talks, Prior's proposals for rolling devolution, the Assembly again, the Forum, the Brooke talks and talks under Sir Patrick Mayhew. They could charitably be described as part of a learning experience, and an even more charitable metaphor would see successive waves, each breaking a little further up the beach, but none succeeding in reaching the harbour wall, and none actually managing to raise a single ship. The received approach at the time was based on the proposition that peacemaking was a matter for peaceable people, that peace could be attained through a centre coalition of moderate parties, which would eventually broaden, and, by commanding increasing public support, would squeeze out the extremists. However, under increasing pressure of violence and counter-violence which drove the communities apart and into separate residential areas, the middle ground tended to narrow rather than widen and the intimidatory control of violent men over whole communities increased.

It was only in the mid-1980s that it began to be accepted that if you wanted to end a war there was little point in talking only to people who were not actually fighting. At this time too there was a realization that the war was both unwinnable and unlosable by both sides. Both had fought to a situation of stasis. The security forces accepted that while the IRA could win, they could not be beaten either, or even suppressed except by means which were not acceptable in a democratic state or to international standards on human rights and were, in any case, likely to be counter-productive. For their part the IRA, while believing that they could not be beaten and could sustain the struggle indefinitely, realized that they could not win either. It took some time, even, for many to realize that there was a difference between not losing and winning. It was this realization which began, perhaps in the early 1980s, the long process of re-educating the republican movement, which had begun to be politicized by the hunger strikes and their aftermath.

Whether John Hume or Gerry Adams was the initiator, the Hume/Adams talks were a process whose time had come, and were an essential prerequisite, a necessary condition for everything that followed. Hume challenged the self-reinforcing, closed-circuit debate within republicanism and was at the same time able to communicate ideas to governments and to begin a debate. Many of the seminal ideas and phrases which were to inform the process and were to set the agenda for the next decade were produced by Hume at this time: the idea of the totality of relationships (whatever that may mean), the idea of a three-stranded process and the idea of a double referendum in order to secure an expression of the will of the Irish people against the use of violence to secure unity. Ultimately the crucial shift in the negotiating stance was to bring Sinn Féin and the loyalist parties into the process as spokesmen for the paramilitaries on both sides. This required some act of faith that there were people in both movements who genuinely wished to make the move away from violence and into politics and should be encouraged to do so. Against this there was a Manichean view that once a gunman, always a gunman, and that such people could not be co-opted into the political process.

Crucial at this time too was the role of Peter Brooke as British secretary of state for Northern Ireland. Brooke was perhaps the most subtle secretary of state, adept at giving coded signals in a rather bumbling way, and very good at decoding the responses, both public and private. His affirmation that Britain had no selfish strategic or economic interest in staying in Northern Ireland, and would leave whenever a majority there so decided, was highly significant in the light of Hume's challenge to the fundamental basis of the republican struggle. It was also an important stage in the development of the principle of consent which was to underpin agreement at a later stage.

This concept was developed in the Anglo-Irish Agreement of 1985 – the work of brilliant civil servants on both sides, smuggled past a suspicious Mrs Thatcher on the grounds that it would secure Irish cooperation in security matters to defeat the IRA. The political purpose of the Agreement was to strengthen the SDLP against Sinn Féin, which had been gaining political ground since the hunger strikes, and to counter alienation in the Catholic community. It also established the principle of the right of the Irish government to be consulted through the Anglo-Irish Ministerial Council and the Maryfield Secretariat. It provoked a unionist howl of rage – 'Ulster says No' – which was simply withstood and which eventually petered out, a salutary lesson to unionists and an important formative experience: they could huff and puff, but governments could go on without them. The Anglo-Irish Agreement was thus a key document in the unfolding peace process. The US ambassador at the time, Bill Shannon, is reported as having said that it would take until the end of the century for its full potential to be realized. He may not be all that far wrong.

Out of the Anglo-Irish Agreement period came the broad acceptance of the three-stranded approach which had been pioneered by John Hume. This was to dominate discussion and to determine the geometry, if not the calculus, of the talks in the years ahead. The first strand concerned the internal arrangements for governing and administering Northern Ireland; the second concerned the North/South arrangements; the third, the relationships between Britain and Ireland. The first was seen as involving the Northern Ireland political parties and the British government, the second brought in the Irish government as well, and the third was seen to be a matter for the governments only.

At this time too a new actor entered the stage, the Irish-American lobby. These were not the gunrunners of Noraid, nor the whining irredentists of traditional Irish-America, but a more assured, more cerebral group, more representative of a new Irish interest in corporate America, Republican as well as Democrat, with more political leverage on the Hill and in the White House, less linked to a purely republican analysis and more concerned to secure an end to conflict and the establishment of democratic and human rights norms. The entrée of this group to the Clinton White House (which has been well documented by Conor O'Clery) and its contacts with Sinn Féin were important in securing the IRA ceasefire. Another influential factor was the shift within the administration which brought the centre of gravity for Irish affairs from the traditionally Anglophile state department to the national security council and the White House. All through this period, against British opposition in matters such as the Adams visa, the Americans were more nearly right than the British.

The British also erred in playing the ceasefire long. The calculation was that the longer the ceasefire went on the more people would get a taste for peace, would isolate the gunmen and make a return to violence impossible. Part of this theory too was that the longer it went on the more Sinn Féin's bargaining power would be weakened and the easier it would become to make a deal with the centre parties. This totally misread the temper of the nationalist community. They had supported the ceasefires as a means of getting Sinn Féin into talks and thought this was the main purpose. In addition the Hume/Adams talks had made Sinn Féin respectable (at some risk to the SDLP) and this made it more difficult to disregard them politically. The successive Drumcree summers had increasingly radicalized the Catholic middle class and driven them closer to the Sinn Féin position. Sinn Féin's propaganda also succeeded in transferring blame to John Major, even for the bomb which ended the ceasefire in 1996. The Unionist tactic was to freeze Sinn Féin out by refusing to talk to them (a tactic they persisted with up to the end) and trying to build the centre ground with the SDLP. The SDLP, however, could not afford to distance itself too far from Sinn Féin without losing its own support, and the Unionist approach, which might have done the trick a couple of years earlier, was bound to fail.

The talks carried out under Sir Patrick Mayhew, although abortive, were not entirely without utility. At one level they can be written off as part of the learning process, but there was engagement, particularly on the first strand elements, which enabled people to learn the vocabulary and some elements of the grammar of negotiation. It is part of Unionist/Tory folklore that agreement had been reached with the SDLP only to be upset by John Hume, eager to maintain solidarity with

Sinn Féin. In reality the proposals were not far advanced on the Convention proposals of the mid-1970s and would not have carried conviction or support in the nationalist community.

John Major too has been unfairly treated by Irish commentators. He invested more time and political capital in the Northern Ireland question than most of his predecessors but was hampered by the parliamentary arithmetic. It was not so much that the Ulster Unionists held the balance of power, but that the Tory party was hopelessly split and that the people who were against him on Ireland were also against him on Europe and on the economy. As it was, it required a change of government and a new prime minister, with no baggage and a huge majority and every prospect of staying in office for two terms, to bring the process finally to the point of decision. Tony Blair was able to build on the work done under the chairmanship of George Mitchell, made more realistic by securing a second IRA ceasefire and the entry of Sinn Féin to talks, this time with a deadline of six months.

Which is why it is time to get back to the model of the double minority and the overlap of nationality. This can now be discussed in the context of changes in Europe which have resulted in a pooling of sovereignty. The Border now scarcely exists in any real sense – there is free movement of goods and capital, free movement of labour, common recognition of qualifications, common standards of protection.

The prime need was to reduce the insecurity of both groups, and especially that of the unionists, who were frozen into immobility by their fear that any change could only worsen their position. The question which had to be addressed in the process was how Britishness and Irishness could live together in the same polity without diminution of the identity or traditions of either, and to deal with the aspirations and fears of both communities. The problem was to find a constitutional envelope which was to contain both. The answer was to unhitch the nation from the state, to accept that national identities could spill across state boundaries and still be protected. In order to remove fears, borders had to be made secure. Unionists had to be reassured that any movement from their entrenched positions would not result in their being sucked into a united Ireland against their will. Nationalists too had to be reassured that they would not be sucked off the shelf of Direct Rule, on which they were comparatively comfortable, into full integration in the United Kingdom, or, worse still, returned to the control of a dominant unionist majority at Stormont. The boundaries between North and South in Ireland, and between east and west in the islands, had to be made secure – but permeable; permeable to ideas, to commerce, to political processes, to cultural movements. In *La fin de la democratie* (translated into English as *Beyond the Nation State*) Jean Gehenna, discussing developments in Europe since the war and looking forward on a global level, argues that boundaries have first to be confirmed so that they can be made irrelevant. These were, perhaps unconsciously, important conceptual underpinnings of the final stages of the negotiations as politicians sought a deal. The other crucial element was the principle of consent: on the one hand, that unionists could not be coerced into a united Ireland and that there could be no change until a majority of the people willed it so, and on the other hand the reassurance to nationalists that the British government would legislate to facilitate change in the future when there was such a majority.

In making a deal it was also important that every party should come away from the table with something, and that no party should get everything it desired – that the gain and the pain would be equally shared around. In the Good Friday Agreement the three strands acted as counterweights to each other. Unionists wanted a Northern Ireland Assembly and an east/west link, nationalists wanted strong North/South bodies. The trick was to find how much each was willing to concede towards the other's demand to secure the maximum realization of its own. Unionists wanted to fill what they called the democratic deficit, the lack of a locally responsible administration for important social and economic programmes. SDLP supporters, who had done quite well out of Direct Rule, were unwilling to risk a return to Stormont. For Sinn Féin it smacked too much of an internal settlement and recognition of Stormont and the legitimacy of Partition. In working out the deal a sort of equilibrium was achieved between the competing forces. Unionists got their Assembly, but with safeguards for minorities, with weighted majorities and parallel consensus. (Indeed such are the safeguards that the system threatens to be unworkable without vast quantities of goodwill.) Nationalists got the cross-border bodies, but with a limited range of functions and clear responsibility to the Oireachtas and the Assembly. The east/west links which were important to unionists were extended to include local representatives, and sweetened for nationalists by including newly emerging devolved administrations in Scotland and Wales. The changes in the Irish Constitution which replaced the territorial claim and the constitutional imperative to unity with an aspiration were matched by the repeal of the remaining vestiges of the 1920 Government of Ireland Act and the Act of Union. The Agreement was set in the context of a preamble which committed all parties to the principle of consent and mutual respect, to non-violence and to securing the decommissioning of weaponry. The various parts were made interdependent and interlocking. The different elements were designed to move forward in concert. No party could achieve its objective without helping the others to achieve theirs.

For the Unionists the Agreement delivered the principle of consent, the changes to the Irish Constitution, the removal of the Anglo-Irish Agreement and the return of local administration to an elected assembly. It also brought the possibility of peace and the beginning of decommissioning. In many ways Sinn Féin came away with fewer of its core demands met – no united Ireland, no independent all-Ireland bodies. This made the other items on its agenda extremely important – prisoners, an equality agenda, respect for Irish culture, a review of policing and the criminal justice system. Prisoners were important not only as a symbol but for their impact on families and communities, and because of the constructive contribution of prisoners and ex-prisoners to the debate within republicanism (and indeed within loyalism). In the discussions, an important contribution was made by the smaller parties, the loyalists and particularly the Women's Coalition. Having been an important lubricant in the process, they came away with less (except for their interest in the general good). They are disadvantaged in the electoral method proposed for the Assembly, and are left with the vestigial potential of the Civic Forum.

Even given the efforts of George Mitchell, the Agreement would not have been achieved without the hands-on involvement and commitment of Tony Blair and Bertie Ahern in the vital closing stages. There were, however, two further hurdles, the referendum and the Assembly election. The referendum debate touched the raw nerves of unionist insecurity and anxiety. There was little doubt for the most part that it would be carried – the question was by how much and whether there could be said to be parallel consensus in both communities. SDLP support was assured. The Agreement confirmed its analysis and the prescience of John Hume. Sinn Féin, after a bit of street theatre, were also on board from the start. The DUP and the UKUP were committed opponents, the loyalist parties were committed supporters. The big question remained what would happen within the Ulster Unionist party.

There is a cruel law of Ulster politics which holds that what pleases your opponent must be bad for you. So the acquiescence of Sinn Féin, which was vital to nationalist acceptance, was a handicap for David Trimble. The Agreement was a complex document which had to be sold as a package. There were individual items which were unpleasant medicine for different parties. It was easy enough for the objectors to pick out these specifics and argue against them. There was one strong voice saying No and several feeble whispers saying Yes. Those advocating Yes were too often addressing different audiences as they courted their own constituencies. Interestingly, too, the opposition was not primarily to the Assembly or the North/South bodies, but to the release of prisoners, to Sinn Féin membership of the Executive without decommissioning, and to changes in policing which threatened the RUC. It may well be, as after Sunningdale, that for many the real objection was to sharing power with nationalists, but the opinion polls do not sustain this. In the event the Agreement was carried by 71 per cent in the North, enough to ensure support in both communities, although the unionist community split almost 50/50. This was enough to ensure support, but also enough to ensure difficulties in the working of the Assembly, with its many checks and balances. The biggest change has been in the nationalist community, which, in voting overwhelmingly for the Agreement in both North and South, has embraced the principle of consent, shown the door to the gunmen and voted for a new future of cooperation and pluralism.

The Agreement is a complex and interlocking document, reflecting the variable geometry of the settlement. The language is ambiguous and much is fudged, as often happens at a late stage in negotiations when there is public pressure for a favourable outcome. The politicians, for instance, could not reach agreement on policing, yet without movement on policing there could be no Agreement, so a commission was promised. Decommissioning, too, was a prerequisite for unionists, and yet the matter was concluded in terms sufficiently vague to allow all to sign up. All these issues were booby-traps for the future, which, with a bit of luck and careful footwork, might yet be avoided.

Cynics in Belfast were saying of the Agreement that the republicans had lost, but were too cute to admit it, and the unionists had won, but were too stupid to know. The overwhelming Yes vote, 95 per cent in the South and 71.2 per cent in the North, does conceal one salient fact. Northern nationalists and republicans, like those in the South, voted 95 per cent for the Agreement. The unionist community split almost 50/50. The Agreement was much more attractive to nationalists. Unionists, despite the substantial advantages gained, were repelled principally by the release of prisoners and the lack of certainty about decommissioning. The DUP and UKUP voted against, while the Orange Order, the Young Unionists and most of the Unionist MPs were opposed.

Once over that hurdle the Assembly elections were another cliffhanger, with Trimble just managing to carry the unionist vote (but with some waverers in the ranks) and Sinn Féin increasing its share of the vote to 15.6 per cent. The number voting for the SDLP remained constant, suggesting that Sinn Féin had pulled in first-time voters, young voters and those who had abstained previously, and calming SDLP fears that Hume/Adams might lead to electoral disaster. Trimble's success, such as it was, owed much to Tony Blair's assurances that decommissioning would proceed in parallel with other parts of the Agreement.

Unionist unease on this front has led to delay in implementation and cries of bad faith from Sinn Féin. Unionists refused to form an Executive until there was some form of decommissioning, Sinn Féin protested that decommissioning was not a precondition to anything in the Agreement. Both are resting on legalistic constructions, but the strong political imperative is for some sort of movement on arms which looks less and less likely to be forthcoming from the IRA. Meanwhile unionists see prisoners being released. It makes no difference to them that half are loyalist prisoners. Their nightmare is of having been trapped in a game where republicans capture all their tricks and then kick over the table and go back to violence. Trimble could probably not survive sitting in an Executive with Sinn Féin without some decommissioning. Without an Executive, North/South bodies cannot be formed, and republicans are likely to lose patience with the political process. Trimble and Adams are therefore caught in the same paradox, each having demanded something the other is unable to deliver. The likelihood is that they will stagger through this phase, but not until the eleventh hour, and not without a good deal of external help. The public mood is for peace, and the process, although it might falter and stutter, shows signs of being irreversible.

It will be noted that the Agreement is not all that far removed from the template developed at Sunningdale. It has been called 'Sunningdale for slow learners'. It may be that Sunningdale was an idea whose time had not come. Since then there have been changes in Europe, which have brought about a dilution of the notion of sovereignty and growing cooperation and mutual interest between successive British and Irish governments. Since then there have also been 3,000 deaths and a growing war-weariness and sense of futility on all sides; furthermore the Irish economy has roared ahead with the Celtic Tiger while the North has at best, stagnated. It must be asked of those people on both sides who brought down Sunningdale whether it was all worthwhile, and of those who continued the violent struggle whether the deaths were justified. This produces a difficult ethical dilemma for some, even as they struggle to secure an end to violence.

Even now, it is only the beginning. There are fires of sectarian bitterness which have smouldered for centuries to be dampened and put out, there is a long process of building trust and removing fear and insecurity, there is the problem of a generation bred into anarchy and contempt for the rule of law, and the danger of arms and personnel passing into organized crime. Above all there is the appalling problem of memory, of whether to draw a line under the atrocities of the past or to face them, and how to help victims and survivors to cope. The victims may fairly claim that there was less recognition of their suffering in the Agreement than they may have deserved. It remains to be seen whether Northern Ireland needs a Truth and Reconciliation Commission on the South African lines. At the very least, what is needed, and has surprisingly often been shown, is heroic charity on the part of survivors who do not seek revenge, only settlement. This is the spirit of Priam, King of Troy, father of Hector, in Michael Longley's powerful poem 'Cease-fire':

> I go down on my knees and do what must be done,
> I kiss Achilles' hand, the killer of my son.[5]

Maybe this is a time for hope, a time when, in the words Seamus Heaney puts into the mouths of the chorus in *The Cure at Troy*, 'hope and history rhyme', a time for belief in miracles and cures and holy wells, for the miracle of self-healing:

> If there's fire on the mountain
> Or lightning and storm
> And a God speaks from the sky
> That means someone is hearing
> The outcry and the birth-cry
> Of new life at its term.[6]

It might just be so.

Notes

1. This paper was first delivered as a lecture at the Institute of Irish Studies, University of Liverpool on 26 October 1998.
2. *The Tain*, trans. Thomas Kinsella (Oxford: Oxford University Press, 1969), pp. 116–17.
3. *The Collected Poems of John Hewitt*, ed. Frank Ormsby (Belfast: The Blackstaff Press, 1991), p. 98.
4. *Collected Poems of John Hewitt*, p. 79.
5. Michael Longley, *The Ghost Orchard* (London: Jonathan Cape, 1995), p. 39.
6. Seamus Heaney, *The Cure at Troy* (London: Faber & Faber, 1990), pp. 77–78.

Mountain-climbing Irish-style:
The Hidden Challenges of the Peace Process

Martin Mansergh

It is a feature of most forms of mountain-climbing that reaching the peak always takes far longer than might be anticipated by line of sight. Behind one steep and arduous slope there is usually another. The Irish peace process has been of that character, and has required the constant and highly motivated engagement not only of government leaders, but also of teams of officials, to whom no short cuts are available, and whose effectiveness depends heavily on the respect and trust that they can establish. (As I shall go on to explain, the term 'mountain-climber' has a somewhat different and more specific connotation in the British context.)

Ireland does not have a political intelligence service. The Gardaí and the Defence Forces engage in intelligence-gathering related to their security tasks. Such work was vital to national survival during the Second World War,[1] and one must presume, even though the history will not be written for many years, that it has saved many lives and thwarted many paramilitary attacks during the thirty-year Troubles that began in 1969. All governments need the best available information on situations, and on the intentions of other parties involved, whether domestic or foreign, to guide their policy- and decision-making. Ireland has had to rely on conventional political and diplomatic methods, and to develop its information-gathering and more proactive powers of persuasion to a high level, not having available to it the short cuts or covert methods or the direct power routinely deployed by many of its larger partners.

There are gains as well as losses. Diplomacy seeks to win trust and respect, as a means to influence and to secure cooperation. One of the ways it can do so is by showing respect for others. The interception of communications, the purchase of influence, the use of agents, deniable military interventions often at arm's length, collusion with or support for insurrectionary armed groups, and covert interference in the internal politics of sovereign countries, which may lead to or involve a multitude of illegal or unethical acts, sometimes even assassination, are all factors that add to much wariness and suspicion in international relations. Fear and suspicion of others' intentions are often the root cause of failure to achieve or sustain rational compromise.

It can be argued, of course, that larger countries have more far-flung interests, that they have many enemies, some overt, some obscure, who have few scruples as to the methods that they use, and that therefore an intelligence capability is essential to national security. Guerilla tactics and/or terrorism are the means by which the weak take on the strong and exploit their vulnerability. The most usual drawbacks of intelligence operations are the absence of any close political control and public accountability; the making of sometimes highly idiosyncratic or paranoid presumptions about the public interest at some remove from the sanction of democratic institutions; and the extension of such methods far beyond the areas for which there may be a strict justification, including prurient curiosity and commercial advantage. Their compatibility with an ethical foreign policy is often strained.

Though relatively small, Ireland too has vital interests to protect, in the European Union, in its relations with the United States, and, above all, in peace, both internationally and on the island of Ireland. Interests and ideals tend to intertwine, but ideals are perhaps best described as those objectives which cannot be immediately reduced to narrow short-term interests or which may even in some instances be opposed to them. Nothing has been of such vital interest to Ireland as a settlement of the recent Northern Ireland Troubles. They have posed a threat to the security, stability and prosperity of the Irish state, less than 50 years in existence when they started. At the same time, the collapse of Stormont between 1969 and 1972 and successive attempts to fill the political vacuum created an opportunity, if not to advance an end to Partition, then to establish what since 1980 has come to be termed 'the totality of relationships' on a new and more equitable footing. This represents something good in its own right, but it may also over time provide the only likely context for peaceful constitutional change, when the democratic conditions for it are fulfilled.

The approach of the Irish government since 1969 has been dominated by the primacy of politics and diplomacy, supported by appropriate security measures, and a determination to find a political route out of conflict, even when confronted by other approaches. British governments in dealing with Ireland over the centuries have used armed power, as well as agents and auxiliaries, to counter popular movements and uprisings. Political initiatives of varying credibility have been another string to the British bow, and have sometimes become the main focus of politics. Prior to the 1994 IRA ceasefire, dialogue with republican paramilitary leaders was mainly left to British intelligence officers (one of whom was known as 'the mountain-climber', interacting through a Derry priest and also by written communication), but their motivation and instructions would always have been open to question. As a 1975 experience showed, they did not necessarily represent what they appeared to be: an inside track for republicans to get to the heart of the real agenda of the British government. In the course of establishing parameters for a post-conflict situation, rosy scenarios could be painted, which could be repudiated, and for which no one was accountable. Such ploys, conscious or otherwise, have occasionally been tried over the years with Irish officials by British ones. There is no substitute for proper agreements, embracing all the affected parties. That form of exploratory dialogue between Sinn Féin and the British was aborted in November 1993 in an atmosphere of mutual recrimination. It was the Irish peace initiative, which the British government was persuaded to opt into in modified form, that led on to the ceasefire and eventually to peace.

Foreign governments, whether allies or enemies of Britain, would from time to time have taken steps to secure their own assessments of the Irish situation, from the French in the late seventeenth and eighteenth centuries to the Germans in the early twentieth century, and no doubt the Americans and Russians as well during the recent Troubles. In this way, they could ward off any collateral damage to themselves, or (I am not including the American government in this) look for opportunities to fish in troubled waters. But Ireland was of little intrinsic strategic significance to any of them. However, quixotic gestures of assistance springing from global ambitions, whether from Qaddafi's Libya in the mid-1980s or from the France of the Directory (or as threatened by the ardent Marquis de Lafayette on leave from America in 1779[2]), could have serious and long-term security and political consequences in Ireland.

The United Irishmen, founded in 1791, were originally an open society dedicated to 'the promotion of constitutional knowledge, the abolition of bigotry in religion and politics, and the equal distribution of the rights of man through all sects and denominations of Ireland'. Within a few years they were driven underground, and Wolfe Tone went as a quasi-diplomatic agent to Paris, where he watched and recorded the fluctuating reactions of the French government, as he heavily lobbied them for an invasion, before taking on a French uniform. Like Casement during the First World War, he was eventually captured by the British, and tried and condemned for treason.

During the later nineteenth century, constitutional action and leadership within a British framework had to compete with inspirational but largely ineffectual secret societies. The 1916 Rising was prepared secretly, but conducted openly, and that was the final coda to the tradition of conventional warfare. The subsequent political victory of Sinn Féin in the 1918 general election, which the British government tried to ignore, was underscored by an increasingly vigorous volunteer campaign using guerrilla tactics. While the principle of the non-coercion of Ulster Unionists in the nascent Northern Ireland was accepted politically by de Valera from August 1921, covert attempts by Dublin in 1922 to destabilize it were ineffective and very counterproductive, consolidating the regime and greatly increasing the vulnerability of the nationalist population. Such tactics were not repeated, and future IRA campaigns were always actively and vigorously opposed by the Irish government.

There was in the 1920s a clear parting of the ways between democratic Irish governments and remnants of the IRA who favoured the use of force to complete a 32-county Republic. Those who founded Fianna Fáil cut loose from a party that claimed to be a shadow government entitled to its own paramilitary army. Successive Irish governments had to crack down on the IRA to uphold their own democratic legitimacy as well as to prevent, as far as possible, their territory being used as a base from which to launch cross-border attacks, contrary to international law. In the 1950s, the increasingly sterile rhetoric of denouncing Partition began to give way to a more pragmatic approach of pursuing political contact and encouraging North–South economic cooperation within a long-term policy framework of seeking unity by agreement. Unity, under an all-Ireland government, was regarded as compatible with maintenance of the existing high degree of autonomy for Stormont, provided there was improved protection for civil rights.

The policy of *détente* between Dublin and Belfast in the mid-1960s, with Lemass–O'Neill and Lynch–O'Neill meetings, soon found itself competing with a growing and more strident civil rights campaign, not prepared to wait patiently for results that would at best arrive long-term. Both governments were caught completely off guard by the suddenness and ferocity of the upsurge of long pent-up anger at second-class citizenship. From the battle of the Bogside and the arrival of British troops in August 1969, the Irish government needed to find its bearings and to assert its relevance, which was at first denied by the British. It had a dearth of up-to-date information. A senior official from the Department of External Affairs was sent north, as also was a journalist employed briefly to produce bulletins on the situation for domestic and international consumption. Conversely, delegations from embattled communities came south, looking for support and protection, including the means of self-defence.

If there was a tension at the political level between, on the one hand, a combination of traditional republicanism and radical opportunism and, on the other hand, a cautious moderation in pursuing long-term goals, there was at the level of the Irish administration a desire to pursue the most rational long-term strategy which would advance the cause of peace with justice, including justice for the nationalist community, leading to ultimate unity by agreement. From the beginning in 1969, many fertile ideas were already in the mind of John Hume. There were dangers for everyone in the growing instability and surge in violence.

The crisis had nevertheless brought to a head the clash between the Lemass/Lynch/Whitaker policy of gradual rapprochement based on North–South contacts and economic co-operation, and the reawakened ideology and instincts of traditional republicanism publicly articulated by Minister Neil Blaney, both of which had to respond to urgent demands for help and assistance. Paradoxically, by the 1960s, North and South, even seen from a strictly nationalist perspective, had grown apart, as Southern politicians with first-hand memories or experiences of Northern conditions moved into retirement or died, and as the South concentrated on exploiting its first real economic break since independence. There was widespread confusion for some years into the Troubles as to whether the chaotic situation heralded the collapse of the Union and whether it called for a renewal of the same tactics which had won the South its independence.

The arms trial in 1970 brought to a head the issue of the degree of assistance that it was appropriate to give the beleaguered nationalist community, whether it should be strictly humanitarian, whether support should be given to self-defence if not a campaign of liberation, or even whether it should attempt to precipitate the internationalization of the problem, though any incursion risked serious blood-shed. The action of the Lynch government put safety and stability first, and in subsequent years courageously opposed support for a growing terrorist campaign, which caused horrific collateral civilian casualties. But in the brief formative period from August 1969 to May 1970 the government had potentially been in a position to exercise some restraining influence on Northern militancy, which was thereafter thrown back largely on its own resources, with some Irish-American and other foreign support.

The arms crisis is open to diverse interpretations, variously seen as a naive but basically well-intentioned covert operation that went wrong, designed to assist nationalists in the event of a renewed and concerted sectarian attack; as primarily an outworking of an internal party struggle; as (the view of the Official IRA and later the Workers' Party) part of a sinister attempt to divide and divert revolutionary socialism, with the by-product of destabilizing Northern Ireland; or as (the view of some unionists) designed to create a paramilitary proxy from the South. However, the proposition that the Provisional IRA was created by elements of the Irish government or ruling party is not sustainable by the evidence, nor is it supported by any serious established historian of the period or of the IRA, nor has it been given any credence by the republican movement. Its major consequence, nevertheless, was to induce great political caution so that for a long time no action open to any risk of misinterpretation would be taken. A severe demarcation preventing any political or official contact with Provisional Sinn Féin, let alone the Provisional IRA, was introduced.

The policy and honourable purpose of successive Irish governments in the 1970s was to bolster constitutional nationalism in Northern Ireland and to seek power-sharing arrangements with an Irish dimension. The Irish government sought, with mixed success, to mobilize the support of Irish-America as well as of the US president and administration for the SDLP and constitutional nationalism against the IRA. This required a considerable intensification of diplomatic effort and information-gathering. Officials from the renamed Department of Foreign Affairs travelled north to canvass moderate nationalist opinion, and at senior level to consult closely with, advise and provide support for leading SDLP members. In America, and at first to a lesser degree at Westminster, legislators were canvassed, as the network of useful contacts was extended. The Friends of Ireland on Capitol Hill and the Four Horsemen played a role in persuading President Carter to promise financial backing for a peace settlement.

One of the sources of concern for the Irish government and causes of mistrust in Anglo-Irish relations was the fear of direct negotiations between the British government and the Provisional IRA, behind the backs of the Irish government and the moderate constitutional parties, all of whom had a direct interest in the terms for ending the conflict. While there were some high-profile meetings, involving Northern Ireland secretary Willie Whitelaw and others, the later conversations during the 1975 ceasefire were conducted by British intelligence officers. While the spurious possibility was held out of a breakthrough on a British declaration of intent to withdraw, based on a cabinet option considered only to be discarded, the dialogue probably fitted more into a counter-insurgency strategy. Though it nearly succeeded, its actual net legacy was to reinforce the will to carry on resistance, even if it involved settling into a long war. In the South, it strengthened the orthodoxy that there should be no contact with terrorist groups, who would only take encouragement from being treated as equal or even privileged interlocutors. The hunger strikes of 1980–81, which raised acute tensions, proved something of an exception, and required much indirect as well as some direct contact, justified on humanitarian grounds and by the need to avert a political disaster. A pragmatic resolution had to be found and was found, but not before eleven men had died. The capture of seats in 1981 North and South marked the emergence of Sinn Féin as an important political force in its own right, even if subordinate to the IRA Army Council.

Throughout the 1980s, despite numerous political initiatives, the military stalemate and political stagnation continued. The Haughey–Thatcher talks, the Prior

Assembly, the New Ireland Forum and the Anglo-Irish Agreement all introduced building-blocks, as had Sunningdale, which could be usefully incorporated into an overall political settlement. But in themselves they led to no breakthrough at the time in terms of bringing about cross-community agreement or a slackening of paramilitary campaigns. Both the Forum and the Anglo-Irish Agreement were designed to boost the constitutional nationalist position of the SDLP vis-à-vis the advance of Sinn Féin, and to provide a spur to the negotiation of a political settlement between constitutional parties. The Anglo-Irish Agreement, in the eyes of its promoters, ended the nationalist nightmare by creating a special channel for moderate nationalists to government, and it was even claimed that it came close to *de facto* or quasi-joint authority, but under Margaret Thatcher this was hardly evident. The SDLP was convinced that it represented British neutrality on the future of Northern Ireland. The next task, having checked the growth of Sinn Féin, was to persuade the republican movement that there was a viable basis for full political participation and the abandonment of armed struggle.

John Hume's controversial attempt to meet with the IRA in 1986 had to be aborted, and in general, as Senator Gordon Wilson was to find some years later, direct public approaches to the IRA were unproductive, since they were on their guard against displaying any sign of weakness. The progress of the IRA engagement with the international body under General de Chastelain has been slow. The tone of IRA statements, even when constructive, is never less than 'macho'.

Because of the moral difficulty of dialogue with even the political proxies of armed groups, the distinction being more one of roles or even the wearing of different hats, clerical involvement and mediation were necessary to provide ethical justification for a step which seemed essential, if conflict were to be brought to an end. This was certainly the case on the Irish side, though in the British case, it was probably for more pragmatic reasons. In 1986, with the knowledge and approval of Cardinal Ó Fiaich, Fr Alex Reid of Clonard monastery approached the Fianna Fáil leader and subsequent Taoiseach Charles Haughey, together with John Hume, to encourage dialogue with Sinn Féin up to the highest level, centred on the concept of self-determination. Post-Enniskillen, which raised in an acute form throughout Ireland questions about any possible continuing justification for a discredited IRA campaign, open dialogue was established over several months between the SDLP and Sinn Féin. There was open and intense ideological debate, which came to no conclusion. Behind the scenes, and in a complementary and supporting fashion, a Fianna Fáil delegation met twice in Dundalk with the Sinn Féin leadership. In the absence of any indication of a commitment to bring violence to an early end, the dialogue could not prudently be sustained. Contact was maintained for the following three years, however, through Fr Reid, and it was not until John Hume came in the autumn of 1991 to Charles Haughey with his proposal for a draft declaration between Taoiseach and British prime minister that a possible basis for a peace initiative was established. In due course, under Haughey's successor Albert Reynolds, direct dialogue was established from the autumn of 1992 by this member of his office with representatives of the Sinn Féin leadership, with the purpose of finalizing a joint declaration that implicitly contained terms for a cessation of conflict.

Based on historical experience, the prospects of bringing this project to fruition were slim, but the prize was so great as to justify serious risks. The risks of exploring a basis for the end of conflict were greatest for the republican movement, given the history of splits and feuds within the wider republican family The broad content of the dialogue has been described elsewhere.[3] Its conduct in complete secrecy and on a basis of trust, despite the political gulf, was vital to any hope of success. Albert Reynolds, not known in other spheres for hiding his light under a bushel, went no further in public than to talk about trying to find 'a formula for peace'. What was treated generally as political rhetoric also had meaning at a much deeper level that made sense to those whom he subsequently took into his trust on the road to the Downing Street Declaration.

Progress was very slow. While one might say that the republican movement was unused to negotiation, the notion of give-and-take and the need to take into account the basic requirements of other parties as well as governments, it was essential for the republicans to secure a degree of internal sanction and agreement for every move, however small. Difficulties of communication and of safely holding meetings in one place with those who needed to be involved also caused delays. It would be fair to say that throughout the process every line was carefully scrutinized for all its meanings and implications by a leadership group. The unity of the movement was paramount.

The draft agreement handed over in June 1993 by Albert Reynolds to the British cabinet secretary was not ideal from the point of view of the Irish government, but was put forward as the basis for further discussion and negotiation. Republicans and even the SDLP leadership seemed to believe that peace justified acceptance of it as it stood. The British government, while interested, was reluctant to engage, and preferred to stick with the more conventional initiative of trying to find a basis for restarting the Brooke–Mayhew talks process, which had stalled after the sessions of 1991 and 1992. For Albert Reynolds, securing an IRA ceasefire was more important than a talks process, which was difficult to restart, and would then be excruciatingly slow. Years could pass, while people continued to be killed, and a successful agreement from which republicans were excluded offered no guarantee of an early end to violence. But the government had continually to adapt the draft declaration, and broaden it out to bring in unionist and loyalist concerns, with the help of clergy familiar with both, to balance the nationalist content of the declaration, and to give Downing Street the confidence to embrace the initiative on agreed terms.

Only Albert Reynolds's extreme persistence, and the vulnerability of the British government to American opinion, together with the embarrassing exposure of many of the detailed exchanges between the British government and Sinn Féin, eventually created the circumstances in which the initiative was embraced. When the Declaration was published, a new climate was created in which there was intense pressure on republicans to bring the IRA campaign to an end, on the basis of promised participation in political negotiations, as well as more immediately in what became the Forum for Peace and Reconciliation organized by the Irish government. While British instincts were at first to treat the Declaration on a take-it-or-leave-it basis, Albert Reynolds embarked on a process of confidence-building and clarification. Only when that was exhausted, and the credibility of Sinn Féin's peace policy threatened, did the IRA finally agree to a ceasefire that was intended to be permanent.

Reynolds's policy was one of swift consolidation, but much momentum was lost when he was driven from office towards the end of 1994. Intensive negotiations between officials on the Framework Document were meant to be the prelude to talks. But this was blocked by unionist rejection of the document as a basis of negotiation and by British and unionist insistence on bringing forward the decommissioning of paramilitary weapons as a precondition for talks. This too became a mountain to be climbed, requiring the intervention of Senator George Mitchell, as a product of the first Clinton visit to Ireland in December 1995. The suggested compromises were brushed aside by the British prime minister John Major in favour of Forum elections six months later. It became clear that the British government was engaged in conscious procrastination, what the Northern Ireland secretary Sir Patrick Mayhew called 'slow bicycling' and Simon Jenkins in *The Times* described as finding another plausible excuse for inertia. It was motivated by a desire to wear down the republican movement, to keep the Ulster Unionists on side, and not least to preserve the British Tory government up to the last moment in the hope that something would turn up to save the government from electoral disaster.

Republicans, feeling that they were being taken for granted, and no doubt to preserve their unity under strain, broke the ceasefire on 9 February 1996. Paradoxically, this served to make it easier to establish a basis for talks. But the imperative was to prevent the return to all-out conflict. The principal opposition party in the Dáil, Fianna Fáil, though severely critical of the breach of the ceasefire, maintained political contact with Sinn Féin, and sought to contribute to an early restoration of the ceasefire. After an interval, the 'Rainbow government' permitted dialogue at official, though not political, level. While the talks started in the absence of Sinn Féin in June 1996, they remained stuck, with endless battles over agenda and procedures and the conditions that should apply to Sinn Féin participation.

After the elections North and South a year later, an intensive effort was made by both governments to reinstate the IRA ceasefire, so that Sinn Féin could participate in the talks from the autumn, when they might be expected to start making some progress. Every summer, the Drumcree stand-off has to be contended with, something that has hitherto defeated all attempts at mediation, but has also been successfully prevented from inflicting serious damage on the peace process.

When the IRA ceasefire was restored, the next difficulty was to find a way of including Sinn Féin in talks, without the Ulster Unionist party abandoning them. All of these exercises involved a great deal of intricate drafting by officials as well as negotiations at the political level, and innumerable bilateral engagements with all the parties. The talks themselves effectively involved three months of opening statements in relation to the various issues, followed by a ground-clearing exercise and the attempt to establish some consensus on the parameters, eventually provided by the twin pillars of the January 1998 Propositions Document and the Framework Document, which remained the lodestar for nationalists. The successive expulsions of the UDP and Sinn Féin for limited periods, because of paramilitary murders by associated organizations, were done in such a way as to ensure that the door remained open.

At a certain moment, the chairman, Senator George Mitchell, assisted by the two governments, had to make a call in order to put together a draft agreement. Neither the Ulster Unionist party nor Sinn Féin wished for discussion on it to be dragged out for any length of time, which would allow the critics of the concessions necessary for an agreement to assemble their forces. Intense negotiations were concentrated over four days, and in the case of Sinn Féin involved going over and over a lengthy series of demands of varying degrees of importance, formulated by backup teams, and providing a response.

The Good Friday Agreement was a major achievement, which repaired many of the faults of the 1920–21 Anglo-Irish settlement. In its inspiration it drew on the creative and constructive elements of every political initiative and movement of the past 200 years. It was a synthesis of the unionist and nationalist/republican positions, protecting the vital interests of all traditions. Its constitutional accommodation incorporated a new and more enlightened self-definition of the Irish nation. It gave legitimacy for the first time to a new dispensation that incorporated Northern Ireland, and changed the basis of future decisions on sovereignty. Agreement was reached as to how self-determination would be exercised, in a manner that again for the first time excluded no one. A fundamental reform of policing, the release of prisoners, North–South institutions and a framework for the decommissioning of illegal arms were agreed.

Most involved understood that implementation of the Agreement would require a whole series of difficult hurdles to be overcome, and so it has proved. The physical challenges of the Drumcree Orangemen and dissident republicans ended in terrible human tragedy but also failure. Establishment of the institutions beyond the Assembly took one and a half years. Agreement on the North–South institutions took some time, but in the end proved to be one of the least difficult obstacles. Throughout the period there was intensive discussion with the pro-Agreement parties to overcome the twin difficulties of devolution and decommissioning. Three high-level political initiatives in 1999, at Hillsborough before Easter, in Downing Street in May, and in Castle Buildings, Stormont, at the end of June and the beginning of July 1999, all came close to success, but ultimately failed. The Mitchell review of the autumn of 1999 eventually brought a breakthrough which finally allowed the Agreement to come fully into force, but it was surrounded by conditions and time limits that led within two months, despite continuous efforts by the Irish government and its officials in particular to avert it, to the suspension of the institutions by the Northern Ireland secretary of state, Peter Mandelson, an event that led to much political recrimination.

The Irish government was determined to adopt a constructive approach. Once again, intensive efforts were made to restore the new institutions on the basis of more viable understandings. The IRA finally crossed the rubicon when it agreed to the international inspection of some of its arms dumps as a confidence-building measure. But failure on one side or the other to fulfil all the commitments agreed in May led to renewed difficulties, when the Unionist first minister David Trimble refused to nominate a Sinn Féin minister to attend meetings of the North–South

Ministerial Council. The legislation to implement the controversial Patten Report was also causing difficulties, going too far for unionists and not far enough for nationalists, with agreement needed on a way forward. All of this required periods of intense discussion and negotiation with the principal parties involved, made more urgent by the approach of the British general election. Securing the Agreement over the period since its ratification has proved as arduous as the negotiation of the Agreement itself or obtaining the ceasefires.

All along there has been an underlying vision that only an inclusive process can secure a lasting peace. The Good Friday Agreement in its balance and sophistication is light years ahead of every alternative, especially in relation to the *status quo ante*. Unlike previous initiatives, this also has the democratic sanction of the people of Ireland, North and South. The effect of overturning the will of the people would in the long run be disastrous. The House of Lords and the Conservative party, in their opposition to Home Rule at the beginning of the twentieth century, played a large part in creating the conditions for the total separation of the 26 counties.[4] Sustaining the settlement will not be easy. There are no doubt many more mountains to be climbed, if the commitment of the parties and peace and stability are to be maintained. This will remain a vital priority for the Irish government, as its continued engagement and willingness to be involved alongside the British government and the parties in solving problems as they arise is a *sine qua non* of the survival of the peace process. The extremely close and cordial working relationship between the Taoiseach, Bertie Ahern, and the prime minister, Tony Blair, has been a key to much of the progress, but good relationships with the parties are equally vital.

Notes

1. Eunan O'Halpin, *Defending Ireland: The Irish State and its Enemies since 1922* (Oxford, 1999).
2. Gilles Perault, *Le secret du roi*. III. *La revanche américaine* (Paris, 1996). Letter of Lafayette to George Washington concerning Ireland: 'I will tell you in confidence, that the project closest to my heart would be to render it free and independent like America; I have found there some secret relations. God willing, we might succeed, and the era of liberty begin finally for the happiness of the world.'
3. Eamonn Mallie and David McKittrick, *The Fight for Peace: The Secret Story behind the Irish Peace Process* (London, 1996). See also Martin Mansergh, 'The Background to the Irish Peace Process', in Michael Cox, Adrian Guelke and Fiona Stephen (eds), *A Farewell to Arms? From 'Long War' to Long Peace in Northern Ireland* (Manchester, 2000).
4. Edward Pearce, *Lines of Most Resistance: The Lords, the Tories and Ireland 1886–1914* (London, 1999).

The Good Friday Agreement:
A Vision for a New Order in Northern Ireland[1]

Peter Mandelson

Harold Wilson said a week is a long time in politics. I have learned since becoming secretary of state for Northern Ireland that some weeks never end. And others, like deadlines, just become extended. I was struck recently by the observation of another elder statesman about the Northern Ireland peace process. At one of many difficult moments he made a speech in Northern Ireland in which he said:

> I realize full well that we are asking much of the parties of the Assembly to work together in the interests of the whole community in Northern Ireland. But I must tell you quite frankly that, having taken the necessary steps to enable a resumption of the political life of Northern Ireland, the people of Britain will not understand any reluctance to take full advantage of it.

I was struck, not because of the words he used, but because this was Edward Heath, speaking in August 1973, as he struggled to create a power-sharing Executive for Northern Ireland. That Executive was duly set up after intensive negotiations at Sunningdale in December 1973, but despite the best efforts of its members, it collapsed in May 1974 in the face of widespread unionist opposition. The intervening years have been cruel. Since the day that Sunningdale fell apart 2,259 men, women and children have been killed in the Troubles. Many thousands more have been injured. And countless people have lost family and friends and lost all hope of any respite. All the result of political failure.

For many, memories of 1974 are still fresh. These are anxious days. I recognize the widespread concern that this process is beginning to falter. The people of Northern Ireland like the Good Friday Agreement, they are proud of their Executive. They like having local voices in charge of local affairs and they want that to continue. It is our duty to make it work, and that of all those who signed up to the Agreement. The prime minister and the Taoiseach, my Irish colleagues and I are doing everything in our power to find a way through these difficulties. But, if there are no clear changes for the better to give confidence that decommissioning will happen, I will put on hold the operation of the institutions in seven days' time.

In all this uncertainty, nobody wants to be reminded of Seamus Mallon's comment that the Good Friday Agreement is 'Sunningdale for slow learners'. So the question I want to consider today is: is history repeating itself? Are we about to squander yet another golden chance to end forever the conflict in Northern Ireland?

The 1973 accord was the best deal possible at the time, agreed as it was against a backdrop of terrorist violence and mass loyalist dissent. And it is true that much of what was agreed late in 1973 was reflected in the settlement of May 1998: an Executive made up of unionist and nationalist politicians; a North–South dimension; and no change in the constitutional status of Northern Ireland without the consent of a majority of the people living there. But, a generation later, those same principles now underpin a very different Agreement – a broader, deeper, fairer Agreement. While the 1974 Executive included both unionist and nationalist representatives, as well as a member of the Alliance party, it did not involve republican ministers and it did not include unionist dissenters. Indeed, the DUP were not even invited to the negotiations from which it emerged. The Good Friday Agreement, on the other hand, was hammered out by political parties of all sizes and all beliefs. Some chose not to contribute, but none can say that they were not given the chance. And the Executive that it conceived is truly representative. It recognizes that everyone who has been a party to the conflict must be a party to its resolution. It recognizes that nationalists and republicans have, historically, felt alienated from the state. And that will only change if we change the very structure of the state. The Good Friday Agreement gave nationalists and republicans an equal stake in the government of Northern Ireland and an equal status in the eyes of that government. It gave all sides of the political debate institutions in which they could all place their trust. This Executive includes two DUP members, whose opposition to the entire process has not stopped them reaping the rewards. And I welcome their contribution – as ministers if not party politicians – because we can only achieve political stability if all sides can claim some ownership of the government that serves them.

The 1973 accord acknowledged the importance of the 'Irish dimension' and took some steps – notably the setting up of a Council of Ireland – towards strengthening Irish involvement in Northern Ireland. Now, we no longer think in terms of an 'Irish dimension', to be tacked on to internal Northern Ireland policies. The Irish government and the Irish people have played a crucial role in bringing the peace process this far. We share the same, unselfish interest. And, when needs be, our two governments will continue to act together in the best interests of all the people of Northern Ireland.

But the Good Friday Agreement sends ripples far beyond the shores and borders of Northern Ireland, for it has created a whole new network of institutional links throughout the United Kingdom and Ireland. Gone is the Anglo-Irish Agreement. In its place we have a framework for enhanced practical cooperation across these islands – a framework that allows us to share what we have in common but respects what makes us different. A framework that disperses the rewards of peace throughout the regions.

The constitutional bottom line was the same in 1973 as it is today: that the future of Northern Ireland should only be decided by, or with the agreement of, the people of Northern Ireland. What was an agreed principle in 1973 was set in stone by the Good Friday Agreement, with changes to Articles 2 and 3 of the Irish Constitution and parallel British constitutional changes, including the repeal of the Government of Ireland Act 1920. But the Good Friday Agreement does more than create the constitutional architecture of a new Northern Ireland, because it builds respect for rights and the principle of fairness into the very fibre of the new

Constitution. It has given us a new Human Rights Commission and an Equality Commission to give Northern Ireland the sort of rights-based society that other countries will look to as a model of excellence. It has given us reforms in the way that Northern Ireland is policed, to correct the extreme religious imbalance which means that there is only one Catholic for every nine Protestants in the service, and to equip the police to meet the challenges of peace with the same courage and determination that distinguished them in times of conflict. And it has the potential, if only we allow it, to redefine the relationship between the people of Northern Ireland and their government.

Northern Ireland has rich traditions across its community. Too often these traditions have had their image sullied by the aggressive demands of a few for rights that cut across the rights of the many. But I believe that at their best these traditions make Northern Ireland what it is – a vibrant, creative society capable of great tolerance and inclusivity. I want to build on, not suppress, these traditions. I want to see a society which celebrates its diversity; a society in which Orange and Gaelic can live side by side in mutual respect, as keen to protect each other's rights as their own. A society at ease with itself does not demand unfettered freedoms or rights without responsibilities. For what value have rights if they are only conferred on people we agree with? I want to see a Northern Ireland with two self-assured traditions but one body of citizens, because it is united by shared language, shared values and shared land, with bonds that are strong enough to encompass diversity of religion, of politics and of custom.

Equally, a healthy, cohesive society is a collection of individuals linked by a shared, respected established order. As long as that order is imposed from outside Northern Ireland, no matter how well meaning the government – or how skilled the Secretary of State! – that vision will elude us. That's why the Good Friday Agreement set the parameters for a new order: because only with self-government can the values and identities of the state truly reflect the values and identities of society.

That is why I am convinced that the collapse of power-sharing in 1974 does not foreshadow the demise of the Good Friday Agreement in 2000. We have not been here before. The Good Friday Agreement is more robust than Sunningdale. Its institutions are more inclusive, more democratic. Its roots in the community go deeper. We have never before had such a comprehensive settlement nor such potential for lasting peace and stability – because we have learned the lessons of Sunningdale. I know, the politicians know and, most important of all, the people of Northern Ireland know that the different basis makes this the best formula we will ever devise. They know, too, that if they throw this chance away it will take another generation before they can claw back the benefits we have so nearly secured.

Just imagine it. Another 30 years. Another 30 years of sectarian division; 30 years of Direct Rule; 30 years of high unemployment, low investment, and sympathy, but not respect, in the eyes of the world. And the Agreement that would emerge from that lost generation would be, give or take the odd dot and comma, exactly the same as the one we have today. Only the wounds will be deeper, the trust harder to build, and the people more cynical than ever about the capacity of their politicians to represent them. Nobody will be in a stronger position than they are now. Just more anguished, more exhausted and more defeated.

I can understand if you are slightly puzzled that, today of all days, you should hear this hymn to the Good Friday Agreement. Why, you may well ask, if the Good Friday Agreement really is the blueprint for a better future in Northern Ireland, is the peace process in such apparent jeopardy? And why insist on decommissioning if it brings down a fair and effective government?

The answer is that the Good Friday Agreement asked everybody to make an investment, to show commitment to the process and faith in each other. It recognized that we could not move into the future until we broke from the past. And that, for many people, was the hardest thing of all. It meant the release of paramilitary prisoners, some of whom had committed the most unspeakable crimes. It meant setting aside generations of often violent hostility and sharing power with old enemies. It meant reform of some of the pillars of Northern Ireland life – the RUC and the criminal justice system – to equip them for the demands of peace, not conflict. And it means decommissioning. To underwrite with actions the paramilitaries' stated commitment to peace. And even at this late, late hour it is within the paramilitaries' power to demonstrate clearly that they are dedicated to this process. To prove to us that the Bill to suspend the institutions is not necessary.

I appreciate the difficulties that this causes. There are many, I know, in the republican movement who are passing from one era of strategy and organization to the next but have not yet reached the logical conclusion of their actions. I know the passions that an attempt to force decommissioning arouses. I am not naive. Surrendering long-fought and hard-line political ground is one thing. Appearing to be forced to surrender altogether is quite another. That's why decommissioning is a voluntary contribution to the process of building trust. But it is also necessary in order to move forward.

During the multi-party talks of 1998, every point of this Agreement was studied in detail then weighed in the round. The result is a finely tuned but hard-won compromise. Every provision, every word, is there for a reason. Any unilateral change of detail or emphasis, no matter how small, would throw it out of balance. Everyone who brokered the Agreement understood this. Unless someone is proposing to renegotiate it, it is this deal that has to be implemented, this deal and all of it.

So if we are to get through the coming period, if we are to keep the peace process on track, then we must guard jealously the integrity of the Good Friday Agreement and maintain the confidence of all parties in its scrupulous fairness. I am under no illusions about the size of the task ahead or the heavy price of failure. These are difficult times but I can assure you that I am not about to give the upper hand to the political dinosaurs who have consistently opposed peace and progress, who thrive on conflict and misery. Northern Ireland's proud traditions grew up in adversity, as its people saw it, to protect their way of life, to express their traditions without fear of attack. They did not live in fear and isolation, did not suffer dreadful losses of friends and family only to flinch now that we are in sight of peace. I have more faith in the people of Northern Ireland than that. Their will, their spirit, their history demands that we make this Agreement work.

The twentieth century was steeped in blood, across the globe and in this small corner of it. It showed, cruelly and indiscriminately, the destructive potential of coercive power. This century will conclusively prove its limits. And I am convinced that history will add Northern Ireland to the roll of nations which proved that force – political or paramilitary – can never supplant democracy.

Note

1. This paper was first delivered as a lecture at the Institute of Irish Studies, University of Liverpool on 4 February 2000.

Hillsborough to Belfast: Is It the Final Lap?[1]

Sir David Goodall

When I chose this title early in January 2000, the institutions established under the Good Friday Agreement were in place and beginning to work. Although the 31 January deadline for General de Chastelain's report on decommissioning was looming, it was possible to hope that by then Sinn Féin would have been able to offer, if not a start to IRA decommissioning, at least enough of an outline timetable for it to enable the general to present a genuinely positive report.

So my intention was to trace the beginnings of the current peace process back as far as the Anglo-Irish Agreement of 1985 – the Hillsborough Agreement; to compare that Agreement with the one reached at Belfast on Good Friday 1998; and to consider in what directions further progress was needed before one could begin to talk with confidence about a 'settlement' of the Irish question having been achieved.

The situation today, with the Good Friday institutions suspended and the IRA having withdrawn from all contacts with General de Chastelain's commission, has rendered such an intention somewhat unreal. Northern Ireland has been plunged back into crisis and there is an ugly possibility that the Belfast Agreement, and the whole approach on which it was based, is facing collapse. It may nevertheless be useful – and help to put the current impasse into perspective – to compare the two Agreements and the rationale behind them. But the question posed in my title now seems decidedly more premature than it did a couple of months ago. So instead of answering it, I shall end by offering a few – necessarily gloomy – reflections on the present stalemate.

In the autumn of 1983, when the preliminary negotiations leading to the Hillsborough Agreement began, the British government had run out of ideas for tackling the Northern Ireland problem. The collapse of the Sunningdale arrangements in 1974 had demonstrated the impracticability of imposing constitutional arrangements which required unionist cooperation in order to work, and which the unionist majority was determined to resist. The SDLP had refused to operate any arrangements which did not include an 'Irish dimension'; and the introduction of such a dimension remained blocked by adamant unionist opposition.

In this situation, the initiative came from the Irish, and personally from the then Taoiseach, Dr Garret Fitzgerald. As explained to the British side at the time, the considerations motivating him were a recognition (1) that Irish unity was simply not attainable in the foreseeable future; (2) that the nationalist minority in the North was alienated from the institutions of government, law and order there; and

(3) that Sinn Féin was capitalizing on this alienation so as to marginalize the SDLP and become a major political force, not just in the North, but in the South too, thereby threatening the stability of the whole island of Ireland. It is a shade ironic to recall now that one of Fitzgerald's primary objectives in initiating the negotiations which led to the 1985 Agreement was to halt the political advance of Sinn Féin.

Fitzgerald proposed that, in order to achieve this, the alienation of the nationalist minority should be ended by associating the Republic with the administration and policing of the North, in return for which the Republic would acknowledge the legitimacy of the Union, if necessary by amending Articles 2 and 3 of the Irish Constitution. In this way (it was argued) the institutions of the British state in the North would be strengthened by being made acceptable to nationalists; the SDLP would be able to show that non-violent nationalism could achieve more for the minority than terrorism; and Sinn Féin and the IRA would be discredited and gradually marginalized.

On the British side, Margaret Thatcher's main concern was to obtain improved cross-border security cooperation against IRA terrorism. But she was reluctantly brought to recognize that no Irish goverment could afford to be seen to be cooperating too closely with British security forces in the North unless it obtained some political quid pro quo in the shape of an 'Irish dimension' in the way the North was governed. Others on the British side recognized also that the particular historical, cultural, geographical and demographic circumstances of Northern Ireland, including the size of the minority community relative to the unionist community and the proximity of the Republic, were such that it was no longer governable without some form of institutionalized recognition of the 'Irishness' of the nationalist minority.

There seemed to be enough commonality between these two positions to justify at least an exploratory negotiation about the possibility of a deal. But unionist hostility to any form of Irish involvement in the affairs of Northern Ireland was so strong that it was clearly impossible for British ministers to think of taking the unionist leadership into their confidence: unionists had made it abundantly clear that their only interest in contributing to such a negotiation would be to wreck it. So the eventual result was an Agreement between the two governments, in which the Northern Ireland political parties were not involved; to which the unionists were bitterly opposed; and which (unlike Sunningdale) was not dependent on their support. But while the Irish government had negotiated in close concert with the SDLP leadership, refusing to accept anything which was unacceptable to John Hume, the British government had been obliged, by unionist intransigence, to negotiate over the heads of the unionist leadership and ride roughshod over their objections.

The central feature of this Agreement was what became known to the negotiators as 'the basic equation': that a strengthened Irish acceptance of the legitimacy of the Union, together with closer cross-border security cooperation, should be balanced by giving the Irish government, on behalf of the Northern nationalist community, a say in the administration of the North in all matters affecting that community. In the course of the negotiations, this basic equation became, in Irish terminology, progressively 'shallower'. The Irish dimension offered by the British stopped well short of the 'joint authority' desired by Garret Fitzgerald, and was limited to a consultative role (although the term 'consultative' was not used), while Irish acceptance of the Union was ambiguously worded and the idea of amending Articles 2 and 3 was dropped.

In addition to these basic provisions, the Agreement contained what was intended as an inducement to the unionists to move to power-sharing, by providing that the Irish government's right to be consulted would apply only to matters which did not become the responsibility of a devolved administration established with the cooperation of 'representatives of both traditions'. There were also provisions relating to human rights; to improving relations between the public and the police; and to cross-border cooperation on a variety of economic and social matters. There was also an important section on 'Legal Matters, including the Administration of Justice'. This required the Conference to consider ways of harmonizing the criminal law on both sides of the border and to seek ways of improving public confidence in the administration of justice, 'considering *inter alia* the possibility of mixed courts in both jurisdictions for the trial of certain offences'.

The watering down of both sides of the 'basic equation', the delays in implementing certain aspects of what had been agreed, and the eventual British refusal to make any change in the courts left both communities in the North dissatisfied in varying degrees. The unionists, indeed, were outraged, as much by the way in which they had been excluded from the negotiations as by the substance of the Agreement itself; while the SDLP continued to withold its support for the forces of law and order in the North. Instead of seeking an accommodation with moderate unionism, John Hume took the momentous decision to explore ways of drawing the IRA's teeth by talking to Sinn Féin, thus in effect forming the 'pan-nationalist front'.

Although it failed in its more ambitious objectives, the Hillsborough Agreement was nevertheless an important step along the road to a comprehensive settlement. In the elections which followed, support for Sinn Féin fell significantly and support for the SDLP increased. Of more enduring and profound importance, the Agreement introduced an irreversible 'Irish dimension' into Northern Ireland by giving the Irish government a consultative role in the administration; it formally committed both governments to the principle of consent; and it established a structure – the Intergovernmental Conference – within which the two governments were obliged to work closely together on Northern Ireland matters. From the practice of regular consultation which this fostered, there developed the mutual understanding and mutual confidence which bore fruit in the joint Downing Street Declaration of 1993 and all that has flowed from it. The fact that Hillsborough was an inter-governmental Agreement, rather than one involving the political parties, also proved a source of strength, since it meant that it could not be brought down unless one or other of the two governments lost its nerve and walked away from it. As a consequence, much though they hated it, the unionists gradually came to recognize the main features of the Agreement – notably the Irish dimension – as facts of life with which (as the Good Friday Agreement showed) they eventually came to terms.

As has often been pointed out, the Good Friday Agreement owes much to the failed Sunningdale Agreement of 1973. But it is also in important respects an extension and development of the Hillsborough Agreement rather than (as union-ists maintain) its supplanter. An expanded 'Irish dimension' is at the heart of the new arrangements, in the form of cross-border institutions responsible to the Dáil and the Northern Ireland Assembly respectively; devolution on a power-sharing basis becomes a reality; the principle of consent is further entrenched; the Irish Republic's territorial claim to the North is ended with the amendment of Articles 2 and 3 of the Irish Constitution; and the Intergovernmental Conference lives on to deal with non-devolved matters. The embryonic references in the Hillsborough Agreement to improving relations between the public and the police, to improving public confidence in the courts and to harmonizing aspects of the criminal law have blossomed (if that is the right word) into the Patten Commission, with its controversial proposals for reforming the RUC, and a review of the criminal justice system, the results of which have yet to surface.

So much for the common threads in the two Agreements. I turn now to some of the differences. One novel element in the Good Friday Agreement is the British–Irish Council – in unionist terminology a 'Council of the Isles'. Lent additional substance by the parallel arrangements for devolution introduced in Scotland and Wales, the establishment of this body enables unionists to claim that the all-Ireland aspects of the Agreement are set within an overarching structure which comprises all the component nations of 'these islands' and is charged with addressing the 'totality of relationships' within them. The Agreement thus accords formal political recognition, for the first time since the Republic of Ireland left the Commonwealth in 1949, to the dense network of ties – of geography, history, language, culture, commerce and family relations – which make the relationship between Britain and Ireland uniquely close as well as uniquely neuralgic.

The significance of this provision in the Agreement could prove to be far reaching; and my original intention had been to develop the theme that a definitive settle-ment of the Irish question – of the Irish–British question – will not be achieved until we have found a way of formulating and institutionalizing the relationship between the two sister islands in terms which reflect its unique character without infringing the national self-respect of all concerned. At present, this can be no more than a very long-term aspiration. But only if it is realized will we have created an environment in which both communities on the island of Ireland can feel fully secure, and in which the existence or disappearance of the border will have ceased to matter.

I still believe this to be a theme of central importance. But the threat which now hangs over the whole peace process makes it necessary to concentrate instead on the other aspects of the Agreement which differentiate it sharply from Hillsbor-ough. One obvious difference is the fact that, unlike Hillsborough, in this case neither the unionists nor the SDLP were excluded from the negotiations. On the contrary, they were major players; and the Ulster Unionist party, in marked contrast to Hillsborough, was a full party to the eventual Agreement. The fact that mainstream unionism, as well as constitutional nationalism, shares ownership of the new Agreement gives it a radically different character from its 1985 prede-cessor, as of course does the fact that it was endorsed by the people of Ireland, North and South, in simultaneous referenda.

But it is not only the Ulster Unionists and the SDLP who are parties to the Agreement, as well as the two governments. Sinn Féin too, on behalf of the republican movement, played its full part in the negotiations and accepted the outcome. And here we come to the most fundamental difference of all. The Hillsborough Agreement, like all the attempts at a settlement which had preceded it, was aimed at providing a constitutional framework within which the 'moderate' representatives of both communities in Northern Ireland would eventually agree to work together (or which they would at least accept as a basis for further progress). The belief was that if a political settlement of this kind could be achieved, the proponents of violence would be marginalized, the Provisionals would lose popular support and peace would eventually follow. The IRA would, in short, eventually be defeated. This might be labelled the 'exclusive' approach – an approach designed to exclude the men of violence and render them increasingly irrelevant; and it envisaged a political settlement being reached first, as a means of achieving peace later.

The Good Friday Agreement, by contrast, and the process leading up to it, reflects an 'inclusive' approach. Persuaded partly by the British government's secret contacts with the IRA and partly by John Hume's exploratory discussions with Gerry Adams, the two governments acted on the assumption that the Provisionals were ready, provided that their representatives were admitted fully and on equal terms into the political process, to abandon the armed struggle and pursue their aims by peaceful means. Instead of looking for a political settlement which would discredit Sinn Féin, erode support for the IRA and thus lead eventually to peace, the two governments decided, with the Downing Street Declaration of December 1993, to go for peace first by including Sinn Féin (and, by extension, the IRA) in the process. The hope was that, with peace once established, a political settlement would then be negotiable in which the demilitarized (or deterrorized) republican movement could be included.

From the British government's point of view, a crucial factor in the decision to make this fundamental change of policy was the message received from the IRA on the 'back channel' in February 1993. As reported by Sir Patrick Mayhew in the House of Commons in November 1993, this said: 'The conflict is over but we need your advice on how to bring it to a close ... we cannot meet the Secretary of State's public renunciation of violence, but it would be given privately as long as we were sure that we were not being tricked.' The IRA may subsequently have disowned that message, but there is no doubt that it was received and that the British government of the day believed it. In the subsequent exchange, the IRA invited the British government to 'open a dialogue in the event of a total end to hostilities'. It is on the meaning of that word 'total' that the whole decommissioning argument turns. Can an end to hostilities be 'total' if a paramilitary organization insists on retaining its armoury for possible future use?

At the outset of the new negotiating process, there were many sceptics, of whom I was one. Given the passionate commitment of the republican movement to getting the British out of Northern Ireland, their atavistic hatred of the British connection, the deeply embedded tradition of republican martyrdom at British hands and the republican lives lost in the course of the 'armed struggle', it seemed impossible to believe that the IRA would in the end allow Sinn Féin to agree on their behalf to any settlement which unionists might find remotely tolerable. If indeed Sinn Féin were to do so, it seemed likely that the republican movement, as so often in the past, would split. Any republican leader who tried to compromise would risk meeting the same fate as Michael Collins. The breakaway group would resume the armed struggle, and we would be back to square one – except that the hard-core practitioners of the armed struggle would (hopefully) have been reduced in numbers and popular sympathy for them in Ireland would have been diminished. Alternatively, the republican movement would hold together, but once it had squeezed maximum political advantage from the peace process, it would find a pretext for turning its back on the negotiations, throw the blame onto the British (never difficult to do in Ireland) and return to violence. In either event we would be driven back into a security confrontation with IRA terrorism and a search for the 'exclusive' settlement against which John Hume had so firmly closed the door.

At various points along the switchback road to the Good Friday Agreement it seemed that one or other of the two unpalatable scenarios I have described was about to materialize and that a different approach was needed. But every time this happened, the prize seemed too great to jeopardize and the argument that there was no alternative to the 'inclusive' approach won the day. The conclusion of the Good Friday Agreement and the subsequent establishment of the Assembly and the Joint Executive seemed conclusive proof that the sceptics were wrong and that the inclusive approach had, against all the odds, succeeded. That one of its effects had been greatly to strengthen the electoral position and standing of Sinn Féin at the expense of the SDLP – the exact opposite of what Garret Fitzgerald had hoped to achieve at Hillsborough in 1985 – was judged to be an acceptable price to pay for peace.

Events following the De Chastelain Commission's negative report at the beginning of February 2000 have thrown serious doubt on this comfortable conclusion. The IRA's failure to respond to David Trimble's remarkable act of faith in allowing the Executive to begin functioning before any decommissioning had taken place, the ambiguous manoeuvre with which Sinn Féin and the IRA tried at the very last minute to avert the consequences of that failure and the ungenerous rhetoric with which Gerry Adams has tried to gloss over the republican movement's share of responsibility for the impasse have done nothing to strengthen unionist or British confidence in the IRA's (or Sinn Féin's) intentions. On the other hand, and allowing that Gerry Adams and Martin MacGuinness (despite their rhetoric) have been sincere in their efforts to persuade the rest of the IRA leadership to put their weaponry 'beyond use', Peter Mandelson's unavoidable decision to suspend the institutions of the Agreement has undoubtedly made their task harder.

The current crisis [of February 2000] has highlighted two fundamental flaws in the Good Friday Agreement: the fudge over decommissioning, which allowed the unionist community (encouraged with singular disingenuousness by the prime minister) to believe that early decommissioning of IRA weapons was an integral part of the package, while allowing republicans to argue that it imposed no obligations on the IRA; and the 'constructive ambiguity' which led unionists to think that the Republic was acknowledging the legitimacy of the Union, while allowing nationalists to read the Agreement as replacing British sovereignty in the North with a kind of Belfast–Dublin condominium. To argue that without these flaws there would have been no agreement is probably true; but the art of finding language which means one thing to one side and something else to the other, although often believed to be the defining skill of the good diplomat, tends in practice to be exposed as trickery the moment the resulting agreement is put to the test. The Good Friday Agreement now faces this moment of truth.

The crucial issue, as it has been all along, is the decommissioning of IRA weapons. That this is an issue of great symbolic importance for both republicans and unionists goes without saying. But it is not, as is often alleged, purely symbolic. The ceasefire called by the IRA on 31 August 1994, which Gerry Adams had insisted was 'complete', was called off without warning on 9 February 1996 with the bombing of Canary Wharf; and as many commentators have noted, the language used by Gerry Adams to denounce Mandelson's suspension of the Executive, with its disingenuously camouflaged threats, is ominously similar to the language which foreshadowed the Canary Wharf attack. In this way Sinn Féin manages to use the IRA's continued military capability as a source of political pressure while at the same time disclaiming any responsibility for doing so. And it is this tactic which makes the decommissioning issue one of practical, and not just symbolic, importance.

On any objective assessment of the balance of advantage, Sinn Féin has done well out of the Good Friday Agreement. From being a political pariah, it is courted and respected by both the Irish and the British governments. Its electoral support, as already noted, has substantially increased on both sides of the border, to a point where it has almost supplanted the SDLP as the main political voice of nationalism in the North, and there is speculation about the possibility of a Fianna Fáil/ Sinn Féin coalition in Dublin. In the United States, Gerry Adams has been all but canonized, and continued financial support from Irish-America is guaranteed. There has been a wholesale release of convicted republican prisoners. Sinn Féin obtained two ministerial portfolios in a devolved Northern Ireland government. A root and branch reform of the RUC has been set in train and British sovereignty over the North has been blurred by the establishment of a whole nexus of cross-border institutions.

That is not, of course, how it looks to the ideologues of the IRA. Their trust in the good faith of the British government is even less than the unionists' trust in the good faith of Sinn Féin. They see a devolved government in the North still led by unionists, the British Army and the RUC still spread across the country and the British government's writ still running there – as Peter Mandelson's unilateral suspension of the Agreement's institutions demonstrated. With the reformulation of Articles 2 and 3 of the Irish Constitution, Ireland's territorial claim to the North has been given up. The sacred goal of expelling the British from Irish soil seems as far away as ever; and on top of all this, they are being pressed to decommission their arms, a gesture of surrender which no Irish republican force has ever made.

What appears to be the IRA's (and Sinn Féin's) present position – that no move of any kind will be made on decommissioning until every provision in the Good Friday Agreement has been fulfilled to their satisfaction – is simply not negotiable, even if it can be relied on as constituting a genuine offer to decommission at the end of the day. No unionist leader could re-enter a devolved administration in cooperation with Sinn Féin on that basis. And so we have the present impasse, with Gerry Adams urging republicans onto the streets, the UUP pressing David Trimble to raise his demands, the 'Real IRA' seeking to resume the armed struggle and the marching season approaching.

A particularly disturbing feature of the present situation is the rift which seems to have opened up between the Irish and British governments. That the institutions of the Agreement have been suspended following the definitive amendment of Articles 2 and 3 of the Irish Constitution is obviously a political embarrassment for the Taoiseach. But his recent speech at the Fianna Fáil Ard Fheis, with its implied equivalence between IRA decommissioning and British demilitarization, and the implication that it would be enough for the IRA to offer some form of commitment to decommissioning only when all nationalist expectations of the Agreement have been realized, will not make things easier for David Trimble – or, indeed, for Peter Mandelson. It suggests that Bertie Ahern is shifting the Irish government's pressure for compromise away from Sinn Féin and back onto the unionists.

All that said, it is hard to believe that the process which began with the Downing Street Declaration, which reached a high point with the conclusion of the Good Friday Agreement, which has brought almost two years' relative cessation of terrorist violence and the establishment of all-party devolved government in Northern Ireland, has at last been tested to destruction. We do not know what may be going on behind the scenes in the way of informal contacts. Perhaps Sinn Féin's aggressive rhetoric does not have to be taken at its face value. Gerry Adams and Martin MacGuinness may be struggling hard to extract from the Army Council some move on decommissioning, or at least a declaration that 'the war is over', which might be balanced by some visible reduction in the British military presence in South Armagh or elsewhere in the North; and this might just be sufficient to enable Peter Mandelson to restore the Executive without forcing David Trimble's resignation. Perhaps, when they look into the abyss, the leaders of the unionist community will bring themselves to accept another fudge rather than see the whole process dissolve back into violence.

All these things are possible; but opinion within Northern Ireland appears to be polarizing and it looks uncomfortably as though the argument within the republican movement has shifted in favour of the hard men. From this vantage point, I can only say that the prospects of saving the Agreement now look no better than fifty-fifty. If the IRA has made up its mind to offer no further concessions of substance on the decommissioning issue, neither the British government nor the present UUP leadership has much room for manoeuvre. Deeply unpalatable though it may be, above all in Dublin, it may be time for the British and Irish governments – and the SDLP also – to start thinking, if only on a contingency basis, about returning to what I have described as the 'exclusive' approach.

Postscript

Since I wrote the foregoing, the switchback ride has continued. The all-party Executive is functioning again, and David Trimble has – provisionally and precariously – survived a challenge from within the unionist movement. The prime minister and the Taoiseach are once more deep in negotiations to resolve interlocking crises over the implementation of the Patten Report, exclusion of Sinn Féin ministers from cross-border meetings, republican and nationalist insistence on increased British demilitarization, and continuing IRA reluctance to move further in the direction of decommissioning its arms. Sinn Féin's onward march threatens the survival of the SDLP. The 'Real IRA' has shown its ability to carry on an armed struggle of its own; and the prospect of a British general election is inhibiting all the Northern Ireland parties from making compromises.

So there is no shortage of issues on which the Good Friday Agreement could still founder. A serious demonstration of strength by the 'Real IRA' could call into question the validity of the whole peace process. There is deepening unionist disillusionment, both with the terms of the Good Friday settlement and with what they see as continuing nationalist (and Irish government) insensitivity to their legitimate concerns. At the same time (at least as viewed from this side of the Irish Sea), there seems to be a growing awareness on the part of unionists and nationalists alike of the benefits which the uncertain peace is bringing to Northern Ireland, and corresponding reluctance to slip back into violent confrontation for the sake of principle. Peace, in short, is within sight of becoming a habit which no one wants to break. To that extent, the odds against the switchback ride ending in derailment have strengthened.

December 2000

Note

1. This paper was first delivered as a lecture at the Institute of Irish Studies, University of Liverpool on 7 March 2000.

Defining Republicanism: Shifting Discourses of New Nationalism and Post-republicanism[1]

Kevin Bean

The pace of events since the first IRA ceasefire in 1994 has been staggering. The nature and speed of these developments have frequently been confusing and erratic, but the pictures of smiling Sinn Féin Executive members seated around the Cabinet table at Stormont alongside their Unionist and SDLP colleagues marks the distance travelled by contemporary republican politicians. Throughout this process a range of commentators, as well as political opponents, have attempted to explain republicanism's apparent transformation from revolutionary armed movement to semi-constitutional party. Many unionists have understandably remained sceptical of the sincerity of this Damascene conversion, while republican critics see the new departure as the abandonment of the movement's traditional goals. Brendan Hughes, a former IRA commander in Belfast, argues that there has been a fundamental shift in Provisional republicanism and that the only real beneficiary of the armed struggle has been the nationalist middle class, which has reaped the rewards of the Good Friday Agreement.[2]

Academic commentators reflect this debate about a possible structural shift within republicanism. For example, Jennifer Todd stresses that Provisionalism has not been transformed into constitutional nationalism, but rather the Sinn Féin leadership has extended the 'ideological repertoire' of republicanism by subordinating traditional long-term goals, which are unachievable in the immediate term, to a more practical agenda of 'radical egalitarian democratic transformist principles'. However, her 'transformist principles' – which include cultural equality, radical reform of the RUC, withdrawal of the British Army and the strengthening of the North–South dimension of the Belfast Agreement – do mark a significant scaling down of republican demands and a redefinition of the scale of the republican project as it has been generally understood during the last thirty years.[3] Henry Patterson also agrees that there has been change, but he sees the 'historical achievement' of the Provisional leadership as its ability to reconcile most republican activists 'to a settlement which contains nothing that can realistically be seen as even "transitional" to a united Ireland'.[4]

A closer examination of the extended ideological repertoire that Todd discusses reveals elements of what might be defined as a 'civic republicanism' and contains ideological themes that could be part of the programme of any new nationalist movement in Western Europe. In an attempt to assess the nature and extent of any alleged paradigm shift in Provisional republicanism I wish to discuss the changes in contemporary Irish republicanism by drawing on some of the perspectives and analyses of the resurgence of nationalism as an international contemporary political phenomenon. In this discussion I wish to challenge the view of Irish republicanism as simply a tradition-driven paradigm in which, in Conor Cruise O'Brien's celebrated phrase, 'the mandate of the dead outweighs that of the living',[5] and instead adopt a structural approach which sees post-republicanism as a facet of wider ideological and political change. By placing the discussion within this framework I hope to show that in these aspects Northern Irish politics are not *sui generis* and that the transformation within republicanism is not simply ideological but organizational. In conclusion, I would like to outline some possible structural determinants of this shift towards the forms of new nationalism.

The resistance of the local to the centralizing forces of globalization and the reemergence of frequently violent ethnic and national conflicts throughout the post-Cold War world, from Kosovo to Congo, has stimulated a growth in the research into the nature and significance of nationalism. In the 1970s, the conflict in Northern Ireland seemed to be an anachronistic throwback to an earlier, more primitive age; commentators stressed its pre-modern and atavistic character. At the beginning of the twenty-first century, discussions of the exceptionalist nature of the conflict no longer seem so compelling as explanations.

Many accounts of nineteenth- and twentieth-century nationalist movements discuss them in relation to the process of state- and nation-building. Gellner, for example, defined nationalism as 'primarily a political principle which holds that the political and national unit should be congruent'.[6] In this reading nationalism has a significant role in the modernization process, in the consolidation of industrialization and in the formation of new social and political elites. Likewise, Anderson's definition of the nation as an 'imagined community' places great stress on nationalism as an agency of modernization and political and social mobilization against both traditional forces and 'external' oppression.[7] These approaches have been influential in our understanding of Irish nationalism and its role in the construction of both national identity and state structures after 1922.

While these approaches are useful and generally valid tools of historical analysis, the emergence of new forms of nationalism and nationalist movements has moved the debate both forwards and backwards at the same time. To some commentators, such as Eric Hobsbawm, the revival of nationalism, especially in its 'ethnic' variety, is a cause for alarm as the dark ancestral gods of blood and soil unleash atavistic, irrational forces across the continent.[8] The experience of the former Yugoslavia is frequently cited as evidence of the dangers of the emerging ethnically based nationalisms.

A useful way to assess contemporary Irish republicanism within the framework of the discourse of the new nationalism is to remind ourselves of the origins of the modern idea of the nation. The French Revolution, the Enlightenment and Romanticism in the late eighteenth and early nineteenth centuries gave birth to the concept of the nation-state along with the contrasting and contradictory concepts of 'civic' and 'ethnic' nationalism. Civic nationalism was rooted in the democratic and secular traditions of the Enlightenment, which stressed the citizen's identification with the state and the nation as a voluntary and conscious choice. This 'Western' tradition was based on the identification and affinity of the citizen with a political community, while the 'Eastern', 'ethnic' tradition was rooted in the concept of the ethnos, a community of fate which defines the 'nation' in terms of 'primordial' elements such as language, culture, tradition and race. With its stress on the *Volk*, this 'Eastern' tradition stressed the irrational and given nature of national identity. As Gellner has argued, these civic and ethnic elements remained in creative tension in the development of nineteenth-and twentieth-century nationalisms which defined the nation-state as a sovereign entity representing, acting and speaking on behalf of a culturally homogeneous people; nationalism, with varying degrees of 'ethnic' or 'civic' emphasis, could thus be described within a variable triad of nation–state–people.

In the literature of contemporary nationalism studies, 'new nationalism' refers to a wave of regionalist, autonomist and separatist movements that represent, in varying degrees, a revolt of the marginalized and the peripheral against the centre and the metropolis. The movements for autonomy/sovereignty in Quebec and Catalonia and devolution in Scotland and Wales are frequently cited as examples of this new nationalism and its clear delineation from classical nationalism's emphasis on nation-state-building. New nationalism represents the fracturing of this linkage and sees a reconnection with the civic elements that were submerged in classical nation-state-building nationalism. According to Nairn, this nationalism is qualitatively different from the anti-modernist and Romantic movements of the nineteenth century and instead represents an engagement with the contemporary world.[9]

Other characteristics mark it out as a different formation from classical nationalism. Breuilly, for example, argues that new nationalism has a specifically 'political' orientation and is frequently driven by the social and economic concerns of key social groups, such as the upwardly mobile managerial and business classes.[10] These movements are also based in regions with a coherent, developed civil society and a certain level of wealth; as such, this is a nationalism of rising expectations rather than the despairing cry of the alienated poor.

Another marked contrast with classical nationalism is the complexity and ambiguity in the relationship between political and cultural nationalism. With its stress on a 'civic' identity rather than an 'ethnic' one, this marks a clear step away from the particularism of descent and blood towards universal values. This can be seen in the emergence of 'identity' politics and a conscious recognition of the plurality of national identities as a feature of political identity rather than a fixed set of cultural characteristics.

These nationalisms are also of a liberal and social democratic character in which self-consciously progressive political and socio-economic themes outweigh the conservative and backward-looking elements of traditional nationalism. It would be wrong, however, to overstate the coherence and clarity of definition of these movements; indeed the literature lays great stress on the frequently contradictory and inchoate nature of the ideology and support that these movements draw upon. McCrone sees this Janus-like character of new nationalism – the ability to incorporate contradictory elements and to shift the ideological pattern of its message – as a reflection both of postmodern politics and of a more diverse social base than that which sustained nineteenth-century nationalism.[11]

It is also a reflection of the relatively recent origin of most of these movements; as an essentially contemporary creation in both ideological and organizational form they reflect the political terrain of their birth and the dominant pragmatic post-ideological politics of the late twentieth century. This contradictory character can be seen in the political goals of these movements; is their ultimate aim 'independence' or some form of 'autonomy'? Their discourse is ambiguous, drawing on concepts of process, transition and movement rather than fixed points and destinations. This studied ambivalence can be best seen in the changing definitions of the nature and structures of political power which have influenced the political framework of new nationalism. This theoretical structure develops the simple triad of people–state–nation into an expanding and developing continuum that relates to both supra-national bodies and the internal distribution of power within a state; new nationalist demands for 'independence within Europe' and devolved power-sharing at all levels show both the application of these ideas in practice and the almost limitless variety of interpretations that can be placed on them in theory.

What I would now like to consider is how far Sinn Féin can be considered to fit into the theoretical shape of new nationalism outlined above. If this is substantially found to be the case then there is a convincing argument that Northern Irish politics has entered a post-republican phase that could bring that polity more closely into line with comparable areas of conflict in Western Europe. However, this assessment does not carry with it implications of 'normalization' or a smooth development of conventional politics; indeed the emergence of new nationalism in Western societies seems to indicate a new politics of instability and challenge to the status quo, albeit within a constitutional framework. As well as bringing us to a closer understanding of the nature of Sinn Féin's politics, this discussion will help to clarify the relationship between the republican movement and the SDLP and whether the 'pan-nationalist front' can be the basis of a new form of post-republican politics.

Before we can do that, we need to arrive at a working definition of the nature and structure of republican politics and ideology. The dominant reading of the formation and development of the republican tradition was significantly influenced by Gellner's discussion of the Eastern, ethnic nationalist tradition. Garvin's stress on the significance of the elitist, Romantic, Pearsian vision in the shaping of the movement's politics[12] and Bowyer Bell's definition of republicanism as a religious cult with a transcendental goal and mandate that derived from the past have been widely influential.[13]

While these readings accurately describe some aspects of the forms of republican ideology they do not fully define the nature and dynamics of an ideology which was much more eclectic and pragmatic than either its critics or supporters would allow. This eclecticism, along with the republican conspiratorial tradition, is a significant factor in explaining the pattern of the paradigm shift in contemporary republicanism, but other structural and conjectural factors are probably more influential in shaping Provisionalism.

Provisionalism reflects the experience of its social base and constituency within the Northern nationalist community; contemporary events and experiences in Northern Ireland have always been more significant in the development of the harder-edged politics of Northern Provisionalism than the Romantic traditions of 1916. The weaknesses of the republican theoretical tradition and a conspiratorial emphasis on organization and agency also contribute to our difficulties in developing a base definition of Provisionalism. In some cases it would appear that republicanism was so devoid of political form that it could be argued that republicanism was whatever the leadership said it was. If we take the current Provisional leadership's own assessment at face value it would appear that before the late 1970s and the emergence of the 'Northern Radicals' around Gerry Adams, republicanism was ideologically and strategically primitive.

The phases in the development of the republican movement are well known and clearly delineated. The 'long war' strategy that had been developed in the late 1970s had been given further impetus by the electoral successes of the 1981 hunger strike. In this period of 'the ballot paper and the Armalite', Provisionalism was clearly revolutionary in strategy, goals and methods. The movement's analysis of the conflict was rooted in an evaluation of Britain's colonial role in the North. Its politics stressed the need for a mass revolutionary movement, led by the cutting edge of armed struggle, to end British domination and create the 32-county socialist republic. This analysis was rooted in traditional nationalist and republican assessments of Britain's imperialist domination of the whole island of Ireland as well as in Third World Marxism, which linked the struggle for national liberation to social and economic transformation.[14]

Starting from this definition, it is clear that there has been something of a shift within Irish republican politics towards the forms of new nationalism as defined above. I would now like to illustrate the extent of that shift by reference to these characteristics of new nationalism, as well as suggesting some possible implications for the development of Sinn Féin and Northern Irish politics in general.

In discussing the shape of new nationalism, the influence of the SDLP and its analysis of the conflict are decisive; however, it would be inaccurate to argue that new nationalism is simply old constitutional nationalism writ large. Although many commentators argue that the SDLP has been the most consistent and successful party in Northern Ireland in the last thirty years and that the Good Friday Agreement is, in Seamus Mallon's words, Sunningdale for slow learners, the ideological influence that it holds over contemporary republicanism may paradoxically be a cause of its electoral decline in the face of the new nationalist challenge of Sinn Féin. In increasingly defining its politics within the broad framework established by John Hume in the 1980s Sinn Féin is not simply becoming the 'green' wing of the SDLP. As recent research has shown, there is a considerable ideological and attitudinal overlap between the members and supporters of the two parties, especially in the rural areas of Northern Ireland.[15] Consequently Sinn Féin could actually overtake the SDLP electorally while operating within the ideological parameters laid down by John Hume. The SDLP's very success in influencing republicanism could thus be the agent of its own electoral retreat.

While this common 'pan-nationalism' could also be the basis for a *de facto* electoral pact, it is not the only factor in the consolidation and growth of Sinn Féin as an electoral force. In common with other new nationalist parties in Western Europe, Sinn Féin has successfully developed and maintained a diverse social constituency and electoral base. Although firmly rooted in the urban nationalist population and traditional rural strongholds, Sinn Féin has been successful in developing a new middle-class constituency. This constituency is more free-floating and unpredictable than that of the republican heartlands, where Sinn Féin acts as a social integration movement and representational party for its social base. This broadening of the electoral base does, however, introduce an element of volatility into Sinn Féin's politics and potential for growth; as a senior republican election strategist noted: 'Riding the two horses of working-class resistance and Catholic new money – unnatural bedfellows – carries with it an inherent contradiction. That contradiction may be masked in a state of political flux but it carries the potential to arrest progress once the political dust has settled … '.[16]

The new departure that emerged during the 1980s brought together many of the ideological and organizational themes of neo-nationalism outlined above. The core of the emerging strategy marked a radical shift in the republican movement's analysis of the nature of the conflict in Northern Ireland and the type of politics needed to achieve what were increasingly seen as long-term goals rather than the stuff of everyday politics. The new nationalist paradigm can clearly be discerned in the pluralist and nuanced assessment of Britain's role in Northern Ireland and in the redefinition of the nature of unionism in terms of multiple national identities within a contested political space.

Along with changes in political style and language came a fundamental shift in the conceptual and discursive framework of the republican position and in the strategic orientation of Provisionalism. The emergence of new nationalist politics meant a gradual shift from a republicanism based on a mass revolutionary movement and armed struggle to a diplomatic and conventional political strategy involving a broad front of Irish nationalism including the Dublin government and the SDLP. Potential international allies, such as Irish-America and the US government, would also have an important role in applying pressure on Britain as part of a long-term transitional strategy. This strategy was rooted in a re-evaluation of Britain's contemporary role in Ireland; secret contacts between the republican leadership and the British government in the late 1980s and 1990s reinforced a developing perception that Britain was no longer involved in Northern Ireland to pursue interests of its own and, furthermore, wanted to withdraw from direct political involvement. In significant aspects of their position republican politicians began to adopt a post-colonial interpretation of the British role in Northern Ireland that stressed crisis management and *raison d'état* rather than colonial domination and atavistic imperialism as explanations for Britain's continued presence.

In the 1990s republican politicians were reflecting these new nationalist themes in their own variants of Hume-speak, using a self-consciously objective tone; the language of this post-republicanism was one of dialogue, engagement, debate, movement, process, transition, reconciliation and conflict resolution. One of the founding documents of this post-republicanism, *Towards a Lasting Peace in Ireland*, written in 1992, discusses British neutrality and Britain's future role as a facilitator and persuader in a process of conflict resolution. The pluralist emphasis of new nationalism is reflected in the political strategy of Sinn Féin: having apparently accepted British assurances of 'no selfish interest', republicans increasingly focused on the 'unionist veto' and winning unionist consent as part of a process of national reconciliation.

Republicans had traditionally considered unionism within the context of the colonial relationship with Britain; republican military-political activity was directed towards British withdrawal, which would allow the Irish people, including the unionists, to exercise the right of self-determination without external interference. This schema has now been inverted, in both the strategic analysis and the practical politics of the Provisionals. Sinn Féin assembly member Francie Molloy argued that the acceptance of the Good Friday Agreement meant that republicans 'are really prepared to administer British rule in Ireland for the foreseeable future. The very principle of partition is accepted.'[17] The new focus is on the shape and nature of political institutions and structures that will be created before British withdrawal. Unionism has moved centre stage in this neo-nationalist analysis and is now assessed as an autonomous political and social force. Something of this pluralistic tone can be heard in the voices of leading republican strategists who increasingly discuss the legitimacy of unionism in pluralist language. Jim Gibney, a South Belfast Sinn Féin representative, has revised the position by arguing that 'the traditional position that a resolution to the problems with the Unionists would have to await the removal of the British government's involvement in Ireland was wrong. We must now accept that there are divided political allegiances within the nation and that Unionists have a dual identity that must be accommodated.'[18] Former Sinn Féin general secretary Tom Hartley has continued the argument on the need for reconciliation with the unionist community and challenged the traditional republican view that it is necessary to focus on the British government if unionist opposition to reunification is to be overcome. Hartley argued that this position made unionists 'a non-people robbed of their power to be a crucial component in the search for a just and lasting settlement on the island … [using] … the language of invitation … In our vision of a united and independent Ireland there must be a place for those who consider themselves British and those who wish to stay British.'[19]

The other side of this coin is an emerging emphasis on the politics of identity within republican discourse. The civic republican themes of equality and citizenship based on affinity emerge most clearly in the justification of Sinn Féin participation in the institutions of the Good Friday Agreement. Drawing on the new discourse of variable power structures within and between states, one of the most significant of New Sinn Féin thinkers, Mitchel McLaughlin, has talked of 'the interplay of several unions' within Northern Ireland (the United Kingdom, the European Union and the physical links between North and South) and stressed the need for a 'historic compromise' between unionism and nationalism:

> That can only be achieved by negotiations that examine and provide for all the elements of a community's identity. The assertion of an absolute and unconditional right to a political union will not produce an agreed Ireland. It is only by focussing on all the unions and on a multiplicity of connecting factors that a compromise can be achieved between nationalists and unionists that will stand the test of time.[20]

McLaughlin continues in a similar vein to stress the necessity for a pluralist republican political project that recognizes that there exists a potentially significant consensus across the full political spectrum of political opinion in Ireland; on the political failures of the past, on the current political realities, and on the consequent need for change ... Political leaders and the political process must demonstrate that there is an effective alternative to conflict. They must devise a constitutional and political framework through a democratic process of negotiation that will accommodate and manage change.[21]

Other aspects of contemporary republicanism reflect these ambiguities concerning the achievement of ultimate goals implicit in the new nationalist paradigm. There have been acknowledgments that the Good Friday Agreement falls far short of republican aims and that it reflects, in Gerry Adams's words, a renegotiation of the terms of the Union. The language of transition and the politics of implicit dynamics contained within the structures established by the Agreement have replaced the clarity and simplicity of traditional republican discourse. This has been presented to republican activists as a new and different phase in a continuing struggle; politics is the continuation of the war by other means.[22] In these ways Sinn Féin has increasingly become an adaptive party, merely representational of its social base as an interest group within the nationalist community. The concept of the universality of the nation, which was central to traditional republicanism, has been replaced by sectional, representational politics and a republicanism that speaks for a community rather than the nation as a whole and negotiates on behalf of its community with other communities within the transitional framework of the new dispensation.

These trends can be seen in the increasing localism and community focus of Sinn Féin politics. Sinn Féin spokespeople talk of the 'republican community' as a distinct entity; the movement's mandate is no longer defined in terms of the historic right of nations to self-determination or a justification of the democratic violence of the oppressed against the repressive forces of imperialism. Instead its mandate is based on a liberal democratic concept of electoral representation within Northern Ireland and defined within the framework laid down by the two governments and the concept of majority consent which had previously been defined as a unionist veto. These themes not only reflect neo-nationalist phraseology and an underlying conception of politics that is at variance with the explicitly revolutionary framework of 1980s republicanism; they mark a fundamental transformation in the ideological and analytical framework of Provisionalism which turns its former worldview on its head and marks a radical departure for politics in the nationalist community in particular and in Northern Ireland in general.

Although Sinn Féin claims a lineage dating back to 1905, in the most significant ideological and organizational respects it is a relatively recently developed party that meets many of the criteria of a neo-nationalist party structure and political shape. Before the 1980s Provisional Sinn Féin was considered by many republicans to be merely a support group for the main focus of republican activity – the armed campaign of the IRA. The 'long war' strategy assigned Sinn Féin a greater importance as a political force under IRA direction. However, the modern history of Sinn Féin as an electoral party does not really begin until the hunger strike in 1981 and the emergence of Sinn Féin as an electoral force within the nationalist community in local government, European and Westminster elections from 1983 onwards.

The significance of the electoral strategy lay not in the contesting of seats – Sinn Féin had done this in the 1950s and there had been a flirtation with electoral politics in the 1970s – but in the implications for the organizational shape and ideological direction of republican politics. The emerging forms of new nationalist parties are often of recent creation and are essentially contemporary in structure and organizational form, unencumbered by a strong party culture and organizational tradition. Many of these characteristics apply to the Sinn Féin party that was created almost anew during the 1980s and 1990s. Although originally rooted in the conspiratorialist organizational tradition, what might be styled New Sinn Féin has developed a significant degree of independence, with many of its new generation of activists coming from outside this militarist tradition. While certain aspects of the party's internal regime and organizational ethos reflect the militarist nature of its origins, the development of a new cohort of activists and middle-ranking leaders in the last twenty years means that in essence Sinn Féin is a new party. As such it is consciously creating itself and inventing a party tradition rooted in the initial interventions in electoral politics and the political successes of the 1990s.[23]

The 'newness' of new nationalist parties lies not only in their relatively recent origins and organizational form, but also in their enthusiastic embrace of postmodern and post-traditional political discourse and practice. Some theorists have argued that in contemporary Western societies, the traditional mass political parties with bureaucratic structures, clearly defined membership and hierarchical power relationships between leaders and followers may be dying. In their place, the argument continues, will appear new 'virtual' political parties with a looser structure constructed around an elite of professional politicians and activists with a large periphery of supporters; politics will be structured around these community networks and an increasingly post-ideological appeal to the electorate through the mass media.[24]

Some elements of these new politics can be discerned in New Sinn Féin. The social and economic terrain of Northern Irish society has many of the salient characteristics of Western post-industrial societies – the decline of traditional industry, a dominant state sector, and the emergence of new social groups as a product of these economic changes – which provide a fertile soil for the emergence of these new political organizational forms. One of Northern Ireland's political contradictions is to combine an 'old-fashioned', deeply ideological conflict with the newly emerging forms and party structures of contemporary post-ideological politics. The everyday organizational and political praxis of New Sinn Féin is the epitome of postmodern politics. Its skilful manipulation of the media, the importance of personalities at local and national level, the constant redefinition of its core ideology and its increasingly post-republican politics suggest an analogy with Tony Blair's New Labour. Although Sinn Féin carries the genetic code of its inheritance – and paradoxically the politics of the new departure blend well with some residual elements of the older militarist ethos – the balance has now tipped decisively towards the politics of new nationalism and its concomitant organizational forms.

Drawing on the extensive community networks and 'non-party' structures as a medium for political and social mobilization within both the traditional 'ghetto'-

based nationalist community and the newly emerging nationalist middle class, the New Sinn Féin party operates with almost a contemporary cadre party structure, which concentrates power at the centre in the hands of republican notables, drawing on both the acquired prestige of struggle and the militarist traditions of obedience to the orders of the leadership. In developing many of these characteristics of a contemporary new nationalist party, republicanism has made a Hegelian leap from a movement that in the early 1980s was almost pre-modern and loosely defined, to a party that embraces all of the techniques and structures of modern politics and is no longer overburdened with traditional ideology and organizational structures.

At a simple descriptive level, Sinn Féin does meet many of the defining criteria of Western European new nationalism; however, it is at a structural level that this analytical framework becomes most useful to our understanding of the trajectory and future pattern of republicanism. It is impossible to evaluate whether the republican leadership has genuinely embraced the values of liberal democracy that these new forms of nationalism embody; looking into the hearts of individuals to assess the significance and depth of a conversion is an activity best left to priests and psychologists. But the analytical tools of political science can help us to evaluate the external determinants that have shaped the republican movement's adoption of elements of new nationalism.

Perhaps the most significant factor in shaping the trajectory has been the relative success of British counter-insurgency and political initiatives, especially since the Anglo-Irish Agreement of 1985. The British policy of political and military containment has effectively placed militant republicanism on the defensive. The defining element of the movement's military-political strategy since the late 1970s has been an attempt to break out of this position by shifting the terrain and, in the 1980s, broadening the battlefield to include the electoral arena. The success of this conflict management and stabilization policy has meant that while republicanism could not be eliminated as a political-military factor, it remained sealed off politically and physically within its traditional base areas.

Wider patterns of socio-economic change and related areas of regime responsiveness in social and economic policy also provided an important context for political development. During the 1980s levels of public expenditure remained high in Northern Ireland in what could be described as Thatcherite Keynesianism. Former Northern Ireland industry minister Richard Needham described this industrial and economic policy as the third arm in the war against the IRA.[25] This Thatcherite Keynesianism can be explained as part of a strategy of containment and conflict management, with the aim of using economic and social change as instruments of political normalization.

One of the most striking features of these and related socio-economic developments has been the emergence of that Catholic middle class which has fuelled the new nationalism of rising expectations. As has been widely recognized, the growth of this middle-class constituency is significant in other ways for the emergence of republicanism as a new nationalist tendency in the European sense. It has strengthened the tendency towards institutionalization within republicanism, given the relationship between social mobility and political and community activism in nationalist areas in the North. This leadership group could also be said to be an organic part of the new Catholic middle class which in turn is itself a result of the growth of the state sector, white-collar and professional employment and relatively high levels of public expenditure in the North. This process of nationalist embourgeoisement has been recorded by Fionnuala O Connor in terms of a 'search for a state',[26] but it is a process that has had a wider impact on politics in the nationalist community as well as a direct reflection in the style, rhetoric and discourse of New Sinn Féin.

Containment strategies have also had an impact on the politics of lower income social groups. The 1980s and 1990s saw a whole series of publicly funded initiatives, such as the Peace and Reconciliation Fund, the European Social Fund and the New Deal, targeted at the unemployed and lower income groups. Given the hegemonic position of the republican movement within the communities targeted by these initiatives and the strength of republican community activism and local government representation, these state strategies have drawn republicans and their community intimately into the embrace of a state that they were once pledged to overthrow by force. These funding mechanisms and the development of a 'community' network provide an important socio-economic basis for the development of the structures of a coherent and self-confident civil society within the nationalist community in Northern Ireland, thus fulfilling one of the essential preconditions for neo-nationalist movements in Western societies. The West Belfast Festival, the growth of the Irish language and a host of community and educational-cultural activities within nationalist areas not only provide evidence of this emerging nationalist civil society as an agency of new nationalist mobilization but also illustrate the complex relationship between cultural and political nationalism.

It may be overstating the case to argue that high levels of public expenditure and the growth of the community sector have blunted the cutting edge of militant republicanism and channelled energies into localized cultural and community projects, but these factors certainly reinforce trends inherent in Sinn Féin's community politics and help establish the preconditions for the organizational institutionalization that has been so significant for the development of new nationalist parties in other areas of Western Europe.[27]

My underlying thesis is that the shifting discourses of republicanism do represent a seismic change and that to a great extent the movement has been constitutionalized. I have attempted to explore the extent and depth of this process by drawing on the comparative literature of other new nationalist movements and by assessing the emerging ideology and strategy of what can increasingly be defined as post-republicanism. The aspects of current Provisionalism that most closely correspond to the new nationalist model are the civic and representational elements of its politics; in its development of pluralistic concepts of identity and citizenship it has moved closer towards mainstream European nationalist politics. Likewise, in its deployment of a discourse of transition and dynamic change it has replaced the old teleological certainties of revolutionary struggle for the 32-county socialist republic with the deliberate ambiguity of an indefinite process driven by demographical determinism towards the less certain goal of 'an agreed Ireland'. In the party structure and political activity of Sinn Féin, the Provisional leadership has enthusiastically adopted some of the features of new nationalism as well as those of contemporary mainstream liberal democratic political parties.

While the Provisionals are clearly moving towards a post-republican position, it would not be entirely accurate at present to define them as a completely mainstream nationalist movement. New Sinn Féin clearly does exist in the persona, style and underlying ideological and strategic framework of the republican leadership, but contemporary republicanism is not monolithic, and its leadership still needs to pay attention both to elements within its coalition of activists and to the emerging contradictions between its traditional voters and its new middle-class constituency. The potential tensions within that coalition will still require a skilful balancing act. However, the main features of republican politics have been fixed by the acceptance of the Belfast Agreement, the participation in the Assembly and the Executive, and the opening up of the arms dumps to inspection. Taken together these stages represent a qualitative change in the direction and shape of the movement that has been emerging since the late 1980s and point towards the development of Sinn Féin as a constitutional nationalist party.

Despite republican confidence and the electoral advance of Sinn Féin into middle-class nationalist constituencies, it remains an open question whether Sinn Féin can overtake the SDLP as the largest nationalist party in Northern Ireland. In a sense the issue is irrelevant because as republicanism has attempted to shift its electoral base and move to a new nationalist position it has increasingly adapted itself to the politics of the SDLP. In seeking wider electoral support in competition with the SDLP it has fought on the political terrain of that party and has increasingly operated within the ideological framework established by John Hume since the 1970s. The politics of pan-nationalism mean that Sinn Féin has distinguished itself from the SDLP as simply the more effective, the more principled and the better organized wing of the new nationalist consensus. Even if Sinn Féin should emerge as the larger of the two parties it will only do so within the broad parameters laid down by the politics of the SDLP and the Belfast Agreement.

On a wider scale, the development of the republican movement since the mid-1980s often unexpectedly illustrates both the attractive power and the contradictory nature of the contemporary nationalist phenomenon. The Janus-like character of nationalism is now something of a cliché, but the evolution and transformation of Irish republicanism from revolutionary movement to party of government within a decade indicates the continuing value of such a description. The academic debate makes it clear that these new forms of nationalism can act as powerful mobilizing agents for a broad range of discontents and potential challenges to the political and social status quo. Irish republicanism has certainly had that function during its recent history. As Melucci has argued in relation to other social movements,

> The ethno-national question must be seen … as containing a plurality of meanings that cannot be reduced to a single core. It contains ethnic identity, which is a weapon of revenge against centuries of discrimination and new forms of exploitation: it serves as an instrument for applying pressure in the political market; and it is a response to the need for personal and collective identity in highly complex societies.[28]

However, the evolution of Irish republicanism indicates that this mobilization function can take different forms in different situations. An important determinant in the transformation of the movement was the ability of the British government and the structures of the state to define the situation and decisively shape the context in which the republican movement was operating.

As the peace process faced serious challenges in areas such as decommissioning and the future of policing in Northern Ireland, many observers believed that the republican leadership's response and continued adherence to its new departure marked the triumph of constitutional nationalism. Discussing the IRA offer to allow international observers to inspect its arms dumps in May 2000, Arthur Aughey believed that this unprecedented action represented the beginning of the end for militant republicanism; he argued that the republican movement had retained a capacity to use violence within democratic politics during the 1990s, but that now the republican leadership was clearly moving towards ending its war. The inspection of the arms dumps and the re-establishment of the political institutions of the Belfast Agreement thus marked significant steps in this choreography of republican transition.[29]

While the precise forms of that transition remain undecided, the general pattern is now reasonably clear. While Northern Ireland society remains structurally divided it will continue to provide the opportunities for nationalist political mobilization. The form and nature of that mobilization will be influenced by the structure of political opportunities, the organizational traditions and repertoires and the social networks and collective identities that have been created by the conflict of the past thirty years. However, looking back on the evolution of Provisional republicanism and the current state of nationalist politics it seems likely that these forces will be decisively post-republican and constitutional rather than revolutionary and republican in form. In this sense, the Sinn Féin ministers in the group photograph around the Cabinet table show not only the distance travelled, but also the main features of the road ahead for New Sinn Féin.

Select Bibliography

Bew, P., and G. Gillespie, *The Northern Ireland Peace Process 1993–1996: A Chronology* (London, 1996).

Gellner, E., *Nationalism* (London, 1997).

Mallie, E., and D. McKitterick, *The Fight for Peace: The Secret Story behind the Irish Peace Process* (London, 1996).

Nairn, T., *Faces of Nationalism* (London, 1997).

O'Brien, B., *The Long War: The IRA and Sinn Féin from Armed Struggle to Peace Talks* (Dublin, 1995).

Patterson, H., *The Politics of Illusion: A Political History of the IRA* (London, 1998).

Smith, A., *National Identity* (Harmondsworth, 1991).

Smith, M.L.R., *Fighting for Ireland: The Military Strategy of the Irish Republican Movement* (London, 1995).

Taylor, P., *Provos: The IRA and Sinn Féin* (London, 1998).

White, R.W., *Provisional Irish Republicans: An Oral and Interpretive History* (London, 1993).

Notes

1. This paper was first delivered as a lecture at the Institute of Irish Studies, University of Liverpool on 11 March 2000.
2. 'Ex-IRA leader attacks Adams', *Daily Telegraph*, 6 March 2000. I am grateful to Jill Callighan for drawing my attention to this article.
3. Jennifer Todd, 'Nationalism, Republicanism and the Good Friday Agreement', in J. Todd and J. Ruane (eds.), *After the Good Friday Agreement: Analysing Political Change in Northern Ireland* (Dublin, 1999).
4. Henry Patterson, 'Towards 2016', *Fourthwrite* (Spring 2000).
5. Conor Cruise O'Brien, *States of Ireland* (London, 1972).
6. Ernest Gellner, *Nations and Nationalism* (Oxford, 1983).
7. Benedict Anderson, *Imagined Communities: Reflections on the Origins and Spread of Nationalism* (London, 1983).
8. Eric Hobsbawm, *Nations and Nationalism since 1780: Programme, Myth and Reality* (Cambridge, 1990).
9. Tom Nairn, *Faces of Nationalism* (London, 1997).
10. John Breuilly, *Nationalism and the State* (Manchester, 1993).
11. David McCrone, *The Sociology of Nationalism* (London, 1998).
12. Tom Garvin, *Nationalist Revolutionaries in Ireland 1858–1928* (Oxford, 1987).
13. J. Bowyer Bell, *The Secret Army: The IRA* (Dublin, 1983).
14. Kevin Bean, *The New Departure: Recent Developments in Irish Republican Ideology and Strategy* (Liverpool, 1994).
15. Jocelyn Evans, Gerard Murray and Jonathan Tonge, 'Constitutional Nationalism and Socialism: The Greening of the SDLP', *British Elections and Parties Review* (2000). I am grateful to Dr Tonge and his colleagues for allowing me to see the results of their work prior to publication.
16. Tony Catney, 'Sinn Féin's Electoral Growth', *Fourthwrite* (Summer 2000).
17. Quoted in Liam Clarke and Michael Jones, 'Trimble shows more flexibility over IRA arms', *Sunday Times*, 28 March 1999.
18. *An Phoblacht*, 2 March 1995.
19. *An Phoblacht*, 2 March 1995.
20. Mitchel McLaughlin, 'The Republican Ideal', in Norman Porter (ed.), *The Republican Ideal: Current Perspectives* (Belfast, 1998), p. 81.
21. McLaughlin, 'The Republican Ideal', p. 76.
22. Anthony McIntyre, 'Gerry Adams, Keeping the Mutterers at Bay', *Parliamentary Brief*, 4(2) (November 1995).
23. Brian Kelly, 'The Invention of Republican Tradition', unpublished paper given at British Association for Irish Studies Conference, Bath 1996. I am grateful to Mr Kelly for allowing me to see his research on the development of republican tradition.
24. Peter Mair, 'Party Organisations: From Civil Society to the State', in Richard Katz and Peter Mair (eds), *How Parties Organise: Change and Adaption in Western Democracies* (London, 1994).
25. Richard Needham, *Battling for Peace* (Belfast, 1998).
26. Fionnuala O Connor, *In Search of a State* (Belfast, 1993).
27. Terry Robson, *The State and Community Action* (London, 2000). See also James Martin, 'The Third Sector', *Fortnight* (November 2000).
28. A. Melucci, *Nomads of the Present: Social Movements and Individual Needs in Contemporary Society* (London, 1989), p. 90.
29. Arthur Aughey, 'The beginning of the end', *The Observer*, 7 May 2000.

Margaret Thatcher and Garret Fitzgerald (above) signing the Anglo-Irish (Hillsborough) Agreement in November 1985. The Agreement introduced an 'Irish dimension' into the running of Northern Ireland, and the links between the Irish and UK governments that it fostered were important in subsequent negotiations. The Agreement bypassed the parties in Northern Ireland, since unionist objections to any negotiations with the Irish government were so strong, and protests against the Agreement were vociferous (below).

American involvement in the peace process exemplifies the importance of 'third parties' in negotiations that many contributors to this book emphasize. President Clinton visited Northern Ireland in 1995 (above), and made his commitment to the resolution of the conflict clear. The patience, tact, persistence and even-handedness of Senator George Mitchell (below) were vital in producing the Good Friday Agreement.

The peace walls in West Belfast separate Protestant and Catholic areas, usually at the request of the residents themselves, and often physically divide streets in apparently 'mixed' areas.

Cluan Place in East Belfast, 2007: a Protestant enclave separated from Catholic Short Strand by a peace wall (one of 11 in Belfast heightened and refortified since the Good Friday Agreement). There have been nine entirely new peace walls constructed in the same period.

The 'Yes' vote in the referendum in 1998 on whether to accept the Good Friday Agreement produced euphoric scenes in Northern Ireland (above).

First Minister Ian Paisley, Deputy First Minister Martin McGuinness, Prime Minister Tony Blair, Taoiseach Bertie Ahern and Secretary of State for Northern Ireland, Peter Hain, pictured after the establishment of the Northern Ireland Assembly in May 2007. Cooperation between the British and Irish governments and the political parties in Northern Ireland seemed finally to have established the region on the path towards normalization. (photo: Paul Faith/AP/PA Photos)

Conflict, Memory and Reconciliation

Paul Arthur

In a reflective article on the tenth anniversary of the release from Robben Island of President Nelson Mandela, the distinguished South African novelist, André Brink, recalls a sense of existential disorientation when he noted a blank wall in the airport building in Port Elizabeth announcing 'YOU ARE NOW HERE'. That was it: a blank wall, no map, no plan. It serves as a useful metaphor for a peace process. A certain amount of disorientation is inevitable, as is the roller coaster between hope and despair. For us the question is which one we 'would choose to define ourselves by: the moments of light or the dark intervals in between. Perhaps neither should be thinkable without the other. If humanity makes sense, it is not because it is capable of the best, or the worst, but of both.'[1]

Let that be our starting point. To start with a blank wall and the question 'where is here?' may be incredibly daunting; and 'we may not be yet,' as Brink asserts, 'where we'd like to be, but at least we are no longer "there" any more. Most importantly, we seem to be on our way "somewhere".' Drawing on the small cell which Mandela occupied for 18 of his 27 years in prison, Brink concludes: 'Our peculiar cell may yet expand to the dimensions of a larger and more human world.' This paper is concerned with such a journey, with the larger issues of time and space rather than more practical concerns of the modalities entailed in conflict transformation.

There

One of the characteristics of an intense conflict is the growth of a cottage industry in navel-gazing. The assumption is that 'our' conflict is unique; that we have nothing to learn from elsewhere; and that indeed the rest of the world is as consumed with our quarrel as we are ourselves. It is incestuous and dangerously static. The Irish poet Louis MacNeice employs a useful metaphor: 'bottled time turns sour upon the sill'.[2] In the Middle East, in Eastern Europe and in Central America I have encountered a similar mindset: a selective obsession with the past, a narrow insularity about the present, and no proper concern with the future. The Czech novelist Milan Kundera captured its essence in *Slowness*: 'the source of fear is in the future, and a person freed of the future has nothing to fear.'[3] Those who are engaged in peace processes know that they have to confront the future. Senator George Mitchell recognized as much in his original Report on Decommissioning. In para. 16 he wrote that 'if the focus remains in the past, the past will become the future, and that is something no one can desire'. So when we speak of 'there' we are thinking less about place and more about space in a temporal and emotional sense. We are acknowledging the baleful role of 'victimhood', which Robert Elias has defined as 'the political economy of helplessness'.[4]

At the most prosaic level we speak of a tiny landmass situated on the northwestern periphery of Europe where the next parish is Boston. It forms, of course, part of a larger island which the French writer Jean Blanchard dismissed as 'une île derrière une île'.[5] In some ways Northern Ireland might act as the model for the optimum size of a political unit. When Prime Minister Harold Wilson established a Royal Commission on the Constitution in the late 1960s the Commissioners took evidence in Northern Ireland. One expert witness gave his definition of the size of a working democracy: the unit, he said, must be small enough for an irate farmer to travel by public transport from the most remote part of the territory to the centre of power, horsewhip the miscreant responsible for official policy and return home before night. Smallness creates its own intimacy and its own perspective. In his (suitably entitled) *Epic*, Patrick Kavanagh describes a dispute between two small farmers. The year was 1939, significant in global terms but not to the inhabitants of this particular locality:

> I have lived in important places, times
> When great events were decided, who owned
> That half a rood of rock, a no-man's land
> Surrounded by our pitchfork-armed claims.
> I heard the Duffys shouting 'Damn your soul'
> And old McCabe stripped to the waist, seen
> Step the plot defying blue-cast steel
> 'Here is the march along these iron stones'.
> That was the year of the Munich bother. Which
> Was more important? I inclined
> To lose my faith in Ballyrush and Gortin
> Till Homer's Ghost came whispering to my mind.
> He said: I made the *Iliad* from such
> A local row. Gods make their own importance.[6]

Admittedly Northern Ireland is larger than, say, Delaware or Rhode Island, but on the world stage it might be argued that little has been heard of the former since it became the first member of the Union (or perhaps since the Civil War when the Du Pont family was producing more than half of all the gunpowder in the United States); nor of the latter since the seventeenth century when Roger Williams imported the notion of true religious freedom. In recent decades Northern Ireland has made its own importance – an importance grounded in political violence.

It has to be said that we operated under an intimidatory political culture long before the recent 'Troubles' became a reality. Towards the end of the nineteenth century an Irish nationalist MP stated that 'violence was the only way of securing a hearing for moderation'.[7] In his comparative analysis Frank Wright comments that in place of what 'metropolitans call peace' Northern Ireland enjoyed at best 'a tranquillity of communal deterrence'.[8] This view is complemented in John Darby's longitudinal study of political violence in the North of Ireland. Darby depicts a polity in which 'the power of intimidation springs from its essentially defensive nature. Local minorities were driven by violence and fear to move to other communities in which they could become part of a majority. They were often willing to encourage the expulsion of ethnic opponents from their new community'.[9] But despite the mayhem the picture is not totally bleak, in that his research indicates that Northern Ireland's conflict is 'remarkable for the limitations on its violence rather than for the violence itself'.[10] That condition produced a paradox that was to be a constraint on mediation. Violence neither reached genocidal levels nor was it sustained enough to induce compromise: 'there has been no resolution because the violence has not been intolerable. By whatever calculus communities compute their interests, the price of compromise is still thought to be greater than the cost of violence.'[11] Later we will need to examine the reasons for the changing calculus.

Given the sad, turbulent history of Ireland, violent acts were revisited after 1969 that were (according to J. Bowyer Bell) 'so natural as to be beyond comment ... [A]ll that was needed was to exploit the existing reality.'[12] Our auditors of violence classified this 'importance' in 1993: 'This small but deeply divided population has generated the most intense political violence of any part of the contemporary UK, the highest levels of internal political violence of any member-state of the European Community, and the highest levels of internal political violence in the continuously liberal democratic states of the post-1948 world.' They went on to make comparisons with other parts of the world: 'If the equivalent ratio of victims to population had been produced in Great Britain in the same period some 100,000 people would have died, and if a similar level of political violence had taken place the number of fatalities in the USA would have been over 500,000, or about ten times the number of Americans killed in the Vietnam war.'[13] They concluded with the devastating remark that our record is not quite so bad as that of the Lebanon; being 'second to the Lebanon' is an unenviable classification.[14]

Those figures might be said to represent the darkness in between the light. They could be countered by another bald fact: this tiny piece of earth, this 'narrow ground', has produced no less than five Nobel laureates in the past 25 years: the Peace People (Mairead Corrigan and Betty Williams) in 1976, Seamus Heaney in 1995, and John Hume and David Trimble in 1998. I want to spend a little time examining this phenomenon because we may be faced with a conundrum: how do we explain so much violence and so many peacemakers? How do we explain the fact that Corrigan and Williams were recognized by the Nobel Peace Institute at the height of political violence; that the movement they led had a more spiritual than secular dimension; that it was briefly in the political firmament and that it could be more easily compared to a shooting star that blazes across the skyline only to burn itself out? We might ask, too, whether a literature laureate belongs in this particular pantheon? And we might query (gently, respectfully) whether John Hume and David Trimble – permanent fixtures in that violent maelstrom of the past three decades – are truly worthy of the award? My instant reply to the latter is that indubitably they deserve their recognition but that it has to be seen in the context of conflict transformation. In other words we are concerned with the temporal and with how we got from 'there' to 'here' in our search for that visionary 'somewhere'. Ultimately we are concerned with 'transcendence'.

'There' has the timeless quality of any intense conflict. I always fall back on an aphorism from another Nobel laureate, Czeslaw Milosz: 'It is possible there is no other memory than the memory of wounds.'[15] That is one of the more profound statements about the condition of victimhood. It calls into play the concept of the 'long war' and a tradition of martyrology. It was part of Irish republican theology, encapsulated in the words of the hunger striker, Terence MacSwiney, in 1920: 'it is not those who inflict the most but those who suffer the most who will conquer.'[16] There can be perfectly understandable reasons why people insist on remembering. It is a way of avoiding oblivion. A Guatemalan human rights activist provides one reason: 'The war created fear, a lack of communication, a lack of confidence, an inability to resolve conflicts. You can't reconcile with the living if you can't reconcile with the dead.'[17] The inmates of Majdanek concentration camp produce another: 'Should our murderers be victorious, should they write the history of this war ... their every word will be taken for gospel. Or they might wipe out our memory altogether, as if we had never existed ... But if we write the history of the period ... we'll have the thankless job of proving to a reluctant world that we are Abel, the murdered brother.'[18] It is also the case that the question 'should we remember?' is 'usually asked by people who have a choice. For many ... there is no choice about remembering ... [it] is not an option, it is a daily torture, a voice inside the head that has no on/off switch and no volume control.'[19]

But if we are in the business of conflict transformation we need to make the distinction between individual and communal suffering on the one hand, and the appropriation of historical trauma for political purposes on the other. The latter is explored by Ian Buruma, who asserts that it 'becomes questionable when a cultural, ethnic, religious, or national community bases its communal identity almost entirely on the sentimental solidarity of remembered victimhood. For that way lies historical myopia and, in extreme circumstances, even vendetta.' A similar view is expressed by the distinguished French jurist, Roger Errera: 'One of the sound foundations of a political society is a true knowledge of its past ... But the affirmation of the rights of memory does not mean that the past must become the only, or the main, value.'[20] I would contend that one of the reasons why we have moved from 'there' to 'here' is that we have been prepared to move beyond memory (as a negative motivation) to acknowledgment (as a form of catharsis). I would go further: our peace process is not solely the property of those who have been rightfully honoured, but belongs to the wider community – to the grass roots, including former combatants, to the diaspora, to the poets, to the transcenders. While there is some merit in the theoretical literature, in the concepts of hurting stalemates and ripe moments, we ignore at our peril the quiet attitudinal changes being nurtured in the undergrowth. Unquestioningly political leadership has a primary role to play in transforming a conflict, in building up trust and credibility, but at the end of the day there has to be a sense of ownership.

Here

A peace agreement is merely one element of a larger peace process, an element that may create some new opportunities but hardly alters all aspects of the conflict. One thing that is imperative is to establish realistic expectations about how much and how quickly a weak and tentative peace agreement can alter the basic nature of a long and profoundly bitter conflict. It is also very important for the leaders on both sides to recognize that the game has changed, that the behaviour necessary to get to a provisional agreement is not always the behaviour appropriate for the post-agreement period: needs and priorities change, interests must be redefined and revisioned, and a joint learning process must be institutionalized and accelerated.

'Here' is the Agreement signed on Good Friday 1998. The fact that it is described under different nomenclatures – the Good Friday Agreement, the Belfast Agreement, or the Agreement reached in the Multi-Party Negotiations, to give it its correct title – is indicative of the necessity for an accelerated joint learning process. If we examine the lifespan of a conflict we can detect three phases: analysis, negotiation and implementation, not all of them totally autonomous. Analysis takes many shapes and forms. It can be part of the normal thrust of political discourse; of informed commentary in the media and academia; in exercises in Track Two diplomacy; in our capacity to tell stories one to each other.

I want to linger on that last point for a few moments. Telling stories, creating narratives, is non-threatening. It can be done in a structured manner as it was in South Africa in what was called the Mont Fleur Project. Pierre Wack suggests that that project was about 'the gentle art of reperceiving'. It was about establishing networks and understandings and ultimately changing hardened opinions. It was about communication.

Communication entails recognition of the other, and 'the awareness of being separate and different from and strange to one another' opens up potentials of creative search for dialogue and for understanding the other. This is also the essence of negotiations. Reaching common ground is not necessarily a product of similar opinions. Lack of communication, lack of dialogue, can lead us to having a wrong cognitive framework 'which is what happens if you prematurely close in on an understanding. There are no correct understandings but there are very bad ones' (Sasson Sofer quoting Z.D. Gurevitch).[21] I would suggest that one of the reasons we were so slow in reaching the negotiation stage was that we were operating under wrong cognitive frameworks – we were not even agreed on the nature of the problem, hence we could not begin to address the elements of a solution.

I want to illustrate this point about the power of dialogue and communication by quoting from one of our Nobel laureates. Seamus Heaney entitled his 1995 Nobel lecture 'Crediting Poetry'. In it he mused on the fact that only

> the very stupid or the very deprived can any longer help knowing that the documents of civilization have been written in blood and tears, blood and tears no less real for being very remote. And when this intellectual predisposition coexists with the actualities of Ulster and Israel and Bosnia and Rwanda and a host of other wounded spots on the face of the earth, the inclination is not only not to credit human nature with much constructive potential but not to credit anything too positive in the work of art.[22]

He was reflecting on Brink's 'dark intervals in between … the moments of light'; or on Edith Wyschogrod's portrayal of the twentieth century as 'the century of man-made mass death'.[23] A death-world manifests itself in the slaughter of the

Great War, which created a postmodern culture of mass death, of necropolis, of impersonality, of the slave labour and concentration camps, of 'the Red Guards in the Cultural Revolution [who] set out to destroy the four olds: old ideas, old culture, old customs and old habits'. Whither the role of the artist in this bleak environment? 'Which is why for years I was bowed to the desk like some monk bowed over his prie-dieu, some dutiful contemplative pivoting his understanding in an attempt to bear his portion of the weight of the world, knowing himself incapable of heroic virtue, but constrained by his obedience to his rule to repeat the effort and the posture. Blowing up sparks for a meagre heat. Forgetting faith, straining towards good works.' Nevertheless he believes that 'art can rise to the occasion'.[24]

Heaney employed his art in this lecture to tell a story based on one of the most harrowing events in our conflict. He recounts what was known as the Kingsmills' massacre of January 1976 when eleven workmen were held at gunpoint on a lonely stretch of the road on their way home. One of the masked executioners demanded that if there were any Catholics among them they were to step out of line. There was only one Catholic and the assumption was that this was a loyalist gang. Heaney continues:

> It was a terrible moment for him, caught between dread and witness, but he did make a motion to step forward. Then, the story goes, in that split second of decision, and in the relative cover of the winter evening darkness, he felt the hand of the Protestant worker next to him take his hand and squeeze it in a signal that said no, don't move, we'll not betray you, nobody needs to know what faith or party you belong to. All in vain, however, for the man stepped out of the line; but instead of finding a gun at his temple, he was pushed away as the gunmen opened fire on those remaining in the line, for these were not Protestant terrorists, but members, presumably, of the Provisional IRA.[25]

Having told this story the poet reflected that it 'is difficult at times to repress the thought that history is about as instructive as an abattoir; that Tacitus was right and that peace is merely the desolation left behind after the decisive operations'.[26] But this dread thought is followed with a moment of light: 'The birth of the future we desire is surely in the contraction which that terrified Catholic felt on the roadside when another hand gripped his hand, not in the gunfire that followed so absolute and so desolate, if also so much a part of the music of what happens.'[27]

I have dwelt on the telling of this particular story for so long because it is significant. Heaney was describing an act of transcendence which can take many forms: an act, a narrative, a person. Its importance lies in the definition provided by Byron Bland: 'connecting what violence has severed'.[28] This particular incident was important in its own right – one of the unnoticed acts of heroism by those who don't make history – and in its telling in the sumptuous surroundings of the Nobel Prize ceremony. Its sentiment was reinforced three years later when in the Oslo Radhus John Hume said: 'I think that David Trimble would agree that this Nobel prize for peace is in the deepest sense a powerful recognition of the compassion and humanity of all the people we represent between us ... Endlessly our people gathered their strength to face another day and they never stopped encouraging their leaders to find the courage [to] resolve this situation so that our children could look to the future with a smile of hope.' One can take examples from other conflicts. Mozambique, at one time listed as the poorest country in the world by the UN, underwent a civil war lasting fifteen years and claiming over one million lives. Yet the anthropologist Carolyn Nordstrom depicts an ethic behind a culture of peace constructed across the wastelands of war: 'Average Mozambicans configured peace as an act of resistance against violence. In delegitimizing violence, people reconstructed a new political culture, one that delegitimized the politics of force.'[29]

It would be foolish to place too much weight on the role of the average person in conflict transformation. I have emphasized it because it seems to me that it has been underplayed. The high politics are much better known because they are in the public domain. One can easily list the landmarks on the road to the 1998 Agreement: a statement by President Jimmy Carter in August 1977; the burgeoning Anglo-Irish diplomatic relationship from 1980 culminating in the signing of the Anglo-Irish Agreement in November 1985; talks between the SDLP and Sinn Féin in 1988, and between an emissary of the British government and a republican representative in 1990–93; the Brooke and Mayhew talks; the Downing Street Declaration; the Framework Document and finally the Agreement itself. Indeed one can examine virtually every Green and White Paper emanating from the British government since 1972 and find elements of them in the final Agreement.

Equally homage has been paid to the exogenous factors: the collapse of the Berlin Wall; the demise of communism as an aggressive ideology in geopolitics; the end of apartheid and South Africa's removal from pariah status; the Oslo Accord; the role of the Clinton presidency. All of these freed republican and loyalist paramilitaries to reassess their old modes of thinking and to learn from peace processes elsewhere. One could mention, too, the place of Track Two diplomacy and suggest that conventional diplomacy may have less to offer than heretofore imagined. For example, the United States Advisory Commission on Public Diplomacy has commented on the effects of the information revolution at a time when the number of societies in transition is unprecedented and where the globalization of issues 'is blurring the separation of foreign affairs and domestic politics'. This calls for the practice of a new kind of diplomacy, such that 'policies and negotiated agreements will succeed only if they have the support of publics at home and abroad'. The Commission borrowed Joe Nye's concept of 'soft power': the 'ability to set the agenda in ways that shape the preferences of others', which 'strengthens American diplomacy through attraction rather than coercion'. Soft power was invoked in Northern Ireland in ways that worked outside the parameters of formal, conventional diplomacy. It appealed beyond the levels of the paramilitaries and the political elite to the wider public at a crucial phase of the process, somewhere between negotiation and implementation, when the public was invited to slough off its historic fatalism and to become proactive in the search for peace. It was yet another indication of the demotic nature of Northern Ireland's political culture whereby political leaders had been unduly influenced by their more extreme supporters to follow an intransigent agenda. The Agreement had an inversionary effect in that the demos ceased being fatalistic and began to urge politicians to work for peace. Beyond American diplomacy we could mention the significance of the European Union and of eminent persons such as Senator George Mitchell and General John de Chastelain, as well as that of NGOs. External actors can have a role to play in depoliticizing extremely contentious issues and can be an enormous asset in assisting countries making the transition out of conflict. The Commission asserts that in 'many ways they can do things better than government. They foster a flexible style that encourages innovation ... They offer the world a winning combination of ... professional skills, a wealth of experience, fresh perspectives, and enormous good will.'[30]

Somewhere

André Brink has reflected on the exhilaration of the first free elections in South Africa in April 1994. They might have been, he says,

> a moment so brief and bright that it appeared all too easy afterwards to discount it as an illusion. But in the long course of history, there are the defining instants in the wind we live by. Without them we must flounder. They keep us going, the dreams that ultimately justify the effort and disillusionment leading to the renewed dedication without which human progress is unthinkable. Those of us who stood in the long queues of that April day to perform the simplest of actions imaginable – drawing a cross on a square – will never forget the exhilaration in what the writer Njabulo Ndebele has called the rediscovery of the ordinary. Nothing could have been more momentous than discovering that all of us, rich or poor, black or white or anything in between, business executive or street sweeper, student or prostitute, were ultimately involved in, and defined by, this part of Africa.[31]

This paper has been more concerned in describing the human condition than in presenting a manual on the modalities of conflict transformation. Each conflict and its resolution creates its own rules. In Ireland the emphasis has been on inclusion, on politics as process rather than zero-sum game and on a proper sense of timescales. As early as 1992 the Sinn Féin strategist Jim Gibney argued that 'a British departure must be preceded by a sustained period of peace and will arise out of negotiation'.[32] In 1995 John Hume spoke of 'the real healing process [which] will take place and in a generation or two a new Ireland will evolve'.[33] I want to close with some considerations on this healing process because in many respects the most difficult phase is that of implementation.

Inherent in a healing process is a capacity to deal with the past, and with the actions of 'spoilers' in the present. We need look no further back than August 1998 and the grotesque tragedy of the Omagh bomb and another 28 lost lives. It was President Clinton on his visit to Omagh on 3 September 1998 who remarked: 'By killing Catholics and Protestants, young and old, men, women and children, even those about to be born, people from Northern Ireland, the Irish Republic and abroad – by doing all that in the aftermath of what the people had voted for in Northern Ireland, it galvanized, strengthened and humanized the impulse to peace.' There have been too many Omaghs. The wounds are raw and deep, the memories scarred and traumatized. But we have to come to terms with all of this. The 1998 Agreement was a start. Besides embracing institutional change it gave implicit recognition to attitudinal change through its comments on rights, on decommissioning, on policing and justice, on prisoners, and on validation. It is explicit when it addresses reconciliation: 'it is essential to acknowledge and address the suffering of the victims of violence as a necessary element of reconciliation ... It is recognized that victims have a right to remember as well as to contribute to a changed society ... An essential aspect of the reconciliation process is the promotion of a culture of tolerance at every level of society ... '.

Our primary task is to establish a culture of tolerance. We have begun. BBC Northern Ireland ran a two-minute radio programme, 'Legacy', every morning for a year in which victims told their stories. It was a powerful indictment of our past and an endorsement of the centrality of narrative. Another has been a monumental tome from four local journalists. The title speaks for itself: *Lost Lives: The Stories of the Men, Women and Children Who Died as a Result of the Northern Ireland Troubles*. In their introduction the authors state that they hope that 'anyone tempted to think of resorting to violence will find in these pages more than 3,600 reasons to think again'. There are other examples. But the wider crucial point has been made by *The Economist* (1 November 1997):

> In their efforts to deal with the past, new democracies have given victims their chance to speak. Wrongs have been exposed. A few culprits have been punished. These are considerable achievements. And by investigating the sins of the former regimes, the new governments have invited their own people to judge them by a higher standard of behaviour. This is the most important achievement of all. The trials and truth commissions of recent years have not really been about the past. Rather, and rather more sensibly, they have been about building a future in which the rule of law prevails, especially over the rulers themselves.

That can be our starting point on the road to 'somewhere'. But we need to move cautiously. In his paper 'Impunity, Reparation and Reconciliation in Latin America' Michael Foley reminds us that it is unseemly 'for anyone to demand of the victims of violence that they forgive. It is reasonable,' he argues, 'and much more respectful, to insist that conditions be created in which it is possible to forgive, to heal, but above all to reclaim one's human dignity.'[34] The South Africans may have shown the way with their Truth and Reconciliation Commission. Brink considers the exercise to be flawed, perhaps even a failure: 'Yet any comparison with situations elsewhere in the world, where a transition has been attempted without such a process, brings to light the profound need for it. Perhaps failure or success is not even important; the test is the "will" to move towards truth, and towards reconciliation.'

Notes

1. André Brink, in *The Observer Magazine*, 13 February 2000, pp. 24–5.
2. Louis MacNeice, 'Ode' (1934) from *Collected Poems* (London: Faber & Faber, 1989), p. 56.
3. Milan Kundera, *Slowness* (London: Faber & Faber, 1996), p. 4.
4. Cited in Padraig O'Malley, *Biting at the Grave: The Irish Hunger Strikes and the Politics of Despair* (Belfast: Blackstaff Press, 1990), p. 19.

5. Cited in Basil Chubb, *The Government and Politics of Ireland* (London: Oxford University Press, 1970), p. 46.
6. *The Bell* (Nov. 1951).
7. Conor Cruise O'Brien, *Parnell and his Party 1880–90* (Oxford: Clarendon Press, 1957), p. 69.
8. Frank Wright, *Northern Ireland: A Comparative Analysis* (Dublin: Gill and Macmillan, 1987), p. xiii.
9. John Darby, *Intimidation and the Control of Conflict in Northern Ireland* (Dublin: Gill and Macmillan, 1986), pp. viii–ix.
10. Darby, *Intimidation*, p. 10.
11. Darby, *Intimidation*, p. 30.
12. Darby, *Intimidation*, p. ix.
13. Brendan O'Leary and John McGarry, *The Politics of Antagonism: Understanding Northern Ireland* (London: The Athlone Press, 1993), p. 12.
14. O'Leary and McGarry, *The Politics of Antagonism*, p. 16.
15. This comment comes from Czeslaw Milosz's Nobel lecture, 8 December 1980.
16. Terence MacSwiney, *Principles of Freedom* (Dublin: Talbot, 1921), p. 26.
17. Peter Canby, 'The Truth about Rigoberta Menchu', *New York Review of Books*, 8 April 1999, p. 248.
18. Edith Wyschogrod, *Spirit in Ashes: Hegel, Heidegger and Man-Made Mass Death* (New Haven: Yale University Press, 1983), p. 126.
19. Marie Smyth, 'Remembering in Northern Ireland: Victims, Perpetrators and Hierarchies of Pain and Responsibility', in Brandon Hamber (ed.), *Past Imperfect: Dealing with the Past in Northern Ireland and Societies in Transition* (Derry: INCORE, 1998), p. 47.
20. Roger Errera, 'Memory, History and Justice in Divided Societies: The Unfinished Dialogue between Mnemosyne and Clio', paper read at a conference on Constitution-Making, Conflict and Transition in Divided Societies (Bellagio, Italy, 1999), p. 16.
21. Sasson Sofer, 'The Diplomat as a Stranger', *Diplomacy and Statecraft*, 8.3 (1997), p. 53.
22. Seamus Heaney, *Opened Ground: Poems 1966–1996* (London: Faber & Faber, 1998), pp. 457–8.
23. Wyschogrod, *Spirit in Ashes*, passim.
24. Wyschogrod, *Spirit in Ashes*, p. 139.
25. Heaney, *Opened Ground*, p. 458.
26. Heaney, *Opened Ground*, p. 456.
27. Heaney, *Opened Ground*, p. 457.
28. Byron Bland, *Marching and Rising: The Rituals of Small Differences and Great Violence in Northern Ireland* (Stanford, CA: Center for International Security and Arms Control, Stanford University, 1996), pp. 10–11.
29. Carolyn Nordstrom, 'Memory, Forgiveness and Reconciliation: Confronting the Violence of History', paper read at the University of Ulster at Magee, Derry, 24 April 1999, p. 7.
30. United States Advisory Commission on Public Diplomacy, *A New Diplomacy for the Information Age* (Washington, DC, 1996), pp. 3–5.
31. Brink, in *The Observer Magazine*, 13 February 2000, p. 25.
32. Cited in Tim Pat Coogan, *The Troubles: Ireland's Ordeal 1966–1995 and the Search for Peace* (London: Hutchinson, 1995), p. 339.
33. Paul Arthur, 'Time, Territory, Tradition and the Anglo-Irish "Peace" Process', *Government and Opposition*, 31.4 (1996), p. 426.
34. Michael Foley, 'Impunity, Reparation and Reconciliation in Latin America', unpublished paper (Derry: University of Ulster, 1999), p. 23.

Keeping Going: Beyond Good Friday

Harvey Cox

Drumcree tl, par, Armagh
Townland is 4 kms NNW of Portadown town centre
Droim Cri 'boundary ridge' … The boundary in question may be the nearby Upper Bann which borders the parish on the east and at an earlier period separated the territories of Clann Bhreasail and Clann Chana … The C of I church marks the site of the medieval parish church.[1]

A bright afternoon in early spring, almost a year after the Good Friday Agreement; we are being plied with tea and explanation just off the Garvaghy road. As it happens, the first of the year's Orange parades to Drumcree church is scheduled for this day. It will not pass up or down the Garvaghy road, and there will be no trouble. But this afternoon the Garvaghy residents feel penned into their little group of estates. They will not leave by the top, or country end, for there lies Dumcree and in any case it is the long way round to town. But they say they are reluctant to leave also by the lower end. The town centre lies across the railway and the Northway bypass. It is hostile territory, and their faces, especially those of the young men, are known. Some time ago a woman, in labour, had to be taken to hospital by a circuitous route because the direct ones were impassable due to the political situation. She lost the baby. On days like this, the residents tell us, they feel a sense of being besieged. There are many days when they feel like this. But they wish to emphasize that this is only the latest phase in a long siege. The Catholics of Portadown have felt ghettoized on the western edge of their own town ever since they settled long ago in 'the tunnel', the Obins Street area, across the tracks from the main part of town.[2] A recent compendium on world conflict situations describes Portadown as 'mixed'.[3] This is demographically true but socially misleading. It is a Protestant town with a Catholic appendix. A grumbling one.

Later, at Drumcree, Harold Gracey of the Portadown Orange Order is in his caravan beside the church. A notice says he has been there for 253 days. He is there to uphold the right of Orangemen to walk to and from the church, via the main road, as they have done for about two hundred years, long before there were housing estates on it. He says they would talk to the Garvaghy residents, but not while they insist on having as a principal spokesman someone who has been charged with a bombing offence in the town. They have offered various compromises, but they cannot compromise on the basic right to walk. Nonetheless, in the summer of 1999, they do not walk. The security forces, the RUC and the British Army, prevent it. All the Orangemen can do is protest with whatever dignity they can muster. They have reserves of dignity; but they cannot control everyone whom their protest attracts.

A stone by the River Bann commemorates the drowning of the Protestants there by the Catholics in 1641. Later that summer, Seagoe churchyard on the Protestant side of the river is bright with flowers; and little Ulster flags, planted on many of the more recent graves. Loyalism is not just for life.

Oh God, oh Portadown!

Outsiders are prone to being misled as to what the Northern Ireland conflict is about (and this is likely to be true of all such conflicts) by a tendency to perceive it as it is so often depicted in the news bulletins. These regularly use, as a locating symbol, a map. Viewers are thus introduced to a Northern Ireland topic by an image of the territory as a whole, as if seen from way above. This implies that Northern Ireland is one relatively undifferentiated territory with one basic conflict going on in it. But what is going on in Portadown is not *simply* a facet of the Ulster conflict. The conflict in Portadown is a conflict *about* Portadown.

In one of those studies that has done more than most to vindicate political science as an activity, John Whyte's *Interpreting Northern Ireland*, the author remarks on the great difficulties facing any attempt to reach general conclusions as to what is the essence of conflict. One clue, he argues, is that 'small though Northern Ireland is, it contains a great variety of situations within it. There are places like south Armagh, which are defiantly nationalist. There are places like north Down, which are happily unionist. There are places ... where unionist and nationalist intermingle, but without the bitterness that is to be found in some other areas.' And, he adds, there are places with every conceivable variety of situation in between.[4]

This self-evident truism has implications for the prospects of building a sustainable peace. For, however much party leaders may have been induced into accommodationist modes by the re-setting (in 1985) of the conflict in a pan-British-Irish context, by whatever mixture of international peace brokering, including the lure and pressure of the American presidency, and their own appraisal of the longer-term interests of their political community, Portadown remains its own place. So too South Armagh will long remain what Toby Harnden terms 'a borderland where strangers fear to tread, a quarrel not just with British rule but with authority per se';[5] the Bogside will carry the sores of Bloody Sunday interminably forward as an indelible part of its identity, and so on.

In the Good Friday Agreement, a new structure of political relationships in Ireland was negotiated by the political leaderships of Irish nationalism and republicanism, the moderate centre, and slightly over half of unionism. Certain issues, notably decommissioning and policing, were left to the future, by careful ambiguity in the one case, and the promise of a commission of enquiry on the other. Nobody could underestimate the huge, potentially crippling, significance of these issues. But equally, an enormous step had been taken to put an overarching political structure in place, guaranteed by the two sovereign governments of the islands and subsequently legitimated by referenda throughout Ireland. The strength of the Good Friday Agreement lies in the commitment of the two governments to its provisions, and in the discernment of most of the people of Northern Ireland that its failure would only be prelude to a long, and quite possibly violent, pause before it would be reconstructed once again on broadly similar lines. Seamus Mallon had this in mind when he famously called Good Friday 'Sunningdale for slow learners', reminding everyone of what had been lost when Sunningdale went down in May 1974.

But Good Friday also had its weaknesses. The unionist community only endorsed it, at the May 1998 referendum, by around 52 per cent. And, arguably, almost everything that happened in Northern Ireland, politically, for the next three years served to put that endorsement under more threat. Collapse cannot even yet, at the time of writing, be ruled out. Yet, despite a series of crises, over parades, policing, prisoner releases and decommissioning, what remained most notable three years on was that the peace process, and its settlement, was still in being, the Executive was in place, and a process of slow bedding in was under way, albeit too slowly for some and too rapidly for others. Even Drumcree 2000 'passed off' with only limited tension. Nonetheless, it had been, and would almost certainly continue to be, a rough ride. Drumcree, and the Portadown situation in general, continued to give its annual notice to the world outside that, whatever top negotiators might agree, the realities are experienced at neighbourhood level, and where these were intractable before, so they remain.

There is now a considerable and growing body of research on peace processes, drawing on experience of many conflicts. As Miall et al. observe in their survey of this work, *Contemporary Conflict Resolution*, 'Peace processes ... are a complex succession of transformations, punctuated by several turning points and sticking points.'[6] Even when settlements are reached, the best engineered political arrangements can collapse later, unless the post-settlement phase is devoted to continuing efforts to secure the foundations of peace. As they see it, there are two basic post-settlement tasks. First, simply to prevent a relapse into war; second, to create a self-sustaining peace. The first step is to take a cold bath of realism and recognize that the settlement, in the form of a political agreement, has been arrived at not as an old-fashioned peace treaty of the sort that used to wind up a war, nor as a great act of peace and reconciliation, but as a means whereby the contending parties have agreed in the first instance to *continue* their conflict by political, i.e. non-military, means. They have done so because of a mutual recognition that the continuance of violence has been hurting both and promising victory to neither. What the settlement is about, in Miall al.'s vivid phrase, is 'Clausewitz in reverse'. Clausewitz, it will be remembered, is famously misquoted as defining war as 'the continuation of politics by other means'. Reversed, this describes a state of political discourse in which contending parties continue to be in a state of earnest struggle, but have agreed, each for their own reasons, to pursue this by non-military means.

At the very least, interpreting things this way serves as an antidote to facile optimism – and to undue pessimism when setbacks occur. These should only be expected. But it also serves as a reminder of what remains to be done. Clearly, the peace process has been and will continue to be hazard to the pressures upon the leaders of unionism and nationalism from those in their camps further away from the negotiating table. The Dutch political scientist Arend Lijphart, in his often cited and pioneering work on consociational (i.e. power-sharing) democracy, noted that one of the most important conditions for the success of such a democracy is that leaders need to be able to retain the support and loyalty of their followers and carry them along, despite being more tolerant and/or compromise-oriented than they. Lijphart explains that by 'followers' he 'does not refer primarily to the mass public, which tends to be rather passive and apolitical almost everywhere, and therefore does not present a great danger to the possibilities of elite accommodation, but refers more specifically to the middle level group that can be described as sub-elite political activists'.[7]

Like Tolstoy's unhappy families, each situation of political conflict is unhappy in its own way; and thus the application to Northern Ireland *specifically* of theory derived from the *general* study of conflict bears its own problems of interpretation. Unionism, for example, is divided. Not since the early 1960s could any Ulster Unionist leader realistically claim to speak for the whole unionist community; nor could we realistically describe non-Agreement unionists as 'followers' of the unionist leadership. On the contrary, a critical problem for the Agreement and post-settlement peacemaking is the relative leaderlessness of unionism. (By contrast, republicanism *appears* impressively cohesive.)

Be that as it may, the prospects of a long-term bedding down of the settlement into a permanent condition of peace – at least in the sense of a level of conflict that is non-lethal and can be lived with by ordinary decent Catholics and Protestants – will depend to a degree on Lijphart's middle-level group of sub-elite political activists, and their relationship with those at the top on whom the task of negotiating and sustaining the settlement has rested. Will these sub-elites support the leaders? What price might they exact for their support? Can the leaders successfully balance the imperative of negotiating compromise with their enemies with that of keeping faith with their friends? Part of the answer will depend on political skills such as trustability and persuasiveness; part also, however, on the political culture of the respective communities, such as those in Portadown. An argument that picks up some of Lijphart's is put forward by a more recent study, Judith Large's *The War Next Door*.[8] Large proposes that we consider three types of actor in the affected population in a conflict. They correspond, from the perspective of making peace, to three foci of activity:

(1) *The top leadership.* These are political (sometimes military) leaders, of high public visibility, playing for high personal stakes; at this level, individual personality is important.
(2) *Middle-range leaders.* These are respected figures in particular social sectors, such as leaders of religious groups or humanitarian organizations, journalists or academics.
(3) *Grassroots.* Local leaders and activists, teachers, community groups etc.

While the top leadership has the responsibility for making a peace settlement, its long-term prospects of success are likely to depend upon the attitudes of those lower down.

In peace processes there is, then, a vital role to be played by people in Large's middle range; and in Northern Ireland this has been so. Relatively neutral, or at least not overtly political, people in the churches or businesses have operated to provide ideas and wider perspectives, to interrogate the ideas and policies of the political activists, to act as go-betweens, to provide safe and neutral venues for behind-the-scenes diplomacy. In peace processes political activists at the middle level can sometimes be freer than their leaderships to sound out positions both within their own side and with counterparts on other sides; a role for middle-level non-politicals can be to facilitate this.

Nonetheless, the middle-level leaderships which can make or break the settlement are not the facilitators and brokers, but those within the political groupings which are negotiating through their leaders, and, more specifically, those particular political parties whose stance vis-à-vis the settlement will determine whether it succeeds or fails. Such people in the Northern Irish case may include backbench MPs and MLAs, councillors and influential party office-holders, but also the paramilitary organizations, the Orange Order, and influential local residents in some areas.

Without the support of middle-level interlocutors and political entrepreneurs, articulators of grassroots sentiment, the top leaders may be able to deal, but cannot, without great difficulty, deliver. But leaders of the middle range will have agendas of their own. These might include having power bases to maintain and political careers to further, which might be enhanced by representing themselves as upholders of the true faith, unsullied by the compromises top negotiators may have had to make. They may represent particular interests or sub-groups within the overall movement the top leader is charged with leading, and these too will have ideologies and agendas specific to themselves. Their relationship with the top leaders is potentially complex. The latter may of course, according to circumstances, find that pressure from the middle and grassroots levels is functional to their own political strategy. A negotiator can point to his hard-line lower leadership as a reason why he cannot make a concession pressed upon him by other parties to negotiation, but which he does not, in any case, wish to make. Conversely, the top leadership may, as a strategic device, encourage the middle level to take stances which further the group strategy but from which the leadership may wish to distance itself. The word 'may' is apposite here. Part of the strategy of a negotiating party may be to foster a sense of confusion amongst its adversaries, and other involved parties, as to just how far its leaders *are* in hock to hardliners, or conversely are manipulating events while denying their responsibility for so doing. The decommissioning issue in Northern Ireland is a classic case of this. Republican leaders left all others guessing as to whether they could not or would not move. Was this the result of genuine pressure or just clever manoeuvring? Only they could say, and they wouldn't.

Middle-range leaders are significant in the handling of circumstances which are not necessarily the stuff of the highest-level constitutional negotiation but are nonetheless vital to the prospect of a transition from a politics of continuous confrontation to one of non-violent contest and adjustment. It is striking, in the Northern Irish case, how much of the month-by-month politics post-Good Friday was not about the basic architecture of the political arrangements agreed on 10 April, but about second-order issues. For instance, to an outside observer, argument by unionists about the name and insignia of the police, or the insistence of Orangemen upon parading down certain roads rather than others, appears simply obtuse. It would seem to indicate a deep malaise within unionism, summed up by Fergal Cochrane as 'the fact that many unionists have hitched their wagons to issues that are peripheral to their traditionally understood perspective of preserving the union'.[9] This suggests that for such unionists, the Union is understood primarily in terms of its symbols and that unionist politics is a politics of identity as much as of power. Indeed it is *only* in the light of such an interpretation that the determination of the Orange Order to adopt its self-destructive attitude to marching makes any sense.

One of the most persistent themes in the voluminous social science literature on Northern Ireland is that of a distinction between two poles within unionism, the one liberal, secular, 'civil' and British, the other particularistic, Ulster-orientated, sectarian and self-absorbed. While many people belong fairly unambiguously in one or the other camp, the two tendencies leak copiously into each other. The problem for the prospects of pro-Agreement unionism is that the second tendency is strongly entrenched in positions where its priorities run counter to the pro-Agreement unionist strategy for preserving the Union. This tendency is not only in a position to exercise constraint, or even veto, on the unionist leadership; its pursuit of identity politics actually plays into the hands of its republican opponents. In turn it would be naive to assume that the republicans have not welcomed and made good use of the opportunity Orange identity politics has presented.

There is a paradox about the emergence of the parades issue which commentators outside Northern Ireland appear barely to have noticed. This is the fact that it emerged not during the 25 years of violent conflict, but only after the first ceasefire had initiated the settlement process. The first of the annual crises at Drumcree/ Garvaghy road was in July 1995, in the summer following the IRA ceasefire of 31 August 1994 and its loyalist response six weeks later. They were to recur annually, accompanied by other parade-induced tensions in Belfast's Lower Ormeau road, in Londonderry over Apprentice Boys parades, and in Co. Antrim, where the loyalist-Orange riposte to being prevented from parading through the largely Catholic village of Dunloy was a prolonged siege of the Catholic church in the Harryville residential area of Ballymena.

If, to cite a phrase, 'the war is over', the emergence of the parades issue clearly indicated that the *conflict* was not. Several elements went into the emergence of the parades issue, all of which related to the politics of the post-ceasefire, settlement-seeking process. The most obvious is that only with the ceasefires could the parades issue have been brought to the fore in the reasonable confidence that it would not spark off a spate of killings. At earlier times during the 25 years to 1994 it would simply have been too dangerous for republicans to protest against parading to the extent that they did from 1995 on. Thus the parades issue itself can be seen not only as a reminder of continuing strife but paradoxically also as a symptom of easement, hard as this might have been to discern at the time.

The initiative to rouse community opposition to Orange parades lay with local republicans and Sinn Féin, who proclaimed 1995 to be a summer of 'angry voices and marching feet'. Again, there were and are sound conflict-related reasons why they should have wished to take this course. 'Clausewitz in reverse' points to the parades issue as a means by which Sinn Féin could keep up the momentum of struggle, show to its supporters that there was no let-up in the campaign, merely a change in tactics, and continue to strengthen its identification with Catholic communities and its stance as their defenders. Sinn Féin knew full well that the parades issue was a way of putting its Orange opponents in the dock of outside opinion, since it is self-evident that, as in the case of the civil rights protests of 1968–69, opinion outside Northern Ireland warms to a reasonable universalistic appeal based on 'rights' (in this case 'community rights') in a way that it will not do to the claims of Irish republicanism as such.

Furthermore, Sinn Féin, and the nationalist community in general, needed to progress with excluding Orange parades from their areas if they were to demonstrate that the peace process was reaping dividends and justifying the cessation of violence. With the coming of the Agreement, Sinn Féin rhetoric shifted from classic Irish republicanism to emphasizing an 'equality agenda' for Catholics in the North (which is where 'civil rights', of course, began in 1968). This means an agenda which emphasizes the Catholic position within a still-partitionist settlement, while recognizing a postponement of the ultimate republican goal to some future date. If Sinn Féin's politics are to mean anything at all, it has to defend and enhance the 'equality agenda' or pack up and leave the field.

Why, however, should the Orange Order and its supporters continue to insist on their right to parade regardless of the cost to their reputation and the risk to the Union? Surely Sinn Féin's tactic of entrapping them in the Drumcree impasse (and those elsewhere) should have been obvious? The crude answer, much peddled by republicans and lapped up by English opinion, is that Orangeism is about asserting dominance over Catholics, particularly by parading through Catholic areas. It can hardly be denied that Orangeism today is a residual legacy of three hundred years or more of a Protestant-British ideology of superiority over the Catholic-Irish world, an ideology which the British in Great Britain have spent most of the last century shedding. But the cruder versions of the anti-Orange critique will not stand up to scrutiny. If the object of the Orange parades has been to inflict insult on Catholics in their areas, it is poorly served by a parading season in which only a small fraction of parades regularly pass through sizeable Catholic districts. The main route of the largest parade of all, in Belfast on 12 July, has always avoided such districts on its way from the centre through south Belfast, though some 'feeder' marches have not done so. Most country demonstrations rotate around different centres annually, thus passing through Catholic districts occasionally but not routinely.[10] There is, in any case, no inalienable human right not to be offended. Moreover, the routes in contention, such as the Garvaghy road and the Lower Ormeau in Belfast, are neither meandering country lanes, nor deliberately chosen to go through Catholic housing estates, but broad thoroughfares linking town or city centres with peripheral districts. The emphasis Orangemen lay on these being 'traditional' routes comes across as extraordinarily hidebound and reactionary. But it also should serve to indicate that the prime motive is the preservation of long-standing practice, not the desire to stir up trouble.

Drumcree parish church was the parish church of the area including most of Portadown when it was little more than a one-street village, and long before the railway age made it into a key junction and industrial town. The first Orange parade to the church for a service took place as long ago as July 1807. Since 1916, moreover, early July has also been the occasion of services commemorating the Battle of the Somme, and the first of the two most contentious parades has taken place on the Sunday nearest to 1 July. Martin Middlebrook, in *The First Day on the Somme*, records that there were on that catastrophic day 32 British Army battalions suffering more than 500 casualties each. Of these battalions four were from Ulster, and number 22 on the list came the Armagh, Monaghan and Cavan Volunteers, with 532 casualties.[11]

Orangeism, moreover, is the spirit of 1688 in aspic. A powerful element in its ideology emphasizes liberty, an opposition to authoritarian rule, and the conscience of the individual, and associates these with the establishment in Britain of liberal democratic norms and institutions. The history may be flawed and simplistic (as whose is not?) and the politics outdated elsewhere in the UK, but the stance is sincerely held. It is, moreover, held in the face of a siege mounted against it, as Orangemen would see it, by a heavily armed terrorist movement which has murdered in large numbers their Brethren, relatives and friends (58 per cent of killings in the Troubles were by republicans) and which has been claiming the rewards of peace without abjuring the means of waging war.

In these circumstances, interference in their traditional marches by Sinn Féin-inspired residents' associations taps into a sense on the part of Orangemen that their way of life is under siege. A complex of political, economic and demographic forces operating since the 1960s means that this sense is well founded. In a body that has fed its imagination for generations on simplistic historical images and brisk slogans, the idea of the siege is potent. So too is the response: 'no surrender!' and 'not an inch'.

If, then, the Good Friday Agreement was hailed outside Northern Ireland as the best piece of good news from the territory in many a long year, the annual recurrence of trouble at Drumcree vividly underlined the fact that the settlement was embedded in a culture of conflict which still had the capacity to smother it. The Drumcree stand-off in July 1998 was the fourth in succession. At one point it threatened to engulf all of Northern Ireland in vicious turmoil reminiscent of the summer of 1969, being averted only when the deaths of the three young Quinn brothers, sixty miles away in Ballymoney, produced a stunned and embarrassed hiatus. To no one's surprise, neither this nor the Omagh bomb of August 1998 prevented 'Drumcree' re-emerging in July 1999, though events there, thanks to strong British preventive measures and some emergence of a will to prudence on the part of the Orange Order, passed off more calmly than had been feared.

It is, in sum, no mere happenstance that the parades issue arose after the armed struggle was 'over', when it had not been present before. The parades issue and the end of the armed phase of the conflict are closely linked. Mobilizing community groups or 'concerned citizens' is about establishing that republicanism is still a 'movement' and that its struggle goes on despite Sinn Féin's transition to electoral, office-holding respectability. But behind this there is a deeper factor involved. The boundary ridge topped by Drumcree church may be an immutable fact of local geography, but political boundaries can and do shift. Drumcree-Garvaghy is a crucial signifier for both republicans and Orangemen: for the republicans signifying that their political struggle, armed or not, has been rewarded by an irreversible change towards the 'equality agenda', and for the Orange Order and its supporters, that there must be a line in the loam beyond which they cannot be pushed.

The Orange Order and its definitions of the situation forms one part of a wider context of unionist grassroots and middle-level pressure acting as a constraint on David Trimble and his negotiating group. The Ulster Unionist party of the 1990s bears a considerable resemblance to the British Labour party of the 1970s and early 1980s, riven as it was between modernizers and an institutionally entrenched bloc of traditionalists. With its leader elected by, and ultimately responsible to, the 860-strong Council, within which the Orange Order holds a built-in block of 120 seats, the Council's relationship to the leader is, appropriately enough, also something akin to a Presbyterian kirk session's relationship to its minister. The leader can only lead with the ultimate consent of the Council, which it can withhold. If it were to do so, the peace process would crash. On 27 November 1999, Trimble secured a vote of 57.9 per cent in favour of activating the power-sharing Executive, but he had to pledge to resign as first minister, with the rest of his colleagues, if by late February 2000 there had been no move towards decommissioning by the IRA. Following Secretary of State Peter Mandelson's suspension of the Executive in March, designed to forestall complete collapse, followed by the IRA's move to open arms dumps to inspection, Trimble returned to the Council on 27 May to obtain support for restoring devolved government. On this occasion he obtained a bare 53 per cent of the Council's vote. But the Unionist party he was leading at Stormont itself represented, along with the Progressive Unionist party's two members, only the barest of majorities among unionist Assembly members (there were 28 declared anti-Agreement unionists to 30 pro-Agreement ones [28 UUP, 2 PUP], but at least four of the latter had been opposed originally to the Agreement).

Pro-Agreement unionism was, thus, only holding on by the skin of its teeth. Indeed, at a crude level of calculation, it could be seen as representing at most the barest plurality of the unionist community at the electoral level (most estimates of unionist support for the Agreement at the 28 May 1998 referendum put it at 51 or 52 per cent), and quite definitely a *minority* tendency of little more than one third at the level of political activists, taking all unionist parties together.

Not the least of the ironies of David Trimble's position in the post-Agreement period was the pressure his leadership came under from younger unionists pursuing a career path far from dissimilar to his own at earlier stages. The most conspicuous example of a middle-level activist with a career agenda of his own was provided by Jeffrey Donaldson, eighteen years younger than Trimble, and for some time a presumptive legatee of the collapse of a pro-Agreement position within the Ulster Unionist party; but there were others such as the 'baby barristers', ambitious and intelligent, if not necessarily far-sighted, young men of the law – like the erstwhile David Trimble. Trimble's critics have the huge asset of non-responsibility for the concessions unionism has had to make in the peace process. His problem is that while there may be those in the unionist community who understand the value of strategic concession to secure the wider objective of peace and stability, it is hard to see this as the basis of a career in unionist politics, whereas the appeal of 'no surrender' and 'not an inch' is obvious. Like Terence O'Neill before him, David Trimble's support lies disproportionately in a constituency which is weakly represented in active unionist politics.[12]

The problem presented on the republican side is parallel and yet different. It would be tempting, but rather facile, to see the IRA as Sinn Féin's equivalent to the Orange Order. The obvious similarity is that of a body within the broader body, acting as an interest in itself and with an elite of its own. But whereas unionism was always more than the political wing of the Orange Order, the nature of Sinn Féin's relationship to the IRA – and who within the movement is really calling the shots, since the emergence of Sinn Féin electorally in the early 1980s – has always been kept (deliberately) obscure.

The key issue on the republican side resides in the fact that in August 1994, and later for the second time in July 1997, the 'armed struggle' was set aside, without defeat but also without victory. As a result, the rules of the game, post-ceasefire, have been quite complex. Failure to win the struggle, which would be signified by some kind of British public intention to withdraw, entailed negotiated compromise. But that undefeatedness also needed recognition in the outcome. Otherwise the Agreement would be repudiated. This was always going to be highly delicate for republicans.

In the twentieth century, wars came to be more difficult to bring to an end short of outright victory by one side or the other. It is almost impossible to declare a draw and go home. One reason is that combatant sides have a need to induce young men to risk their lives. Hence they sacralize the cause, turn their dead into martyr heroes. This reached its apogee in 1914–18 in Britain and with its Irish republican equivalent in 1916 and 1919–21. But that means the war must go on, and must result in vindication of the struggle, because the dead must be seen not to have died in vain. Yeats referred, in 'Easter 1916', to the power of 'MacDonagh's bony thumb'. Over the shoulders of Sinn Féin negotiators in the 1990s gazed the smiling, futureless eyes of Bobby Sands.

An extensive literature including Kevin Toolis's illuminating *Rebel Hearts: Journeys within the IRA's Soul*[13] and Toby Harnden's *Bandit Country* shows an IRA deeply embedded in its heartlands in rural Ulster, where each republican village has a Bobby Sands or three of its own, acting as a warning and a mute rebuke awaiting any republican negotiator seen to give too much away. In electoral terms, Sinn Féin has much less to risk than pro-Agreement unionists. Its voters will not go anywhere else. But Sinn Féin does face the risk that the more it becomes accepted and routinized the more it will be seen as simply another set of politicians. Miall et al. point out the danger in all conflict situations of erstwhile leaders becoming 'metropolitanized' and leaving resentful erstwhile followers behind.[14]

But the risk to the peace process from the republican side is more military than political. Clearly, the weaponry in paramilitary hands will continue to be considerable, whatever becomes of decommissioning in general. The ability to use it, the know-how of bomb-making and bomb-planting, is undecommissionable. Already, in the months following Good Friday, it was believed that a large part of the IRA's technical 'staff' had gone over to out-and-outers such as the 'Real IRA'.

Steeped as republicanism has been in the Pearsean doctrine that 'Ireland unfree shall never be at peace', the political stance of such people should occasion no surprise. They and their equivalents elsewhere are the virtually unavoidable residue of all conflict situations – but no less lethal for that. Ireland's own experience of 1922–23 is itself testimony. About 4,000 people (possibly slightly fewer) died in the civil war, greatly outnumbering those who died in the Anglo-Irish conflict that preceded the 1921 Treaty. Republican true believers guard a strong, if narrow, vision of a pure ideal that must not be compromised. But, ideology apart, low-intensity, irregular conflict notoriously produces warlords, people with local power for whom war is a way of life – and, through intimidation and exploitation, a rewarding one. The isolation and grinding down of the capabilities of warlordism thus has an important part to play in the transition to peace. The Omagh bomb of August 1998 showed how much damage armed irreconcilables could do, their alienation from the political process placing them in a position of being a self-appointed antinomian elite.

On the other hand, while republican militancy, as the Omagh bomb demonstrated, has the capacity to kill and disrupt, its capacity to derail the peace process is likely to be limited, *unless* it is able to mount a sustained campaign coinciding with peace-eroding forces operating within the main unionist–republican relationship. Arms decommissioning was clearly at the core of this relationship, post-Good Friday. The tortured history of this issue would fill a book in itself. Suffice it to reiterate the point of how little argument there was in Ireland in the period after the Good Friday Agreement about its actual constitutional substance or its longer-term implications, while the vast bulk of the argument and rancour centred upon *process*: in particular, to what degree the Agreement entailed decommissioning by the IRA before Sinn Féin could participate in the new institutions, or indeed whether the Agreement required decommissioning at all.

It is worth underlining just how astonishingly radical a departure the Agreement was, from the core positions of both Sinn Féin and unionism. It may be precisely because both sides *had* moved so far from their 'home-base' positions that for both sides decommissioning represented the *ne plus ultra*, the line they could not cross, because so many had already been crossed. Seen in this light, decommissioning was not one last difficulty on a long road, but the ultimate test of how far one side could push the other, in part via the pressures of the sponsoring governments. The view has often been expressed, especially outside Northern Ireland, that decommissioning is a purely symbolic issue. Those who take this line usually decline to indicate, this being so, just *who* should climb down and 'get real'. In any case, the bloody civil war of 1922–23 was, arguably, fought over symbolism. Only those fortunates for whom political symbols are largely uncontentious have the luxury of dismissing them as 'mere' symbols.

The Provisionals' statement at the time of the first ceasefire, 31 August 1994, made it clear that they saw this as the action of an undefeated force, taken of its own free will and not under duress. Freedom to deploy or dispose of its weapons was a key signifier of the movement's continued autonomy as a political actor. In his revealing memoir of the Albert Reynolds government, Sean Duignan reports

Martin McGuinness as speaking 'frankly about the need to dispose of armaments': 'We know the guns will have to be banjaxed'.[15] On the other hand, being constrained to 'hand them over' would be tantamount to surrender. As McGuinness said to *Guardian* reporters Rusbridger and Freedland in February 1999, 'What do they want me to do? Do I have to lie down in the middle of the road and allow them to walk on top of me? I can't do it. I can't get the IRA to surrender.'[16] Brian Keenan, in April 1999, was even blunter: 'I do not know where they get this word decommissioning [from p. 20 of the Agreement perhaps?]. It strikes me that what it means is surrender. There will be no surrender.'[17] Of course 'decommissioning', as a term, was deliberately selected *not* to imply necessarily 'handing over'. Common usage, however, wasn't always so precise.

But the implication of McGuinness's position was huge. It meant that Sinn Féin was demanding to be treated by everyone else as a fellow democratic party while itself declining to adhere to democratic norms. It would bargain as a political party, while retaining what others were bound to see as a capacity, unique among the involved political parties, to reinforce its democratic bargaining power by extra-democratic means (to put it mildly). Others would simply have to trust that the IRA weaponry would not be used; the experience of Sinn Féin as a partner in government, and the fulfilling of its equality agenda, would make the weaponry irrelevant. The guns would 'rest in peace'.

There was, and there is, no particular reason why non-republicans should believe this. At most, they have been faced with taking a gamble on it. The precedent of Canary Wharf, when the first ceasefire broke down after 17 months, is an ever-present reminder that the peace process is continuously hazard to the balance of opinion within the IRA Army Council. Be that as it may, the IRA constitutes a critical constituency for Sinn Féin. The IRA might remain in ceasefire mode, but self-evidently the non-decommissioning of weapons, at least under any kind of pressure, is for its members a key article of faith. (Slogans painted up in republican areas proclaim 'not a pound, not one bullet' in possibly unselfconscious paralleling of the long-standing unionist 'not an inch'.) The unity of the main republican movement has been one of its principal assets, especially in contrast with unionism, and the leadership, quite rightly from its point of view, was never going to jeopardize this, especially while there remained the slightest chance that republicans might gain the rewards of the Agreement without conceding on decommissioning. That decommissioning had the capacity to wreck the Agreement was implicitly recognized in the wording of the document, which was intended to kick the issue into touch. But it could not remain there indefinitely. The impasse *seemed* to be broken with the IRA's concession of international inspection in May 2000. The implication of this was that the republicans would retain their caches of arms, but they had put their own bona fide that they would not be used into the international public domain. Not exactly banjaxing; but a deft breakthrough in peace-brokering which got the process over another sticking point. There would be more.

When the IRA declared its 'total' ceasefire on 31 August 1994, to be followed shortly after, on 13 October, by that of the Combined Loyalist Military Command, the Northern Irish conflict of the modern era had lasted a quarter of a century and cost 3,173 lives within the territory and around 200 more outside. It was, as a much reproduced slogan put it, 'time for peace'. It was also, however, a time for much caution and wariness, as few could be sure what it all meant, or even whether, or for how long, it would last.

In the event, the ceasefire lasted for just over 17 months, to 9 February 1996, when the IRA's massive bomb at Canary Wharf signalled its end. Further bombings and killings ensued before the ceasefire was restored following the Labour election victory of May 1997. The speed with which the process of settlement-seeking now proceeded to Agreement, signed at Belfast on 10 April 1998, suggested that Seamus Mallon's slow learners had, after all, been quite quick on the uptake on the three-and-a-half years' journey from the first ceasefires.

The fact that the prospects for the Good Friday Agreement remained highly uncertain more than three years on from April 1998 only served to reinforce the point that the term 'peace *process*' is extremely apt. We are used to wars which have definite beginnings and endings. We know where we are when the news comes through from the Appomattox Court House, from the Forest of Compiègne, from Lüneberg Heath. But Northern Ireland's was a conflict, not a war in the older sense. It was not declared but it evolved. From ceasefire to Agreement and after, it remained unclear whether the conflict had ended or simply mutated. To ensure the former amid many signs of the latter required *process*, as it always will in the numerous conflicts which are not quite wars. Peace, thus, needs to be seen as a path, not an achieved state. It will be prone to setbacks as well as forward steps, with periods of pause, of seeming disintegration as well as of consolidation.

The gaining of negotiated consent to an 'agreed Ireland' in an agreed British–Irish relationship, in April and May 1998, was a huge landmark and achievement, but it was nonetheless a building resting upon insecure foundations. Arguably, the rush from ceasefire to all-inclusive settlement left many behind and left a huge post-settlement task still to be undertaken to secure its grounding in a culture of peace. In a comment in his autobiographical account, *Minority Verdict*, in 1995, Maurice Hayes implies that, in his view, the attempt at that time to complete a settlement was premature:

> What more than anything is needed in Northern Ireland as a precursor to political activity is a build up of trust. Too much energy is squandered in a search for great and complete constitutional constructs that will solve all problems at once, and for all time. At every possible occasion, negotiators tackle the most difficult and divisive issues first. They head off for the North Face of the Eiger, without first travelling the foothills of trust.[18]

Arguably, however, the converse was also true. If, without trust, there could be no lasting settlement, it is valid to argue that trust could not emerge while there remained all to play for in the shaping of a constitutional construct.

Almost everything that occurred in the peace process from Good Friday onwards served to emphasize how much the prospect of the Agreement bedding down depended not just on the leaders who had made it but upon critical elements within their followings – elements capable of issuing vetos. A political leader can deliver if he or she has built up a loyalty, a following and a fund of trust on which to draw, or at least a following that, notwithstanding misgivings, can see that it basically has no alternative option, no exit strategy. Neither Adams nor Trimble fully enjoyed this. In purely party political terms, Trimble's position was much the more precarious. In votes, the anti-Agreement unionists were breathing down his neck. He was extremely fortunate that there was no electoral test of the Agreement for two years or more from June 1998, but it was clear in the two Unionist Council votes of November 1999 and May 2000 that his support stood at a dangerously low level and appeared to be diminishing with each concession he was obliged to make. The dubious loyalty of several middle-range unionist leaders, including Geoffrey Donaldson MP, as well as the turmoil in the Orange Order, left him exposed, clutching a Nobel peace prize and a diminishing base of adherents. In these circumstances one might have hoped that Adams and Sinn Féin, who did not appear to be in any electoral danger (quite the contrary) would see the sense of trying to ease the Trimble path. But they also had their loyalty and exit problems. True, their electorate appeared solid, but it had nowhere else to go. The problem was with the IRA, and Adams and co. could not deliver it for decommissioning; perhaps, also, they would not. A token measure of decommissioning of some sort would have been an extremely effective use of the weaponry in political terms. It would have posed for the unionists an unanswerable question; Sinn Féin, whatever the outcome, would have emerged still formidably armed *and* smelling of essence of rose. Clearly, however, decommissioning was hugely difficult. The principal reason republicans have tended to give (apart from a legalistic reading of the text of the Agreement) has been that the giving up of arms was simply not part of the Irish nationalist tradition. By the same token, of course, neither was making an Agreement like that of April 1998.

Transitions from war to peace always imply threats to the many for whom violence has become a way of life. There will be those left without an activity defining a role in society, a means of attaining personal prestige, of compensating for social or personal deficits, and, not least, for some, of making profit. This is particularly the case with conflicts of the Ulster (or the Yugoslav) variety. Those bound to be threatened by a farewell to arms in Ulster must include hardline ideologues disaffected by the compromises negotiated into the Agreement; those local warlords left to fight on alone or fade from the scene; and those who have made a 'killing' in the financial sense under the cover of political conflict and who will hope to continue so to do. In practice, these are overlapping descriptions – several caps for the same heads.

Out of these conditions there are likely to be plenty of occasions of continuing post-agreement destabilization. In the Ulster case, in particular, the emergence of a 'Troubles' economy, involving racketeering and smuggling and 'legitimate' enterprises developed as funding sources for paramilitaries, has long been noted as part of the scene. Add to this the pattern of local warlordism in the former cockpits of violence, such as north Belfast or South Armagh, and the emergence in recent years of the drugs scene, and we have a cocktail of possible destabilizations.

There is, however, a difference between turbulence and collapse. The former, given the history of the last thirty years, is only to be expected. What matters is what capacity it has to jeopardize the survival and enhancement of the peace process.

Naturally, for the first few years, the diagnosis must be interim and tentative. We have seen the Omagh bomb, killing 29 people on 15 August 1998. The tragedy gave everyone pause; but it did not bring down the peace – it did not even produce reprisals. We have seen 'turf wars' amongst various groups of loyalist organizations; but these are localized in impact. And we have seen the parades and decommissioning issues. All of these the Agreement and the peace process have survived. The greatest threat to Good Friday has always been its possible repudiation at the polls by the unionist electorate. Even here, however, unionist politicians engaged in criticizing the Agreement, or in claiming betrayal, must know that with the two governments unbudgeable in their joint commitment, now of many years' standing, to the basic framework of the Agreement, oppositionists have nowhere to go but into the desert to sulk. For some, the grand sulk, perfected over many years, is the only political style they know. But the hard experience of unionists, since the 1985 Hillsborough Agreement, is that this is a sterile position which only passes more of the shaping of the future into the hands of others. Both contemporary politics and demographics indicate further that it is as untenable a position as the old politics of territorial domination ultimately proved also to be.

Recollecting his feelings on hearing the news of the 31 August 1994 ceasefire, Seamus Heaney has said, 'I had the physical pleasure of that bright Sunday morning after the ceasefire. There was also the political and psychological brightness of the moment. I do believe that whatever happens, a corner was turned historically in 1994. We've passed from the atrocious to the messy, but the messy is a perfectly OK place to live.'[19]

True. It is. For the time being. It took another three and a half years of pretty dispiriting mess to get to Good Friday 1998 and there was and probably still is more to come. The first task, getting from ceasefire to comprehensive settlement, was achieved (remarkably speedily, but largely because so much foundation work had already been done). The second, securing the settlement against breakdown, remains uncompleted, its prospects uncertain. There is, however, a third stage. Martin Woollacott, in exploring 'Why peace processes are breaking down all over',[20] reminds us that many of the peace processes of the 1990s did not wholly deserve the name. He puts this down to 'perhaps too much concentration on skilful ways of moving conflict from a violent phase to a non-violent phase and not enough on tackling fundamental differences'. Denial – a self-deceiving refusal to see, know or accept unpleasant or uncomfortable facts – is ubiquitous both amongst those involved in conflict *and* amongst those who would intervene and mediate. This points to the need to follow up the process of achieving and securing a negotiated settlement with a more fundamental and long-term task, that of creating a culture of peace. UNESCO, declaring 2000 an International Year for the Culture of Peace, defines this as 'all the values, attitudes and forms of behaviour that reflect respect for life, for human beings and their dignity, and for all human rights. It is the rejection of violence in all its forms and a commitment to the principles of freedom, justice, solidarity, tolerance and understanding between groups and individuals.'[21] In British–Irish relations, and in Northern Ireland in particular, that's an agenda for a generation or two. A start has been made; the important thing is marking realistically what has been achieved, and how much remains to be done; and keeping going.

Postscript

Writing a postscript in 2006 prompts the taking of a long view. So it all depends what you mean by peace. An end to violence, at long last (net of a good deal of localized thuggery and a possibly irreducible few fatal incidents)? Yes. An embedded political settlement with a reasonable prospect of longevity? Maybe, sometime, never? Anyhow not yet. Peace as *shalom*, wholeness, reconciliation, atonement – in themselves contested concepts? Too much, too soon, to expect.

One of the premises of this volume was that lessons could be learned from the 'long road to peace' in Northern Ireland that might have resonance elsewhere. In retrospect, one might well wish to be more cautious and modest. If there is one principal lesson, though, it might still be that of the importance of keeping going. Over the years since the Good Friday (Belfast) Agreement (GFA) the British and Irish governments have persisted in just that. The road map, set out in general in the Downing Street Declaration (1993) and in specific detail in the GFA (1998), has been adhered to. Consistency of purpose on the part of the sovereign powers has been key. The journey might have halted for lengthy periods, but the fault for this lay within Northern Ireland, not in Dublin and London. We might note here that, almost uniquely since the 1960s, both governments enjoyed continuity of tenure, and even of leadership, throughout these years – an imponderable, but probably important, plus factor. Whether the stalling on the road from Good Friday was due more to the IRA's long delaying of its decision to decommission weapons in a publicly verifiable way, or to the unionist community's use of any available obstacle to sharing power, especially with Sinn Féin, remains to some degree a matter of political judgment.

It was inevitably going to take time and consistent pressure to get the IRA into full demilitarized mode, as part of Sinn Féin's acceptance into democratic legitimacy. But as opinion polls and successive elections post-1998 showed, every delay by the IRA in verifiably disposing of the bulk of its arms drove unionist voters into the anti-Agreement camp (prop. I.R.K. Paisley). Not for the first time since the late 1960s, unionist moderates, or more accurately, accommodationists, found themselves standing on rapidly shrinking ground. Probably only full and transparent decommissioning by June 2000 could have saved Trimble and his UUP from eclipse. As it was, this did not occur until September 2005.

It is tempting to see a parallel in the overtaking of the SDLP by Sinn Féin. But the reason for it is different. Once Sinn Féin had signed up to the Agreement, and the IRA, with or without its arms, went into credible ceasefire mode, the SDLP became a party without a clear political space, save to represent those Catholics who could not stomach the friends of Gerry Adams. The two moderate parties, the SDLP and the UUP, might, in theory, have operated more at elections to assist each other; but in practice, the balance of advantage for both parties was always going to lie in maximizing votes within their respective communities rather than seeking them across the divide.

So the result of the fallout from the GFA was that the future of Northern Ireland came, after the Assembly election of November 2003, to lie with those on both sides who had long represented the most irreconcilable positions – a situation reinforced by the UK general election of June 2005, in which the UUP was all but wiped out. Only the most soft-headed of optimists could take comfort from this. Nevertheless, extreme positions have the advantage of being hard to outflank. It is almost a political commonplace to point out that it was de Gaulle who rescued France from its Algerian imbroglio and Nixon who went to China (an irony not lost, no doubt, on the opera-loving David Trimble). Now that a power-sharing administration has been set up, the astonishing reality of the DUP following those above examples by starring in it alongside Sinn Féin has been brought about by several factors. Among these have been the removal of the obstacle of IRA weaponry; the DUP's seeing off its rivals in the UUP; and the lure of office. But also the fact that while the official British position after April 1998 was that there was no 'plan B', it was pretty clear that, unofficially, one *did* exist – an ever closer relationship between London and Dublin. Even so, a reality check is in order – a compulsory grand coalition, in which both major parties have a veto, may well prove unsustainable in practice.

We might also note, in conclusion, the significance of factors operating outside Northern Ireland since 1998 but having a powerful bearing on the dynamics of the situation. Item: the evolution of the United Kingdom. With the creation of devolved administrations in Edinburgh and Cardiff (both housed in prestigious new premises) and the likelihood that these will, in time, acquire further powers, the re-establishment of such a regime in Northern Ireland, the original home of devolution, looks even more than before part of the logic of the times, and its absence more like the persistence of a quasi-colonialist anomaly. Item: the terrorist attacks in New York on 9/11, as well as those in Madrid, Bali and of course London on 7/7 cannot but have had implications for the decommissioning issue and Sinn Féin's specious finessing of its own position in regard to the IRA and its weaponry. Perhaps the Irish peace process benefited from the excesses of al-Qaida elsewhere. Item: while an obsessive eye on population trends has always marked the Northern Irish political scene, a quite unforeseen new demographic started to operate in the early 2000s – immigration, both of people settling and of migrants, especially from Eastern Europe. One of the biggest challenges for the fledgling police service (PSNI) was the violence associated with this new sectarianism. How this factor might play in the longer run is anyone's guess. What it, along with the other items, does show is that Northern Ireland, for all its self-absorption, is not as much 'a place apart' as we are sometimes inclined to think.

Notes

1. Patrick McKay, *A Dictionary of Ulster Place Names* (Belfast: Queen's University, 1999), p. 61.
2. Peter Mulholland, 'The View from Drumcree' (MA dissertation, Department of Social Anthropology, Queen's University, Belfast).
3. Patrick Brogan, *World Conflicts: Why and Where They Are Happening* (London: Bloomsbury, 1989).

4. John Whyte, *Interpreting Northern Ireland* (Oxford: Oxford University Press, 1999), p. 243.
5. Toby Harnden, *Bandit Country: The IRA and South Armagh* (London: Hodder and Stoughton, 1999), p. 334.
6. Hugh Miall et al., *Contemporary Conflict Resolution* (Oxford: Polity Press, 1999), p. 183.
7. Arend Lijphart, *Democracy in Plural Societies* (London: Yale University Press, 1977), p. 53.
8. Judith Large, *The War Next Door* (Stroud: Hawthorn, 1977).
9. Fergal Cochrane, 'Disagreeing to Agree', *Fortnight*, 385 (May 2000), p. 13.
10. Neil Jarman and Dominic Bryan, *Parade and Protest* (Coleraine: University of Ulster, 1996).
11. Martin Middlebrook, *The First Day on the Somme* (London: Allen Lane, 1971).
12. See Marc Mulholland, *Northern Ireland at the Crossroads* (London: Macmillan, 2000).
13. Kevin Toolis, *Rebel Hearts: Journeys within the IRA's Soul* (London: Picador, 1995).
14. Miall et al., *Contemporary Conflict Resolution*, ch. 7, pp. 183–215.
15. Sean Duignan, *One Spin on the Merry-Go-Round* (Dublin: Blackwater, 1996), p. 151.
16. *The Guardian*, 5 February 1999.
17. *The Guardian*, 6 April 1999.
18. Maurice Hayes, *Minority Verdict: Experiences of a Catholic Public Servant* (Belfast: Blackstaff, 1995), p. 317.
19. *The Guardian*, 30 April 1996.
20. *The Guardian*, 22 December 2000.
21. *Peace Movement*, 1(2) (Summer 2000), p. 5.

Religion and Identity in Northern Ireland[1]

Marianne Elliott

During 1992–93 I acted as one of the seven commissioners of the Opsahl Commission: an independent enquiry into ways forward in Northern Ireland, which produced its report in June 1993.[2] The Commission was a novel exercise in democracy, which sought to involve the people of Northern Ireland in the debate about its future. It received submissions from some 3,000 people and held public meetings and oral hearings throughout the region. The report made a number of recommendations which were subsequently endorsed in public opinion polls in Northern Ireland, Britain and the Republic of Ireland.[3] Most of these recommendations stemmed from the people's sense of frustration and helplessness after a quarter of a century of violence and deadlock and their desire to have more control over their own future. To do so, they recognized, would also involve their taking responsibility for the situation, past and present. This recognition – that the source of the conflict lies inside rather than outside the province, with the people themselves – was the uncomfortable conclusion of most of those addressing the Commission. There is no 'quick fix' to Northern Ireland. This is why the Opsahl Commission recommended a series of 'building blocks' to help the different communities build up trust and experience of working together before they could arrive at some common ground on Northern Ireland's long-term future.

The exercise showed that opinion had shifted considerably since the onset of the Troubles in 1969. But it also highlighted a continuing gulf of understanding between Protestant and Catholic, however anxious the individual to reach accommodation. There is still a sense that the other community is a different people and ignorance is preventing any overall sense of a shared culture. Basic ignorance about what the other faiths teach is rampant. Thus cocooned within their respective communities and traditions, most people in Northern Ireland have had little experience of the other community outside their workplace. There is an almost total lack of neutral venues where their differences can be explored in safety. Northern Ireland is not a zone of conflicting polarities, as many believe. There are too many shades of grey, too many people who 'pick and mix' from a range of identities, for that.[4] But there are certain fundamentals to the mainstream religions which their adherents rarely lose even when they cease to be practising members. It is these core differences which this paper seeks to analyse.

Table 1. Religion and national identity in Northern Ireland, 1968–89

	1968		1978		1986		1989	
	Prot.	Cath.	Prot.	Cath.	Prot.	Cath.	Prot.	Cath.
	%	%	%	%	%	%	%	%
British	39	20	67	20	65	9	68	8
Irish	20	76	8	69	3	61	3	60
Ulster	32	5	20	6	14	1	10	2
N. Irish	–	–	–	–	11	20	16	25

Source: Edward Moxon-Browne, 'National Identity in Northern Ireland', in Peter Stringer and Gillian Robinson (eds), *Social Attitudes in Northern Ireland* (Belfast: Blackstaff Press, 1991), p. 25.[5]

I

The oral hearings of the Opsahl Commission closed with two schools assemblies in Derry and Belfast. In Derry the sub-group discussing culture and identity produced the following motion: 'Our culture and identity is influenced more by our religion than by any other factor'. A number of Catholic sixth-formers subsequently voiced their bewilderment to their friend, who had been part of the group, at the choice of such a motion. On an earlier occasion the same school group had told the Commission that they opposed integrated education[6] not so much because their religion would be in any way diluted, but because their Irish culture would be.[7] Interestingly, it was the same consideration which inspired greater hostility towards educational integration among Sinn Féin supporters than among Catholics generally.[8] Throughout the hearings these core differences between Protestants and Catholics emerged time and time again: the centrality of religion to the identity of the one, of Irish history, language and culture to the other. The bogeyman for Catholics was the state and its representatives, that for Protestants the Catholic Church itself.

This fear of Catholicism as a powerful political system was found by the Commission at every level of the Protestant community. It is the one element which unites an otherwise very diverse, even divided community.[9] It is the main defining element of their Britishness and the perceived link with a Protestant power.[10] The Commission was told repeatedly of Protestants' reluctance to call themselves Irish. There has been a decline in Protestants' sense of Irishness which, while never high before the Troubles, plummeted sharply after their outbreak (see Table 1).

'Irishness' is perceived by Protestants as something not only Catholic, but also highly politicized, something which has been 'hijacked' by the republicans. It is this which dictates Protestant attitudes to the Irish Republic, which they see not as a modern democracy but as the incarnation of their worst nightmare: a hostile Catholic state, out to destroy Protestantism itself. Protestants, we were told by a former moderator of the Presbyterian Church,

> see the political situation in clearly religious perspectives … they see the attempt to bring about a 'United Ireland' not only as an attack upon their political and constitutional wellbeing, but also as an attack upon their religious heritage and an attempt to

establish in Northern Ireland the dominance of the Roman Catholic Church and people
... They see every aspect of the political, cultural, educational, medical, industrial, social
and religious life of the Republic dominated, and often controlled, by the power and
influence of the Roman Catholic Church ...[11]

In such a rapidly changing society as that of the Republic of Ireland, people have
genuine difficulty accepting the sincerity of such views of their state as 'priest-
ridden'. The recommendation of the Opsahl Commission which received scarcely
any mention in the otherwise vigorous and positive reception of the report in the
Republic was that on the Catholic Church in Ireland:

> 4.1. In the light of the widespread and deep fear and mistrust we encountered among
> Northern Protestants about the Catholic nature of Southern society ... we believe that
> the government of the Republic of Ireland must move – and be seen to move – to make
> good the claim in the 1916 Declaration that it cherishes all the children of the Irish
> nation equally.
>
> Recalling the Irish Hierarchy's declaration to the New Ireland Forum that it did not
> wish to have the moral teaching of the Catholic Church become the criterion of consti-
> tutional law or to have its principles embodied in civil law, and its reference to the need
> for a balanced examination of the role of the Church in a changing Ireland, we urge that
> this examination – and a public debate on it – should take place now. To this end we
> suggest the setting up ... of a wide-ranging public inquiry into the role of the Catholic
> Church in Ireland.[12]

This was in June 1993 and I have to say now that this recommendation may not
have been the dead letter that I once thought it. The joint Downing Street Declaration of the British and Irish governments on 14 December 1993 does signify a
genuine reaching out by the latter to the Protestant people of Northern Ireland. It
contains the following undertaking:

> The Taoiseach will examine with his colleagues any elements in the democratic life
> and organisation of the Irish state that can be represented to the Irish government in
> the course of political dialogue as a real and substantial threat to their way of life and
> ethos, or that can be represented as not being fully consistent with a modern democratic
> and pluralist society, and undertakes to examine any possible ways of removing such
> obstacles.

No such inquiry was established. But in the aftermath of a number of scandals
affecting the Church during 1993–94 (notably the case of the paedophile priest,
Brendan Smyth), a very wide-ranging public debate on the role of the Catholic
Church in the Republic is under way.

Conscious of how antiquated their fears of 'popery' sound, most Ulster Protestants have great difficulty defining their identity in public. In private they were
more forthcoming. 'There is the notion that you have to be Catholic to be Irish',
we were told in Auchnacloy – a border town in County Tyrone – but this was
the Catholic Church teaching the children biased history and hatred of anything
British, and Catholic teachers in schools would force their views on the children
since 'Catholics are taking their lead from Rome and Rome is out to get rid of
Protestants'. Despite the Catholic Church's relaxation of directives concerning the

religion of children of mixed marriages, even the leaders of the Protestant churches think the Catholic Church has not made sufficient concessions in this area.[13]

It is no surprise, therefore, to find ordinary Protestants still convinced that the Catholic Church's views on the family, education and mixed marriage are part and parcel of some great conspiracy to destroy Protestantism entirely. It is the Church which urges its adherents to bigger families, which forces mixed religion couples to bring up the children as Catholics (every Protestant commenting on this knew all about the *Ne Temere* decree of 1908 on Catholic marriage – most Catholics had never heard of it).[14] There is more hostility to mixed marriages among Protestants than among Catholics, even liberal-minded Protestants thinking it 'something that's morally wrong'. Similar hostility is expressed to attendance at any kind of service in a Catholic church, only half of church-going Protestants claiming that they would do so.[15] Members of the Orange Order are required to 'scrupulously avoid countenancing (by his presence or otherwise) any act or ceremony of Papish worship'.[16] The Rev. Ian Paisley's frequent reference to 'Jesuitical' conspiracies,[17] particularly in connection with the Republic's former territorial claim over Northern Ireland, struck a real chord. Although there are only 13,000 Free Presbyterians in Northern Ireland (i.e. followers of the fundamentalist Protestant church led by Paisley), over a quarter of the Protestant electorate regularly votes for his party, the Democratic Unionist Party. Further, an estimated 100,000 Protestants belong to the male-only Orange Order – a staggering 38 per cent of the Protestant male population – which requires its members to 'strenuously oppose the fatal errors and doctrines of the Church of Rome'.[18]

Given the view that the Catholic Church's ultimate aim is to destroy Protestantism, recent demographic trends were contributing to an apocalyptic psychology among some Protestants. The 1991 census showed a rising Catholic population (41.4 per cent, up from 34.7 per cent in 1971, against 54 per cent Protestant; see Fig. 1), with Catholic majorities in almost every local authority west of the Bann, South Down and North Antrim. In Belfast – whose city council is the most notoriously anti-nationalist in the province – there has been an increase in the number of Catholics from 32.2 per cent in 1971 to 42.5 per cent in 1991.[19]

Protestants in these areas and along the border with the Republic have felt most beleaguered. The IRA's border attacks were seen as 'ethnic cleansing' and Protestants selling out to Catholics were condemned by their co-religionists. Since Protestants generally still think of the Catholics as a 'fifth column', awaiting their moment to remove the constitutional link with Britain, the threat these figures seemed to hold out of a future end to a Protestant majority was a factor in the escalating numbers of murders of Catholics by loyalist terrorists in the two years prior to the 1994 ceasefires.[20]

All social surveys show Protestants to be less tolerant of Catholics moving into their neighbourhood than the reverse. The experience of the Waterside district of Derry and Protestant North and West Belfast is perceived as a portent of things to come. In Derry most Protestants have moved out of the city and into the Waterside in the last twenty years, consciously ghettoizing themselves from a city now deemed Catholic – a microcosm of how they would see themselves in a united Ireland.[21] In Belfast the Commission was told that the Protestant population of

Figure 1. Population of Northern Ireland from the 1991/2001 censuses

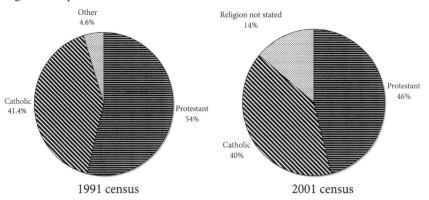

the Shankill in West Belfast had dropped from 76,000 to 27,000 and in North Belfast from 112,000 to 56,000 over the previous twenty years. There is 'a sense of siege, of retreat, almost of defeat', commented one community worker from the Shankill.[22] Protestants see neighbouring Catholic areas bursting at the seams while their own community is declining. Since the onset of the Troubles coincided with the virtual collapse of heavy industry in Northern Ireland (where the workforce was predominantly Protestant), the Protestant working class is experiencing new levels of unemployment and deprivation, once largely Catholic phenomena. Given the anti-discrimination legislation introduced in the last two decades – much of it to redress undoubted discrimination against Catholics – Protestants see all the economic gains as having been on the Catholic side, and they consider bogus the statistics which show Catholics still twice as likely to be unemployed.[23] It is, after all, in Catholic culture to complain. The sentiments expressed in a satirical song at the beginning of the Troubles still find echoes today:

> Come all you boys that vote for me, come gather all around.
> A Catholic I was born an' reared an' so I'm duty bound
> To proclaim my country's misery and express our Papish hope,
> To embarrass all the Orangemen an' glorify the Pope.
> Chorus: Sing fol dol do dee, it's great to be in the Nationalist game,
> We don't attempt solutions, we have only to complain.[24]

II

Catholics are baffled and embittered by such attitudes. Surely it is they who have been the victims in the past? They see themselves as being the most reasonable, making all the overtures for good community relations and pointing to the local councils with nationalist majorities having adopted power-sharing as policy. They find puzzling Protestant rejection of things Irish and their general ignorance of what Catholics believe. 'It's funny how little they know about us,' commented one Catholic in South Armagh. 'They have a picture of the South as a wee red-haired fella with a freckly face pulling a donkey loaded with turf … and that the people are all ruled by the church and things like this.'[25]

This comment highlights a general Catholic belief in a continuing Protestant tendency to see them as an inferior breed. Yet there has always been a superiority/inferiority dichotomy in Catholic thinking, the belief that they hold the moral high ground inducing a sense of pity for Protestants whose culture they see as sterile and impoverished compared to their own. At its more extreme this superiority/inferiority syndrome induces a self-righteousness and moral elitism. Republicans are particularly skilled at exploiting Catholics' shared memory of disadvantage and any effort to break away from it risks the accusation of 'selling out'. John Hume, leader of the SDLP, has little time for such 'whingeing' among his own community, suggesting that it suits many to persist in this kind of 'grievance mentality', rather than attempting to remedy the cause of their complaint.[26]

It is because of such 'shared memory of disadvantage' that Catholics are so unwilling to accept that Protestant fears might be genuine. Fear of the Catholic Church's power is simply a cover for pure bigotry; Protestant determination to cling to the Union with Britain a ploy to maintain their 'ascendancy' over the Catholics.[27] The use of the word 'ascendancy' by Catholics when speaking of their Protestant compatriots is instructive. Originally defined in the eighteenth century to describe exclusive Protestant rule of Ireland, it is a word embedded in the Catholic psyche. It acquired a new resonance after the creation of the Northern Ireland state in 1921 and the embers of resentment are easily ignited. It is such memories which unite SDLP and Sinn Féin supporters (though they agree on little else) against anything savouring of restored majoritarian unionist rule.

Now although I think such Catholic perceptions of Protestant motivation no longer accurate, and the Commission was made aware of a certain grudging admiration among Protestants for many aspects of Catholic culture – notably a greater ability to organize at community level – nevertheless, historically, the tendency to see Catholics as an inferior breed is real enough. Protestants think they are culturally more inclined to the useful scientific subjects, while Catholics prefer 'soft' subjects such as history and the arts[28] – hence the perceived economic backwardness of the South in the past, with which Protestants normally associated the Northern Catholics. Much of this they attributed to 'priestly tyranny', keeping the Catholics in ignorance and superstition. Catholics were encouraged by their priests to believe in fairies, Dr Bob Curran's Protestant grandmother told him when he was a child in the Mourne Mountains. 'As long as they believed in the supernatural – fairies, cures, visions and miracles – the priests had them in their grip. Catholics would believe anything which you told them – not like Protestants who were altogether much more sensible.'[29]

Such attitudes to the Irish are part of British culture, which can be documented from at least the time of Gerald of Wales in the twelfth century.[30] At the time of the Reformation the image was transferred to the Irish Catholics generally. In Ulster in particular, the absence of a Catholic gentry and later of a Catholic middle class seemed to confirm the stereotype, for Catholics have remained largely lower class and rural.[31] Travellers in eighteenth- and nineteenth-century Ulster were struck by the lengths to which Protestants would go to avoid being confused with the Catholic Irish. In 1812 John Gamble recorded an encounter with an innkeeper named O'Sullivan near Larne: 'he was very anxious to assure me that he wasn't

Catholic, despite the name, but descended from a Huguenot' – 'a zealous Protestant would as soon call his son Judas as Pat'.[32] But nothing caused more irritation to Catholics in past centuries than to be lorded over by Protestants who were sometimes intellectually and socially their inferiors. For the centrality of status in Gaelic culture had transferred itself to that of the Irish Catholics in early modern times. One of the aspects of the eighteenth-century penal laws most resented by Catholics was the ban on Catholics owning or carrying arms, thereby denying their middling and upper ranks the external status symbols of a gentleman.[33] A natural deference to their social betters had also been a trait of Gaelic society – and in many cases it was transferred to the new landlords (it was the settlers who were resented, more for their lowly social status than for their religion). Likewise this natural deference was misinterpreted as the sign of a slavish mind and entered Protestant folk stereotype of Catholics, defying even the recent emergence of a Catholic middle class, noted earlier:

> Come all you loyal Ulstermen, rejoice that we're together,
> We Catholics in the Middle Class have never had it better ...
> And if some have not got houses or employment we don't grumble,
> Why don't they beg and grovel, can't they follow our example ...
> My son will go to Clongoes Wood[34] and stay there till he's twenty,
> And learn there how to scrape and bow and pass himself with gentry.[35]

III

The kind of mutual incomprehension of the other community's core values outlined above owes not a little to the way in which they are expressed. 'The talks failed for lack of language', wrote Professor Edna Longley of the breakdown of interparty talks on the future of Northern Ireland in November 1992.[36] Certainly Catholics and Protestants in Northern Ireland appear to have different thought patterns. Recent social surveys have found social attitudes consistently different – even if they share a general religious conservatism.[37] The self-image of the Northern Protestant is that of a straight, uncomplicated, trustworthy, direct, plain-speaking individualist, as against the dissembling, untrustworthy, Jesuitical Catholic.[38] 'The SDLP speak with a forked tongue,' a group of Protestants from Castledawson in County Londonderry told the Opsahl Commission. 'The Republic can always wriggle out of things,' we were told by another group in Auchnacloy. 'Northern Protestants believe that Catholics do not say what they mean,' the Rev. Sydney Callaghan told the Commission, 'that they are profligate with words, past masters of the art of the fine point, the innuendo and the half-truth.'[39] Whereas the unionists tend to see hidden agendas and seek a cautious, step-by-step approach, the nationalists think in terms of frameworks and big solutions.

Ingrained cultural differences have meant that the two communities have frequently bypassed each other in every attempt at compromise and the differences in outlook have fed into many other areas of the Northern Ireland crisis, notably law, justice and security. There is a collective sense among Catholics that their whole community is treated unfairly in these areas: 'the army asked me what religion I was and I felt intimidated', commented a Catholic from Keady in South Armagh.

'When I see a member of the security forces I feel initimidated and guilty, even though I haven't done anything', a Catholic sixth-former told the Opsahl Commission's schools assembly in Belfast – and from all over the province the Commission heard evidence that those with Catholic-sounding names were more likely to be harassed by the security forces and stopped at checkpoints.[40]

> In the different religious/national traditions there have developed different visions of righteousness, radically different versions of justice. In a significant part of the Ulster Protestant tradition justice tends to emphasise honest dealing, getting one's deserts, acting rightly, fair procedures and the punishment of the guilty. Communal justice is not so central.
>
> In the Irish Catholic tradition there has developed a victim theology whereby the community sees itself as the victim and making sure the oppressor gets his deserts … Peace comes after justice and justice is the right framework. Reconciliation in this perspective is seen merely as giving the other a place in our framework, not together trying to create something new.
>
> This radical difference in perspective between the two communities is one of the reasons why they have such difficulty understanding each other.[41]

A 1993 analysis by Paul Burgess also presents a disturbing finding that the major Protestant and Catholic communities do not share a common morality. Hence the 'moral ambivalence' and 'double standards' which pervade Northern Irish society and permit otherwise peaceable people to perceive terrorist acts by one side as less morally reprehensible than those by the other. Burgess's survey shows that sectarian stereotypes are acquired from an early age through the segregated schools, often unconsciously transmitted by the teachers themselves (though more influentially, by the parents). This is why the government's well-intentioned 'Education for Mutual Understanding' programme has failed. With limited, frequently non-existent contact between schools of different denominations, it is taught by teachers who have not been specially trained and inevitably carry their own cultural baggage in the politically partisan nature of education in Northern Ireland. 'I have seen these so-called inter-school contact programmes,' one Catholic teacher told Paul Burgess. 'We take our lot to the swimming pool along with the neighbouring Protestant school. What actually happens is our kids stay up one end of the pool while they stay down the other.'[42] Little wonder that the programme evokes cynicism and a sense of futility among the schoolchildren at whom it is directed. 'It is not us, but our parents and teachers who need EMU,' commented one sixth-former at the oral hearings of the Opsahl Commission in Dungannon, Tyrone in February 1993.[43]

Sectarian consciousness is pervasive in Northern Ireland. It is not the monopoly of one community or the other and is often far removed from what we commonly call bigotry. It can be instinctive even to the most liberally minded and provides fertile ground for the kind of insider humour about prejudice and difference which most Northern Irish people engage in from time to time. It is there because difference has been institutionalized, locked, sometimes imperceptibly, into the social fabric of people's lives. It is a difference preserved and exaggerated by the very high levels of segregation in Northern Irish society. Some 83 per cent of Catholics and Protestants questioned in 1992 said most or all of their relatives were of the same denomination, and educational, sporting and social life, and now increasingly housing, are confined within one community.[44] The Opsahl Commission was told repeatedly of once mixed communities having become predominantly one-denominational as a result of the Troubles, of working-class males in particular deterred by fear from moving outside the safety of their own areas, even to take up much-needed employment, of the problems of attending integrated schools which might involve travel through areas dominated by the other community.[45] One of the most notable aspects of the rapid thaw in atmosphere following the 1994 ceasefires was a visible increase in public mobility, particularly in the Belfast area.

In March 1993 leading Northern Ireland journalist David McKittrick analysed unpublished data from the 1991 census and produced statistics for such increasing segregation which startled even those who knew it was occurring. He concluded that:

- Some 50 per cent of Northern Ireland's 1.5 million populace lived in areas which were over 90 per cent Protestant or Catholic.
- Less than 110,000 people live in substantially mixed areas, and even here there may be internal separation by the numerous 'peace lines' (20-foot-high walls physically separating Catholics and Protestants).
- In the last twenty years the number of wards exclusively Catholic or Protestant have increased from 43 to 120 and 56 to 115 respectively.
- In Belfast 35 of the 51 wards are now over 90 per cent Protestant or Catholic.

A community worker on the almost exclusively Protestant Shankill Road in Belfast neatly summarized the lifelong cycle of segregation thus:

> Young people start off in primary school: they are segregated. They go to secondary school: they are segregated. They leave school, no hope probably of getting a job … so they go to a youth training programme. There are separate YTPs [Youth Training Programmes] for Catholics and Protestants … Because they don't have any money they are stuck in their own areas, so they don't get to see other people with other religions or other cultures.[46]

It is this lifelong separation of the communities which has caused stereotypes to take the place of understanding in Northern Ireland. When the two communities do mix in the workplace, good relations are maintained by polite fancy footwork, tiptoeing around potentially controversial topics. 'Sectarianism … is the ghost at the feast of much of polite society in Northern Ireland,' Ken Logue told the Opsahl Commission. It 'depends essentially on a popular culture which invokes religion as a boundary marker between the two communities'. It can operate without any overt signs of such sectarian consciousness. The stereotypical cues of appearance, name, school, cultural values and speech are the unspoken language of everyday discourse.[47]

IV

We still await authoritative research into the historical background to this gulf of understanding. The Ulster Catholic in particular must be one of the most under-researched figures in Irish history. And yet to grow up as a Catholic in Northern Ireland – particularly in working-class areas – is to grow up convinced that you occupy the moral high ground, a descendant of the true Gael, your ancestors deprived of their land, your religion persecuted. Protestants are perceived as not entirely Irish, and Catholicism itself as possessing some kind of organic unity with Irishness, the very landscape suffused with both. 'It is perhaps inevitable that our poetry should be provincial,' wrote the Ulster Protestant poet Roy McFadden in 1946, ' … concerned with appearances, seeing the tree and the field without the bones beneath.'[48]

Although the Catholic tendency to think in terms of 'native' and 'planter' is on the wane, particularly among the young, traditionally Catholics have believed that they are 'the Irish properly so-called, trodden and despoiled'. The words are those of Theobald Wolfe Tone, generally held to have been the founder of modern republican nationalism at the end of the eighteenth century. But this perception has been part of the Irish Catholics' 'origin legend' since the seventeenth century.[49] The satirical song of the Troubles, cited earlier, points to the centrality of this belief in Northern nationalism.

> Our allegiance is to Ireland, to her language and her games,
> So we can't accept the border boys, as long as it remains,
> Our reason is the Gaelic blood that's flowin' in our veins,
> An' that is why our policy is never known to change.[50]

Protestants of all social categories are ambivalent about the cultural aspects of Irishness. On the one hand they reject it as subversive, used, as it undoubtedly has been, by extreme nationalists to exclude Protestants from the Irish fraternity. On the other hand they resent this narrow political focus and some are taking action to redress it – many Protestants are now showing a particular interest in Irish history and the Irish language, once unknown in Protestant schools.[51] 'Nationalists have defined Protestants out of being Irish,' Dr Chris McGimpsey of the Ulster Unionist party told the Commission. 'Nationalism is seen to be exclusively defined in terms of a 32-county state and a united Ireland. Many Protestants feel very Irish. Linking Irishness to a specific ideology has done tremendous damage.'[52]

The truth of this claim of the 'faith and fatherland' reading of Irishness is indisputable. A 1905 *Irish History Reader* published by the Christian Brothers included the following instructions:

> The teacher should dwell with pride, and in glowing words on Ireland's glowing past … her devotion through all the centuries to the Faith brought by her National Apostle … their interest should be aroused in that widespread movement, the creation of earnest men, that has already effected so much for Ireland in the revival of her native language, native music, and native ideals; they must be taught that Irishmen, claiming the right to make their own laws should never rest content until their native Parliament is restored; and that Ireland looks to them, when grown to man's estate, to act the part of true men in furthering the sacred cause of nationhood.[53]

But equally Ulster Protestants were more likely to reject a common Irish identity in past centuries. The following early-nineteenth-century warning of the combined political and religious threat awaiting Protestants who flirted with separatism and nationalism was a common one:

> From experience of th[is] event [the 1798 rebellion] … Irish Protestants ought to be convinced that the political separation of their country from Britain by a popular insurrection must involve their extinction and that consequently an infrangibly determined adherence to their British connexion is necessary for their safety.[54]

There is not much sense here of an ethnic Britishness among Protestants to match the ethnic Irishness of the later Gaelic revival. This is because their identity as a Protestant people was already well established – a religious identity which did not require racial underpinnings except in very specific periods of threat. The racial undertones of nationalist theory in nineteenth- and twentieth-century Europe have made it more difficult for Ulster Protestants to explain their identity in purely religious terms, however accurate it is in reality. But Britishness is more a declaration of political affiliation than an accurate label for that identity. A recognition of its inadequacies is one of the reasons for the collective loss of confidence among Northern Ireland's Protestant community.

There is already a search under way among some Protestants for an equivalent 'origin legend' to that of the Gaels for the Catholics. The argument is that Ulster has always been a distinct 'nation'; that Protestants are not 'Johnny-come-latelys', but descendants of the ancient Celtic people of Ulster, the Ulaid, the people of the Ulster Cycle and the heroic tales of Cuchullain – the central theme of which is the struggle of the Ulster people against the rest of Ireland. This claim provided an alternative origin legend for those arguing for an independent Ulster against the territorial claims over the province made by the Republic's constitution until 1999. In other words it is the Protestants who are the 'natives', not those of Gaelic stock. It is interesting that this origin legend should extract the same romantic views from the past for incorporation into a future state as the Gaelic revival did for the future Irish state: notably a rejection of materialism and an idealization of life on the land. An extension of this version of pre-history is to see the Scottish settlers who came over at the time of the Ulster Plantation as descendants of the ancient Ulaid, who had been pushed into the north-east, then to Scotland, returning in the seventeenth century to reclaim what was rightfully theirs.[55]

In fact the Gaels, like the Ulaid before them, were simply a warrior elite who absorbed indigenous peoples. It is impossible to trace lineage back beyond the eleventh and twelfth centuries – though the learned classes were kept busy creating bogus lineages into early modern times. It is unlikely that anyone in modern Northern Ireland can trace an unbroken lineage to either the ancient Celts or the Gaels. There is one important rider to all of this, however: the Gaels did succeed in imposing their culture not only over the whole of Ireland, but over Scotland as well, so that the 25,000 Scots mercenaries (Gallowglasses) operating in Ulster by the sixteenth century were Gaelic in culture and Catholic in religion.[56] What differentiated most of the Scottish settlers at the time of the Ulster Plantation from the resident populace and families of Scots descent was their religion, not their race. It simply cannot be proven that the settlers were Celts. Gaelic-speaking is not evidence – the Gaels and the Celts were different peoples.

This is a mirror image of the thesis of organic links between Catholicism, Irishness and territory which has dominated Catholic and nationalist readings of the past since the seventeenth century and which still surfaces in the popular tendency to see Protestantism as alien to Irish culture. The process whereby this image of the Catholic Gael was constructed has long been recognized by scholars. Less noticed – but equally important in the identikit of the Ulster Protestant – was the similar cultural creation of the Ulster Scot. In this account the Ulster Plantation of the early seventeenth century introduced a hardy breed of Scots. Endowed with the Calvinist work ethic and a no-nonsense independence of spirit, they turned the province into the economic success story which it was when the myth was fully developed in the nineteenth century and gave to Ulster that distinctive quality which separates it from the rest of Ireland.[57] All of this ignores the distinctiveness of Ulster long before the Plantation; the impact of Catholic Scots (not least in the Plantation itself where some 20 per cent of settlers were Catholic); the pre-existence of linen production which would provide the base for the economic miracle; the high proportion of mixed marriages; and the general cultural mix which has gone to make Ulster Catholics more like the Ulster Protestants than like their co-religionists elsewhere in the country.

This does not deny the fact, however, that even in the seventeenth century one was already deemed English, Scots or Irish according to one's religion. Not until the very end of the eighteenth century do some Irish Protestants call themselves Irish. Until then to be Protestant in Ireland was to be English – not of course a term readily adopted by the Ulster Presbyterians, who used terms such as 'Scots', 'Hiberno-Scots', and – on those occasions when a common Protestant identity was assumed in the face of a Catholic threat (such as the 1690s, the 1820s–40s and during the Troubles) – 'British'.[58] It was this reluctance by the Ulster Presbyterians to think of themselves as Irish which prompted Wolfe Tone's famous 'common name of Irishman' plea – though even he never lost that instinctive Protestant dislike of Catholicism as a system, notable in his other call to give Catholics rights and liberty to make them think more like Protestants – a forerunner of Terence O'Neill's infamous, though equally well-intentioned, remark: 'Give them jobs and houses and they will live like Protestants.'[59]

Contemporary Protestant rejection of Irishness therefore has a long history and it occurred long before it was taken over by an equally exclusive nationalism at the turn of the twentieth century. In many ways it is unhistorical to expect Ulster Protestants to readily accept an Irish identity, though many have. While Irish culture still has an identifiable link with Catholicism it will continue to be suspected by the bulk of Protestants, for it is dislike and fear of the latter which has informed their religion and shaped their identity for the last four centuries.

There can be no doubt then that twenty-five years of violence have polarized people in Northern Ireland to a greater extent than before. Peace – which has been sustained since the republican and loyalist cease-fires of August and October 1994 – is beginning to transform the situation. But it will not do so overnight and will not remove the underlying causes of the Troubles. The poverty, discrimination, massive unemployment, a dependency culture[60] which will be rocked by the consequent scaling down of security expenditure, and the sectarian and cultural divisions outlined above will take longer to resolve. But it is these divisions which are increasingly recognized by the people of Northern Ireland themselves as the underlying cause of the Troubles. The events of the past twenty-five years have been a deeply humbling experience. The experience of the Opsahl Commission has shown that there is a greater willingness than ever before among people to admit and explore the prejudices which have divided them. The Commission's report, and other recent commentaries, also show a fracturing of the old quasi-monolithic Catholic/ Protestant identities; a fracturing which, particularly within the Protestant community, created a deep sense of decline and despondency and was the backdrop to the escalation of Protestant paramilitarism before the two ceasefires. That fracturing, however, may be the necessary precondition for a recognition of what unites rather than what divides the communities. There is a small but significant increase in the number of people who accept a common Northern Irish identity (see Table 1) and the Opsahl Commission revealed a growing desire among nationalists to be given a more legitimate role within Northern Ireland (see Appendix 3), whereas once reunification of the island would alone have satisfied them. It is not yet an equality which many Protestants would easily accept. But even here there is a recognition that religious misunderstandings and prejudice have artificially divided sectors of the populace (notably in deprived working-class areas) who had more in common than they had with other social sectors within their own community or with the Irish or British governments with which they had traditionally identified. The Opsahl Commission (1993), the Downing Street Declaration (1993), the republican and loyalist ceasefires (1994), the 'Framework' proposals (1995), the Good Friday Agreement (1998) and a host of other local, national and international initiatives, are products of an ongoing peace process which started on the ground in Northern Ireland in 1992. At the heart of all these developments is a recognition that the problems in Northern Ireland will only be resolved from the bottom up, by its people learning to live and work together, prior to any decision about long-term constitutional structures.

Postscript

I have chosen to include the main recommendations of the Opsahl Commission among the appendices. Opsahl was an in-depth examination of public opinion at a time when demands for a sustained peace process were gathering momentum, and, although an independent report unlike the others, it provides a good insight into the wider public debate which formed the backdrop to the political talks.

Postscript 2006

In my original essay, I argued that the root of the problems in Northern Ireland was conflicting religious identities. Since then, the relationship between religious identity and conflict has become an urgent issue globally. That urgency has not yet reached the political classes in Northern Ireland, though it has reached most of those who study the conflict. It is very difficult to find any serious theoretical study of sectarianism and there is widespread misunderstanding of where it comes from and how it works.[61] No one likes to admit to being sectarian. Irish people generally think it is confined to the North; Catholics think it confined to Protestants; 'polite' Protestants think it confined to Loyalists, and each demonizes the other. Meanwhile 'Rome burns': peace walls in Belfast are increasing in height and number; sectarian attacks (and murders) are continuing beyond the official end of the Troubles; polarization of formerly mixed communities is significantly up since 2001, as shown by Shirlow and Coulter in this volume.[62]

On this issue, the recommendations of the Opsahl Commission (Appendix 3) now look fuzzy, which is why I here reproduce my essay on religion and identity (pp. 240–45) and that of Eric Gallagher on the role of the Churches (pp. 245–48), which were part of its report. They are still relevant. The declining confidence among working-class Protestants is still an issue. The growing secularization and prosperity of the Irish Republic has only marginally scaled down Protestant perceptions of Catholicism as poor, priest-ridden and politically dangerous, while among nationalists, north and south, there is little appreciation of just how fundamental Catholicism is to their Irish identity, even if the Catholic Church no longer figures so prominently in their lives.

As this new edition goes to press, the international monitoring commission has declared decommissioning achieved; there have been historic meetings between the DUP and the Catholic hierarchy and between Sinn Féin and Protestant Church leaders; and the political institutions have been restored on a power-sharing basis. Perhaps, belatedly, the time may not be far distant when we can finally look in depth at the centuries-old religious identities that have long underpinned our conflict.

Notes

1. Reprinted, with minor alterations, from Winston A. Van Horne (ed.), *Global Convulsions: Race, Ethnicity and Nationalism at the End of the Twentieth Century* (New York: SUNY Press, 1997), pp. 149–67, reproduced by kind permission of the publisher.
2. T. Opsahl, P. O'Malley, M. Elliott, R. Lister, E. Gallagher, L. Faulkner and Eric Gallagher, *A Citizens' Inquiry: The Opsahl Report on Northern Ireland* (ed. Andy Pollak; Dublin: Lilliput Press, 1993).
3. *Northern Ireland and the Opsahl Proposals: A Tri-Partite Poll* (Dublin: Irish Marketing Surveys, June 1993), summarized and extracted in *A Citizens' Inquiry*, 2nd edn, pp. 435–44.
4. Opsahl Commission, submission no. 531: Prof. Edna Longley. The Opsahl Commission Submissions have been deposited with the Linenhall Library in Belfast and are accessible to the public.
5. I am grateful to Dr Moxon-Browne for granting me permission to reproduce his findings. See also an analysis of similar findings in John Whyte, *Interpreting Northern Ireland* (Oxford: Oxford University Press, 1990), pp. 67–69.
6. Schools in Northern Ireland are generally divided by religion. In 1993, integrated schools accounted for only 1 per cent of school-age children (i.e. 14 out of a total of 1,336 schools, most of them at primary level). But the integrated movement is very recent and is gaining ground. It is still vigorously opposed by the Catholic hierarchy, inspires caution within the leadership of the Church of Ireland and Methodist Church, but is welcomed by the Presbyterian Church. Growing numbers of laity, however, are positively inclined.

7. Opsahl Commission, oral hearing, Dungannon, 5 February 1993, Omagh Christian Brothers School. Catholics in Castledawson told the Commission likewise.

8. Whyte, *Interpreting Northern Ireland*, p. 47.

9. See also Rosemary Harris, *Prejudice and Tolerance in Ulster: A Study of Neighbours and 'Strangers' in a Border Community* (Manchester: Manchester University Press, 1972), p. xi.

10. This emerged particularly during the Opsahl Commission's Derry schools assembly discussion group on Culture and Identity.

11. Opsahl Commission, submission by the Rev. Robert Dickinson; also presentation by the Witness Bearing Committee of the Reformed Presbyterian Church, oral hearing, Shankill Road, Belfast, 18 February 1993.

12. *A Citizens' Inquiry*, p. 120.

13. *Sectarianism: The Report of the Working Party on Sectarianism. A Discussion Document for Presentation to the Inter-Church Meeting* (Belfast: Irish Inter-Church Meeting, 1993), p. 133.

14. Opsahl Commission, Auchnacloy focus group; see also classic Protestant statement in letter signed 'L.S. Coleraine', *Belfast Newsletter*, 13 March 1989; also one signed 'Ulster Loyalist', *Irish News*, 11 April 1992.

15. Peter Stringer and Gillian Robinson (eds), *Social Attitudes in Northern Ireland: The Second Report 1991–1992* (Belfast: Blackstaff Press, 1992), p. 141.

16. *Sectarianism: A Discussion Document*, p. 147.

17. See for example his comments on President Mary Robinson's controversial visit to West Belfast in his interview with Jim Dougal, BBC Radio Ulster, 'A Week in Politics', August 1993.

18. *Sectarianism: A Discussion Document*, pp. 144–45.

19. *The Irish Times*, 14 November 1992, report based on the 1991 census.

20. Fionnuala O Connor, *In Search of a State: Catholics in Northern Ireland* (Belfast: Blackstaff Press, 1993), p. 145; Opsahl Commission, submission no. 402, the Witness Bearing Committee of the Reformed Presbyterian Church of Ireland, on how Catholics were feared by the majority Protestant community as 'subversive aliens'.

21. Opsahl Commission, Waterside focus group; also *Irish News*, 11 April 1992.

22. Opsahl Commission, submission by Jackie Redpath and oral hearing, Shankill Road, Belfast, 18 February 1993.

23. Opsahl Commission, oral hearing, Shankill Road, Belfast, 18 February 1993, particularly the Rev. Jack Magee and Roy Montgomery; Fintan O'Toole, 'On the other foot', *The Irish Times*, 30 November 1993.

24. Linenhall Library, Belfast, Northern Ireland Political Collection: 'A New Song for Nationalist Heroes'.

25. Opsahl Commission, Keady focus group.

26. O Connor, *In Search of a State*, p. 93.

27. Opsahl Commission, Keady focus group; also O Connor, *In Search of a State*, pp. 370–71.

28. Terence Brown, 'British Ireland', in Edna Longley (ed.), *Culture in Ireland: Division or Diversity?* (Proceedings of the Cultures of Ireland Group Conference; Belfast: Institute of Irish Studies, 1991), pp. 71–72.

29. Opsahl Commission, submission no. 325, Dr Bob Curran; *Belfast Newsletter*, 14 April 1988: 'Culture gap divides Ulster from Eire'; *Belfast Newsletter*, 7 October 1987: Ian Paisley's comments on a Catholic–Methodist conference; A.D. Buckley, 'Uses of History among Ulster Protestants', in Elizabeth Tonkin et al. (eds), *History and Ethnicity* (London: Routledge, 1989), p. 187.

30. Anne Laurence, 'From the Cradle to the Grave: English Observation of Irish Social Customs in the Seventeenth Century', *The Seventeenth Century*, 3(1) (1988), pp. 63–84; D.W. Hayton, 'From Barbarian to Burlesque: English Images of the Irish c. 1660–1750', *Irish Economic and Social History*, 14 (1988), pp. 5–31.

31. Marianne Elliott, *The Catholics of Ulster: A History* (Harmondsworth: Penguin, 2000); S.J. Connolly, 'Catholicism in Ulster, 1800–1850', in Peter Roebuck (ed.), *Plantation to Partition* (Belfast, 1981), pp. 157–71.

32. John Gamble, *A View of Society and Manners in the North of Ireland, in the Summer and Autumn of 1812* (London, 1813), pp. 63, 83–84.

33. Marianne Elliott, *Wolfe Tone: Prophet of Irish Independence* (New Haven and London: Yale University Press, 1989), p. 112.

34. Clongowes Wood, prestigious Catholic boarding school in the Irish Republic.

35. Linenhall Library, Belfast, Northern Ireland Political Collection: 'Song of the Middle Class Catholic'.

36. Opsahl Commission, submission no. 531: Professor Edna Longley.

37. Stringer and Robinson (eds), *Social Attitudes in Northern Ireland: Second Report*, p. 36; *The Guardian*, 19 March 1993: 'Divided loyalties'; only 23,933 out of 342,059 pupils were reported as attending integrated schools in January 1992.

38. See my *Watchmen in Sion: The Protestant Idea of Liberty* (Derry: Field Day Pamphlet, No. 8, 1985).

39. Cited in *A Citizens' Inquiry*, p. 37.

40. Opsahl Commission, submissions by Gabriel O'Keefe and Dr Brian Gaffney; also oral hearings, 4 and 16 February 1993.

41. Opsahl Commission, submission by Pax Christi Ireland.

42. Paul Burgess, *A Crisis of Conscience* (Aldershot: Avebury, 1993), particularly ch. 7.

43. Opsahl Commission, oral hearings, Dungannon, 5 February 1993, discussion of submission no. 422, Cookstown High School.

44. Stringer and Robinson (eds), *Social Attitudes in Northern Ireland: Second Report*, p. 36. The Opsahl Commission was also made aware of the polarization in charitable and voluntary organizations: Nick Acheson, submission no. 360 and oral hearing, Belfast, 17 February 1993.

45. See for example Opsahl Commission, submissions nos. 340, North Belfast Women; 466, Community Development Trust; 540, Elizabeth Groves; 142, CBI Northern Ireland. But the most revealing comments and information on this issue came in the oral submissions of these four parties, Belfast, February 1993.

46. *The Independent* (London), 22 March 1993; David McKittrick, 'Apartheid deepens on streets of Ulster', *The Independent on Sunday*, 21 March 1993.

47. Opsahl Commission, submission no. 472, Ken Logue; also his oral presentation, Shankill Road, Belfast, 18 February 1993.

48. Quoted in Patrick G. Curley, 'Northern Irish Poets and the Land since 1800' (MA dissertation, Queen's University Belfast, 1977), p. 88.

49. Elliott, *Wolfe Tone*; Thomas Bartlett, *The Fall and Rise of the Irish Nation: The Catholic Question 1690–1830* (Dublin: Gill and Macmillan, 1992), p. 295; Bernadette Cunningham, 'The Culture and Ideology of Irish Franciscan Historians at Louvain, 1607–1650', in Ciaran Brady (ed.), *Ideology and the Historians* (Historical Studies, XVII; Dublin: Lilliput Press, 1992), pp. 11–30; Opsahl Commission, submission no. 132, Centre for Research and Documentation, also oral hearing, 19 February 1993.

50. Linenhall Library, Belfast, Northern Ireland Political Collection, 'Song of the Middle Class Catholic'.

51. Opsahl Commission, submission no. 422, Cookstown High School, Lower Sixth Form;

also schools assembly, Belfast; I am grateful also for information from Aídan Mac Poílin of the Ultach Trust in Belfast.

52. Opsahl Commission, oral hearing, Newtownards, 21 January 1993.

53. Belfast Public Library, Bigger Collection, *Irish History Reader* (Dublin: Gill and Son, 1905); see also the Ulster Folk and Transport Museum, School Textbook Collection.

50. Quoted in R.R. Adams, *The Printed Word and the Common Man: Popular Culture in Ulster 1700–1900* (Belfast: Institute of Irish Studies, 1992), p. 143.

55. *Cru'thne: The Reawakening of an Ancient Kindred* (Portadown: Ulster Motherland Movement, n.d.); see also Ian Adamson, *The Identity of Ulster: The Land, the Language and the People* (Belfast: Pretani Press, 1982); J. Michael Hill, 'The Origins of the Scottish Plantations in Ulster to 1625: A Reinterpretation', *Journal of British Studies*, 32 (January 1993), pp. 24–43, for a more scholarly claim that many settlers were 'Celtic … ethnically'.

56. Ciaran Brady, 'The Failure of the Tudor Reform', in *idem*, M. O'Dowd and B. Walker, *An Illustrated History of Ulster* (Belfast: Institute of Irish Studies, 1990), p. 90.

57. See Raymond Gillespie, 'Continuity and Change: Ulster in the Seventeenth Century', in Roebuck (ed.), *Plantation to Partition*, pp. 124–26; Ian McBride, 'Ulster and the British Problem', in Richard English and Graham Walker (eds), *Unionists in Modern Ireland* (Basingstoke, 1996), pp. 1–18.

58. S.J. Connolly, *Religion, Law and Power: The Making of Protestant Ireland, 1660–1760* (Oxford: Clarendon Press, 1992), pp. 118–19.

59. Quoted in Eric Gallagher and Stanley Worrall, *Christians in Ulster, 1968–1980* (Oxford: Oxford University Press, 1982), p. 17.

60. The Northern Ireland economy receives British government subsidies totalling some £1.5 billion per annum; a further £0.5 billion is expended on the police and army and £500 million has been paid in compensation to businesses etc. in the course of the Troubles.

61. Notable exceptions are Joseph Liechty and Cecilia Clegg, *Moving Beyond Sectarianism: Religion, Conflict and Reconciliation in Northern Ireland* (Dublin: Columba Press, 2001) and John Fulton, *The Tragedy of Belief: Division, Politics and Religion in Ireland* (Oxford: Clarendon Press, 1991).

62. Although small beginnings are being made. The Northern Ireland Housing Executive is promoting the idea of mixed-community housing estates, the first in Enniskillen (October 2006); the Liverpool Institute of Irish Studies is mounting a study on such mixed estates prior to the Troubles.

Getting to Know the 'Other': Inter-church Groups and Peace-building in Northern Ireland[1]

Maria Power

The Catholic, Nationalist, Republican community are not British – so you get an anti-Britishness inside the Nationalist, Republican, Catholic community. Whereas inside the Protestant community, you get the same phenomenon expressed as anti-Catholicism. So, they define themselves over and against Catholicism – they are not Catholics. So, it works in the two communities in two slightly different ways but the end result is the same: you end up with a divided community.[2]

The conflict in Northern Ireland is one of contradictory identities based upon, among other things, differing political aspirations and religious affiliations, leading to communal identity defining itself along these lines. The result of this has been the creation of an oppositional identity in which the two communities generally classify themselves according to who they are not, rather than who they are. In *The Journey Towards Reconciliation*, John Paul Lederach describes this as a three-stage process. During the first stage, those involved 'begin to see in another person, not the sameness [they] share, but the differences between [them] that [they] identify as negative. [They] attach to those differences a negative judgement, a projection that this person is a threat to [them] and is wrong.' This separation from the 'other' in turn leads to feelings of superiority, which finally prompts a process of dehumanization and a belief that morally they stand above the other group.[3] Marc Gopin has summed up this experience, commenting: 'It is typical of conflict-generation thinking to formulate one's identity in opposition to another's identity, to form one's self as part of an ingroup verses the outgroup.'[4] In Northern Ireland this has resulted in the development of boundaries which are challenging to cross, both psychologically and, during times of heightened violence and tension, physically.

Religion plays a large role in the creation of these boundaries, providing a means of defining cultural and political as well as religious values and beliefs, producing 'a popular culture which invokes religion as a boundary marker between the two communities.'[5] In the 2001 Census, 85.5 per cent of the population readily identified themselves with a religious denomination[6] and the Protestant and Catholic Churches are still viewed as the largest institutions of civil society. Indeed, as David Stevens points out, 'the churches are present in every community in Northern Ireland. Much of the voluntary effort in this society is focused around churches and they contribute enormously to social capital.'[7] As a result, the Churches have generally been analysed purely in terms of the conflict in Northern Ireland. Endless articles and books are devoted to the issues of identity politics and the contribution of the Protestant and Catholic Churches to their development.[8]

However, religion is a multi-faceted entity containing elements of the 'peaceable kingdom' as well as the 'holy war,'[9] and as Jimmy Carter, former president of the United States of America, points out:

> Historically and currently, we all realize that religious differences have often been a cause or a pretext for war. Less well known is the fact that the actions of many religious persons and communities point in another direction. They demonstrate that religion can be a potent force in encouraging the peaceful resolution of conflict.[10]

Northern Ireland has been no exception to this phenomenon, with numerous church groups working ecumenically to promote peace and reconciliation within communities deeply fractured by the conflict. They have done so by directly challenging the notions of oppositional identity and feelings of moral superiority felt by the two communities by offering participants a 'safe space in which to step out of [their] comfort zone'[11] through which they can get to know something of the beliefs and attitudes of the 'other side'. Such work affords them an opportunity to learn more about their own faith and culture and, consequently, to replace their oppositional identity with an identity based on a firmer knowledge of their own and the 'other's' belief system. These ecumenical groups can slowly remove the feelings of threat and fear felt by participants, to be replaced by understanding, an acceptance of common bonds and a respect for the differences between the two communities. Through this process, inter-church groups eventually bring more peaceful relationships to their area.

This essay will focus on the historical development of such local inter-church peace initiatives, exploring in particular the means through which they challenge accepted notions of communal identity. It will demonstrate that these are often surprisingly low-key endeavours that take years rather than months to produce results. Such activities reveal that through the work of local churches, religion has consistently been used as a means of reconciliation, long before the cease-fires and subsequent European peace funding made cross-community work safe and acceptable. This essay first provides a short account of the different forms of ecumenical peace and reconciliation activity occurring in Northern Ireland since the Troubles began in the late 1960s, before going on to examine in detail the development of a number of Ecumenical Communities, whose work provides a reflection of all the methods employed by local inter-church groups within their communities.

I

Interaction between the Protestant and Catholic Churches in Northern Ireland has been taking place in some form since the early 1960s, with the Glenstal and Glencree Conferences[12] providing the initial opportunities for clergy to meet with one another and discuss doctrinal issues. However, it was the Vatican Council's *Decree on Ecumenism*[13] in 1964 that greatly eased matters and prompted a growth in contact, as Catholics now had their Church's blessing to engage with the Protestant Churches. Since the conflict began in Northern Ireland, numerous inter-church initiatives have sprung up, ranging from dialogue between church leaders to small ecumenical prayer initiatives founded in the wake of terrorist atrocities.

These groups, which are too numerous to count, have been broadly categorized as national-level ecumenical dialogue, peace and reconciliation education initiatives and local inter-church groups. Although each of these forms of inter-church contact uses vastly differing methods, they are all united in one fundamental aim: a desire to comprehend the perspective and identity of the 'other' community. They do so by creating positive attitudes towards each other in place of the oppositional identities described by Gopin and Lederach. They use whatever means are available to them, developing peaceful relationships between themselves before moving their mission out into the wider community.

National-level ecumenical dialogue has been the most high-profile of all the forms of inter-church contact. Although contact between the church leaders had been taking place during the late 1960s, national-level ecumenical dialogue began formally in 1973 with the Ballymascanlon talks, which eventually became the Irish Inter-Church Meeting. These were attended by representatives of the leaderships of the Protestant and Catholic Churches, with the exception of the Free Presbyterian Church, which protested outside the first meeting.[14] The focus of these meetings was initially doctrinal, centring on matters such as the role of Mary in the Church and salvation, and they were 'basically a structure for conversation between the member churches of the [Irish Council of Churches] and the Catholic Church.'[15] As time progressed, the Inter-Church Meeting became more ambitious in its scope and began to tackle problems that were of common concern to member churches, the most notable being sectarianism, on which a discussion document was produced in 1993.[16] The main concern of these talks was the creation of understanding between the different denominations involved. They achieved this aim, producing a sizeable number of pamphlets and discussion documents outlining the similarities and differences between the denominations on a number of issues. Through this they dispelled a number of the misconceptions and myths that have contributed to the development of an oppositional identity within both the Protestant and Catholic communities. In addition, the friendships formed between individual members through these gatherings are cited as one of their key achievements, as the insights into the 'other' community's belief systems are often reported back to the participants' congregations.

The work of the Irish Inter-Church Meeting has been much criticized. It has been accused of being little more than a 'talking shop'. The central problem with the Irish Inter-Church Meeting lies not in the actual work that it does (although this, unlike other forms of inter-church work, has remained fairly static), but in the use that it has made of the documents produced, and the friendships and understanding developed. The results of the dialogue have failed to move further than the immediate circle of those involved and it has not disseminated its work beyond those already committed to inter-church relationships. Ecumenical dialogue between the church leaders, and by association through the Irish Inter-Church Meeting, is fundamentally problematic. According to Revd Dr John Dunlop: 'the political and cultural suspicion [in this] environment has inhibited inter-church relations in Ireland', and the issues under discussion, both doctrinal and social, carried 'with them a tremendous emotional charge which has made building relationships across these divisions difficult.'[17] Furthermore, 'some people perceived the first inter-church meeting as some sort of peace conference,[18] thereby placing a burden of expectation upon the participants, making their work seem essentially flawed as they have never meaningfully addressed the issue of the conflict in Northern Ireland.[19] Nevertheless, although beset by problems, national-level ecumenical dialogue has contributed something to inter-church work. By tackling issues such as sectarianism and providing materials for other groups to work with, it has helped to improve people's understanding of communal identities. Moreover, despite its failure to move forward, it has provided much-needed impetus for many local organizations and has been a symbol of the church leaderships' acceptance of such contact.

This momentum has, in part, been picked up by the peace and reconciliation education initiatives that support groups wishing to undertake community relations or reconciliation work, which challenge traditionally accepted notions of communal identity. These organizations have been in existence, in some form, since the early 1970s when the Irish School of Ecumenics was founded by Fr Michael Hurley SJ. This was followed in the 1980s and 1990s by others, such as Youth Link: Northern Ireland, the Evangelical Contribution on Northern Ireland (ECONI), which works with the evangelical community, and Mediation Northern Ireland. They operate by developing courses through which local inter-church groups can explore issues relating to their identity, in a controlled manner and with the help of a skilled facilitator. Such courses, in the words of Lynda Gould, a facilitator from ECONI, 'make it easier for people to connect with the issues' of identity, politics, history and religion by enabling Protestants and Catholics to realize 'that they have been told the story one way; part of [the course's role] is to turn the coin over and say "there is another side to this"'.[20] In doing so, participants are encouraged to think about their identity and that of the 'other' community in a different way. Here, the presence of a facilitator is vital:

> If it is a group who are wanting to get into discussion – I would have a number of exercises which are aimed at getting people to think, to be more aware of their own identity and their perspectives, and these are the tools for getting them to structure what sharing they may do with one another. I think that the biggest role of a facilitator is giving them some handles through which to talk about their experience and giving them permission to do so. Often my role there is to describe a few examples and give them a feel for it. I get people to think what are the three things in the past 30 years that have made the deepest impact on me? [It could be] something as simple as that and I get them to draw it on a piece of paper and to talk about it in groups of four. They would maybe have never got into that unless someone who had facilitated them – it is giving handles and giving permission.[21]

This granting of 'permission' to explore issues relating to identity is one of the key contributions made by these initiatives to the development of inter-church relations and their identity work. The work of these education initiatives and of national-level dialogue both acted as a backdrop to what was going on at a local level, and it was this work within communities that provided the most inventive methods of challenging oppositional identity and demonstrated the ability of church groups to act as peacemakers.

II

Inter-church groups have been working within local communities since the first, a clerical study group, was founded in 1964. All use contrasting approaches to their work but each aims to deal with the issue of identity, which they see as one of the key barriers to the promotion of Christian reconciliation within Northern Ireland. Much of this is done by providing a safe space through which people can get to know each other and, in doing so, dispel the myths that cause oppositional identity to develop. A variety of methods are employed including parent and toddler groups, unemployment advice centres, adult education classes, women's and ecumenical prayer groups and the church fora which aim to act as the 'churches' voice' within the local area.

Ecumenical Communities played a central role in the development of inter-church projects within communities. Their work provides an excellent case study of the development of local level inter-church relations, as their efforts have encompassed all of the techniques employed since the late 1960s. Furthermore, these communities have been at the forefront of the development of reconciliation work in Northern Ireland and, as such, have clearly demonstrated the positive influence that the churches can have there. Between 1965 and 1992, seven were founded in order to 'include Protestants and Catholics who share a common life and [to] engage in... reconciliation'.[22] They were initially established as a means of providing respite from the violence of the late 1960s and 1970s. Thus, the Corrymeela Community, founded in 1965, and the Christian Renewal Centre, established in 1974, demonstrated the value of providing a place to which people could retreat from the pressures of living in an area of ongoing conflict. In doing so, they provided places of shelter, away from the inner cities, in which Protestants and Catholics could come together and pray while getting to know and understand something of each other's culture and faith.

By 1980, however, it was becoming obvious that retreat and removal from everyday life was not going to be effective for everyone, and that some form of work *within* local neighbourhoods needed to be undertaken. The newly founded groups, recognizing this need, started to concentrate upon more geographically defined areas, working in places of deprivation and conflict, providing social welfare as well as opportunities for prayer and reconciliation. The location of each of these groups has been crucial to their role in the inter-church relationships, and their membership and work has been constantly rooted in the area that they aim to serve. These Ecumenical Communities operated in extremely segregated areas, with social and economic deprivation characterizing the life experience of both Catholic and Protestant residents. These circumstances were compounded by the spectre of paramilitarism, as Church of Ireland Archbishop, Robin Eames, commented: 'they are not fighting each other on the Malone Road. It took me years to understand the implications of that remark. There are two communities here, and one is involved in violence, suffering, unemployment and injustice. The demarcation is class.'[23]

The walls erected as peacelines between Protestant and Catholic communities served as a stark, physical reminder to local residents of their sectarian divisions and served to sharpen the distrust between the two groups. 'Nobody could imagine the fear that the residents had to live under. It was a fact of life in [such] area[s] that everyone had to be on the constant look-out. The residents felt it was a potential killing field and were terrified for their lives.'[24] These peacelines shaped every aspect of the residents' lives, determining for example where children could play and which shops they could use. Over the past thirty years this pattern of separation has been perpetuated by the ongoing socialization processes of the two communities, and as one commentator has pointed out 'many children born into working-class households will grow up in districts where they will never have the opportunity to encounter someone from the other ethno-political tradition.'[25] Thus, the cycle of mistrust and fear has been passed from generation to generation, making the peacelines 'the only 30 foot high wall which neither side thinks is high enough.'[26]

It was in this atmosphere of fear, violence and deprivation that the Peaceline Ecumenical Communities were founded: the Lamb of God Community in 1977 in North Belfast between the two communities of New Lodge and Tiger's Bay, the Columba Community in 1980 in Derry,[27] the Cornerstone Community in West Belfast's Springfield Road in 1982. This was followed by the Columbanus Community of Reconciliation, which, although founded in 1983 in a neutral and increasingly salubrious section of the Antrim Road, was close enough to an interface to be able to minister to the communities there.[28] Finally, the Currach Community was born out of the experience of Cornerstone members in 1992 and was located on the opposite side of the Springfield Road peaceline, to offer support to a new housing development. These organizations promoted a model of Christian reconciliation and living that had been developed through tentative contacts between a few people who believed that their faith in God should override ethno-religious labels. Their value lay not only in their pioneering work in enabling the two communities to understand and respect each other's identity, but also in their commitment to longevity and consistency within the localities that they aimed to serve.

These communities all worked on or near peacelines and were primarily established to present an alternative definition of identity to the communities in which they worked, based upon a desire for Christian reconciliation. One member described them as:

> a Christian Ecumenical Community ... on the peaceline. We are in the middle of Protestant and Catholic and that is really where we want to be. We feel that we are something of a parable of possibility for the peaceline ... people coming together to pray and to share their faith ... doesn't make them into an amorphous mass. We still maintain our identities but we work together.[29]

Their founding stories are remarkably similar: the Lamb of God Community was established by a group of people who had met one another at a charismatic prayer group. The Columba Community was created because of its members' experiences of praying together and those involved wanted to aid those who had been affected by the conflict. Each of these peaceline communities was established through the vision and desire of a small group of people and evolved from well-established ecumenical prayer groups, at which the participants had begun to recognize the value of meeting members of the other community. For them, 'there was simply a strong desire to build relationships and encourage a faith journey together with people of different Christian Churches'.[30]

The five Ecumenical Communities founded after 1977 wanted their houses to be viewed as safe havens for both Protestants and Catholics, becoming a physical manifestation of their belief that people of different Christian traditions could live together without major conflict. Their stated aims provide a clear illustration of this: the Lamb of God Community aimed to 'encourage each other on the faith journey; to build stronger relationships between different traditions; to reach out together to the wider community'.[31] The Columba Community saw its role as incorporating prayer, community, evangelization, repentance and reconciliation.[32] Cornerstone sought 'to enable the people of the Shankill and of the Falls to discover the bonds that unite them and to respect their differences that arise from tradition and culture'.[33] The Columbanus Community of Reconciliation wanted 'to give a practical example of what a more united church, a more just society and a more peaceful world would be like; to challenge the sectarianism, injustice and violence prevalent in Northern Irish society'.[34] Finally, the Currach Community stated that 'Our *raison d'être* is to bring people together, to help them discover what they have in common, what their differences are and to begin to value the commonness and the difference'.[35] Their primary aim was to bring local Protestants and Catholics together and their methods were based upon a need to stress commonality while creating acceptance and understanding of difference, thereby promoting reconciliation.

III

A common methodological model has emerged from the experiences of these Ecumenical Communities. While the schemes employed were not entirely the same, in their engagement with their local communities each has moved through three phases: prayer and outreach, community relations work and social action. The communities added each of these new aspects to their work at roughly the same time. In doing so, they placed further emphasis upon their desire to promote more peaceful community relations within a Christian framework, through encouraging understanding and friendships. Through prayer and outreach they remained committed to their ecumenical origins with regular prayer groups, while establishing relationships with the wider community enabled them to gain trust and acceptance within the area. These relationships allowed them to begin working more directly on community relations issues and establishing social action projects. Here each Peaceline Community would implement some practical measures aimed at alleviating the problems of the area. It is no coincidence that these developments occurred at around the same time for each of these communities, as outside influences, such as the political peace process and the resultant influx of reconciliation funding, have had a profound influence upon the methods and work of these groups.

From the outset, these communities understood the need to adopt a low-key approach to their work, understanding that this was fundamental to gaining the trust needed to carry out their schemes of communal reconciliation. As one of the community leaders put it:

We knew that we could not come in here and start doing what we thought that the area needed. That would have been unhealthy. What we needed to do was to come in here and be part of the community around here, talk to them and dialogue with them because we wanted to be part of the area as well and through that we would learn what would emerge.[36]

Initially, each of the Peaceline Ecumenical Communities remained close to their roots as places of prayer and fellowship for the local Catholic and Protestant communities. This was reflected in the first stage of their evolution: prayer and outreach. Prayer has played a consistent role within the work of these groups and has underlined all their methods of engagement with the Protestant and Catholic communities. It was used as a means of interacting initially with the locality before attempting to introduce new projects. This can be seen most clearly in the case of two communities, the Lamb of God and the Cornerstone, both based in Belfast.

The Lamb of God Community was originally housed on the top two floors of a hairdressing salon in Duncairn Gardens, North Belfast. The salon was run by two members of the community and eventually became a thrift shop. According to one of the founding members, 'This provided revenue for the Community and also gave the vital means of contact with the surrounding area.'[37] They adopted a low-key approach that allowed them to build trust and it was through the contacts made with the customers that Lamb of God was able to found its prayer ministry. As with most of its work, the community took a simple and reactive approach, helping people when asked rather than offering services to the surrounding area. This outreach work grew as they realized that there was a need for counselling within the area. This was developed by a religious sister who, with the help of other community members, answered the need in the locality for a place where people could go, 'just to unburden and to talk and just to be listened to,'[38] particularly about the violence in the area. Consequently, the community began to be viewed as a safe haven, and their early work built up and enabled them to fulfil their founding aim of reaching out into the wider community.

The experience of the Cornerstone Community, while similar to that of Lamb of God, highlights the importance of the local setting in the development of the Peaceline Communities. Once more, prayer was the main focus, with members praying together twice daily and a large amount of time at the weekly community meeting being devoted to scripture or prayer. This focus was almost immediately translated into outreach work, which developed organically in response to surrounding events. This they saw as an expression of their aims: 'We have tried to further our work of peace and reconciliation by having groups of Catholics and Protestants in to share views and prayer and by visiting local people and groups',[39] commented one member in 1986. The initial link between their prayer and outreach work came with the establishment of their bereavement and crisis visiting. This was initiated by a local Catholic priest, Fr Gerry Reynolds, after a member of the UDR had been killed by the IRA. Thus, nearly every time a sectarian atrocity was committed locally during the 1980s, a member of Cornerstone 'would go in and sit with the family and if [they] found it appropriate would say a prayer'.[40] In addition to this, Cornerstone became active in promoting inter-church prayer groups, establishing a women's prayer group that allowed those involved to pray and talk together once a month. Gradually the members of the community became engaged in prayer initiatives outside the house itself. The most successful of these were the Shankill pilgrimages founded in 1994, through which members of the Catholic parishes of the Falls attended a service at a Protestant church on the Shankill. Such schemes were a tangible manifestation of the reconciling vision of Cornerstone, as one of the members pointed out: 'We see our visits as planting new seeds of friendship and prayer between the congregations of the church in the Shankhill and those in the Falls'.[41]

As a result of adopting such low-key approaches, these Peaceline Ecumenical Communities began to be viewed as safe havens within the area, building up the trust that would be so vital to the implementation of their communal identity schemes. This acceptance manifested itself in different ways. For example, the Currach Community was asked to be a spokesperson for the local area:

> After about a year and a half there was an incident here that showed us very clearly that we were accepted as a group. There was a threat to close the gate [that acts as a peace-line]. A meeting was called and they were going to the police to make a statement. [They decided] if that didn't work they'd go to the City Hall and someone piped up 'well we should send somebody from the Community House', which meant that they were going to send one of us to go and represent the area. That was within two years. That was a very rewarding experience for us.[42]

By the late 1980s they had, through their prayer and outreach, fulfilled their initial aims and began to plan to make a larger impact upon the area through community relations work and practical schemes that were constantly informed by their prayer and outreach experiences.

The second stage of the Peaceline Communities development, community relations work, represented their first attempt to go beyond prayer and bring the two communities together to address some of the major points of division. Here the communities demonstrated the value of using dialogue through prayer as a means of bringing the Protestant and Catholic participants to an understanding of each other's identities. However, the Ecumenical Communities understood that this was a long-term process that would involve them dealing with their own identity issues before attempting to work within the local communities. As one member commented, 'you have to know what you are about yourself'[43] before attempting to deal with other people's identities. Once this internal trust had been achieved, the communities moved on to working with members of the local community, drawing participants from their existing prayer groups and the congregations of neighbouring churches. These communities took a two-stage approach to the issue of identity, starting first with its religious aspects before moving on to the political when the paramilitary cease-fires made this possible.

This work was initially discreet and simple, using prayer and seasons in the liturgical calendar, such as Lent or Christmas, as a means of communication. Subsequent changes in the political situation enabled them to address issues, such as the effect that paramilitary violence had upon the neighbourhood, more directly. The earliest attempts at community relations work came in the 1980s and 'brought

Christians from all denominations… to worship, to discuss in small groups, to listen to speakers from various backgrounds'. [44] As one of the participants points out, these meetings were valuable in offering a safe space for people to meet and talk to one another. One describes the experience thus:

> we made out lists of how we perceived others and what we really believed … I think that was the main part of the exercise … so that we began to see how other people see us and the things that we do that hurt them and the things that they do that hurt us. [45]

The results confirmed for the facilitators their belief that the two communities shared a great deal in common, similarities that they could eventually harness to promote reconciliation. For example, the facilitators of one group found that 'It was a very honest course, people were very wounded but one of the first positive things that they discovered was that they had the same fears, which was very interesting, and the same thoughts about God'. [46] Through these earliest exercises in community relations work the participants felt more equipped to pray together and engage in the tentative conversations regarding religious belief and identity that were to underpin later work. In providing such opportunities, the Ecumenical Communities began to dispel the myths and notions of otherness that produced feelings of moral superiority and fear. They did so by providing a forum in which Protestant and Catholic participants could learn about the similarities in their respective identities, while understanding the differences.

The move from discussing religion to exploring issues related to politics, and in some cases history, was taken slowly by the Ecumenical Communities and demonstrated a desire to continually challenge the Protestant and Catholic communities' accepted definitions of one another. Generally, the communities started anew with fresh groups of people rather than continuing with those who had previously been in their prayer groups. This was mostly due to the timescale involved, as this shift towards working on political issues only started to gain momentum after the paramilitary ceasefires in 1994. The communities had to adopt a low-key approach to this work, taking into account the needs of the groups involved, rather than just implementing one of the standard community relations courses made available to them by the growth of the peace and reconciliation education initiatives.

This need for sensitivity is illustrated clearly by the experience of a women's group founded in 1993 by the Currach Community in West Belfast. Much of the work done in the early stages with this group of Catholic and Protestant women was very practical, dealing with cooking and crafts, and, according to the group's leader, 'it took us two to three years before they would do anything serious, even look at their own stress levels'. [47] Once trust had been established within the group, they felt able to do more serious work, looking for example at their own identity and that of their families:

> We've done *From the Personal to the Political* looking at how I, as an individual, am not cut off from the politics. People think that it has nothing to do with me, but by the very fact that I deny it I am political because I am affecting what goes on up there by not doing anything about it. We bonded with a group in Dublin and we have had four residential weekends with them. We took some history around the time *Michael Collins* had been made. Then we had two of the women whose husbands had been [leaders] in the Orange

Order and they told us what that was about, they brought in the sashes and explained what that was about. We went to Stormont and visited there and when we came back some of the nationalists were saying how strange they found it and here we were walking around this place and trying to say this is where my government lives. The Protestant women were saying that they felt the same way too [about the Stormont Government] 'they never seemed to be organising things for us, they were always away from us'. So we began to realise the commonness of alienation. We talked about that. That is the kind of thing that we can be about now.[48]

For the participants these meetings 'stand out as times when we took risks with each other in expressing our fears and prejudices. While each of the courses encouraged us to be articulate about our own beliefs and traditions we also learnt to listen respectfully and to appreciate the experience of others'.[49] These experiences clearly illustrate the value of such work in combating oppositional identity. Through the guidance of the Ecumenical Communities, people were able to explore issues relating to their own identity and that of the other community in a safe and neutral environment. In doing so, those taking part in such exercises were reversing the three-stage process described by Lederach – moving from judgement of differences, group separation and dehumanization to acknowledgement of similarities and shared experiences, acceptance of difference, and, finally, friendship and understanding.

The community relations work undertaken by the Ecumenical Communities raised a number of issues regarding the socio-economic problems in the surrounding areas, which it was felt erected a further barrier between the Protestant and Catholic communities. In the mid-1990s, this led to the final stage in the Peaceline Communities' development: the social action project, through which they attempted to offer practical help to their localities and in doing so developed another avenue through which the question of identity could be tackled. This was based upon the idea that 'if you get people of different political groups working together, tackling common problems, then you will overcome the hostilities gradually by getting people to focus on things other than differences, focusing on commonalties'.[50] Such schemes enabled those involved to realize that the problems they faced, such as alcoholism, deprivation, unemployment and alienation, were the same for both communities. This work was always carried out in partnership with the local community, with the services being offered ranging from emergency crèches for the children of victims of violence to the establishment of an alcohol and drugs addiction centre in Derry.

The Columba Community's foundation of a rehabilitation centre for alcoholics in 2001 is a clear example of this type of scheme. The White Oaks Rehabilitation Centre was established as a result of a perceived need within the local community. As one of the members commented:

Now I think the Community felt that drink was a problem in the city, so we've moved into that area, because some lady came and banged at the door with her shoe, and broke the door in and said, 'Nobody is listening to me'. And I think at that stage we felt maybe we should listen to this. Anybody who comes breaking the door downstairs has something to say.[51]

The Centre offers a thirty-day residential programme designed to help addicts, based upon the twelve-step programme used by Alcoholics Anonymous. For the members of Columba, White Oaks represented a natural progression in their work, signifying a continuation of their engagement with the two communities in Derry, enabling them to work towards an understanding of identity through practical means rather than discussion and therefore reconciliation at a deeper level than before.

The work of the Lamb of God and Cornerstone Communities also served to illustrate the variety of this social action work and the ways through which the matter of identity was addressed. Lamb of God founded a crèche in 1992, where local children 'would be taken care of and allowed to play'[52] after an atrocity. By 2005, this crèche had become one of the Community's central projects and was providing regular, rather than emergency, childcare for the area. From this initial project Shalom House evolved, offering services to develop the 'emotional, social, personal and spiritual'[53] needs of the community. Lamb of God began to run GCSE courses in Maths and English for people wishing to return to education, a drop-in centre and a spiritual programme based upon prayer and meditation. Cornerstone's social action was developed though a family worker and a youth worker, employed in 1990 and 1993 respectively, as a response to a perceived need within the community. With the establishment of these posts, Cornerstone began to offer services such as counselling as well as events such as an inter-community senior citizens' club and youth clubs. The social action projects offered by these Ecumenical Communities were holistic rather than purely material and focused upon alleviating the deprivation of the local community through practical action rather than charity. By engaging in such methods, they contributed to reconciliation in two key ways: first, they centred upon a long-term need to improve the lives of both communities through the provision of services. These, they argued, had the potential to bring stability by treating the consequences of the violence, such as increased alcoholism. Secondly, and perhaps most potently, they provided another means through which Protestants and Catholics, who perhaps would not be comfortable with other methods of community relations contact, could work together. As a result, they demystified those of whom they would previously have been ignorant and fearful.

IV

In their work with local communities, Ecumenical Communities placed themselves at the very heart of the conflict in Northern Ireland. In doing so, they demonstrated the effectiveness of religion in resolving conflict and promoting reconciliation. By ministering to those most affected by the violence and socio-economic deprivation, they provided Protestants and Catholics with an alternative, more peaceful way of relating to one another. While the Peaceline Ecumenical Communities in Northern Ireland have not been the only ones working in such ways, they have been the centre of this movement, often leading the way when it came to implementing new ideas. A desire to reconcile the two communities in Northern Ireland defined everything that the Peaceline Ecumenical Communities did. Using their understanding of the destructive nature of oppositional identity, they developed innovative and effective ways of gently challenging sectarianism. As communities they have been constantly aware of the need to change, reacting to events while retaining their initial vision of practical Christian reconciliation. Herein lies the key to their success: they listened to the Protestant and Catholic communities themselves, rather than imposing the kind of 'top-down approach' that character- izes so much of the community relations work currently being carried out in the Province. They used any methods at their disposal and employed these to demys- tify the beliefs, values and experiences of the 'opposed' community, in a setting that encouraged debate and supported those who found the process difficult or painful. As a result, participants came genuinely to know and understand members of the other community, rather than persisting with the negative judgements that have pervaded Northern Irish society and have helped to escalate tensions within local communities. The methods and ideas of the Peaceline Ecumenical Communi- ties, especially their use of prayer as a means of initially gaining the trust of local communities, have the potential to be one of the most potent forces available to resolve conflict and build peace, especially in a region where the majority of the population 'belong' to a religion. Their work has effectively demonstrated that local communities need to feel safe, both emotionally and physically, when engaging in reconciliation programmes, and only then will people begin to work through their identity issues in relation to the 'Other' and recognize the similarities that they share.

Notes

1. I am grateful to the Economic and Social Research Council (award number PTA-026- 27-0247) for their support which enabled me to complete the research for this essay and to Professor Arthur Williamson at the University of Ulster for his helpful comments.
2. Author's interview with Revd Dr John Dunlop, Belfast, 14 January 2000.
3. John Paul Lederach, *The Journey Towards Reconciliation* (Scotdale: Herald Press, 1999), pp. 47–49.
4. Marc Gopin, *Between Eden and Armageddon: The Future of World Religions, Violence and Peacemaking* (Oxford: Oxford University Press, 2000), pp. 148–49.
5. Ken Logue, cited in Marianne Elliott, 'Religion and Identity in Northern Ireland', in Winston A. van Horne (ed.), *Global Convulsions: Race, Ethnicity, and Nationalism at the End of the Twentieth Century* (New York: State University of New York Press, 1997), pp. 149–67, 158.
6. Figure calculated by the author from data in Peter Brierley (ed.), *UK Christian Handbook: Religious Trends 1998–99* (London: Christian Research, 1999) and NISRA, 'Northern Ireland Census 2001 Key Statistics', Table KS07a, http://www.nisra.gov.uk/ census/pdf/Key%20Statistics%20ReportTables.pdf, accessed 26 July 2005. Such high levels of religious self-identification indicate clearly the salience of religious identity in Northern Ireland, especially when one takes into account the fact that it is not compul- sory to answer this question on the census form. On average 91 per cent of the popula- tion has answered this question since 1971.
7. David Stevens, 'The Churches and Ten Years of the Peace Process', in *Beyond Sectari- anism? The Churches and Ten Years of the Peace Process* (Belfast: Community Relations Council, 2005), p. 10. A detailed account of this contribution can be found in Derek

Bacon, *Communities, Churches and Social Capital in Northern Ireland* (Centre for Voluntary Action Studies, University of Ulster, 2003).

8. For a fuller discussion of this see Maria Power, *From Ecumenism to Community Relations: Inter-Church Relations in Northern Ireland 1980–2005* (Dublin: Irish Academic Press, 2007), pp. 1–3.

9. Elise Boulding, cited in Chadwick F. Alger, 'Religion as a Peace Tool', *The Global Review of Ethnopolitics*, 1(4), June 2002, pp. 94–109, 94. This article contains a useful summary of the debates surrounding the use of religion in conflict resolution processes.

10. Jimmy Carter, 'Foreword', in Douglas Johnston and Cynthia Sampson (eds), *Religion, the Missing Dimension of Statecraft* (Oxford: Oxford University Press, 1994), pp. vii–viii, vii.

11. Author's interview with Maire Foley and Graeme Thomson, Ploughshare, Bangor, Co. Down, 9 November 2005.

12. Glenstal and Greenhills are annual inter-denominational theological conferences. The Glenstal Conference grew out of 'a mixed lay-clerical group of Dublin Catholic intellectuals interested in religion and theology' who in 1963 began to develop contacts with members of the Church of Ireland clergy. Consequently, it was suggested by the Abbot of Glenstal that an ecumenical conference be held there in 1964 on the subject of the Liturgy. The first Greenhills Conference was held in January 1966 as a one-day inter-church conference and was initiated by the Revd Dr J. G. McGarry of Maynooth, who felt that the relative proximity of the location to Northern Ireland would make it 'more readily accessible to participants from Northern Ireland [and] would … be appropriate and meet a real need'. See Michael Hurley, 'The Preparation Years', in *The Irish Inter-Church Meeting: Preparation and Development* (Belfast: IICM, 1998), pp. 8–9.

13. *Decree on Ecumenism: Unitatis Redintegratio*, 21 November 1964 (Boston: Pauline Books and Media, 1964).

14. For a description of these initial meetings see Eric Gallagher and Stanley Worrall, *Christians in Ulster 1968–1980* (Oxford: Oxford University Press, 1982), p. 78.

15. Author's interview with Revd Dr David Stevens, Irish Council of Churches, Belfast, 13 February 2002.

16. *Sectarianism, a discussion document: The Report of the Working Party on Sectarianism* (Belfast: Department of Social Issues of the IICM, 1993).

17. Interview with Dunlop.

18. Interview with Stevens.

19. See Power, *From Ecumenism to Community Relations*, pp. 27–71.

20. Author's interview with Lynda Gould, Training Officer, ECONI, Belfast, 16 May 2001.

21. Author's interview with Revd Doug Baker, Mediation Northern Ireland, Belfast, 4 October 2000.

22. Churches Advisory Group, *A Directory of Cross-Community Church Groups and Projects in Northern Ireland 1999* (Belfast: Community Relations Council, 1999), p. 27.

23. Archbishop Robin Eames, cited in Margaret Carey and Carmel Roulston, *The Cornerstone Community, A Report for the Annual Review* (University of Ulster, September 1996), p. 6. The Malone Road is a middle-class area situated in South Belfast close to Queen's University.

24. *Life on the Interface, 'Report on a Community Group Conference'* (Belfast, 1991), cited in Brendan Murtagh, 'Image Making Versus Reality: Ethnic Division and the Planning Challenge of Belfast's Peace Lines', in William J. V. Neill, Diana S. Fitzsimons and

Brendan Murtagh (eds), *Reimaging the Pariah City: Urban Development in Belfast and Detroit* (Aldershot: Avebury, 1995), pp. 209–30, 209.

25. Colin Coulter, *Contemporary Northern Irish Society An Introduction* (London: Pluto, 1999), p. 75.

26. *The Guardian*, 6 August 1986, cited in Murtagh, 'Image Making Versus Reality', p. 213.

27. Although this community does not actually operate on a peaceline its methods and ethos are similar enough to those of its Belfast counterparts to be included here.

28. As one of their members later stated, the community was founded there in order to 'avoid undue pressure from either side, it was necessary that we should be situated on neutral ground, [although] we are very near to both Protestant and Catholic troubled areas and hope increasingly to be able to serve both communities across the divide'. Eileen Mary Lyddon writing to *Encounter and Exchange* (1986), reprinted in *We Plough the Fields and Scatter* (booklet produced by the Columbanus Community of Reconciliation c. 1994). This community closed in 2003 as a result of funding difficulties.

29. Author's interview with Mr Tom Hannon, Director of the Cornerstone Community, 28 January 2000.

30. *Questionnaire on the Experiences of the Ecumenical Communities: The Lamb of God Community, Belfast*, 11 September 2001.

31. *Questionnaire: the Lamb of God Community*.

32. The Columba Community, *Columba House* (information leaflet, n.d.).

33. Cornerstone Community, *Information Leaflet* (n.d.).

34. *Columbanus Community of Reconciliation: An Introduction* (leaflet, n.d. but around 1994).

35. Author's interview with Noreen Christian, leader of the Currach Community, Belfast, 21 October 1999.

36. Ibid.

37. *Questionnaire: the Lamb of God Community*.

38. Ibid.

39. *Cornerstone Contact*, 1986.

40. Interview with Tom Hannon.

41. *Cornerstone Contact*, Winter 1999.

42. Author's interview with Noreen Christian, leader of the Currach Community, Belfast, 13 February 2002.

43. Author's interview with members of the Lamb of God Community, Belfast, 12 February 2002.

44. Author's interview with the Columba Community, 14 February 2002.

45. Interview with the Lamb of God Community.

46. Ibid.

47. Interview with Noreen Christian, 2002.

48. Ibid.

49. *Cornerstone Contact*, Spring 1999.

50. Author's interview with Cardinal Cahal Daly, Belfast, 3 February 2000.

51. Interview with Columba Community, June 2005.

52. Interview with the Lamb of God Community.

53. Lamb of God Community, *Shalom House* (information leaflet, n.d.).

Enduring Problems: The Belfast Agreement and a Disagreed Belfast

Peter Shirlow and Colin Coulter

There is a common concern to explain why the 'long war' in Northern Ireland became the 'long peace'.[1] Such analyses are important but most of them have been driven by an examination of political actors and their actions, and have under-examined the significance of factors such as social class, habituation and the experience of violence in undermining the delivery of meaningful 'mutual respect'.[2] Evidently at the political level several obvious stalemates have been broken with regard to the main political parties. They all now either accept (in some cases reluctantly) the principle of consent or (cautiously) endorse the validity of power-sharing. Political problems endure but even the most durable of these, the Democratic Unionist Party's (DUP) 'requirement' that Sinn Féin (SF) must divest itself of military linkage, is slowly dissolving. Within the ranks of the DUP the clarion call of 'Not an Inch' has been transformed into a process of inching slowly towards a devolved power-sharing administration.

In this chapter we seek not only to explore some of the limitations of the Belfast Agreement but also to highlight how the social reality of enduring segregation maintains ethno-sectarian relationship. Such relationships undermine the development of shared space. Territorial entrapment remains and is a forceful reminder that the political process may be advancing but not in the manner required to challenge the nature of spatial separation and thus much of what constitutes identity formation.

The Belfast Agreement achieved some key principles and developed structures that will evolve and bed down, but the agreement and the political leadership offered has not and probably will not challenge the edifice of ethno-sectarianism. We are thus trapped in a situation in which Northern Irish society will remain shaped and directed by 'trustworthy' factors such as segregating living, fear, suspicion and resource competition.[3] Without the removal of such unambiguous divisions, and with the reality that Northern Ireland's constitutional future remains uncertain, it is evident that the undermining of sectarian relationships, in whatever form, remains a central goal of conflict transformation.

The Belfast Agreement

The document that emerged from the multiparty negotiations at Stormont was inevitably detailed, multifaceted and wide ranging. The terms of the Belfast Agreement sought to address and resolve three different sets of relationships understood to be at the heart of the 'Northern Ireland problem'. In more specific terms, the political deal struck at Stormont set out to 'nurture' and 'heal' relations between the 'two communities' in Northern Ireland, between people living either side of the Irish border and between the various peoples who live either side of the Irish Sea. The first of these relationships is of course the most substantial concern of any solution to the Northern Irish conflict and it is, therefore, the one with which we will concern ourselves most.

The basis of such relationships was to be 'parity of esteem' and the principles of 'mutual respect'. But the Belfast Agreement came late with regard to equality building. For over two decades fair employment legislation had done much to dent and undermine allegations of discrimination. Imbalances remained, but they were not at the level that once motivated direct political action. Similarly, the housing issue, once such an emotive problem, had also been largely resolved. What did remain were issues regarding territoriality and the divisions that they caused. The location of jobs in predominantly Protestant areas has been shown to undermine the employment of Catholics, especially in lower-paid jobs. The same is the case regarding jobs located in Catholic areas.[4] Such 'chill factors'[5] were not mentioned in the Belfast Agreement even though, as shown below, the impact that they have remains significant.

The 'two tribes' model advanced within the Belfast Agreement meant that it offered little to those who advanced non-sectarian discourses. The bolstering and official recognition of these cultural blocs upheld the power and authority of division. It also motivated the rise in a process of concession-seeking as opposed to forcing political leaderships to imagine shared solutions needed to challenge the complexity of a divided society. In rewarding the politics of concession-seeking, the Belfast Agreement promoted oppositional political codes and approaches.

The Agreement aimed to allay the enduring fears of the unionist community that they might be duped into a united Ireland. So it stated quite categorically that 'Northern Ireland in its entirety remains part of the United Kingdom' (Annex A Part 1 (1)). Yet the Agreement also set out to accommodate nationalists' aspirations that they might in the future become citizens of a united Ireland. The evident reality was that the border issue had not been resolved and the *de facto* constitutional holding operation that was put in place meant that unionists remained concerned and republicans/nationalists ambitious.

The binary sense of giving and taking was also evident with regard to policing and Articles 2 and 3 of the Irish Constitution.[6] The Belfast Agreement sought to redress the grievances of nationalists by promising a 'new beginning to policing'. Conversely, the dissolution of the Royal Ulster Constabulary (RUC) and the creation of the Police Service of Northern Ireland (PSNI) have failed to gain full and unequivocal support from within the republican community. More importantly, the dissolution of the RUC furthered a unionist interpretation that concessions were only going in one direction, towards the nationalist/republican community.

In the spirit of better cross-border relations, the Irish government committed itself to the revision of Articles 2 and 3 of the 1937 Constitution, which had proved so profoundly offensive and threatening for many unionists. The existing claim upon the territory of Northern Ireland would be replaced by an expression of kinship with people living north of the border and an aspiration that Irish unity would in time be achieved through purely peaceful means.[7] The rewriting of these Articles was hardly a seismic shift within the Republic of Ireland, where ideology was driven more by lifestyle than by recalling de Valera's attempt to build state republicanism. At best unionists viewed the constitutional changes as the removal of a territorial claim that they believed should not have existed in the first place. Not only did the Agreement fail to recognize the durability of sectarianism, but in view of the muddled concession-giving in which it was presented, it furthered the unionist sense of alienation. Furthermore, the capacity of those who wished to advance non-constitutional political discourses was narrowed by the rise in electoral power of political tribalism.

Tribal Power

The Belfast Agreement did not silence the meaning of constitutional desire and the capacity to resist the 'other' political bloc through new forms of conflict. If anything, the Belfast Agreement became a site within which the diversity between constitutionally committed ethnic blocs was to be played out. The issues of parading, housing and victimhood were to become the new arenas within which distrust and suspicion between the dominant ethno-sectarian blocs were to be publicly raised. In reality, the Agreement, and the eventual political administration it ushered forth, merely managed polarization. There was no desire to tackle segregation in schooling, residence and work.

The closure of the Jubilee Maternity Hospital, in a predominantly Protestant part of South Belfast, meant that 'Protestant' babies would be born in the Royal Victoria Hospital (located within Republican West Belfast), and led to unionist outrage. This anger was compounded by the fact that the decision (based upon an improvement in service delivery) was taken by Bairbre de Brún of SF, the then Minister of Health. Nigel Dodds from the DUP, while Environment Minister, moved a bus stop in North Belfast so that Protestants would not have to wait at a stop within Catholic 'territory'. Decisions on road building and the location of other services were constantly placed under the ethno-sectarian lens of resource competition. 'Mutual respect' within such decision making has constantly struggled against such tribal allegiances. Clientelist politics echoed the serving of ethno-sectarian interests that had been embedded within the Agreement.[8]

The polarization of political opinion that has unfolded over the last few years represents a substantial threat, not only to the peace process but to the building and development of conflict transformation. The overall political aim, shared by the British and Irish states, was to bolster the position of the Ulster Unionist Party (UUP) and the Social Democratic and Labour Party (SDLP). These essentially middle-class parties were viewed by the British and Irish states as reasonable brokers who would deliver some constitutional middle ground. This in turn would highlight how the more vociferous voices of SF and the DUP were irrelevant within an emergent 'post-nationalist' consensus.

This strategy was profoundly undermined by several factors. First, the slow rate of military thaw within armed republicanism provided space for Ian Paisley to mobilize a unionist electorate disenchanted by what they viewed as unequal concessions and the failure of the IRA to simply disappear. Secondly, a significant share of the middle classes, who located few vested interests in local politics, chose a non-voting path in favour of conspicuous consumption and in so doing brought down middle-class consensus politics. Thirdly, the political tensions caused by truncated de-militarization, a lack of consensus building and new modes of contention led to the disputes at Drumcree, Holy Cross and the robbery of the Northern Bank. It was not that the governance model envisaged within the Agreement had failed but that the tensions between communities had remained without any positive counter-balances.

Despite some signs of political maturity, such as DUP members sharing platforms with SF politicians, it is evident that the discourse of belligerent unionism remains tied to constantly 'exposing' the link between the IRA and SF. Within such a logic of 'undeniable' linkage, the DUP began a successful assault upon David Trimble, whose 'lundyism' had permitted SF into the Executive without a 'significant' decommissioning of weaponry. The DUP also played upon unionist fears that the IRA was still in existence by pointing to the 'realities' of gun running in Florida, the case of the Columbia Three and the Stormont 'spy ring'. These 'trump cards', which maintained DUP hostility, are slowly being undermined by the decline in such incidents and the wider recognition that Gerry Adams has managed IRA disengagement. Eventually, the subtlety of republican shifts has not been lost upon the DUP, who pushed SF's participation in the Policing Boards as the final prerequisite for the return of devolution. It is difficult to comprehend that SF led the IRA to a place that is more agreeable to the DUP. A more cynical commentary would contend that the republican leadership mobilized unionist intransigence to disguise their own interpretation that militant republicanism had to be disengaged so as to advance SF's political mandate.

In essence the demobilization of armed republicanism has been achieved, but at a pace that was too slow to allow the UUP to remain dominant within unionism. The unequivocal message that emerged from unionists who voted was that republicans could not be trusted until they had been brought to heel, while for republicans it is evident that unionists cannot be trusted to accept their bona fides and mandate. By now even the most positive advocates of the Agreement must accept that the restoration of devolution was based upon accessing power and not upon meaningful and agreed consensus building. The central message from the main political parties is that 'you will respect our mandate', not that 'we have earned your respect'.

The strengthening of the more insistent and vociferous political voices in electoral terms was not forecast by academic commentators, such as Brendan O'Leary, who had championed a form of consensus building that would marginalize ethnic chauvinists. O'Leary even went so far as to predict that 'Sinn Féin and the DUP would do very well under fresh elections only if they run on moderated platforms.'[9] As has been indicated by the 125 per cent increase in votes for the DUP between the 1997 and 2005 Westminster elections (Table 1), the rejection of certain aspects of the Agreement has grown in both fervour and intent, and there were few signs that moderation had won the unionist day. For the DUP, political culture is tied to an unswerving commitment to an ethnically defined conception of territorial sovereignty. It was a simple and direct message that wooed some UUP members, who had become disillusioned by that party's pro-Agreement stance. Unionist voters have increasingly chosen not to vote or have moved to a more demanding unionist position. The 37.5 per cent growth in votes for SF also indicates that electoral choices are increasingly being based upon the delivery of a clearly defined cultural and political identity. Indeed, the SDLP's flirtation with post-nationalism and Europeanized notions of identity construction has been a far from successful political strategy.

Table 1. Westminster vote 1997 and 2005

Political party	Number of votes 1997	Number of votes 2005	% Change
Democratic Unionist Party	107,348	241,856	+125
Sinn Féin	126,921	174,530	+37.5
Ulster Unionist Party	258,439	127,314	−50.7
Social Democratic and Labour Party	190,844	125,626	−34.7

Source: www.ark.ac.uk/elections

The difficulty for Sinn Féin was that the new art of governance could not be seen to have eclipsed defined notions of sovereignty. Thus they have won political support through the contention that the Agreement will lead to a united Ireland and that the demands that they make, upon the two states and unionists, are tied to the genuine voice of Irish nationalism. Such a political discourse has been read as a championing of the republican/nationalist cause, without any admission of compromise or evident ideological shifts.[10] The overall winners, in political terms, have been those who have exposed their ethnic credentials under the guise of rights, while disguising the concessions that they have made. The UUP and SDLP, who openly presented their concessions, have been slowly deserted by an electorate that has sought ethnically defined refuges.

Governance strategies that were based upon the constructive ambiguity of the Agreement were never capable of establishing ongoing negotiations, especially when it was evident that such ambiguities provided alternative perceptions and meanings. The Agreement established 'objectives' of inter-community governance instead of direct legal guidelines and because of this there remained multiple interpretations of what the means and ends actually entailed. For unionists, decommissioning meant a short-term disbanding of armed groups, but for republicans it meant a consultative and ongoing process. Northern Ireland's identities and their presentation were too embedded to get political interlocutors to change basic positions and interests. The Agreement as articulated by competing political discourses was also undermined by a failure to harness a greater sense of stability and 'normality' on the ground. Even though there has been a significant shift from the violence of the 1970s and 1980s, events such as Drumcree and Holy Cross encouraged the need for identity-based hegemony within a political process that increasingly did not indicate any emancipation from ethno-sectarian discourse. Thus normality remained a disputed concept with regard to group-based discourses.

Segregated Places

The population of Belfast is divided more or less equally between the two main ethno-sectarian groups. As shown in Tables 2a and 2b, the majority of people from a Catholic or Protestant community background live in places in which at least 81 per cent of people are from the same ethno-religious background. Just over two-thirds of Catholics (67.3%) and 73 per cent of Protestants live in such places. A mere 10.7 per cent of Catholics and 7 per cent of Protestants live in places that are between 41–60 per cent Catholic or Protestant, locations that could be described as mixed.

Table 2a. Segregation of Belfast Catholics within Catholic-dominated areas

% of area population Catholic	% of total Belfast Catholic pop. resident in area
0–20	4.7
21–40	3.6
41–60	10.7
61–80	13.8
81–90	9.3
91–100	58.0

Source: Census of Population, 2001.

Table 2b. Segregation of Belfast Protestants within Protestant-dominated areas

% of area population Protestant	% of total Belfast Protestant pop. resident in area
0–20	3.4
21–40	7.3
41–60	7.0
61–80	9.3
81–90	28.4
91–100	44.6

Source: Census of Population, 2001.

For many residents of segregated places, the borders or interfaces between unionist/loyalist and republican/nationalist spaces are not merely boundaries between communities but are important markers in the definition of discursively constructed space. Interface walls reduce contact with the 'other' community whose cultural designations are generally viewed as culturally, politically and socially 'offensive'. The capacity of segregation to turn territory into symbolic signs of cultural and political differentiation is both considerable and undeniable.

Interfaces are also a constant reminder of harm done and of threat implied. Their existence presents a script from which community loyalty can be read. Interfaces both undermine and regulate inter-community relationships, through compressing territory into sites that remain the most notable places of ethno-sectarian resistance and violent re-enactment.

The militarized barricades that constitute lines of division have become self-sustaining features. Somewhat ominously, there were 16 interface walls in 1994, the first year of the paramilitary ceasefires. Since then most of these have been either extended or heightened. Nine additional walls have been constructed due to interface-related violence since 1998. For example, the loyalists who drove the Holy Cross dispute were only persuaded to end their protest once guarantees were given that an interface wall and security cameras were placed between them and the republican/nationalist population of Ardoyne, in what a senior Ulster Defence Association leader labelled the 'pipe bombing, wall getting campaign'.

The obvious fact is that violence and menace have created significant psychological burdens and prejudiced attitudes that lead to restricted mobility between antagonistic communities. 'Chill factors' remain, associated with the experience and perception of danger. Fear and avoidance of the 'other' community is influenced by territoriality and ethno-sectarian practices and leads to abnormal patterns of consumption, leisure and labour market activity that impinge upon social relationships. For many residents of segregated areas, the ideological role of ethno-sectarian disputation still influences social and productive relationships. Low levels of inter-community mobility are either linked to a prejudiced position or to a perceived or actual fear of entering a community within which an individual or group will immediately become an 'unprotected' minority. Evidently, the crossing of ethno-sectarian boundaries is linked to wider ethno-sectarian notions within which the 'other' community is viewed as threatening. The work of Shirlow and Murtagh[11] has shown that the levels of social, cultural and economic interaction between communities are low and that the reasons for these abnormal mobility patterns are firmly attached to an emotional landscape of fear, prejudice, loathing, the experience of violence and the more obvious marking of space through hostile imagery and graffiti.

Most respondents interviewed by Shirlow and Murtagh[12] felt relatively safe within their own community, but had reservations, at best, about entering areas dominated by the 'other' community. The lack of interaction between communities was similar and no one group was disadvantaged more than any other. Enclaved communities, places that were surrounded by the 'other' community, suffered most and residents within them generally undertook extensive journeys to access services. Larger and more homogeneous communities, within which an extensive range of facilities are located, produced more internalized mobility patterns.

In general it was found that only one in eight respondents worked in areas dominated by the 'other' community. In addition, 78 per cent of respondents provided examples of at least three publicly funded facilities (notably health centres, libraries, leisure centres and welfare offices) that they did not use because they were located on the 'wrong' side of an interface. In some communities, upwards of 75 per cent of the survey respondents refused to use their closest health centre if it was located in a place dominated by the 'other' community. Over half of all respondents (58%) travel at least twice as far as they have to, usually into neutral areas or areas dominated by co-religionists, in order to access two or more private sector facilities. 82 per cent of respondents whose nearest benefit office was located in the territory dominated by the 'other' community used facilities located in areas dominated by their 'own' community, even though this meant making longer journeys. These disruptions to everyday living are significant in that interface areas contain the most apparent forms of social exclusion and deprivation within Belfast. Somewhat depressingly, the evidence collected by Shirlow and Murtagh also suggested that around one in eight respondents have forgone health services when such facilities are located on the 'wrong' side of the interface.

A mere 18 per cent of respondents undertook, on a weekly basis, consumption-based activities in areas dominated by the 'other' community. It is generally assumed that fear of being attacked by the 'other' community is central in determining low levels of inter-community contact. However, a subjective reading of such information masks a series of relationships complicated by age, gender and intra-community threat. Nearly 60 per cent of respondents who did not carry out shopping and other consumption activities in areas dominated by the 'other' community gave as the reason what they recognized as fear of either verbal or physical violence. Around 9 per cent stated that they would not make such trips due to a desire not to spend money in areas dominated by the 'other' community, which they deemed to be based upon 'loyalty' to their own community.

Many more women (31%) than men (9.8%) stated that they would be afraid to walk through their own community after dark. However, the dissimilarity in the responses received from men and women narrows significantly when respondents were questioned on whether they would 'feel safe when walking through an area dominated by the other community at night'. The percentage share that would not undertake such a journey after dark rose to 92.2 per cent and 94.2 per cent of men and women respectively.

The impact of segregation upon daily lives illustrates how the nature of fear and prejudice still motivates alternative political identities. At present no major political party articulates the de-segregation of society, each choosing instead to represent the electorate's fears. In many instances the political instability that still exists reflects the limitations of the Agreement and the inability of devolution to substantially alter the nature of conflict.

Violence Endures

Over the period of the peace process, those operating within the orbit of the British and Irish states have sought, predictably, to place an unequivocally positive slant on the course that Northern Ireland has taken since the cease-fires. The speeches of Tony Blair and Bertie Ahern have been littered with references to historic developments and new dawns. The Northern Ireland Tourist Board[13] seeks to entice visitors to the region with the reassurance that '[m]uch has happened in the past few years and old perceptions of the North have had to be rewritten'. Infomercials in the Irish press strive to depict the regional capital Belfast as a 'thriving' city in which new investments are helping to sustain growth at levels unimaginable a decade ago.

Despite more creative and managerial mechanisms within which to roll out conflict transformation, it is evident that violence has remained a constant feature of Northern Irish society since the cease-fires of 1994. A common form of violence has been a series of sectarian attacks upon symbolic sites such as churches, Orange Halls and GAA clubs. According to Jarman[14] there were 594 reported attacks upon these symbolic sites between 1996 and 2004. Jarman also concluded that there were a staggering 6,623 recorded sectarian incidents in North Belfast during the same period.

There have been 1,129 recorded punishment attacks since 1994, the year of the first paramilitary cease-fires (Table 3). As with more recent violence, such attacks were rare between the cease-fires and the advent of the Agreement and declined even more significantly in the wake of the IRA's commitment to demobilize in 2005. There were virtually no punishment attacks in 1995 and relatively few between 1996 and 2000. The onset of instability following the various suspensions of the Northern Ireland Assembly (NIA) between 2000 and 2004 was matched by a near doubling of such assaults. The attempts in 2004 to re-establish the NIA heralded a small decline in this particular form of violence. A common suggestion among unionists and the media is that such violence declines during periods of political negotiation and resumes when dialogue breaks down.

Table 3 Punishment attacks in Northern Ireland 1994–2004

Year	Assaults	% of all assaults 1994–2004
1994	122	10.8
1995	3	0.2
1996	24	2.1
1997	72	6.3
1998	72	6.3
1999	73	6.4
2000	136	12.0
2001	186	16.4
2002	173	15.3
2003	156	13.8
2004	112	9.9
Total	**1,129**	**100**

Source: Authors' calculations

Between 1994 and early 2005 225 people were murdered (Table 4b). The significance of a declining violent death rate is evident given that in the previous ten years there were 857 violent deaths. This equals a 74 per cent decline between these two periods. The nature of violence has also altered such that there were no violent deaths recorded among police officers or members of the prison service or related army personnel after 1999. In sum, 13 security-related personnel were killed in the more recent period (1994–2005) compared with 272 in the preceding decade (Table 4a). Civilians constituted 67 per cent of all victims in the earlier period compared to 94 per cent in the post-1994 period. The share of violent deaths among civilians has declined at a much slower rate (64%) than has been the case among security-related personnel (95%).

Table 4a. Politically motivated killings in Northern Ireland 1983–93

Year	Non-civilians	Civilians	Total
1983	33	44	77
1984	28	36	64
1985	29	26	55
1986	24	37	61
1987	27	68	95
1988	39	55	94
1989	23	39	62
1990	27	49	76
1991	19	75	94
1992	9	76	85
1993	14	70	84
Total	**272**	**575**	**857**

Source: Authors' calculations

Table 4b. Politically motivated killings in Northern Ireland 1994–April 2005

Year	Non-civilians	Civilians	Total
1994	5	49	54
1995	0	12	12
1996	2	12	14
1997	4	29	33
1998	2	42	44
1999	0	7	7
2000	0	18	18
2001	0	17	17
2002	0	15	15
2003	0	7	7
2004/05	0	4	4
Total	**13**	**212**	**225**

Source: Authors' calculations

The violence linked to the Drumcree event in 1998 witnessed a doubling of deaths compared to all deaths between 1995 and early 1997. The high death rate in 1999 is a result of the Omagh bombing. Many of the violent deaths that have occurred in the past decade have been centred upon loyalist feuds, but there have also been ethno-sectarian murders in segregated communities, such as the murder of Danny McColgan in Rathcoole and Steven Keyes in Upper Ardoyne.

Since 1994 there have been 2,505 shooting incidents (Table 5b). This is around half the total number of shooting incidents between 1983 and 1993. There is less variation with regard to shootings than is the case with regard to other forms of violence, although 1995 witnessed a dramatic fall in such acts. There was some growth in shooting incidents around the time of the Holy Cross dispute and also linked to the instability created by various political crises. As shown in Table 5b, the use of bombs fluctuated within the 1994–2004 period, and as with shooting

Table 5a. Shooting and bombing incidents 1983–93

Year	Shootings	Bombing devices used
1983	424	367
1984	334	248
1985	238	215
1986	392	254
1987	674	384
1988	538	458
1989	566	420
1990	557	286
1991	499	368
1992	506	371
1993	476	289
Total	**5,204**	**3,660**

Source: Authors' calculations from data supplied by PSNI

Table 5b. Shooting and bombing incidents 1994–2004

Year	Shootings	Bombing devices used
1994	348	222
1995	50	2
1996	125	25
1997	225	93
1998	211	243
1999	125	100
2000	302	135
2001	355	444
2002	350	239
2003	229	88
2004	185	69
Total	**2,505**	**1,660**

Source: Authors' calculations from data supplied by PSNI

incidents the number of such acts halved in comparison to the 1983–93 period (Table 5a). Most of the bombing devices used were pipe bombs, which are less destructive than the majority of bombs used in earlier periods. Pipe bombs have been largely used by loyalist paramilitary groups within interface areas. They are small rudimentary weapons that are essentially used as hand grenades. Their use in rioting and the intimidation of families within interface communities became commonplace during and immediately after the Holy Cross dispute. There has, however, been a decline in the use of pipe bombs post-2003, although recorded sectarian attacks grew in the period 2005–06.

Table 6 examines data on intimidation cases reported to the Northern Ireland Housing Executive as a result of civil disturbances between 1989–99 and 2000–01. Just over half (52%) of all incidents took place in Belfast. One of the striking features of the data is the dramatic rise in the number of reported cases post-1998. With regard to housing intimidation within the Shankill district, most was linked to inter-community-based loyalist violence. Despite this, the majority of intimidation has been against spatially vulnerable minority populations within distinct social housing arenas. The rise in intimidation, from as low as 56 cases in 1998–99 to 1,108 cases in 2000–01, highlights the nature and extent of violence as a result of the environments created by political instability. It should also be noted that these figures do not record those persons who moved from their homes within the private housing sector because of intimidation.

Table 6 Profile of intimidation cases by Housing Management District

District	1998–99	1999–2000	2000–01	Total	%
Belfast 1 West	3	21	34	58	3
Belfast 2 East	3	26	40	69	4
Belfast 3 West	3	32	36	71	4
Belfast 7 South	9	60	90	159	9
Belfast 4 North	1	40	104	145	8
Belfast 5 Shankill	1	11	238	250	15
Belfast 6 North	18	28	110	156	9
Total Belfast	41	218	652	908	52
Total Northern Ireland	56	549	1,108	1,713	100

Source: Data supplied by NIHE

The obvious effect of such violence was that it eroded the goodwill experienced in the immediate ceasefire period, and at the same time created a new generation who experienced dramatic violent events. The problem with the Belfast Agreement was not merely that it remained unsustainable, but that the insecurity and political mayhem that came about forged new versions of victimhood and risk at the hands of the ethno-sectarian 'other'.

Conclusion

Belfast's slow transition from 'troubled' city to a less violent city is under way. Yet the impact of decades of conflict endured encourages the 'logic' of spatial separation between a constitutionally divided people. Memory and the reproduction of low-level violence are intertwined in the promotion of ethno-sectarian attitudes. The fear of unionists that they will be subsumed within a united Ireland, and the related desire of Irish nationalists for constitutional re-unification, means that the conflict cannot be resolved. Conflict resolution will not obtain in a discord driven by the Irish border's existence, for even the removal of that construct will produce instability. However, conflict transformation contains the possibility that uncertainty can be framed by democratic dialogue and not by violent responses to future constitutional instability.

Conflict transformation and the reduction and near removal of violence are achievable, but only through a politics that confronts mythic reiteration of community belief. The peace accords and the return of political devolution did not undermine political antagonisms, which remain ingrained within the continuation of various forms of partition and the territorialization of wider cultural, social and economic allegiances. In the short term at least there is little capacity for a shared Northern Irish identity to be forged. Without such an identity shift or a move towards non-sectarian class politics, the capacity to shift attitudes remains problematic.

Northern Ireland is a more agreeable and less threatening place, but its future remains disagreed. There has been no shift regarding national faithfulness and electoral outcomes, a reality that is furthered by those interested in non-constitutional politics failing to mobilize politically. Given the failure of political development around a third tradition it is obvious that political power brokers will seek a settlement for their own community as opposed to meaningful compromise between communities.

For there to be greater success Northern Ireland needs governance structures that shift from serving ethno-sectarian interests. An honest and enduring recognition that the potential development of civil society is subdued by persistent ethno-sectarian relationships is also required. In addition, the formation of the built environment, where state and private enterprise dominates land use, where security consciousness has produced fragmented spatial arrangements, and where clientelist politics promotes resource competition, is also of concern. Civil enterprise in any post-conflict situation must claim a pivotal role in shaping and designing a less contested city. Neutral spaces and their protection are fundamentally important in the presentation of more normalized social conditions. At present the desire to de-segregate a divided city remains as a minority pursuit and is only articulated by those who challenge ethno-sectarian belonging.

The essential problem that affects Belfast is that geography matters in a way that is explicit and obvious. The cantonization of life is a forceful impediment to the delivery of a new and agreed city. The debate on developing a less contested city will remain undermined by the ability of political entrepreneurs to mobilize space as a crucial variable within identity construction. Fear and residential segregation impede the search for work, the uptake of training and education and the use of public services. In addition, fear creates socio-spatial burdens that are mostly endured by socially deprived communities. The potential to reconstruct Northern Ireland's production and consumer arenas, in order that they respond to equality of opportunity and parity of esteem, is a major factor in the creation of long-term political stability. Few, if any, of the policies that aim to challenge socio-economic dislocation link the realities of spatialized fear to the reproduction of social deprivation and communal polarization.

The analysis of fear and prejudice underpins the need to translate policy and political rhetoric about segregation into practice, and to connect practice with the reality of sectarianized habituation. Given the sectarian nature of political control in Northern Ireland, much of the commentary dedicated to challenging segregation and ultimately the reproduction of fear is ambiguous and difficult to distinguish in the detail of policy-making instruments. Belfast, despite change, remains a sectarianized place.

Notes

1. Michael Cox, Adrian Guelke and Fiona Stephen (eds), *A Farewell to Arms? Beyond the Good Friday Agreement* (Manchester: Manchester University Press, 2006).
2. Colin Coulter, *Contemporary Northern Irish Society: An Introduction* (Belfast: Pluto Press, 1998).
3. J. Darby, 'A Truce rather than a Treaty? The Effects of Violence on the Irish Peace Process', in Cox, Guelke and Stephen (eds), *A Farewell to Arms?*, pp. 212–23.
4. Peter Shirlow, 'Measuring Workforce Segregation: Religious Composition of Private-Sector Employees at Individual Sites in Northern Ireland', *Environment and Planning A*, 38(8), 2006, pp. 1545–59.
5. Chill factors refer to a fear of entering an area dominated by the 'other' community.
6. Peter Shirlow, 'Devolution in Northern Ireland/Ulster/the North/Six Counties: Delete as Appropriate', *Regional Studies*, 35(8), 2001, pp. 743–75.
7. Paul Bew, 'Myths of Consociationalism: From Good Friday to Political Impasse', in Cox, Guelke and Stephen (eds), *A Farewell to Arms?*, pp. 57–68.
8. Arthur Aughey, 'The 1998 Agreement: Three Unionist Anxieties', in Cox, Guelke and Stephen (eds), *A Farewell to Arms?*, pp. 89–108.
9. Brendan O'Leary, 'Elections Not Suspensions', *The Guardian*, 13 July 2001, p. 13.
10. Jon Tonge, 'Polarisation or New Moderation? Party Politics since the GFA', in Cox, Guelke and Stephen (eds), *A Farewell to Arms?*, pp. 70–88.
11. Peter Shirlow and Brendan Murtagh, *Belfast: Segregation, Violence and the City* (Belfast: Pluto Press, 2006).
12. The survey questioned a population of nearly 9,000 people. This is the largest body of work ever undertaken on interfaced communities.
13. Northern Ireland Tourist Board, *Visitor Guide 2006*, available at www.discovernorthernireland.com.
14. Neil Jarman, *No Longer a Problem? Sectarian Violence in Northern Ireland* (ICR, 2005).

Appendices

The Sunningdale Agreement (December 1973)

1. The Conference between the British and Irish Governments and the parties involved in the Northern Ireland Executive (designate) met at Sunningdale on 6, 7, 8 and 9 December 1973.
2. During the Conference, each delegation stated their position on the status of Northern Ireland.
3. The Taoiseach said that the basic principle of the Conference was that the participants had tried to see what measure of agreement of benefit to all the people concerned could be secured. In doing so, all had reached accommodation with one another on practical arrangements. But none had compromised, and none had asked others to compromise, in relation to basic aspirations. The people of the Republic, together with a minority in Northern Ireland as represented by the SDLP delegation, continued to uphold the aspiration towards a united Ireland. The only unity they wanted to see was a unity established by consent.
4. Mr Brian Faulkner said that delegates from Northern Ireland came to the Conference as representatives of apparently incompatible sets of political aspirations who had found it possible to reach agreement to join together in government because each accepted that in doing so they were not sacrificing principles or aspirations. The desire of the majority of the people of Northern Ireland to remain part of the United Kingdom, as represented by the Unionist and Alliance delegations, remained firm.
5. The Irish Government fully accepted and solemnly declared that there could be no change in the status of Northern Ireland until a majority of the people of Northern Ireland desired a change in that status. The British Government solemnly declared that it was, and would remain, their policy to support the wishes of the majority of the people of Northern Ireland. The present status of Northern Ireland is that it is part of the United Kingdom. If in the future the majority of the people of Northern Ireland should indicate a wish to become part of a united Ireland, the British Government would support that wish.
6. The Conference agreed that a formal agreement incorporating the declarations of the British and Irish Governments would be signed at the formal stage of the Conference and registered at the United Nations.
7. The Conference agreed that a Council of Ireland would be set up. It would be confined to representatives of the two parts of Ireland, with appropriate safeguards for the British Government's financial and other interests. It would comprise a Council of Ministers with executive and harmonising functions

and a consultative role, and a Consultative Assembly with advisory and review functions. The Council of Ministers would act by unanimity, and would comprise a core of seven members of the Irish Government and an equal number of members of the Northern Ireland Executive with provision for the participation of other non-voting members of the Irish Government and the Northern Ireland Executive or Administration when matters within their departmental competence were discussed. The Council of Ministers would control the functions of the Council. The Chairmanship would rotate on an agreed basis between representatives of the Irish Government and of the Northern Ireland Executive. Arrangements would be made for the location of the first meeting, and the location of subsequent meetings would be determined by the Council of Ministers. The Consultative Assembly would consist of 60 members, 30 members from Dáil Éireann chosen by the Dáil on the basis of proportional representation by the single transferable vote, and 30 members from the Northern Ireland Assembly chosen by that Assembly and also on that basis. The members of the Consultative Assembly would be paid allowances. There would be a Secretariat to the Council, which would be kept as small as might be commensurate with efficiency in the operation of the Council. The Secretariat would service the institutions of the Council and would, under the Council of Ministers, supervise the carrying out of the executive and harmonising functions and the consultative role of the Council. The Secretariat would be headed by a Secretary-General. Following the appointment of a Northern Ireland Executive, the Irish Government and the Northern Ireland Executive would nominate their representatives to a Council of Ministers. The Council of Ministers would then appoint a Secretary-General and decide upon the location of its permanent headquarters. The Secretary-General would be directed to proceed with the drawing up of plans for such headquarters. The Council of Ministers would also make arrangements for the recruitment of the staff of the Secretariat in a manner and on conditions which would, as far as is practicable, be consistent with those applying to public servants in the two administrations.

8. In the context of its harmonising functions and consultative role, the Council of Ireland would undertake important work relating, for instance, to the impact of EEC membership. As for executive functions, the first step would be to define and agree these in detail. The Conference therefore decided that, in view of the administrative complexities involved, studies would at once be set in hand to identify and, prior to the formal stage of the conference, report on areas of common interest in relation to which a Council of Ireland would take executive decisions and, in appropriate cases, be responsible for carrying those decisions into effect. In carrying out these studies, and also in determining what should be done by the Council in terms of harmonisation, the objectives to be borne in mind would include the following:

(1) to achieve the best utilisation of scarce skills, expertise and resources;
(2) to avoid in the interests of economy and efficiency, unnecessary duplication of effort; and

(3) to ensure complementary rather than competitive effort where this is to the advantage of agriculture, commerce and industry.

In particular, these studies would be directed to identifying, for the purposes of executive action by the Council of Ireland, suitable aspects of activities in the following broad fields:

(a) exploitation, conservation and development of natural resources and the environment;
(b) agricultural matters (including agricultural research, animal health and operational aspects of the Common Agriculture Policy), forestry and fisheries;
(c) co-operative ventures in the fields of trade and industry;
(d) electricity generation;
(e) tourism;
(f) roads and transport;
(g) advisory services in the field of public health;
(h) sport, culture and the arts.

It would be for the Oireachtas and the Northern Ireland Assembly to legislate from time to time as to the extent of functions to be devolved to the Council of Ireland. Where necessary, the British Government will cooperate in this devolution of functions. Initially, the functions to be vested would be those identified in accordance with the procedures set out above and decided, at the formal stage of the conference, to be transferred.

9. (i) During the initial period following the establishment of the Council, the revenue of the Council would be provided by means of grants from the two administrations in Ireland towards agreed projects and budgets, according to the nature of the service involved.
(ii) It was also agreed that further studies would be put in hand forthwith and completed as soon as possible of methods of financing the Council after the initial period which would be consonant with the responsibilities and functions assigned to it.
(iii) It was agreed that the cost of the Secretariat of the Council of Ireland would be shared equally, and other services would be financed broadly in proportion to where expenditure or benefit accrues.
(iv) The amount of money required to finance the Council's activities will depend upon the functions assigned to it from time to time.
(v) While Britain continues to pay subsidies to Northern Ireland, such payments would not involve Britain participating in the Council, it being accepted nevertheless that it would be legitimate for Britain to safeguard in an appropriate way her financial involvement in Northern Ireland.

10. It was agreed by all parties that persons committing crimes of violence, however motivated, in any part of Ireland should be brought to trial irrespective of the

part of Ireland in which they are located. The concern which large sections of the people of Northern Ireland felt about this problem was in particular forcefully expressed by the representatives of the Unionist and Alliance parties. The representatives of the Irish Government stated that they understood and fully shared this concern. Different ways of solving this problem were discussed; among them were the amendment of legislation operating in the two jurisdictions on extradition, the creation of a common law enforcement area in which an all-Ireland court would have jurisdiction, and the extension of the jurisdiction of domestic courts so as to enable them to try offences committed outside the jurisdiction. It was agreed that problems of considerable legal complexity were involved, and that the British and Irish Governments would jointly set up a commission to consider all the proposals put forward at the Conference and to recommend as a matter of extreme urgency the most effective means of dealing with those who commit these crimes. The Irish Government undertook to take immediate and effective legal steps so that persons coming within their jurisdiction and accused of murder, however motivated, committed in Northern Ireland will be brought to trial, and it was agreed that any similar reciprocal action that may be needed in Northern Ireland be taken by the appropriate authorities.

11. It was agreed that the Council would be invited to consider in what way the principles of the European Convention on Human Rights and Fundamental Freedoms would be expressed in domestic legislation in each part of Ireland. It would recommend whether further legislation or the creation of other institutions, administrative or judicial, is required in either part or embracing the whole island to provide additional protection in the field of human rights. Such recommendations could include the functions of an Ombudsman or Commissioner for Complaints, or other arrangements of a similar nature which the Council of Ireland might think appropriate.

12. The Conference also discussed the question of policing and the need to ensure public support for and identification with the police service throughout the whole community. It was agreed that no single set of proposals would achieve these aims overnight, and that time would be necessary. The Conference expressed the hope that the wide range of agreement that had been reached, and the consequent formation of a power-sharing Executive, would make a major contribution to the creation of an atmosphere throughout the community where there would be widespread support for and identification with all the institutions of Northern Ireland.

13. It was broadly accepted that the two parts of Ireland are to a considerable extent interdependent in the whole field of law and order, and that the problems of political violence and identification with the police service cannot be solved without taking account of that fact.

14. Accordingly, the British Government stated that, as soon as the security problems were resolved and the new institutions were seen to be working effectively, they would wish to discuss the devolution of responsibility for normal policing and how this might be achieved with the Northern Ireland Executive and the Police.

15. With a view to improving policing throughout the island and developing community identification with and support for the police services, the governments concerned will cooperate under the auspices of a Council of Ireland through their respective police authorities. To this end, the Irish Government would set up a Police Authority, appointments to which would be made after consultation with the Council of Ministers of the Council of Ireland. In the case of the Northern Ireland Police Authority, appointments would be made after consultation with the Northern Ireland Executive which would consult with the Council of Ministers of the Council of Ireland. When the two Police Authorities are constituted, they will make their own arrangements to achieve the objectives set out above.

16. An independent complaints procedure for dealing with complaints against the police will be set up.

17. The Secretary of State for Northern Ireland will set up an all-party committee from the Assembly to examine how best to introduce effective policing throughout Northern Ireland with particular reference to the need to achieve public identification with the police.

18. The Conference took note of a reaffirmation by the British Government of their firm commitment to bring detention to an end in Northern Ireland for all sections of the community as soon as the security situation permits, and noted also that the Secretary of State for Northern Ireland hopes to be able to bring into use his statutory powers of selective release in time for a number of detainees to be released before Christmas.

19. The British Government stated that, in the light of the decisions reached at the Conference, they would now seek the authority of Parliament to devolve full powers to the Northern Ireland Executive and Northern Ireland Assembly as soon as possible. The formal appointment of the Northern Ireland Executive would then be made.

20. The Conference agreed that a formal conference would be held early in the New Year at which the British and Irish Governments and the Northern Ireland Executive would meet together to consider reports on the studies which have been commissioned and to sign the agreement reached.

The Anglo-Irish (Hillsborough) Agreement (November 1985)

The Government of Ireland and the Government of the United Kingdom:

Wishing further to develop the unique relationship between their peoples and the close co-operation between their countries as friendly neighbours and as partners in the European Community;

Recognising the major interest of both their countries and, above all, of the people of Northern Ireland in diminishing the divisions there and achieving lasting peace and stability;

Recognising the need for continuing efforts to reconcile and to acknowledge the rights of the two major traditions that exist in Ireland, represented on the one hand by those who wish for no change in the present status of Northern Ireland and on the other hand by those who aspire to a sovereign united Ireland achieved by peaceful means and through agreement;

Reaffirming their total rejection of any attempt to promote political objectives by violence or the threat of violence and their determination to work together to ensure that those who adopt or support such methods do not succeed;

Recognising that a condition of genuine reconciliation and dialogue between unionists and nationalists is mutual recognition and acceptance of each other's rights;

Recognising and respecting the identities of the two communities in Northern Ireland, and the right of each to pursue its aspirations by peaceful and constitutional means;

Reaffirming their commitment to a society in Northern Ireland in which all may live in peace, free from discrimination and intolerance, and with the opportunity for both communities to participate fully in the structures and processes of government;

Have accordingly agreed as follows:

A
STATUS OF NORTHERN IRELAND

ARTICLE 1

The two Governments
(a) affirm that any change in the status of Northern Ireland would only come about with the consent of a majority of the people of Northern Ireland;
(b) recognise that the present wish of a majority of the people of Northern Ireland is for no change in the status of Northern Ireland;
(c) declare that, if in the future a majority of the people of Northern Ireland clearly wish for and formally consent to the establishment of a united Ireland, they will introduce and support in the respective Parliaments legislation to give effect to that wish.

B
THE INTERGOVERNMENTAL CONFERENCE

ARTICLE 2

(a) There is hereby established, within the framework of the Anglo-Irish Intergovernmental Council set up after the meeting between the two Heads of Government on 6 November 1981, an Intergovernmental Conference (hereinafter referred to as 'the Conference'), concerned with Northern Ireland and with relations between the two parts of the island of Ireland, to deal, as set out in this Agreement, on a regular basis with
   (i) political matters;
   (ii) security and related matters;
   (iii) legal matters, including the administration of justice;
   (iv) the promotion of cross-border co-operation.
(b) The United Kingdom Government accept that the Irish Government will put forward views and proposals on matters relating to Northern Ireland within the field of activity of the Conference in so far as those matters are not the responsibility of a devolved administration in Northern Ireland. In the interest of promoting peace and stability, determined efforts shall be made through the Conference to resolve any differences. The Conference will be mainly concerned with Northern Ireland; but some of the matters under consideration will involve cooperative action in both parts of the island of Ireland, and possibly also in Great Britain. Some of the proposals considered in respect of Northern Ireland may also be found to have application by the Irish Government. There is no derogation from the sovereignty of either the Irish Government or the United Kingdom Government, and each retains responsibility for the decisions and administration of government within its own jurisdiction.

ARTICLE 3

The Conference shall meet at Ministerial or official level, as required. The business of the Conference will thus receive attention at the highest level. Regular and frequent Ministerial meetings shall be held; and in particular special meetings shall be convened at the request of either side. Officials may meet in subordinate groups. Membership of the Conference and of sub-groups shall be small and flexible. When the Conference meets at Ministerial level an Irish Minister designated as the Permanent Irish Ministerial Representative and the Secretary of State for Northern Ireland shall be joint Chairmen. Within the framework of the Conference other Irish and British Ministers may hold or attend meetings as appropriate: when legal matters are under consideration the Attorneys General may attend. Ministers may be accompanied by their officials and their professional advisers: for example, when questions of security policy or security co-operation are being discussed, they may be accompanied by the Commissioner of the Garda Siochána and the Chief Constable of the Royal Ulster Constabulary; or when questions of economic or social policy or co-operation are being discussed, they may be accompanied by officials of the relevant Departments. A Secretariat shall be established by the two Governments to service the Conference on a continuing basis in the discharge of its functions as set out in this Agreement.

ARTICLE 4

(a) In relation to matters coming within its field of activity, the Conference shall be a framework within which the Irish Government and the United Kingdom Government work together
   (i) for the accommodation of the rights and identities of the two traditions which exist in Northern Ireland; and
   (ii) for peace, stability and prosperity throughout the island of Ireland by promoting reconciliation, respect for human rights, co-operation against terrorism and the development of economic, social and cultural co-operation.
(b) It is the declared policy of the United Kingdom Government that responsibility in respect of certain matters within the powers of the Secretary of State for Northern Ireland should be devolved within Northern Ireland on a basis which would secure widespread acceptance throughout the community. The Irish Government support that policy.
(c) Both Governments recognise that devolution can be achieved only with the co-operation of constitutional representatives within Northern Ireland of both traditions there. The Conference shall be a framework within which the Irish Government may put forward views and proposals on the modalities of bringing about devolution in Northern Ireland, in so far as they relate to the interests of the minority community.

C
POLITICAL MATTERS

ARTICLE 5

(a) The Conference shall concern itself with measures to recognise and accommodate the rights and identities of the two traditions in Northern Ireland, to protect human rights and to prevent discrimination. Matters to be considered in this area include measures to foster the cultural heritage of both traditions, changes in electoral arrangements, the use of flags and emblems, the avoidance of economic and social discrimination and the advantages and disadvantages of a Bill of Rights in some form in Northern Ireland.
(b) The discussion of these matters shall be mainly concerned with Northern Ireland, but the possible application of any measures pursuant to this Article by the Irish Government in their jurisdiction shall not be excluded.
(c) If it should prove impossible to achieve and sustain devolution on a basis which secures widespread acceptance in Northern Ireland, the Conference shall be a framework within which the Irish Government may, where the interests of the minority community are significantly or especially affected, put forward views on proposals for major legislation and on major policy issues, which are within the purview of the Northern Ireland Departments and which remain the responsibility of the Secretary of State for Northern Ireland.

ARTICLE 6

The Conference shall be a framework within which the Irish Government may put forward views and proposals on the role and composition of bodies appointed by the Secretary of State for Northern Ireland or by Departments subject to his direction and control including

the Standing Advisory Commission on Human Rights;
the Fair Employment Agency;
the Police Authority for Northern Ireland;
the Police Complaints Board.

D
SECURITY AND RELATED MATTERS

ARTICLE 7

(a) The Conference shall consider
(i) security policy;
(ii) relations between the security forces and the community;
(iii) prisons policy.
(b) The Conference shall consider the security situation at its regular meetings and thus provide an opportunity to address policy issues, serious incidents and forthcoming events.

(c) The two Governments agree that there is a need for a programme of special measures in Northern Ireland to improve relations between the security forces and the community, with the object in particular of making the security forces more readily accepted by the nationalist community. Such a programme shall be developed, for the Conference's consideration, and may include the establishment of local consultative machinery, training in community relations, crime prevention schemes involving the community, improvements in arrangements for handling complaints, and action to increase the proportion of members of the minority in the Royal Ulster Constabulary. Elements of the programme may be considered by the Irish Government suitable for application within their jurisdiction.

(d) The Conference may consider policy issues relating to prisons. Individual cases may be raised as appropriate, so that information can be provided or inquiries instituted.

E
LEGAL MATTERS, INCLUDING THE ADMINISTRATION OF JUSTICE

ARTICLE 8

The Conference shall deal with issues of concern to both countries relating to the enforcement of the criminal law. In particular it shall consider whether there are areas of the criminal law applying in the North and in the South respectively which might with benefit be harmonised. The two Governments agree on the importance of public confidence in the administration of justice. The Conference shall seek, with the help of advice from experts as appropriate, measures which would give substantial expression to this aim, considering inter alia the possibility of mixed courts in both jurisdictions for the trial of certain offences. The Conference shall also be concerned with policy aspects of extradition and extra-territorial jurisdiction as between North and South.

F
CROSS-BORDER CO-OPERATION ON SECURITY, ECONOMIC, SOCIAL AND CULTURAL MATTERS

ARTICLE 9

(a) With a view to enhancing cross-border co-operation on security matters, the Conference shall set in hand a programme of work to be undertaken by the Commissioner of the Garda Siochána and the Chief Constable of the Royal Ulster Constabulary and, where appropriate, groups of officials, in such areas as threat assessments, exchange of information, liaison structures, technical co-operation, training of personnel, and operational resources.

(b) The Conference shall have no operational responsibilities; responsibility for police operations shall remain with the heads of the respective police forces, the Commissioner of the Garda Siochána maintaining his links with the

Minister for Justice and the Chief Constable of the Royal Ulster Constabulary his links with the Secretary of State for Northern Ireland.

ARTICLE 10

(a) The two Governments shall co-operate to promote the economic and social development of those areas of both parts of Ireland which have suffered most severely from the consequences of the instability of recent years, and shall consider the possibility of securing international support for this work.

(b) If it should prove impossible to achieve and sustain devolution on a basis which secures widespread acceptance in Northern Ireland, the Conference shall be a framework for the promotion of co-operation between the two parts of Ireland concerning cross-border aspects of economic, social and cultural matters in relation to which the Secretary of State for Northern Ireland continues to exercise authority.

(c) If responsibility is devolved in respect of certain matters in the economic, social or cultural areas currently within the responsibility of the Secretary of State for Northern Ireland, machinery will need to be established by the responsible authorities in the North and South for practical co-operation in respect of cross-border aspects of these issues.

The Opsahl Commission (June 1993)[1]

POLITICS AND THE CONSTITUTION

1.1 On the process towards future government

In the event of the current talks process failing, the British Government, in consultation with the Irish Government, should set up a special Commission to put forward views and recommendations. These should be the basis for further consultation with the political parties and, if necessary, for direct consultation with the people of Northern Ireland. This Commission should also consider how best the people should be consulted, given that simple majorities do not work in a divided society.

1.2 On future government

Given that majority rule in Northern Ireland is not a viable proposition, and the unionist community will not accept any administration that gives an executive role to anyone outside the United Kingdom, the following proposal is put forward. 'Provided that Irish nationalism is legally recognised (see next recommendation), a government of Northern Ireland should be put in place, based on the principle that each community has an *equal voice* in making and executing the laws or a veto on their execution, and equally shares administrative authority.' This government should be free to discuss and negotiate its relationships, institutional and other, with the Irish Government.

1.3 On the legal recognition of nationalism

Recognising the nationalist community and its aspirations in law could start a process which would change thinking in both communities. 'Parity of esteem' between the two communities should be given approval, promoted and protected legally. Such recognition could be made operational at the highest level by an Act of Parliament. The Opsahl Commission recommends that the Government moves to examine the feasibility of drafting such legislation. It should be stressed that this legal recognition of Irish nationalism should not mean the diminution of 'Britishness' for unionists.

1.4 On the training of politicians

The Opsahl Commission believes there is a need for education and training for political leadership in Northern Ireland, as happens in the USA, Germany and Sweden. Such training programmes should be tailored both to present and prospective politicians and should involve the study of other democratic systems, and particularly those representing pluralism at its best; briefings on economics, the environment and other relevant issues; and community relations training.

1.5 On the position of Sinn Féin

There was widespread agreement in submissions that any settlement which had entirely excluded Sinn Féin from the negotiating process would be neither lasting nor stable, and that some way should be found to involve them in future talks. However, most authors felt that before Sinn Féin could earn a seat at the negotiating table, it would have to renounce its justification of the use of violence.

The Opsahl Commission believes that marginalising Sinn Féin in Northern Ireland by means of the broadcasting ban, excluding it from local council committees, and removing funding from community groups in the areas where it is strongest, only plays into the hands of those who prefer the use of violence, and is a policy that should be reconsidered. It therefore recommends that the Government open informal channels of communication with Sinn Féin with a view to testing that party's commitment to the constitutional process, without resort to or justification of violence. It also believes that the broadcasting ban in the Republic should be reconsidered.

LAW, JUSTICE AND SECURITY

2.1 On the need for public debate about reform

The Commission endorses a suggestion that key organisations in Northern Irish society – such as churches, public services bodies, trade unions, businesses and others – should be challenged to set up working groups to look at how their particular organisation could contribute to 'an improvement of law and order with a view to ensuring justice.'

2.2 On reducing the violence

The reduction and eventual elimination of political violence is clearly the most important and difficult task in Northern Ireland. No submission believed a 'military solution' could achieve this. Many believed that the way forward lay in the eventual involvement of the paramilitary organisations in a peace-seeking process. Most of these thought that an extended cessation of violence was the 'sine qua non' for any talks with either the IRA or their loyalist counterparts. A clear distinction would have to be made between talks on the constitutional future, which should involve constitutional political parties, and peace talks to bring the conflict to an end, which could involve the paramilitaries.

In this regard the Commission endorses the proposal from a mediation group it met during the oral hearings that the security forces and the IRA should each make exploratory, unilateral moves towards reducing the violence, clearly signalling such moves to the other side. It recommends that the Government – either directly or through intermediaries – open discussions with Sinn Féin with a view to persuading the IRA first to move towards a de-escalation in the level of violence and eventually to a ceasefire.

2.3 On policing

Unless genuine representatives of the nationalist community are given an executive role in policing, nationalists cannot take responsibility for it. It is unreasonable to expect a police force made up largely of members of one community to be acceptable to the other community in a divided society like Northern Ireland. The Commission believes that nationalist support for and significant recruitment to the RUC will only take place in the context of new political structures for the region, in which power and authority go hand in hand with responsibility.

In the interim – while being conscious of the extremely difficult and dangerous work the RUC are forced to undertake in the current security situation – the Commission suggests that a study should be initiated into alternative decentralised and multi-level models of policing, as exist in most other European countries outside the UK and Ireland. Suggested reforms it also endorses include: the takeover of the functions of the Independent Commission for Police Complaints by the Ombudsman's office; the immediate introduction of at least visual recording of police interviews; relieving the RUC of responsibility for making decisions on the routing of Orange and other controversial marches; and immediate steps to be taken by the Chief Constable (and the General Officer Commanding the army) to resolve the widespread problem of harassment by the security forces, particularly of young nationalist men.

2.4 On strengthening the protection of human rights

Given the widespread agreement expressed both in submissions and among the political parties, the Commission strongly recommends the enactment of a Bill of Rights for Northern Ireland as soon as possible. To enact such a Bill in the form of incorporating the European Convention on Human Rights into domestic law, accompanied by a review of the available domestic remedies, would be relatively simple.

2.5 On discrimination

The Commission endorses the recommendation of the Standing Advisory Commission on Human Rights that the 1989 Fair Employment Act's provisions should be extended to protect not just people's employment rights, but also their rights in the provision of goods and services.

2.6 On criminal justice

The Commission endorses a number of the proposals put forward by the Committee on the Administration of Justice and others for improving the fairness and accountability of the criminal justice system: a) the single judge in the Diplock Courts should be joined by one or two judicial or lay assessors, as is the practice in other jurisdictions where jury trials are not the legal norm; b) the inquest process in Northern Ireland requires reform, particularly because of the long delays in bringing cases to court; c) the introduction of a charge of manslaughter in cases involving the intentional use of lethal force, where the latter is excessive in the circumstances; d) an independent appeals tribunal or commissioner to investigate cases of people claiming to have been unfairly convicted, with the power to refer a matter back to the courts; e) the ending of indeterminate sentences for prisoners under 18 convicted of terrorist offences, and a re-examination of the life sentence review system.

THE ECONOMY AND SOCIETY

3.1 On economic cooperation with the Republic

The Commission endorses the many submissions in favour of greater cross-border economic cooperation, and proposes that the creation of an appropriate cross-border economic institution be an immediate priority of the Irish Government and any new Northern Ireland government set up in accordance with recommendation 1.2.

3.2 On a strategic regional plan

The Commission believes that the proposal from a range of groups for a strategic regional plan embracing both social and economic goals should be pursued vigorously and without delay.

3.3 On tackling deprivation

The Commission believes the Government's 'Targeting Social Need' programme has the potential to make a real contribution to tackling deprivation in Northern Ireland. However, it needs to be given a higher priority in the allocation of resources, clearer goals, stronger monitoring procedures, and to be pursued with more vigour and urgency.

3.4 On community development

The Commission welcomes the Government's recent statement of support for community development in Northern Ireland, which needs to be backed up with adequate resources to reflect the priorities of the communities themselves. It recommends that the 'political vetting' of community groups should be replaced by procedures which ensure strict accountability in the use of funds. It urges support for the establishment of local community development trusts, defined as independent, non-profit-making organisations bringing together the public, private and voluntary sectors with people of a local area in order to renew it 'physically, socially and in spirit.'

3.5 On women in politics

The Commission believes that the work of women in civil society in Northern Ireland should be more securely supported and funded, and their important contribution to the political life and the search for a settlement in the region should be recognised. It urges:

(a) the political parties to set targets for the number of women MPs and local councillors representing them;
(b) the Northern Ireland Office to set targets for the number of women on public bodies;
(c) the political parties to give higher priority to the social issues which are of particular concern to many women.

It also supports calls for a comprehensive regional strategy on child care, which is at a low level compared to other European countries.

3.6 On poverty and social security

The Commission draws attention to the failure of social security benefits and the social fund to prevent poverty among a significant proportion of the population in Northern Ireland, and urges full compensation to social security recipients for the proposed imposition (after the 1994 budget) of VAT on domestic fuel.

3.7 On integrated housing

The Commission suggests that the Housing Executive should examine the feasibility of setting up a number of 'pilot' integrated housing schemes, with subsidised rents and other support mechanisms, in order to encourage those who wish to be involved in the necessary process of reversing the drastic segregation of housing in Northern Ireland.

CULTURE, RELIGION, IDENTITY AND EDUCATION

4.1 On the Catholic Church in Ireland

Conscious of continuing deep Protestant fears about Irish Catholicism and recalling the Irish hierarchy's declaration to the New Ireland Forum that it did not wish to have the moral teaching and principles of the Catholic Church embodied in constitutional or civil law, the Commission urges that now is the time for a balanced examination of the role of the Church in a changing Ireland. To this end it urges the setting up – by a university or other reputable independent body – of a wide-ranging public inquiry into the role of the Catholic Church in Ireland.

4.2 On churches and confidence-building

The Commission also urges the hierarchy to consider such confidence-building steps as: offering communion to inter-church couples when requested; altering the rules for mixed marriages; and not putting obstacles in the way of parents who want to send their children to integrated schools. It also supports the proposal for a Christian Centre for Social Investigation to do research and sponsor debate on the religious divides in Irish society.

4.3 On the Protestant churches in Northern Ireland

The Commission believes that the Protestant churches should re-examine and – where they can – revise any of their formulations that give offence to Catholics. It draws attention to the view expressed strongly at the Initiative '92 schools assemblies that pupils wanted mixed Catholic-Protestant religious education classes, where questions of belief, culture and identity can be discussed frankly and openly.

4.4 On churches and community understanding

The Commission believes that Protestant church and community leaders should acknowledge, on behalf of their community, that Catholics suffered discrimination for many years. They should encourage Protestants to see themselves as Irish people with British citizenship and take pride in the Christianity and culture they share with their Catholic neighbours. Equally it believes Catholic church and community leaders should give credit, on behalf of their community, to Protestants for changes in attitude which have taken place. They should encourage their community to view the emblems of 'Britishness' which they dislike as part of the culture of their fellow Irishmen and women, and respect them as such.

4.5 On integrated education

While not pretending that integrated education by itself can solve the problems of a divided society like Northern Ireland, the Commission is convinced that integrated schooling at all levels – from nursery to sixth-form – is a valuable aid to the kind of reconciliation which will necessarily have to accompany any political and other accommodations. It suggests to the Irish hierarchy that it should follow the example of the English hierarchy and investigate the possibility of setting up 'shared schools' as part of the process of ecumenism.

4.6 On school projects for understanding

The Commission urges that action should be taken on some of the many projects suggested in submissions to further contact and debate between schools and universities, ranging from a shared nursery on Belfast's 'peace line' to joint heritage collection projects.

4.7 On a common Irish history and culture

Using the arguments outlined in the schools assemblies, the Commission recommends that a common Irish history course be introduced in all schools in Northern Ireland and, eventually, in the whole of Ireland. It was made aware of a real desire by many Northern Protestants to regain their sense of Irishness, and to re-acquaint themselves with Irish history, culture and the language, which they believe have been expropriated by nationalists as political weapons. The Commission believes that Irish culture has a great potential for uniting people in Northern Ireland, and urges all its proponents to ensure that it is made unthreatening and attractive to Northern Protestants.

SECTION 9
CULTURE, RELIGION, IDENTITY: THE ARTICULATION OF CONFUSION

Culture and Identity

Few would question the idea that, central to our problems in Northern Ireland is a conflict, even a confusion, of identity. The 'troubles' and attendant political developments have shattered old certainties. Nationalism and unionism are no longer the monoliths they once were. The IRA's brand of republicanism has alienated many from the nationalist cause, and the Commission found little confirmation among ordinary nationalists – whatever about their political leaders – of the Protestant perception of nationalists as 'winning'. Nor was there much foundation for some nationalists' belief that unionists seek only to continue their ascendancy. Although we are still forced to use the language of stereotypes for analysis, the stereotypes no longer apply. This is the reason for the withdrawal into private life and apparent apathy of so many Northern Irish people – the fragmentation of the old identities, the abuses to which this has given rise, but the inability to arrive at anything new which carries the same clarity.

It is difficult to articulate confusion. Yet if there was one common denominator in most of the submissions to the Opsahl Commission, it was the attempt to do just this. One presentation by a group of evangelical clergy, while outlining their traditional fears of 'political catholicism', recognized their past neglect of biblical teachings on justice. 'The troubles have been a humbling experience … the old certainties have gone, there's a sense we don't know what we want.' There is still much suspicion, but also a new will to understand, if people can be given some help to do so.

There can be little doubt that religious practice in Northern Ireland has sectarian and politicized undertones, however subconscious – a definition of oneself against the idea of 'the other'. There still is a frequent resort to stereotypes and 'a demonization of one side by the other' to justify one's own stance; the ideal of religion removed from the 'political' sphere to the realms of private conscience and practical Christian concern for the common good is still a long way off. There is, however, a recognition, particularly among the young, that such politicized religion is part of the problem and there was criticism of clerics participating in party politics.

For many Protestants, religion is a far more important element in defining their identity than their 'unionism' or 'Britishness'. Their attitudes to the Republic of Ireland are explained almost entirely in religious terms: Catholicism is seen not just as a religion, but as a threatening political system with international dimensions. Catholicism and Irish nationalism are seen as two parts of the same system, with Articles 2 and 3 of the Irish Constitution symbolic of its threat. Catholicism is still perceived as an authoritarian religion, wielding considerable power over its flock, and the stance of the Catholic clergy on integrated education was cited repeatedly as an example of this. There is still a belief among some Protestants that the Catholic Church teaches hatred of Protestantism. Protestant fears and mistrust of the Catholic Church are so deeply and sincerely felt that both the Catholic Church itself, and leaders of society in the Republic of Ireland, must move to allay them. In the opinion of the Commission it is time for an in-depth examination of the role of the Church in the Republic, paying particular attention to its perceived influence in the ethos of such state-funded and controlled sectors as health and education. It is specifically concerned about the continuing threat to the existence and ethos of the Republic's only Protestant-run general teaching hospital, the Adelaide, and points to the effect such a threat has in reinforcing the poor image of the Republic among Northern Protestants. The Commission also supports those submissions which asked the Catholic Church to be more sensitive to the needs of couples in mixed marriages and of Catholic parents who wish to have their children educated in integrated schools.

There is also a sense that Protestants' culture is 'rubbished', 'vilified nationally and internationally'. 'We are treated like white South Africans', commented one person from the Shankill Road. There is a defensiveness about Protestant culture, which is not helped by a certain inarticulateness and inability to explain, let alone share it.

Catholics do not have the same problem with Protestantism as a religion and are more tolerant of Protestants as individuals. They do not understand Protestant fears of their Church. They are baffled and offended by Protestant 'anti-popery'; at the offensive treatment of Catholicism in some evangelical writings; and the political consequences of this – one submission pointed to advertisements for such literature in UDA newsletters. Because of a lack of understanding of the religious reasons for such attitudes (and the past failure of Protestants to explain them), the belief persists among many Catholics that Protestants cling to the connection with Britain simply to retain their 'ascendancy'. The Catholic complaint is still with the politicians and the state; they still have a sense of being victimised and 'pigeonholed' politically because of their religion. There is resentment among west Belfast Catholics, in particular, that they are perceived as being highly politicized and treated accordingly.

Much of the defensiveness of Protestants comes from ignorance of their own history and of Irish history generally, a sense that history will be used as a weapon against them, and a tendency in consequence to dwell on those events in which they too were victims, and to ignore the rest. In this sense, all sides in Northern Ireland are prisoners of a victim theology which sees the other side as the aggressor.

But do Protestants really need to be so defensive and apologetic about their culture? We think not. There was less sign than in the past of the nationalist tendency to view Protestants as somehow un-Irish; only a few submissions used the old planter/native stereotypes, and these came almost exclusively from people from the South or older border nationalists. Very many Protestants can boast as sound a Gaelic lineage as Catholics (if they only studied their own history). In this respect, the new trend of Protestants tracing links with pre-historic Ulster is a beginning, though the tendency to claim exclusive 'ownership' is the reverse image of the IRA's version of Irish history. No one group has a monopoly of Irishness or indeed Ulsterness.

The Commission was made aware of a strong desire among many Protestants to be 'made to feel at ease with their Irishness'. The belief is still there that nationalists generally have appropriated the Irish language and Irish history as political weapons. The truth of this was recognized by many nationalists. But few Protestants acknowledged that they too had contributed by their own rejection of both. There is a clear desire among nationalists to move away from such exclusiveness. This, unfortunately, has taken the form of omitting Irish history from some Catholic schools because it is potentially divisive. Yet there was a desire among both Catholic and Protestant sixth-formers at the schools' assemblies that both Irish history and the Irish language be made available in all schools. Perhaps, too, if more were known about the history of Ulster, more common ground might be established.

For their part, Protestants should look at the anti-Catholic nature of some of their culture. The emphasis by the Orange Order on marches seem singularly unimaginative. Its continued insistence that these should take traditional routes, even when the areas through which they pass have become predominantly Catholic, is indefensible, and transmits the negative signal about their culture which many Protestants wish to deflect. The Commission points out that such marches do not accord well with the qualifications as laid down for Orangemen by their own organization: 'He should cultivate truth and justice, brotherly kindness and charity, concord and unity and obedience to the laws; his deportment should be gentle and compassionate, kind and courteous.' One submission suggests that a summer festival would give people a way of celebrating Protestant and Orange culture without emphasizing religious antagonisms.

Protestants privately acknowledge injustices which existed under the Stormont regime, but few will say as much, and they resent being reminded of them. Yet Catholics desire this simple recognition, and it would win considerable respect if made.

Time and time again we heard Protestants talk of Catholics' greater proficiency at organizing themselves; what once would have been dismissed as a herd-like tendency, now wins admiration and an acceptance that in the voluntary and community sector Protestants have much to learn. Certainly there are signs of a weak political culture generally among Northern Ireland Protestants and a recognition that the public voice of Protestantism sounds bigoted.

The Churches were considered not to have done enough either to represent the fears of their communities or to take a lead in assuaging them. It is all very well for the religious leaders to act in unison, the Commission was told, but the 'trickle-down effect' is perceived as very limited. However, submissions reflected considerable debate and movement amongst a wide range of clergy and a recognition that they can do more. The Churches should encourage more explanation of their theologies and their cultural and political implications. In the Belfast schools' assembly there was a demand for more religion to be taught, not less. A purely secular atmosphere in schools is not what most young people want. Rather, they asked for 'mixed' religious education classes, where they could actually hear other young people talking about their religion. The discussion groups preceding the assemblies were a model of what could happen: frank discussions about beliefs and identities. Could existing integrated schools and those state schools that are mixed – as well as schools linked through the Education for Mutual Understanding (EMU) programme – run pilot projects along these lines and involve the respective Churches?

The Catholic Church bears a particular responsibility for this (given the depth of Protestant suspicion outlined above). The submission from the Inter-Church Group on Faith and Politics pointed to a number of ways in which the Catholic Church could help defuse 'the deep-seated distrust among Protestants, of Catholic ecclesiastical power', among them 'offering communion to inter-church couples when requested, or not putting obstacles in the way of those who wish to give experiments in integrated education a fair trial, or altering some of the rules for mixed marriages'.

Protestants in the South should be encouraged to talk to their co-religionists in the North, and explain that they do not feel threatened. Northern Protestant clergy, for their part, should be sensitive to elements conducive to sectarianism in their own statements and practices. A more thoughtful and concerned religious leadership could not be imagined than those representing the Presbyterian Church and Government Committee, who appeared at the first week's oral hearing in Belfast. And yet they had difficulty explaining the implications of one of Presbyterianism's central doctrinal documents: the Westminster Confession of Faith, with its description of the Pope as the 'anti-Christ'. Many Catholics were also critical of their Church's stance on integrated education, pointing to the obstacles placed in the way of some Catholic parents wishing to send their children to integrated schools.

While Catholics were comfortable with their Irish identity, the difficulties for Protestants in this sphere was a recurring theme. Many felt no difficulty in being British and 'Irish only in the geographical sense'. However, others echoed the outgoing Presbyterian moderator, Dr John Dunlop, in asking 'How can Protestants claim to be Irish when their neighbours are being killed in the name of Ireland?' Many Protestants addressing the Commission admitted to being less inclined to call themselves Irish because of the 'troubles'.

If the schools' assemblies were taken as a guide, many young Protestants west of the Bann appeared to see themselves as British rather than Irish, while those in the east were more open to seeing themselves as Irish first. Young Catholics west of the Bann were less inclined to recognize a common local identity than those in the east, where an identity with the geographic region of Northern Ireland was stronger, regardless of religion. But there is more duality and confusion than is generally recognized. Where older Protestants spoke of the monarch, the British constitution and the Protestant succession, young Protestants had difficulty defining their Britishness and tended to point to things like sport. Family traditions seemed paramount: where the family was highly politicized, the young felt strongly British (although, even here, there was a sense of being second-class British citizens). Where Irish history was offered at school, Protestant pupils felt more comfortable in accepting an Irish identity, when coupled with British citizenship. Given such attitudes, there appears to be a case for offering people in Northern Ireland some way of recognizing such mixed identity, other than the simple option of holding British or Irish passports.

The young Catholics at the schools' assemblies defined their Irishness almost entirely in terms of culture; there was a desperate eagerness that it should be shared and little sign that they wanted it used as a political weapon. 'As a Protestant who has never had a problem with embracing my Irishness', writes Sam McAughtry in his submission, 'I have been aware for many years that this single gesture brings with it more warmth and goodwill from Catholics than any other Protestant response within the context of our divisions.'

In fact, nationalists have come a long way since the 1960s. They have reconsidered their history in a way that unionists have not. Unionism could benefit from a similar reconsideration – 'we need to take the history of our antagonism seriously'. 'Britishness' needs to be redefined in the context of Northern Ireland. Political Britishness, defined simply in terms of the political connection, no longer gives Protestants the confidence in their identity that they once had. Religion is clearly the most fundamental element in defining Protestant identity and, if that is generally explained and recognized, they could have, and be given, more confidence in the future. Equally, Irishness needs to be redefined as something more pluralist than at present; it was, after all, happily used by Protestant and Catholic alike until the foundation of Northern Ireland.

A number of other specific suggestions were made to the Commission, such as the organization of local festivals, including Orange festivals. One innovative scheme was for a Northern version of the schools-based heritage collection project, based on the one mounted in the Republic in the 1950s, 'which not only established a valuable cultural archive, but also created a shared sense of cultural, communal history and identity among the pupils who collected the material'. Another was for a community-based Centre for the Media, Arts and Communication, to be established on the Belfast 'peace line' to increase awareness of the culture and tradition of both sides.

Catholics concerned about the Irish language and culture should condemn their use for divisive political ends and generally should help Protestants to feel more at ease by recognizing Protestant culture as part of an Irish identity. There should be a progressive depoliticizing of cultural beliefs, with attempts to find new Northern Irish symbols and emblems with which both traditions can identify. A monolithic national identity is inappropriate to the experiences of the people of Northern Ireland: 'In practice its citizens pick 'n' mix from a range of cultural choice … Thus acknowledgement of *de facto* affiliation to two islands must inform any new institutional framework.' There are many signs that the British government and the Northern Ireland Office have recognized this need; there are fewer from the Republic.

Religion

Church apologists have consistently argued that the Northern Ireland problem is not religious. Land, power and nationhood are identified as the issues. But when the good land and power have for centuries been in the hands of a group on one side of the traditional religious divide, and when the lack of both land and power has been experienced by a group on the other side, a religious content in the struggle is inevitable. When Protestants claim to be British and when Catholics assert their Irishness and want to be rid of any British connection, the mixture of religion and national identity makes for a volatile brew.

While both sides may in some ways deny that they are engaged in a religious war, their art forms and mores tell a different story. Loyalist murals depict warriors ready for action under the words 'For God and Ulster' emblazoned on gable walls. Republicans, on the other hand, have for generations thought, spoken and written in terms of blood-sacrifice. They have their hagiography of the men and women who have died 'for the cause'. The suffering of those who died on hunger strike is still compared with the sufferings and sacrifice of Christ on the cross. Every one of the more than 3000 people who have been killed in the present 'troubles', irrespective of whether or not they were paramilitary activists, has been given a Christian burial.

Religion may or may not be the prime cause of the conflict: it is certainly a potent component of it – probably more so for Protestants than for Catholics. It was evident in more than one submission that the real 'hate figures' for Protestants are likely to be the priest and the Pope – the human personification of Roman clericalism – while for Catholics it is most certainly the loyalist politician, the RUC and the UDR (now the RIR), rather than the Protestant clergyman or minister.

It simply comes to this: the Northern Ireland conflict is in part economic and social, in part political and constitutional, and also in part religious, and damagingly so. Accepting the religious factor in the equation, are the Churches obliged to respond? Have they any obligation to do anything?

In so far as the Churches succeed in relieving suffering; in persuading activists to lay down their arms; in persuading others not to take them up; in providing ideas or suggestions that may lead to a settlement, or indeed in reaching out and mediating, they may be considered as part of the solution. In so far as they fail to do any or all of these things, they are part of the problem. Responsibilities and obligations consequently rest on all the Churches. They cannot assert that they are not affected or involved in a struggle which is tearing apart Northern Ireland society, causing deaths and destruction on a scale even the greatest pessimist would have considered impossible twenty-five years ago.

What then has been the contribution of the Churches, good or bad, to the Northern Ireland problem over the last quarter of a century? Let it be said at once that in the early 1900s and as late as 1912, when the Home Rule crisis came to a head, the Churches had no hesitation in taking sides. There was no doubt about the stance of any of them. The newspaper reports and public rallies of the period are witness to adamant Protestant Church opposition to Home Rule and to Catholic Church approval of it.

Not so in the years of the current unrest. The mainstream Churches at least have organized no public religious–political rallies and engaged in no public agitation, whatever may be the inner wishes and aspirations of their members.

The Commission received over fifty written submissions from official church bodies and individual clergy and lay people. These included important voices from the three main Protestant Churches, in the form of key Presbyterian and Methodist committees and three Church of Ireland bishops. Regrettably, the Northern Catholic bishops did not contribute, although members of religious orders and individual priests did.

In both the written submissions and oral hearings, the Commission had clear evidence of a wealth of Christian compassion in Northern Ireland over the years. The relatives of the murdered have been comforted, counselled and helped; refugee and rest centres have been provided when needed; housing has been made available through Church-based housing associations; Christian organizations and communities like Corrymeela have been at work supporting the victims of violence; holidays for children from ghettos have been arranged on a cross-community basis year after year by Church-related organizations and by associations whose aims and members are avowedly Christian. There is much worth in what has been done.

Nonetheless, the Churches would be ready to admit that all this is only a fraction of what needs to be done. At best they can hope only to provide a back-up and to complement what the state can and ought to provide. In any case, only the Churches can say what more they could have done. The submission of the Irish Council of Churches referred to the many thousands of pounds contributed through the Churches Emergency Fund to organizations and groups engaged in cross-community and ameliorating projects. However, all the money distributed has come from Germany, the United States and Britain. None of the Irish Churches seem to have contributed to the Fund.

The late Cardinal Conway once reflected that perhaps the Catholic Church should have been more concerned about unemployment and other social issues. The other Churches could well have said the same. The gospel the Churches profess to believe, preach and practise has much to say, in addition to its insistence on the grace of God, about the search for justice, concern for the poor and equal rights, and love for self, neighbour and enemy. Those are the criteria and principles that the Churches must apply to what they say to politicians and to what the politicians wish to propose.

How then have the Churches measured up to that obligation? The Commission was reminded that the Presbyterian Church had published studies on Irish republicanism and loyalism; that the Methodist Church's Council on Social Welfare had done work on poverty and deprivation in Northern Ireland and on the Anglo-Irish Agreement. It was aware of books by Cardinal Daly and Archbishop Eames, calling for the application of Christian principles to any solution offered for Northern Ireland's agony.

The Commission took note of the reference in the Irish Council of Churches' submission to the recommendations of the 1976 report from the Working Party on Violence in Ireland, appointed by the Catholic Hierarchy and the Protestant Churches of the Council. The report recommended that the Churches should actively support peace and reconciliation movements; they should support the principle of a Bill of Rights to protect minorities; there should be action by the Churches to ensure that they are not compromised by paramilitary organizations at funerals and commemorations; there should be urgent experiments in the youth service to make it both non-denominational and appealing to those young people hitherto not attracted to it; a joint committee should be established to consider closer contact and co-operation between Catholic and other schools; the Churches should set an example to society in the place they give to women; a sustained programme of education within the Churches should be initiated to make their members more aware of the political and social implications of Christianity for Irish society, and of democratic methods for promoting justice and peace; and a Christian Centre of Social Investigation should be set up, to conduct research into the problems underlying the conflict and to monitor progress in removing discrimination and other injustices related to the occurrence of violence. The Commission regrets that there is much unfinished business as far as many of these recommendations are concerned, notes that they are as relevant now as they were then, and calls for renewed action on them.

How have the Churches in Northern Ireland discharged the ministry of reconciliation? The late Bishop Philbin of Down and Connor once wrote that the world could with justification keep aloof from the Churches as long as the Churches kept aloof from one another. What then has been happening in Northern Ireland?

The Commission learned from both written submissions and oral hearings that there has been a marked development in ecumenical services and in the growth of cross-community prayer and Bible study groups. However, it was claimed that the majority of Catholic clergy attending those services come from the religious orders (rather than from priests in parishes), and the majority of Protestants also appear to be from non-congregational or non-parish sectors. Furthermore, it was claimed that the lay attendances are for the most part Catholic. This seems to bear out a comment made by the late Professor John Whyte in his posthumously published book *Interpreting Northern Ireland* that more than 50 per cent of both Presbyterians and Methodists are opposed to such ecumenical services. The intensity of that opposition may be gauged from some sentences in a written submission made to the Commission by a former moderator of the Presbyterian Church.

> Many unionists see ecumenism as but another means of undermining their Protestant heritage by blurring the fundamental differences between the Reformed and Unreformed faiths. It is clear that in all the Protestant Churches, whatever the clergy may pretend or even wish, the people are determined that their Protestant faith and heritage are not for sale.

So much for reaching out in ecumenical services. What of actual attempts to make peace? Probably the full story of such initiatives will never be completely known. The Commission is aware that meetings between churchmen – whether or not officially accredited – and republican and loyalist activists have taken place which have never been publicized. Some of those encounters have not been without positive effects. However, it should be noted that the much publicized 1974 Feakle encounter between leading Protestant churchmen and the IRA had far from unanimous support inside the Protestant Churches, and one of the party was publicly disavowed by his superiors. The Peace People, the unnumbered peace groups and organizations, the Sadie Pattersons, Ruth Agnews and others whose names are history, the Gordon Wilsons of today, are witnesses to the fact that somewhere along the line the Churches have succeeded in producing persons who are prepared to work and struggle as well as to pray for peace. Tragically, more is needed to end the conflict..

There is one other factor to be considered. To a remarkable extent, the Churches have succeeded in maintaining 'quality of life' inside their own communions and particularly within individual parishes and congregations. Members of those congregations have been able to attain a degree of caring for each other and norms of acceptable behaviour that might not have been expected. At a minimum, thousands of adults and young men and women have been encouraged and persuaded to refrain from activity that would foment or increase unrest. It is, of course, undeniable that large numbers, who at one time were under the tutelage of the Churches, have resorted to violence.

At a time when the credibility of the Churches is increasingly being called into question, their maintainance of a regular pattern of worship and practice, often in the face of intimidation and danger, has been no mean achievement.

The summaries of the written submissions in Part II give some indication of the record – good and bad, successful and failed, encouraging and depressing – of the Churches in Northern Ireland over the last quarter century of strife. There has been concern; there has been action of different kinds, but there is still an alarming amount to be accomplished.

Notes

1. Taken from *The Opsahl Commission: 100 ideas about ways forward for Northern Ireland and its people* (Belfast, 1993).

The Downing Street Joint Declaration (December 1993)

1. The Taoiseach, Mr Albert Reynolds TD, and the Prime Minister, the Rt Hon. John Major MP, acknowledge that the most urgent and important issue facing the people of Ireland, North and South, and the British and Irish Governments together, is to remove the causes of conflict, to overcome the legacy of history and to heal the divisions which have resulted, recognising that the absence of a lasting and satisfactory settlement of relationships between the peoples of both islands has contributed to continuing tragedy and suffering. They believe that the development of an agreed framework for peace, which has been discussed between them since early last year, and which is based on a number of key principles articulated by the two Governments over the past 20 years, together with the adaptation of other widely accepted principles, provides the starting point of a peace process designed to culminate in a political settlement.

2. The Taoiseach and the Prime Minister are convinced of the inestimable value to both their peoples, and particularly for the next generation, of healing divisions in Ireland and of ending a conflict which has been so manifestly to the detriment of all. Both recognise that the ending of divisions can come about only through the agreement and co-operation of the people, North and South, representing both traditions in Ireland. They therefore make a solemn commitment to promote co-operation at all levels on the basis of the fundamental principles, undertakings, obligations under international agreements, to which they have jointly committed themselves, and the guarantees which each Government has given and now reaffirms, including Northern Ireland's statutory constitutional guarantee. It is their aim to foster agreement and reconciliation, leading to a new political framework founded on consent and encompassing arrangements within Northern Ireland, for the whole island, and between these islands.

3. They also consider that the development of Europe will, of itself, require new approaches to serve interests common to both parts of the island of Ireland, and to Ireland and the United Kingdom as partners in the European Union.

4. The Prime Minister, on behalf of the British Government, reaffirms that they will uphold the democratic wish of a greater number of the people of Northern Ireland on the issue of whether they prefer to support the Union or a sovereign united Ireland. On this basis, he reiterates, on behalf of the British Government, that they have no selfish strategic or economic interest in Northern

Ireland. Their primary interest is to see peace, stability and reconciliation established by agreement among all the people who inhabit the island, and they will work together with the Irish Government to achieve such an agreement, which will embrace the totality of relationships. The role of the British Government will be to encourage, facilitate and enable the achievement of such agreement over a period through a process of dialogue and cooperation based on full respect for the rights and identities of both traditions in Ireland. They accept that such agreement may, as of right, take the form of agreed structures for the island as a whole, including a united Ireland achieved by peaceful means on the following basis. The British Government agree that it is for the people of the island of Ireland alone, by agreement between the two parts respectively, to exercise their right of self-determination on the basis of consent, freely and concurrently given, North and South, to bring about a united Ireland, if that is their wish. They reaffirm as a binding obligation that they will, for their part, introduce the necessary legislation to give effect to this, or equally to any measure of agreement on future relationships in Ireland which the people living in Ireland may themselves freely so determine without external impediment. They believe that the people of Britain would wish, in friendship to all sides, to enable the people of Ireland to reach agreement on how they may live together in harmony and in partnership, with respect for their diverse traditions, and with full recognition of the special links and the unique relationship which exist between the peoples of Britain and Ireland.

5. The Taoiseach, on behalf of the Irish Government, considers that the lessons of Irish history, and especially of Northern Ireland, show that stability and well-being will not be found under any political system which is refused allegiance or rejected on grounds of identity by a significant minority of those governed by it. For this reason, it would be wrong to attempt to impose a united Ireland, in the absence of the freely given consent of a majority of the people of Northern Ireland. He accepts, on behalf of the Irish Government, that the democratic right of self-determination by the people of Ireland as a whole must be achieved and exercised with and subject to the agreement and consent of a majority of the people of Northern Ireland and must, consistent with justice and equity, respect the democratic dignity and the civil rights and religious liberties of both communities, including:

   • the right of free political thought;
   • the right to freedom and expression of religion;
   • the right to pursue democratically national and political aspirations;
   • the right to seek constitutional change by peaceful and legitimate means;
   • the right to live wherever one chooses without hindrance;
   • the right to equal opportunity in all social and economic activity, regardless of class, creed, sex or colour.

   These would be reflected in any future political and constitutional arrangements emerging from a new and more broadly based agreement.

6. The Taoiseach however recognises the genuine difficulties and barriers to building relationships of trust either within or beyond Northern Ireland, from

which both traditions suffer. He will work to create a new era of trust, in which suspicion of the motives or actions of others is removed on the part of either community. He considers that the future of the island depends on the nature of the relationship between the two main traditions that inhabit it. Every effort must be made to build a new sense of trust between those communities. In recognition of the fears of the Unionist community and as a token of his willingness to make a personal contribution to the building up of that necessary trust, the Taoiseach will examine with his colleagues any elements in the democratic life and organisation of the Irish State that can be represented to the Irish Government in the course of political dialogue as a real and substantial threat to their way of life and ethos, or that can be represented as not being fully consistent with a modern democratic and pluralist society, and undertakes to examine any possible ways of removing such obstacles. Such an examination would of course have due regard to the desire to preserve those inherited values that are largely shared throughout the island or that belong to the cultural and historical roots of the people of this island in all their diversity. The Taoiseach hopes that over time a meeting of hearts and minds will develop, which will bring all the people of Ireland together, and will work towards that objective, but he pledges in the meantime that as a result of the efforts that will be made to build mutual confidence no Northern Unionist should ever have to fear in future that this ideal will be pursued either by threat or coercion.

7. Both Governments accept that Irish unity would be achieved only by those who favour this outcome persuading those who do not, peacefully and without coercion or violence, and that, if in the future a majority of the people of Northern Ireland are so persuaded, both Governments will support and give legislative effect to their wish. But, notwithstanding the solemn affirmation by both Governments in the Anglo-Irish Agreement that any change in the status of Northern Ireland would only come about with the consent of a majority of the people of Northern Ireland, the Taoiseach also recognises the continuing uncertainties and misgivings which dominate so much of Northern Unionist attitudes towards the rest of Ireland. He believes that we stand at a stage of our history when the genuine feelings of all traditions in the North must be recognised and acknowledged. He appeals to both traditions at this time to grasp the opportunity for a fresh start and a new beginning, which could hold such promise for all our lives and the generations to come. He asks the people of Northern Ireland to look on the people of the Republic as friends, who share their grief and shame over all the suffering of the last quarter of a century, and who want to develop the best possible relationship with them, a relationship in which trust and new understanding can flourish and grow. The Taoiseach also acknowledges the presence in the Constitution of the Republic of elements which are deeply resented by Northern Unionists, but which at the same time reflect hopes and ideals which lie deep in the hearts of many Irish men and women North and South. But as we move towards a new era of understanding in which new relationships of trust may grow and bring peace to the island of Ireland, the Taoiseach believes that the time has come to consider together

how best the hopes and identities of all can be expressed in more balanced ways, which no longer engender division and the lack of trust to which he has referred. He confirms that, in the event of an overall settlement, the Irish Government will, as part of a balanced constitutional accommodation, put forward and support proposals for change in the Irish Constitution which would fully reflect the principle of consent in Northern Ireland.

8. The Taoiseach recognises the need to engage in dialogue which would address with honesty and integrity the fears of all traditions. But that dialogue, both within the North and between the people and their representatives of both parts of Ireland, must be entered into with an acknowledgement that the future security and welfare of the people of the island will depend on an open, frank and balanced approach to all the problems which for too long have caused division.

9. The British and Irish Governments will seek, along with the Northern Ireland constitutional parties through a process of political dialogue, to create institutions and structures which, while respecting the diversity of the people of Ireland, would enable them to work together in all areas of common interest. This will help over a period to build the trust necessary to end past divisions, leading to an agreed and peaceful future. Such structures would, of course, include institutional recognition of the special links that exist between the peoples of Britain and Ireland as part of the totality of relationships, while taking account of newly forged links with the rest of Europe.

10. The British and Irish Governments reiterate that the achievement of peace must involve a permanent end to the use of, or support for, paramilitary violence. They confirm that, in these circumstances, democratically mandated parties which establish a commitment to exclusively peaceful methods and which have shown that they abide by the democratic process, are free to participate fully in democratic politics and to join in dialogue in due course between the Governments and the political parties on the way ahead.

11. The Irish Government would make their own arrangements within their jurisdiction to enable democratic parties to consult together and share in dialogue about the political future. The Taoiseach's intention is that these arrangements could include the establishment, in consultation with other parties, of a Forum for Peace and Reconciliation to make recommendations on ways in which agreement and trust between both traditions in Ireland can be promoted and established.

12. The Taoiseach and the Prime Minister are determined to build on the fervent wish of both their peoples to see old fears and animosities replaced by a climate of peace. They believe the framework they have set out offers the people of Ireland, North and South, whatever their tradition, the basis to agree that from now on their differences can be negotiated and resolved exclusively by peaceful political means. They appeal to all concerned to grasp the opportunity for a new departure. That step would compromise no position or principle, nor prejudice the future for either community. On the contrary, it would be an incomparable gain for all. It would break decisively the cycle of violence and the intolerable suffering it entails for the people of these islands, particularly

for both communities in Northern Ireland. It would allow the process of economic and social co-operation on the island to realise its full potential for prosperity and mutual understanding. It would transform the prospects for building on the progress already made in the Talks process, involving the two Governments and the constitutional parties in Northern Ireland. The Taoiseach and the Prime Minister believe that these arrangements offer an opportunity to lay the foundations for a more peaceful and harmonious future devoid of the violence and bitter divisions which have scarred the past generation. They commit themselves and their Governments to continue to work together, unremittingly, towards that objective.

The Framework Document (1995)

A NEW FRAMEWORK FOR AGREEMENT
A shared understanding between
the British and Irish Governments
to assist discussion and negotiation involving
the Northern Ireland parties

1. The Joint Declaration acknowledges that the most urgent and important issue facing the people of Ireland, North and South, and the British and Irish Governments together, is to remove the causes of conflict, to overcome the legacy of history and to heal the divisions which have resulted.

2. Both Governments recognise that there is much for deep regret on all sides in the long and often tragic history of Anglo-Irish relations, and of relations in Ireland. They believe it is now time to lay aside, with dignity and forbearance, the mistakes of the past. A collective effort is needed to create, through agreement and reconciliation, a new beginning founded on consent, for relationships within Northern Ireland, within the island of Ireland and between the peoples of these islands. The Joint Declaration itself represents an important step towards this goal, offering the people of Ireland, North and South, whatever their tradition, the basis to agree that from now on their differences can be negotiated and resolved exclusively by peaceful political means.

3. The announcements made by the Irish Republican Army on 31 August 1994 and the Combined Loyalist Military Command on 13 October 1994 are a welcome response to the profound desire of people throughout these islands for a permanent end to the violence which caused such immense suffering and waste and served only to reinforce the barriers of fear and hatred, impeding the search for agreement.

4. A climate of peace enables the process of healing to begin. It transforms the prospects for political progress, building on that already made in the Talks process. Everyone now has a role to play in moving irreversibly beyond the failures of the past and creating new relationships capable of perpetuating peace with freedom and justice.

5. In the Joint Declaration both Governments set themselves the aim of fostering agreement and reconciliation, leading to a new political framework founded on consent. A vital dimension of this three-stranded process is the search, through dialogue with the relevant Northern Ireland parties, for new institutions and

structures to take account of the totality of relationships and to enable the people of Ireland to work together in all areas of common interest while fully respecting their diversity.

[...]

9. The primary objective of both Governments in their approach to Northern Ireland is to promote and establish agreement among the people of the island of Ireland, building on the Joint Declaration. To this end they will both deploy their political resources with the aim of securing a new and comprehensive agreement involving the relevant political parties in Northern Ireland and commanding the widest possible support.

10. They take as guiding principles for their co-operation in search of this agreement:

    (i)   the principle of self-determination, as set out in the Joint Declaration;
    (ii) that the consent of the governed is an essential ingredient for stability in any political arrangement;
    (iii) that agreement must be pursued and established by exclusively democratic, peaceful means, without resort to violence or coercion;
    (iv) that any new political arrangements must be based on full respect for, and protection and expression of, the rights and identities of both traditions in Ireland and even-handedly afford both communities in Northern Ireland parity of esteem and treatment, including equality of opportunity and advantage.

11. They acknowledge that in Northern Ireland, unlike the situation which prevails elsewhere throughout both islands, there is a fundamental absence of consensus about constitutional issues. There are deep divisions between the members of the two main traditions living there over their respective senses of identity and allegiance [...]

12. In their search for political agreement, based on consent, the two Governments are determined to address in a fresh way all of the relationships involved. Their aim is to overcome the legacy of division by reconciling the rights of both traditions in the fullest and most equitable manner. [...]

13. The two Governments will work together with the parties to achieve a comprehensive accommodation, the implementation of which would include interlocking and mutually supportive institutions across the three strands, including:

    (a) structures within Northern Ireland (paragraphs 22 and 23) – to enable elected representatives in Northern Ireland to exercise shared administrative and legislative control [...]
    (b) North/South institutions (paragraphs 24–38) – with clear identity and purpose, to enable representatives of democratic institutions, North and South, to enter into new, co-operative and constructive relationships [...]
    (c) East-West structures (paragraphs 39–49) – to enhance the existing basis for co-operation between the two Governments [...]

Constitutional Issues

14. Both Governments accept that agreement on an overall settlement requires, inter alia, a balanced accommodation of the differing views of the two main traditions on the constitutional issues in relation to the special position of Northern Ireland.

15. Given the absence of consensus and depth of divisions between the two main traditions in Northern Ireland, the two Governments agree that such an accommodation will involve an agreed new approach to the traditional constitutional doctrines on both sides. This would be aimed at enhancing and codifying the fullest attainable measure of consent across both traditions in Ireland and fostering the growth of consensus between them.

16. In their approach to Northern Ireland they will apply the principle of self-determination by the people of Ireland on the basis set out in the Joint Declaration: the British Government recognise that it is for the people of Ireland alone, by agreement between the two parts respectively and without external impediment, to exercise their right of self-determination on the basis of consent, freely and concurrently given, North and South, to bring about a united Ireland, if that is their wish; the Irish Government accept that the democratic right of self-determination by the people of Ireland as a whole must be achieved and exercised with and subject to the agreement and consent of a majority of the people of Northern Ireland.

17. New arrangements should be in accordance with the commitments in the Anglo-Irish Agreement and in the Joint Declaration. They should acknowledge that it would be wrong to make any change in the status of Northern Ireland save with the consent of a majority of the people of Northern Ireland. If in future a majority of the people there wish for and formally consent to the establishment of a united Ireland, the two Governments will introduce and support legislation to give effect to that wish.

18. Both Governments recognise that Northern Ireland's current constitutional status reflects and relies upon the present wish of a majority of its people. They also acknowledge that at present a substantial minority of its people wish for a united Ireland. Reaffirming the commitment to encourage, facilitate and enable the achievement of agreement over a period among all the people who inhabit the island, they acknowledge that the option of a sovereign united Ireland does not command the consent of the unionist tradition, nor does the existing status of Northern Ireland command the consent of the nationalist tradition. Against this background, they acknowledge the need for new arrangements and structures – to reflect the reality of diverse aspirations, to reconcile as fully as possible the rights of both traditions, and to promote cooperation between them, so as to foster the process of developing agreement and consensus between all the people of Ireland.

19. They agree that future arrangements relating to Northern Ireland, and Northern Ireland's wider relationships, should respect the full and equal legitimacy and worth of the identity, sense of allegiance, aspiration and ethos of both the unionist and nationalist communities there. Consequently, both Governments commit themselves to the principle that institutions and arrangements in

Northern Ireland and North/South institutions should afford both communities secure and satisfactory political, administrative and symbolic expression and protection. In particular, they commit themselves to entrenched provisions guaranteeing equitable and effective political participation for whichever community finds itself in a minority position by reference to the Northern Ireland framework, or the wider Irish framework, as the case may be, consequent upon the operation of the principle of consent.

20. The British Government reaffirm that they will uphold the democratic wish of a greater number of the people of Northern Ireland on the issue of whether they prefer to support the Union or a sovereign united Ireland. On this basis, they reiterate that they have no selfish strategic or economic interest in Northern Ireland. For as long as the democratic wish of the people of Northern Ireland is for no change in its present status, the British Government pledge that their jurisdiction there will be exercised with rigorous impartiality on behalf of all the people of Northern Ireland in their diversity. It will be founded on the principles outlined in the previous paragraph with emphasis on full respect for, and equality of, civil, political, social and cultural rights and freedom from discrimination for all citizens, on parity of esteem, and on just and equal treatment for the identity, ethos and aspirations of both communities. [...] This new approach for Northern Ireland, based on the continuing willingness to accept the will of a majority of the people there, will be enshrined in British constitutional legislation embodying the principles and commitments in the Joint Declaration and this Framework Document, either by amendment of the Government of Ireland Act 1920 or by its replacement by appropriate new legislation, and appropriate new provisions entrenched by Agreement.

21. As part of an agreement confirming the foregoing understanding between the two Governments on constitutional issues, the Irish Government will introduce and support proposals for change in the Irish Constitution to implement the commitments in the Joint Declaration. These changes in the Irish Constitution will fully reflect the principle of consent in Northern Ireland and demonstrably be such that no territorial claim of right to jurisdiction over Northern Ireland contrary to the will of a majority of its people is asserted, while maintaining the existing birthright of everyone born in either jurisdiction in Ireland to be part, as of right, of the Irish nation. [...]

Structures in Northern Ireland

22. Both Governments recognise that new political structures within Northern Ireland must depend on the co-operation of elected representatives there. They confirm that cross-community agreement is an essential requirement for the establishment and operation of such structures. [...]

North/South Institutions

24. Both Governments consider that new institutions should be created to cater adequately for present and future political, social and economic interconnections on the island of Ireland [...]

25. Both Governments agree that these institutions should include a North/South body involving Heads of Department on both sides and duly established and maintained by legislation in both sovereign Parliaments. This body would bring together these Heads of Department representing the Irish Government and new democratic institutions in Northern Ireland, to discharge or oversee delegated executive, harmonising or consultative functions, as appropriate, over a range of matters which the two Governments designate in the first instance in agreement with the parties or which the two administrations, North and South, subsequently agree to designate. [...]

    In relevant posts in each of the two administrations participation in the North/South body would be a duty of service. Both Governments believe that the legislation should provide for a clear institutional identity and purpose for the North/South body. It would also establish the body's terms of reference, legal status and arrangements for political, legal, administrative and financial accountability. The North/South body could operate through, or oversee, a range of functionally-related subsidiary bodies or other entities established to administer designated functions on an all-island or cross-border basis.
    [...]

27. Both Governments envisage regular and frequent meetings of the North/South body [...]

28. The two Governments envisage that legislation in the sovereign Parliaments should designate those functions which should, from the outset, be discharged or overseen by the North/South body; and they will seek agreement on these, as on other features of North/South arrangements, in discussion with the relevant political parties in Northern Ireland. It would also be open to the North/South body to recommend to the respective administrations and legislatures for their consideration that new functions should be designated to be discharged or overseen by that body; and to recommend that matters already designated should be moved on the scale between consultation, harmonisation and executive action. Within those responsibilities transferred to new institutions in Northern Ireland, the British Government have no limits of their own to impose on the nature and extent of functions which could be agreed for designation at the outset or, subsequently, between the Irish Government and the Northern Ireland administration. Both Governments expect that significant responsibilities, including meaningful functions at executive level, will be a feature of such agreement. The British Government believe that, in principle, any function devolved to the institutions in Northern Ireland could be so designated, subject to any necessary savings in respect of the British Government's powers and duties, for example to ensure compliance with EU and international obligations. The Irish Government also expect to designate a comparable range of functions.

29. Although both Governments envisage that representatives of North and South in the body could raise for discussion any matter of interest to either side which falls within the competence of either administration, it is envisaged, as already mentioned, that its designated functions would fall into three broad categories:

consultative: the North/South body would be a forum where the two sides would consult on any aspect of designated matters on which either side wished to hold consultations. Both sides would share a duty to exchange information and to consult about existing and future policy, though there would be no formal requirement that agreement would be reached or that policy would be harmonised or implemented jointly, but the development of mutual understanding or common or agreed positions would be the general goal;

harmonising: in respect of these designated responsibilities there would be, in addition to the duty to exchange information and to consult on the formulation of policy, an obligation on both sides to use their best endeavours to reach agreement on a common policy and to make determined efforts to overcome any obstacles in the way of that objective, even though its implementation might be undertaken by the two administrations separately;

executive: in the case of these designated responsibilities the North/South body would itself be directly responsible for the establishment of an agreed policy and for its implementation on a joint basis. It would however be open to the body, where appropriate, to agree that the implementation of the agreed policy would be undertaken either by existing bodies, acting in an agency capacity, whether jointly or separately, North and South, or by new bodies specifically created and mandated for this purpose.

30. In this light, both Governments are continuing to give consideration to the range of functions that might, with the agreement of the parties, be designated at the outset [...]

33. By way of example, the category of agriculture and fisheries might include agricultural and fisheries research, training and advisory services, and animal welfare; health might include co-operative ventures in medical, paramedical and nursing training, cross-border provision of hospital services and major emergency/accident planning; and education might include mutual recognition of teacher qualifications, co-operative ventures in higher education, in teacher training, in education for mutual understanding and in education for specialised needs. [...]

36. Both Governments expect that there would be a Parliamentary Forum, with representatives from agreed political institutions in Northern Ireland and members of the Oireachtas, to consider a wide range of matters of mutual interest. [...]

38. Both Governments envisage that this new framework should serve to help heal the divisions among the communities on the island of Ireland; provide a forum for acknowledging the respective identities and requirements of the two major traditions; express and enlarge the mutual acceptance of the validity of those traditions; and promote understanding and agreement among the people and institutions in both parts of the island. The remit of the body should be dynamic, enabling progressive extension by agreement of its functions to new areas. Its role should develop to keep pace with the growth of harmonisation and with greater integration between the two economies.

East–West Structures

39. Both Governments envisage a new and more broadly-based Agreement, developing and extending their co-operation, reflecting the totality of relationships between the two islands, and dedicated to fostering co-operation, reconciliation and agreement in Ireland at all levels.

40. They intend that under such a new Agreement a standing Intergovernmental Conference will be maintained, chaired by the designated Irish Minister and by the Secretary of State for Northern Ireland. It would be supported by a Permanent Secretariat of civil servants from both Governments.

41. The Conference will be a forum through which the two Governments will work together in pursuance of their joint objectives of securing agreement and reconciliation amongst the people of the island of Ireland and of laying the foundations for a peaceful and harmonious future based on mutual trust and understanding between them.

42. The Conference will provide a continuing institutional expression for the Irish Government's recognised concern and role in relation to Northern Ireland. The Irish Government will put forward views and proposals on issues falling within the ambit of the new Conference or involving both Governments, and determined efforts will be made to resolve any differences between the two Governments. The Conference will be the principal instrument for an intensification of the co-operation and partnership between both Governments, with particular reference to the principles contained in the Joint Declaration, in this Framework Document and in the new Agreement, on a wide range of issues concerned with Northern Ireland and with the relations between the two parts of the island of Ireland. It will facilitate the promotion of lasting peace, stability, justice and reconciliation among the people of the island of Ireland and maintenance of effective security co-operation between the two Governments.

43. Both Governments believe that there should also be provision in the Agreement for developing co-operation between the two Governments and both islands on a range of 'East-West' issues and bilateral matters of mutual interest not covered by other specific arrangements, either through the Anglo-Irish Intergovernmental Council, the Conference or otherwise.

44. Both Governments accept that issues of law and order in Northern Ireland are closely intertwined with the issues of political consensus. For so long as these matters are not devolved, it will be for the Governments to consider ways in which a climate of peace, new institutions and the growth of political agreement may offer new possibilities and opportunities for enhancing community identification with policing in Northern Ireland, while maintaining the most effective possible deployment of the resources of each Government in their common determination to combat crime and prevent any possible recourse to the use or threat of violence for political ends, from any source whatsoever.

45. The Governments envisage that matters for which responsibility is transferred to new political institutions in Northern Ireland will be excluded from consideration in the Conference, except to the extent that the continuing responsibilities of the Secretary of State for Northern Ireland are relevant, or

that cross-border aspects of transferred issues are not otherwise provided for, or in the circumstances described in the following paragraph.

46. The Intergovernmental Conference will be a forum for the two Governments jointly to keep under review the workings of the Agreement and to promote, support and underwrite the fair and effective operation of all its provisions and the new arrangements established under it. Where either Government considers that any institution, established as part of the overall accommodation, is not properly functioning within the Agreement or that a breach of the Agreement has otherwise occurred, the Conference shall consider the matter on the basis of a shared commitment to arrive at a common position [...] However, each Government will be responsible for the implementation of such measures of redress within its own jurisdiction. There would be no derogation from the sovereignty of either Government; each will retain responsibility for the decisions and administration of government within its own jurisdiction.

47. In the event that devolved institutions in Northern Ireland ceased to operate, and direct rule from Westminster was reintroduced, the British Government agree that other arrangements would be made to implement the commitment to promote co-operation at all levels between the people, North and South, representing both traditions in Ireland, as agreed by the two Governments in the Joint Declaration, and to ensure that the co-operation that had been developed through the North/South body be maintained.

48. Both Governments envisage that representatives of agreed political institutions in Northern Ireland may be formally associated with the work of the Conference, in a manner and to an extent to be agreed by both Governments after consultation with them. This might involve giving them advance notice of what is to be discussed in the Conference, enabling them to express views to either Government and inviting them to participate in various aspects of the work of the Conference. Other more structured arrangements could be devised by agreement. [...]

Protection of Rights

50. There is a large body of support, transcending the political divide, for the comprehensive protection and guarantee of fundamental human rights. Acknowledging this, both Governments envisage that the arrangements set out in this Framework Document will be complemented and underpinned by an explicit undertaking in the Agreement on the part of each Government, equally, to ensure in its jurisdiction in the island of Ireland, in accordance with its constitutional arrangements, the systematic and effective protection of common specified civil, political, social and cultural rights. They will discuss and seek agreement with the relevant political parties in Northern Ireland as to what rights should be so specified and how they might best be further protected, having regard to each Government's overall responsibilities including its international obligations. Each Government will introduce appropriate legislation in its jurisdiction to give effect to any such measure of agreement.

51. In addition, both Governments would encourage democratic representatives from both jurisdictions in Ireland to adopt a Charter or Covenant, which might reflect and endorse agreed measures for the protection of the fundamental rights of everyone living in Ireland. It could also pledge a commitment to mutual respect and to the civil rights and religious liberties of both communities, including:

    • the right of free political thought,
    • the right to freedom and expression of religion,
    • the right to pursue democratically national and political aspirations,
    • the right to seek constitutional change by peaceful and legitimate means,
    • the right to live wherever one chooses without hindrance,
    • the right to equal opportunity in all social and economic activity, regardless of class, creed, gender or colour.

52. This Charter or Covenant might also contain a commitment to the principle of consent in the relationships between the two traditions in Ireland. It could incorporate also an enduring commitment on behalf of all the people of the island to guarantee and protect the rights, interests, ethos and dignity of the unionist community in any all-Ireland framework that might be developed with consent in the future, to at least the same extent as provided for the nationalist community in the context of Northern Ireland under the structures and provisions of the new Agreement.

53. The Covenant might also affirm on behalf of all traditions in Ireland a solemn commitment to the exclusively peaceful resolution of all differences between them including in relation to all issues of self-determination, and a solemn repudiation of all recourse to violence between them for any political end or purpose.

Conclusion

54. Both Governments agree that the issues set out in this Framework Document should be examined in the most comprehensive attainable negotiations with democratically mandated political parties in Northern Ireland which abide exclusively by peaceful means and wish to join in dialogue on the way ahead.

55. Both Governments intend that the outcome of these negotiations will be submitted for democratic ratification through referendums, North and South.

56. Both Governments believe that the present climate of peace, which owes much to the imagination, courage and steadfastness of all those who have suffered from violence, offers the best prospect for the Governments and the parties in Northern Ireland to work to secure agreement and consent to a new political accommodation. To accomplish that would be an inestimable prize for all, and especially for people living in Northern Ireland, who have so much to gain from such an accommodation, in which the divisions of the past are laid aside for ever and differences are resolved by exclusively political means. Both Governments believe that a new political dispensation, such as they set

out in this Framework Document, achieved through agreement and reconciliation and founded on the principle of consent, would achieve that objective and transform relationships in Northern Ireland, in the island of Ireland and between both islands.

57. With agreement, co-operation to the mutual benefit of all living in Ireland could develop without impediment, attaining its full potential for stimulating economic growth and prosperity. New arrangements could return power, authority and responsibility to locally-elected representatives in Northern Ireland on a basis acceptable to both sides of the community, enabling them to work together for the common welfare and interests of all the community. The diversity of identities and allegiances could be regarded by all as a source of mutual enrichment, rather than a threat to either side. The divisive issue of sovereignty might cease to be symbolic of the domination of one community over another. It would instead be for decision under agreed ground-rules, fair and balanced towards both aspirations, through a process of democratic persuasion governed by the principle of consent rather than by threat, fear or coercion. In such circumstances the Governments hope that the relationship between the traditions in Northern Ireland could become a positive bond of further understanding, co-operation and amity, rather than a source of contention, between the wider British and Irish democracies.

58. Accordingly, the British and Irish Governments offer for consideration and strongly commend these proposals, trusting that, with generosity and goodwill, the peoples of these islands will build on them a new and lasting agreement.

Summary

FRAMEWORK FOR ACCOUNTABLE GOVERNMENT IN NORTHERN IRELAND

With the purpose of restoring democracy to Northern Ireland, as part of an overall settlement, it:

- Proposes a 90 member Assembly, elected by PR, with substantial legislative and administrative powers over Northern Ireland affairs
- Proposes a system of detailed checks and balances, including weighted voting on contentious business
- Envisages a system of departmental committees and Chairmen, reflecting party strengths, to take over many of the current responsibilities of Northern Ireland Ministers.
- Suggests a separately elected Panel of 3, operating unanimously in a monitoring and referees role in relation to the Assembly.

FRAMEWORK FOR AGREEMENT

With the purpose of promoting agreement and reconciliation it:

- Reaffirms the Downing Street Declaration principles of democracy, consent and peaceful democratic means

- Proposes Irish recognition of the need to remove the territorial claim to jurisdiction over Northern Ireland, contrary to the will of its people, and British recognition of the need to ensure that its constitutional legislation is consistent with the Downing Street Declaration
- Proposes a North/South Body in which elected representatives from the Assembly, acting with the authority of that Assembly, and answerable to that Assembly could, by agreement, carry out designated functions, including executive functions, in clearly defined areas to the benefit of both North and South
- Ensures that extensions of powers can take place, but only with the agreement of the Assembly
- Proposes a new Agreement to develop and extend co-operation between the Republic of Ireland and the UK
- Suggests ways of dealing with fundamental breaches of a settlement without creating Joint Sovereignty or Authority over Northern Ireland
- Proposes involvement of the Assembly in the Anglo-Irish Conference while ensuring that the Conference would not deal with matters exclusive to the Assembly
- Re-asserts the importance of protecting civil rights.

The Good Friday (Belfast) Agreement (April 1998)

1. We, the participants in the multi-party negotiations, believe that the agreement we have negotiated offers a truly historic opportunity for a new beginning.
2. The tragedies of the past have left a deep and profoundly regrettable legacy of suffering. We must never forget those who have died or been injured, and their families. But we can best honour them through a fresh start, in which we firmly dedicate ourselves to the achievement of reconciliation, tolerance, and mutual trust, and to the protection and vindication of the human rights of all.
3. We are committed to partnership, equality and mutual respect as the basis of relationships within Northern Ireland, between North and South, and between these islands.
4. We affirm our total and absolute commitment to exclusively democratic and peaceful means of resolving differences on political issues, and our opposition to any use or threat of force by others for any political purpose, whether in regard to this agreement or otherwise.
5. We acknowledge the substantial differences between our continuing, and equally legitimate, political aspirations. However, we will endeavour to strive in every practical way towards reconciliation and rapprochement within the framework of democratic and agreed arrangements. We pledge that we will, in good faith, work to ensure the success of each and every one of the arrangements to be established under this agreement. It is accepted that all of the institutional and constitutional arrangements – an Assembly in Northern Ireland, a North/South Ministerial Council, implementation bodies, a British-Irish Council and a British-Irish Intergovernmental Conference and any amendments to British Acts of Parliament and the Constitution of Ireland – are interlocking and interdependent and that in particular the functioning of the Assembly and the North/South Council are so closely inter-related that the success of each depends on that of the other.
6. Accordingly, in a spirit of concord, we strongly commend this agreement to the people, North and South, for their approval.

CONSTITUTIONAL ISSUES

1. The participants endorse the commitment made by the British and Irish Governments that, in a new British-Irish Agreement replacing the Anglo-Irish Agreement, they will:

   (i)   recognise the legitimacy of whatever choice is freely exercised by a majority of the people of Northern Ireland with regard to its status, whether they prefer to continue to support the Union with Great Britain or a sovereign united Ireland;

   (ii) recognise that it is for the people of the island of Ireland alone, by agreement between the two parts respectively and without external impediment, to exercise their right of self-determination on the basis of consent, freely and concurrently given, North and South, to bring about a united Ireland, if that is their wish, accepting that this right must be achieved and exercised with and subject to the agreement and consent of a majority of the people of Northern Ireland;

   (iii) acknowledge that while a substantial section of the people in Northern Ireland share the legitimate wish of a majority of the people of the island of Ireland for a united Ireland, the present wish of a majority of the people of Northern Ireland, freely exercised and legitimate, is to maintain the Union and, accordingly, that Northern Ireland's status as part of the United Kingdom reflects and relies upon that wish; and that it would be wrong to make any change in the status of Northern Ireland save with the consent of a majority of its people;

   (iv) affirm that if, in the future, the people of the island of Ireland exercise their right of self-determination on the basis set out in sections (i) and (ii) above to bring about a united Ireland, it will be a binding obligation on both Governments to introduce and support in their respective Parliaments legislation to give effect to that wish;

   (v)   affirm that whatever choice is freely exercised by a majority of the people of Northern Ireland, the power of the sovereign government with jurisdiction there shall be exercised with rigorous impartiality on behalf of all the people in the diversity of their identities and traditions and shall be founded on the principles of full respect for, and equality of, civil, political, social and cultural rights, of freedom from discrimination for all citizens, and of parity of esteem and of just and equal treatment for the identity, ethos, and aspirations of both communities;

   (vi) recognise the birthright of all the people of Northern Ireland to identify themselves and be accepted as Irish or British, or both, as they may so choose, and accordingly confirm that their right to hold both British and Irish citizenship is accepted by both Governments and would not be affected by any future change in the status of Northern Ireland.

2. The participants also note that the two Governments have accordingly undertaken in the context of this comprehensive political agreement, to propose

and support changes in, respectively, the Constitution of Ireland and in British legislation relating to the constitutional status of Northern Ireland.
[...]

STRAND ONE

DEMOCRATIC INSTITUTIONS IN NORTHERN IRELAND

1. This agreement provides for a democratically elected Assembly in Northern Ireland which is inclusive in its membership, capable of exercising executive and legislative authority, and subject to safeguards to protect the rights and interests of all sides of the community.

The Assembly

2. A 108-member Assembly will be elected by PR(STV) from existing Westminster constituencies.
3. The Assembly will exercise full legislative and executive authority in respect of those matters currently within the responsibility of the six Northern Ireland Government Departments, with the possibility of taking on responsibility for other matters as detailed elsewhere in this agreement.
4. The Assembly – operating where appropriate on a cross-community basis – will be the prime source of authority in respect of all devolved responsibilities.

Safeguards

5. There will be safeguards to ensure that all sections of the community can participate and work together successfully in the operation of these institutions and that all sections of the community are protected [...]
[...]

Executive Authority

14. Executive authority to be discharged on behalf of the Assembly by a First Minister and Deputy First Minister and up to ten Ministers with Departmental responsibilities.
15. The First Minister and Deputy First Minister shall be jointly elected into office by the Assembly voting on a cross-community basis [...]
[...]
25. An individual may be removed from office following a decision of the Assembly taken on a cross-community basis, if (s)he loses the confidence of the Assembly, voting on a cross-community basis, for failure to meet his or her responsibilities including, inter alia, those set out in the Pledge of Office. Those who hold office should use only democratic, non-violent means, and those who do not should be excluded or removed from office under these provisions. [...]

Relations with other institutions

[...]

34. A consultative Civic Forum will be established. It will comprise representatives of the business, trade union and voluntary sectors, and such other sectors as agreed by the First Minister and the Deputy First Minister. It will act as a consultative mechanism on social, economic and cultural issues. The First Minister and the Deputy First Minister will by agreement provide administrative support for the Civic Forum and establish guidelines for the selection of representatives to the Civic Forum.

[...]

STRAND TWO

NORTH/SOUTH MINISTERIAL COUNCIL

1. Under a new British/Irish Agreement dealing with the totality of relationships, and related legislation at Westminster and in the Oireachtas, a North/South Ministerial Council to be established to bring together those with executive responsibilities in Northern Ireland and the Irish Government, to develop consultation, co-operation and action within the island of Ireland – including through implementation on an all-island and cross-border basis – on matters of mutual interest within the competence of the Administrations, North and South.

2. All Council decisions to be by agreement between the two sides. Northern Ireland to be represented by the First Minister, Deputy First Minister and any relevant Ministers, the Irish Government by the Taoiseach and relevant Ministers, all operating in accordance with the rules for democratic authority and accountability in force in the Northern Ireland Assembly and the Oireachtas respectively. Participation in the Council to be one of the essential responsibilities attaching to relevant posts in the two Administrations. If a holder of a relevant post will not participate normally in the Council, the Taoiseach in the case of the Irish Government and the First and Deputy First Minister in the case of the Northern Ireland Administration to be able to make alternative arrangements.

[...]

13. It is understood that the North/South Ministerial Council and the Northern Ireland Assembly are mutually inter-dependent, and that one cannot successfully function without the other.

[...]

18. The Northern Ireland Assembly and the Oireachtas to consider developing a joint parliamentary forum, bringing together equal numbers from both institutions for discussion of matters of mutual interest and concern.

19. Consideration to be given to the establishment of an independent consultative forum appointed by the two Administrations, representative of civil society, comprising the social partners and other members with expertise in social, cultural, economic and other issues.

[...]

BRITISH-IRISH COUNCIL

1. A British-Irish Council (BIC) will be established under a new British-Irish Agreement to promote the harmonious and mutually beneficial development of the totality of relationships among the peoples of these islands.
2. Membership of the BIC will comprise representatives of the British and Irish Governments, devolved institutions in Northern Ireland, Scotland and Wales, when established, and, if appropriate, elsewhere in the United Kingdom, together with representatives of the Isle of Man and the Channel Islands.
   [...]

BRITISH-IRISH INTERGOVERNMENTAL CONFERENCE

1. There will be a new British-Irish Agreement dealing with the totality of relationships. It will establish a standing British-Irish Intergovernmental Conference, which will subsume both the Anglo-Irish Intergovernmental Council and the Intergovernmental Conference established under the 1985 Agreement.
   [...]

RIGHTS, SAFEGUARDS AND EQUALITY OF OPPORTUNITY

Human Rights

1. The parties affirm their commitment to the mutual respect, the civil rights and the religious liberties of everyone in the community. Against the background of the recent history of communal conflict, the parties affirm in particular:

   - the right of free political thought;
   - the right to freedom and expression of religion;
   - the right to pursue democratically national and political aspirations;
   - the right to seek constitutional change by peaceful and legitimate means;
   - the right to freely choose one's place of residence;
   - the right to equal opportunity in all social and economic activity, regardless of class, creed, disability, gender or ethnicity;
   - the right to freedom from sectarian harassment; and
   - the right of women to full and equal political participation.

United Kingdom Legislation

2. The British Government will complete incorporation into Northern Ireland law of the European Convention on Human Rights (ECHR), with direct access to the courts, and remedies for breach of the Convention, including power for the courts to overrule Assembly legislation on grounds of inconsistency.
3. Subject to the outcome of public consultation underway, the British Government intends, as a particular priority, to create a statutory obligation on public authorities in Northern Ireland to carry out all their functions with due regard to the need to promote equality of opportunity in relation to religion and

political opinion; gender; race; disability; age; marital status; dependants; and sexual orientation. [...]

4. The new Northern Ireland Human Rights Commission (see paragraph 5 below) will be invited to consult and to advise on the scope for defining, in Westminster legislation, rights supplementary to those in the European Convention on Human Rights, to reflect the particular circumstances of Northern Ireland, drawing as appropriate on international instruments and experience. These additional rights to reflect the principles of mutual respect for the identity and ethos of both communities and parity of esteem, and – taken together with the ECHR – to constitute a Bill of Rights for Northern Ireland. Among the issues for consideration by the Commission will be:

- the formulation of a general obligation on government and public bodies fully to respect, on the basis of equality of treatment, the identity and ethos of both communities in Northern Ireland; and
- a clear formulation of the rights not to be discriminated against and to equality of opportunity in both the public and private sectors.

New Institutions in Northern Ireland

5. A new Northern Ireland Human Rights Commission, with membership from Northern Ireland reflecting the community balance, will be established by Westminster legislation, independent of Government, with an extended and enhanced role beyond that currently exercised by the Standing Advisory Commission on Human Rights [...]

6. Subject to the outcome of public consultation currently underway, the British Government intends a new statutory Equality Commission to replace the Fair Employment Commission, the Equal Opportunities Commission (NI), the Commission for Racial Equality (NI) and the Disability Council. Such a unified Commission will advise on, validate and monitor the statutory obligation and will investigate complaints of default.

7. It would be open to a new Northern Ireland Assembly to consider bringing together its responsibilities for these matters into a dedicated Department of Equality.
   [...]

Comparable Steps by the Irish Government

9. The Irish Government will also take steps to further strengthen the protection of human rights in its jurisdiction. [... The] Irish Government will:

- establish a Human Rights Commission with a mandate and remit equivalent to that within Northern Ireland;
- proceed with arrangements as quickly as possible to ratify the Council of Europe Framework Convention on National Minorities (already ratified by the UK);
- implement enhanced employment equality legislation;
- introduce equal status legislation; and

• continue to take further active steps to demonstrate its respect for the different traditions in the island of Ireland.

A Joint Committee

10. It is envisaged that there would be a joint committee of representatives of the two Human Rights Commissions, North and South, as a forum for consideration of human rights issues in the island of Ireland. The joint committee will consider, among other matters, the possibility of establishing a charter, open to signature by all democratic political parties, reflecting and endorsing agreed measures for the protection of the fundamental rights of everyone living in the island of Ireland.

Reconciliation and Victims of Violence

11. The participants believe that it is essential to acknowledge and address the suffering of the victims of violence as a necessary element of reconciliation. They look forward to the results of the work of the Northern Ireland Victims Commission.
12. It is recognised that victims have a right to remember as well as to contribute to a changed society. The achievement of a peaceful and just society would be the true memorial to the victims of violence. The participants particularly recognise that young people from areas affected by the troubles face particular difficulties and will support the development of special community-based initiatives based on international best practice. [...]
13. The participants recognise and value the work being done by many organisations to develop reconciliation and mutual understanding and respect between and within communities and traditions, in Northern Ireland and between North and South, and they see such work as having a vital role in consolidating peace and political agreement. Accordingly, they pledge their continuing support to such organisations and will positively examine the case for enhanced financial assistance for the work of reconciliation. An essential aspect of the reconciliation process is the promotion of a culture of tolerance at every level of society, including initiatives to facilitate and encourage integrated education and mixed housing.

RIGHTS, SAFEGUARDS AND EQUALITY OF OPPORTUNITY

ECONOMIC, SOCIAL AND CULTURAL ISSUES

1. Pending the devolution of powers to a new Northern Ireland Assembly, the British Government will pursue broad policies for sustained economic growth and stability in Northern Ireland and for promoting social inclusion, including in particular community development and the advancement of women in public life.
2. Subject to the public consultation currently under way, the British Government will make rapid progress with:

(i)   a new regional development strategy for Northern Ireland [...]

(ii) a new economic development strategy for Northern Ireland [...]

(iii) measures on employment equality included in the recent White Paper ('Partnership for Equality') and covering the extension and strengthening of anti-discrimination legislation, a review of the national security aspects of the present fair employment legislation at the earliest possible time, a new more focused Targeting Social Need initiative and a range of measures aimed at combating unemployment and progressively eliminating the differential in unemployment rates between the two communities by targeting objective need.

3. All participants recognise the importance of respect, understanding and tolerance in relation to linguistic diversity, including in Northern Ireland, the Irish language, Ulster-Scots and the languages of the various ethnic communities, all of which are part of the cultural wealth of the island of Ireland.

4. In the context of active consideration currently being given to the UK signing the Council of Europe Charter for Regional or Minority Languages, the British Government will in particular in relation to the Irish language, where appropriate and where people so desire it:

- take resolute action to promote the language;
- facilitate and encourage the use of the language in speech and writing in public and private life where there is appropriate demand;
- seek to remove, where possible, restrictions which would discourage or work against the maintenance or development of the language;
- make provision for liaising with the Irish language community, representing their views to public authorities and investigating complaints;
- place a statutory duty on the Department of Education to encourage and facilitate Irish medium education in line with current provision for integrated education [...]

5. All participants acknowledge the sensitivity of the use of symbols and emblems for public purposes, and the need in particular in creating the new institutions to ensure that such symbols and emblems are used in a manner which promotes mutual respect rather than division. Arrangements will be made to monitor this issue and consider what action might be required.

DECOMMISSIONING

[...]

3. All participants accordingly reaffirm their commitment to the total disarmament of all paramilitary organisations. They also confirm their intention to continue to work constructively and in good faith with the Independent Commission, and to use any influence they may have, to achieve the decommissioning of all paramilitary arms within two years following endorsement in referendums North and South of the agreement and in the context of the implementation of the overall settlement.

[...]

SECURITY

1. The participants note that the development of a peaceful environment on the basis of this agreement can and should mean a normalisation of security arrangements and practices.
2. The British Government will make progress towards the objective of as early a return as possible to normal security arrangements in Northern Ireland, consistent with the level of threat and with a published overall strategy, dealing with:

   (i) the reduction of the numbers and role of the Armed Forces deployed in Northern Ireland to levels compatible with a normal peaceful society;
   (ii) the removal of security installations;
   (iii) the removal of emergency powers in Northern Ireland; and
   (iv) other measures appropriate to and compatible with a normal peaceful society.
   [...]
5. The Irish Government will initiate a wide-ranging review of the Offences Against the State Acts 1939–85 with a view to both reform and dispensing with those elements no longer required as circumstances permit.

POLICING AND JUSTICE

1. The participants recognise that policing is a central issue in any society. They equally recognise that Northern Ireland's history of deep divisions has made it highly emotive, with great hurt suffered and sacrifices made by many individuals and their families, including those in the RUC and other public servants. They believe that the agreement provides the opportunity for a new beginning to policing in Northern Ireland with a police service capable of attracting and sustaining support from the community as a whole. They also believe that this agreement offers a unique opportunity to bring about a new political dispensation which will recognise the full and equal legitimacy and worth of the identities, senses of allegiance and ethos of all sections of the community in Northern Ireland. They consider that this opportunity should inform and underpin the development of a police service representative in terms of the make-up of the community as a whole and which, in a peaceful environment, should be routinely unarmed.
2. The participants believe it essential that policing structures and arrangements are such that the police service is professional, effective and efficient, fair and impartial, free from partisan political control; accountable, both under the law for its actions and to the community it serves; representative of the society it polices, and operates within a coherent and co-operative criminal justice system, which conforms with human rights norms. [...]
3. An independent Commission will be established to make recommendations for future policing arrangements in Northern Ireland including means of encouraging widespread community support for these arrangements within the agreed framework of principles [...]

4. The participants believe that the aims of the criminal justice system are to:
   - deliver a fair and impartial system of justice to the community;
   - be responsive to the community's concerns, and encouraging community involvement where appropriate;
   - have the confidence of all parts of the community; and
   - deliver justice efficiently and effectively.
5. There will be a parallel wide-ranging review of criminal justice (other than policing and those aspects of the system relating to the emergency legislation) to be carried out by the British Government through a mechanism with an independent element, in consultation with the political parties and others. [...]
6. Implementation of the recommendations arising from both reviews will be discussed with the political parties and with the Irish Government.
7. The participants also note that the British Government remains ready in principle [...] to devolve responsibility for policing and justice issues. [...]

PRISONERS

1. Both Governments will put in place mechanisms to provide for an accelerated programme for the release of prisoners, including transferred prisoners, convicted of scheduled offences in Northern Ireland or, in the case of those sentenced outside Northern Ireland, similar offences (referred to hereafter as qualifying prisoners). Any such arrangements will protect the rights of individual prisoners under national and international law.
2. Prisoners affiliated to organisations which have not established or are not maintaining a complete and unequivocal ceasefire will not benefit from the arrangements. The situation in this regard will be kept under review. [...]

VALIDATION AND IMPLEMENTATION

1. The two Governments will as soon as possible sign a new British-Irish Agreement replacing the 1985 Anglo-Irish Agreement, embodying understandings on constitutional issues and affirming their solemn commitment to support and, where appropriate, implement the agreement reached by the participants in the negotiations which shall be annexed to the British-Irish Agreement.
2. Each Government will organise a referendum on 22 May 1998. [...] The Irish Government will introduce and support in the Oireachtas a Bill to amend the Constitution as described in paragraph 2 of the section 'Constitutional Issues' [...]

AGREEMENT BETWEEN THE GOVERNMENT OF THE UNITED KINGDOM OF GREAT
BRITAIN AND NORTHERN IRELAND AND THE GOVERNMENT OF IRELAND

[...]

ARTICLE 1

The two Governments:

(i)   recognise the legitimacy of whatever choice is freely exercised by a majority of the people of Northern Ireland with regard to its status, whether they prefer to continue to support the Union with Great Britain or a sovereign united Ireland;
[...]

(iii) acknowledge that while a substantial section of the people in Northern Ireland share the legitimate wish of a majority of the people of the island of Ireland for a united Ireland, the present wish of a majority of the people of Northern Ireland, freely exercised and legitimate, is to maintain the Union and accordingly, that Northern Ireland's status as part of the United Kingdom reflects and relies upon that wish; and that it would be wrong to make any change in the status of Northern Ireland save with the consent of a majority of its people;

(iv) affirm that, if in the future, the people of the island of Ireland exercise their right of self-determination on the basis set out in sections (i) and (ii) above to bring about a united Ireland, it will be a binding obligation on both Governments to introduce and support in their respective Parliaments legislation to give effect to that wish;

(v)   affirm that whatever choice is freely exercised by a majority of the people of Northern Ireland, the power of the sovereign government with jurisdiction there shall be exercised with rigorous impartiality on behalf of all the people in the diversity of their identities and traditions and shall be founded on the principles of full respect for, and equality of, civil, political, social and cultural rights, of freedom from discrimination for all citizens, and of parity of esteem and of just and equal treatment for the identity, ethos and aspirations of both communities;

(vi) recognise the birthright of all the people of Northern Ireland to identify themselves and be accepted as Irish or British, or both, as they may so choose, and accordingly confirm that their right to hold both British and Irish citizenship is accepted by both Governments and would not be affected by any future change in the status of Northern Ireland.
[...]

ARTICLE 3

(1) This Agreement shall replace the Agreement between the British and Irish Governments done at Hillsborough on 15th November 1985 which shall cease to have effect on entry into force of this Agreement.
[...]

The Report of the Northern Ireland Victims Commission (Sir Kenneth Bloomfield, 1998)

THE ORIGINS AND REMIT OF THE COMMISSION

Initial Announcement

1.1 The intention of establishing a Commission 'to look at possible ways to recognise the pain and suffering felt by victims of violence arising from the troubles of the last 30 years, including those who have died or been injured in the service of the community' was announced by the Secretary of State for Northern Ireland in Belfast on 24 October, 1997. It was made clear that this initiative had been discussed with the Prime Minister who, 'from his discussions and meetings with people across Northern Ireland, felt that not enough attention had been paid to those who had suffered'. In announcing that I had been asked to lead such a Commission, Dr Mowlam noted that I had been asked 'to have particular regard to the possibility of establishing a new memorial reflecting both the sorrows of the past and hope for a stable future'.

Terms of Reference

1.2 On 19 November 1997 the Secretary of State wrote to me with the following formal Terms of Reference:

'To lead the Commission and to examine the feasibility of providing greater recognition for those who have become victims in the last thirty years as a consequence of events in Northern Ireland, recognising that those events have also had appalling repercussions for many people not living in Northern Ireland'

and asking me to consult various organisations concerned with the welfare of the bereaved and disabled, as well as with community groups, churches and political parties, and to make recommendations to her.

Ambit of the Review

1.3 In a subsequent lengthy discussion with the Secretary of State about the scope of the work, I was able to confirm that I could consider practical measures to deal with pain and suffering experienced by victims alongside the issue of a memorial project or scheme, and that I should of course acknowledge the special obligation owed by the State to people killed or injured in the course of protecting persons or property or in providing essential public services.

Establishing the Commission

1.4 I also established that, in being asked to lead the Commission, it was not implied that further Commissioners should or would be appointed. My first task would be to oversee the provision of administrative support, and in this I was most fortunate to secure the services of Mary Butcher, whose previous work for the Northern Ireland Office had given her extensive contacts throughout the community. Mary has been a tower of strength throughout this work. I was clear from the outset that this must not be a 'one man Commission'; I would rather seek to work with a very wide range of interests and people both inside and outside Northern Ireland, and in particular with those who had suffered in a very direct way from the violence of the last three decades. I hope that all of those whom I met or who wrote to me (many of whom had suffered themselves) will feel they have played a part in shaping this Report.

[…]

HOW TO PROCEED FROM HERE

Summary of Recommendations

8.1 My recommendations so far may be summarised as follows:

(a) there should be a comprehensive review of the 'fitness for purpose' of Criminal Injuries compensation in serving the needs of victims of violence (para 5.11);

(b) employers should be sensitive to the special circumstances of victims and their carers, and specific action should be taken by public sector employers to assure this (para 5.13);

(c) in dealing with victims within the social security and other systems officials should be sensitive and understanding in their approach (para 5.16);

(d) effective targeting of the special needs of victims should be a specific sub-set of the Targeting Social Need objective (para 5.17);

(e) a senior official should be designated to take immediate responsibility for a better co-ordinated approach to the problems of victims within Government (para 5.17);

(f) the recommendations of the SSI-led study on 'Living with the Trauma of the Troubles' should be energetically implemented by those interests to which they are directed (para 5.23);

(g) victims should be given the best comprehensive advice, locally differen-tiated, on where to turn for support (para 5.25);

(h) victims must, as the barest minimum, be as well served as former prisoners in terms of their rehabilitation, future employment etc. (para 5.26);

(i) in the interests of giving victims an effective 'champion', existing organ-isations meeting their needs require more and more secure funding, and there is a strong case for a powerful 'umbrella' organisation to give them a stronger voice in bidding for resources and urging changes in policy or practice (para 5.27);

(j)   in the longer term, the interests of victims should be made the concern of a Standing Commission or a Protector or Ombudsman for Victims;

(k)   a much higher priority should be given to treatment of and local research into chronic physical pain (para 5.30); the question of a Trauma Centre and the availability of residential psychiatric care for young people should also be addressed (para 5.30);

(l)   the recent Code of Practice for Victims of Crime should be conscientiously observed and critically monitored (para 5.35);

(m) the possibility of benefiting from some form of Truth and Reconciliation Commission at some stage should not be overlooked (para 5.37);

(n)   every effort should be made to persuade and enable those with information about the 'disappeared' to disclose it (para 5.38);

(o)   Government should not overlook the special claims of communities uprooted from their homes and farms (para 5.39);

(p)   consideration should be given to the creation of a fund to assist in particular children and young people affected by the death or injury of a parent (para 6.5);

(q)   the Government should consider the possibility of supporting efforts towards peace and reconciliation originating in Great Britain and not just in Northern Ireland (para 6.6);

(r)   consideration should be given, if and when the churches consider it appropriate, to the designation of a 'Memorial and Reconciliation Day' (para 6.19);

(s)   at the appropriate time, consideration should be given to a Northern Ireland Memorial in the form of a beautiful and useful building within a peaceful and harmonious garden (para 7.13);

(t)   such a project should be called simply 'the Northern Ireland Memorial' (para 7.18).

Publication of the Report

8.2 There has been intense interest in the work of this Commission, and I hope and **recommend** that this Report should be published in its entirety and widely distributed. In particular, I would urge that it be provided gratis to all those who have taken the trouble to assist the Commission in its deliberations.

Consultation on Recommendations

8.3 Thereafter, I **recommend** that a reasonable time (of up to three months) should be allowed for interested individuals to react to the Report and recommendations. As I have explained, I have tabled in Appendix 1 a list of all the suggestions made to me, in case wider opinion should favour some course I have not been disposed to recommend.

Association with wider Political Development

8.4 As I write, the course of action beyond this will depend critically upon the progress of wider political development. If the basis for an accord is subsequently endorsed by referenda, with the prospect of significant early transfer of functions to locally elected political leaders, then action within the ambit of a prospective new administration might have to be deferred; although even in that event, certain of the key areas may continue to be a concern of the Secretary of State for Northern Ireland. Subject to this, however, I would **recommend** the earliest possible identification of and action upon practical steps of the kind canvassed in Chapter 5 of the Report.

Timing and Appropriateness

8.5   On the other hand, the development of ideas for a memorial project or scheme must be subject to sensitive considerations of timing and appropriateness. While no-one can guarantee that there will be no further victims, it could seem grotesque to contemplate a memorial if, unhappily, full-scale violence were to resume. The question of memorialisation can only appropriately be addressed after the definitive entry into the new and more forward looking era in the life of Northern Ireland. It should be a matter for the representatives of the people of Northern Ireland after, but not before, they have found common ground. Even then, there are strong arguments that some seemly interval should elapse.

8.6   It may nevertheless be worth considering now, rather than later, how projects of the kind canvassed in this Report might, at the appropriate time, be advanced. I would see a need for several stages of consideration.

A Commission to Develop a Project

8.7   The first such stage would be the determination by the political administration of the general nature of the project they wished to pursue. This might then appropriately be remitted to a high-level appointed Commission, with membership representing the victims of violence, architecture and the fine arts, landscape gardening and/or arboriculture, archive skill and experience and so on. They would be charged to prepare a more detailed design brief, and to make proposals seeking the necessary capital and running costs. I would emphasise the prime importance of ensuring that any Memorial can be afforded and properly cared for over the long term. The wonderful work of the War Graves Commission shows that this can be done.

Choice and Management of a Project

8.8   After a design brief is prepared, the project should be the subject of a prestigious international competition, and the Ad Hoc Commission should select appropriate persons of distinction in relevant fields to judge that competition. On approval of the project, the political administration would need to decide upon long-term responsibility for its management, which might be vested in a body of Trustees, with appropriate administrative support.

The Patten Report (1999)

[...]

20

SUMMARY OF RECOMMENDATIONS

The following is a list of all the recommendations in this report:

Human Rights

1. There should be a comprehensive programme of action to focus policing in Northern Ireland on a human rights-based approach. [para. 4.6]
2. There should be a new oath, taken individually by all new and existing police officers, expressing an explicit commitment to upholding human rights. The text might be as follows –

   'I hereby do solemnly and sincerely and truly declare and affirm that I will faithfully discharge the duties of the office of constable, and that in so doing I will act with fairness, integrity, diligence and impartiality, uphold fundamental human rights and accord equal respect to all individuals and to their traditions and beliefs.' [para. 4.7]

3. A new Code of Ethics should replace the existing, largely procedural code, integrating the European Convention on Human Rights into police practice. Codes of practice on all aspects of policing, including covert law enforcement techniques, should be strictly in accordance with the European Convention on Human Rights. [para. 4.8]
4. All police officers, and police civilians, should be trained (and updated as required) in the fundamental principles and standards of human rights and the practical implications for policing. The human rights dimension should be integrated into every module of police training. [para. 4.9]
5. Awareness of human rights issues and respect for human rights in the performance of duty should be an important element in the appraisal of individuals in the police service. [para. 4.10]
6. A lawyer with specific expertise in the field of human rights should be appointed to the staff of the police legal services. [para. 4.11]
7. The performance of the police service as a whole in respect of human rights,

as in other respects, should be monitored closely by the Policing Board. [para. 4.12]

Accountability

8. An entirely new Policing Board should be created, to replace the present Police Authority. [para. 6.2]
9. The statutory primary function of the Policing Board should be to hold the Chief Constable and the police service publicly to account. [para. 6.3]
10. The Policing Board should set objectives and priorities for policing over a 3 to 5 year period, taking account of any longer term objectives or principles set by the Secretary of State or successor. It should then be responsible for adopting a 3 to 5 year strategy, prepared by the Chief Constable through a process of discussion with the Board, which should reflect the objectives and priorities set by the Board. [para. 6.5]
11. The Board should be responsible for adopting an Annual Policing Plan, developed by the Chief Constable, through a process of discussion with the Board, on the basis of objectives and priorities set by the Board, and within the agreed 3 to 5 year strategy. [para. 6.6]
12. The Board should be responsible for negotiating the annual policing budget with the Northern Ireland Office, or with the appropriate successor body after devolution of policing. It should then allocate the police service budget to the Chief Constable and monitor police performance against the budget. [para. 6.7]
13. The Board should monitor police performance against the Annual Policing Plan and the 3 to 5 year strategy. It should watch crime trends and patterns, and police performance in public order situations. It should also follow such things as recruitment patterns and trends, including fair employment and equal opportunities performance, and training needs. It should assess public satisfaction with the police service and, in liaison with the Police Ombudsman, patterns and trends in complaints against the police. [para. 6.8]
14. The Board should have the responsibility for appointing all chief officers and civilian equivalents and for determining the length of their contracts. All appointments should be subject to approval by the Secretary of State (and successor after devolution) and the Chief Constable should be consulted in relation to the appointment of subordinate chief officers and civilian equivalents. The Board should have the power to call upon the Chief Constable to retire in the interests of efficiency and effectiveness subject to the approval of the Secretary of State (and successor) and to the right to make representations as at present. Similarly, the Board should have the same power in relation to other chief officers and civilian equivalents exercisable subject to the approval of the Secretary of State (and successor) and to the same right to make representations and after consultation with the Chief Constable. The Secretary of State should have power to require the Policing Board to call upon the Chief Constable to retire on the same grounds but this power should be exercisable only after consultation with the Board and subject to the same right to make

representations already referred to. Additionally, after devolution the relevant Northern Ireland minister should have power to call for the retirement of the Chief Constable on the same grounds but this should be subject to the agreement of the Policing Board and the approval of the Secretary of State with an equivalent right to make representations. The Board should be the disciplinary authority for chief officers and civilian equivalents. [para. 6.9]

15. The Policing Board should coordinate its work closely with other agencies whose work touches on public safety, including education, environment, economic development, housing and health authorities, as well as social services, youth services and the probation service, and with appropriate nongovernmental organizations. [para. 6.10]

16. The Policing Board should have 19 members, 10 of whom should be Assembly members drawn from the parties that comprise the new Northern Ireland Executive, selected on the d'Hondt system, who should not at the same time hold ministerial office in the Executive. [para. 6.11]

17. The nine independent members of the Board should be selected from a range of different fields – including business, trade unions, voluntary organizations, community groups and the legal profession – with the aim of finding a group of individuals representative of the community as a whole, with the expertise both to set policing priorities and to probe and scrutinise different areas of police performance, from management of resources to the safeguarding of human rights. Their appointments should be for four years; but if it were necessary for the purpose of continuity to ensure that not all Board positions fell vacant at the same time as elections to the Assembly, some of these appointments could be for an initial period of two years. [para. 6.12]

18. The independent members should be appointed by the Secretary of State, in consultation with the First Minister and the Deputy First Minister, until such time as responsibility for policing is devolved, at which point the appointments should be made by the First Minister and the Deputy First Minister acting together. Until devolution, the Secretary of State should also determine the remuneration and expenses of Board members, in consultation with the First Minister and the Deputy First Minister. [para. 6.13]

19. A Board member of high quality and standing in the community should be appointed by the Secretary of State to be the first chairman of the Board, with the agreement of the First Minister and the Deputy First Minister, for an initial term of four years. [para. 6.14]

20. Responsibility for policing should be devolved to the Northern Ireland Executive as soon as possible, except for matters of national security. [para. 6.15]

21. The powers of the Policing Board proposed in this report, in relation to both government (as now represented by the Secretary of State) and the Chief Constable, should in no way be diminished when the government role in the tripartite arrangement passes to the Northern Ireland Executive. [para. 6.15]

22. The provisions of the Police (Northern Ireland) Act 1998 should be simplified so that the respective roles of the Secretary of State (or successor), the Policing Board and the Chief Constable are clear. [para. 6.16]

23. The provision, in Section 39 of the Police (Northern Ireland) Act 1998, that

the Secretary of State may issue guidance to the police as to the exercise of their functions, should be repealed. [para. 6.18]

24. The Chief Constable should be deemed to have *operational responsibility* for the exercise of his or her functions and the activities of the police officers and civilian staff under his or her direction and control. [para. 6.21]

25. The Policing Board should have the power to require the Chief Constable to report on any issue pertaining to the performance of his functions or those of the police service. The obligation to report should extend to explaining operational decisions. If there is a disagreement between the Board and the Chief Constable over whether it is appropriate for a report to be provided on a particular matter, it should be for the Chief Constable to refer the question to the Secretary of State for a decision as to whether the Board's requirement should stand. [para. 6.22]

26. The Policing Board should have the power, subject only to the same limitation set out in paragraph 6.22, to follow up any report from the Chief Constable by initiating an inquiry into any aspect of the police service or police conduct. Depending on the circumstances, the Board should have the option to request the Police Ombudsman, the Inspectorate of Constabulary or the Audit Office to conduct or contribute to such an inquiry, or to use the Board's own staff, or even private consultants for such a purpose. [para. 6.23]

27. Each District Council should establish a District Policing Partnership Board (DPPB), as a committee of the Council, with a majority elected membership, the remaining independent members to be selected by the Council with the agreement of the Policing Board. The chair of the DPPB should be held by an elected member, with rotation between parties from year to year. [para. 6.26]

28. The District Policing Partnership Board in Belfast should have four subgroups, covering North, South, East and West Belfast. [para. 6.27]

29. There should be monthly meetings between the DPPB and the police District Commander, at which the police should present reports and answer questions and the Board should reflect community concerns and priorities to the police. The views expressed by DPPBs should be taken fully into account by the police and by the Policing Board in the formulation of policing plans and strategies at the central level. [para. 6.30]

30. The DPPB should submit an annual report to the District Council, and publish it. [para. 6.31]

31. The approved administration costs of the DPPB should attract a 75% grant from the Policing Board, the remaining 25% to be funded by the District Council. [para. 6.32]

32. District Councils should have the power to contribute an amount initially up to the equivalent of a rate of 3p in the pound towards the improved policing of the district, which could enable the DPPB to purchase additional services from the police or other statutory agencies, or from the private sector. [para. 6.33]

33. It should be the aim of every police beat manager to have a consultative forum in his or her patrol area. [para. 6.34]

34. The Policing Board should maintain regular contact with the DPPBs, through

periodic meetings of chairpersons, annual conferences, seminars, training courses and by including them in the circulation of information. [para. 6.35]

35. The Policing Board should meet in public once a month, to receive a report from the Chief Constable. [para. 6.36]

36. District Policing Partnership Boards should meet in public once a month, and procedures should allow for members of the public to address questions to the Board and, through the chair, to the police. [para. 6.37]

37. The police service should take steps to improve its transparency. The presumption should be that everything should be available for public scrutiny unless it is in the public interest – not the police interest – to hold it back. [para. 6.38]

38. The Police Ombudsman should be, and be seen to be, an important institution in the governance of Northern Ireland, and should be staffed and resourced accordingly. The Ombudsman should take initiatives, not merely react to specific complaints received. He/she should exercise the power to initiate inquiries or investigations even if no specific complaint has been received. The Ombudsman should be responsible for compiling data on trends and patterns in complaints against the police, or accumulations of complaints against individual officers, and should work with the police to address issues emerging from this data. He/she should have a dynamic cooperative relationship with both the police and the Policing Board, as well as other bodies involved in community safety issues. He/she should exercise the right to investigate and comment on police policies and practices, where these are perceived to give rise to difficulties, even if the conduct of individual officers may not itself be culpable, and should draw any such observations to the attention of the Chief Constable and the Policing Board. The Ombudsman should have access to all past reports on the RUC. [para. 6.41]

39. New legislation on covert policing should be fully compliant with the European Convention on Human Rights and should have the same application in Northern Ireland as in the rest of the United Kingdom. [para. 6.43]

40. There should be a commissioner for covert law enforcement in Northern Ireland. [para. 6.44]

41. There should be a complaints tribunal, comprising senior members of the legal profession, with full powers to investigate cases referred to it (either directly or through the Police Ombudsman) involving covert law enforcement operations. [para. 6.45]

42. There should be a substantial strengthening of financial accountability, including: a fully costed Annual Policing Plan; a strong audit department within the Policing Board, staffed by experts in budgeting, financial management and value for money programmes; and more systematic use of the Audit Office to study police resource management, either at the behest of the Policing Board or on its own initiative. [para. 6.46]

43. The Chief Constable should be designated a sub accounting officer, in addition to the Chief Executive of the Policing Board, so that either or both may be called, together with the Permanent Under Secretary as principal accounting officer, to give evidence to the Public Accounts Committee. [para. 6.47]

Policing with the Community

44. Policing with the community should be the core function of the police service and the core function of every police station. [para. 7.9]
45. Every neighbourhood (or rural area) should have a dedicated policing team with lead responsibility for policing its area. [para. 7.10]
46. Members of the policing team should serve at least three and preferably five years in the same neighbourhood. They should wear their names clearly displayed on their uniforms, and their uniforms should also bear the name of the locality for which they are responsible. [para. 7.11]
47. All probationary police officers should undertake the operational phases of their probationary training doing team policing in the community. [para. 7.12]
48. Where practicable, policing teams should patrol on foot. [para. 7.13]
49. Neighbourhood policing teams should be empowered to determine their own local priorities and set their own objectives, within the overall Annual Policing Plan and in consultation with community representatives. [para. 7.14]
50. The Northern Ireland police should, both at a service-wide level and at patrol team level, conduct crime pattern and complaint pattern analysis to provide an information-led, problem-solving approach to policing. All police officers should be instructed in problem-solving techniques and encouraged to address the causes of problems as well as the consequences (the priority being to train beat managers and their teams); and they should be regularly appraised as to their performance in doing so. [para. 7.16]
51. DPPB members and other community leaders should be able to attend police training courses in problem-solving techniques. [para. 7.17]

Policing in a Peaceful Society

52. Police stations built from now on should have, so far as possible, the appearance of ordinary buildings; they should have low perimeter walls, and be clearly visible from the street; but they should have security features, which may be activated or reinforced as necessary. [para. 8.5]
53. Existing police stations should – subject to the security situation in their areas and to health and safety considerations – be progressively made less forbidding in appearance, more accessible to public callers and more congenial for those working in them. The public reception areas inside police stations should be made more welcoming, and civilian receptionists could replace police officers. [para. 8.6]
54. District police commanders should have discretion to decide in consultation with their local community how best to balance their resources between static posts and mobile patrols. [para. 8.7]
55. Police cars should continue to be substituted as patrol vehicles in place of armoured Landrovers, and the use of armoured Landrovers should be limited to threatening situations. [para. 8.8]
56. As soon as possible (that is, as soon as the incidence of deployment ceases to be regular) armoured Landrovers should be moved to depots, to be kept in

reserve for use in public order policing for as long as this contingency may be required. [para. 8.9]

57. The word 'Police' should be painted onto the sides of Landrovers. [para. 8.10]

58. The role of the army should continue to be reduced, as quickly as the security situation will allow, so that the police can patrol all parts of Northern Ireland without military support. [para. 8.11]

59. For as long as the prospect remains of substantial public order policing demands on the scale seen at Drumcree in recent years, the army should retain the capacity to provide support for the police in meeting those demands. [para. 8.12]

60. Provided the threat of terrorism in Northern Ireland diminishes to the point where no additional special powers are necessary to combat it, legislation against terrorism should be the same in Northern Ireland as in the rest of the United Kingdom. [para. 8.14]

61. In the meantime, with immediate effect, records should be kept of all stops and searches and other such actions taken under emergency powers. [para. 8.14]

62. The three holding centres at Castlereagh, Gough barracks and Strand Road should be closed forthwith and all suspects should in future be detained in custody suites based in police stations. [para. 8.15]

63. Video recording should be introduced into the PACE custody suites. [para. 8.16]

64. Responsibility for inspecting all custody and interrogation suites should rest with the Policing Board, and Lay Visitors should be empowered not only to inspect the conditions of detention (as at present), but also to observe interviews on camera subject to the consent of the detainee (as is the case for cell visits). [para. 8.16]

65. The question of moving towards the desired objective of a routinely unarmed police service should be periodically reviewed in the light of developments in the security environment. [para. 8.19]

Public Order Policing

66. The Northern Ireland police should have the capacity within its own establishment to deal with public order emergencies without help from other police services and without more than the present level of support from the army. [para. 9.6]

67. It should be a condition for the approval of a parade that the organizers should provide their own marshals, and the organizers and the police should work together to plan the policing of such events. This should involve as appropriate the representatives of the neighbourhoods involved in the parade route. [para. 9.9]

68. Marshal training should be further developed, with an appropriate qualification on successful completion of the training. All parades should be marshalled and, as soon as practicable, it should be a requirement that all potentially contentious parades requiring a decision or determination by the Parades

Commission should be marshalled by qualified personnel. [para. 9.10]

69. An immediate and substantial investment should be made in a research programme to find an acceptable, effective and less potentially lethal alternative
to the Plastic Baton Round (PBR). [para. 9.15]

70. The police should be equipped with a broader range of public order equip-
ment than the RUC currently possess, so that a commander has a number of
options at his/her disposal which might reduce reliance on, or defer resort to,
the PBR. [para. 9.16]

71. The use of PBRs should be subject to the same procedures for deployment, use
and reporting as apply in the rest of the United Kingdom. Their use should be
confined to the smallest necessary number of specially trained officers, who
should be trained to think of the weapon in the same way as they would think
of a firearm, that is as a weapon which is potentially lethal. Use of PBRs should
in the first instance require the authorisation of a district commander. This
should be justified in a report to the Policing Board, which should be copied to
the Police Ombudsman. Wherever possible, video camera recordings should
be made of incidents in which the use of PBRs is authorised. [para. 9.17]

72. Officers' identification numbers should be clearly visible on their protective
clothing, just as they should be on regular uniforms. [para. 9.18]

73. The Policing Board and, as appropriate, the Police Ombudsman should actively
monitor police performance in public order situations, and if necessary seek
reports from the Chief Constable and follow up those reports if they wish.
[para. 9.19]

74. Guidance governing the deployment and use of PBRs should be soundly
based in law, clearly expressed and readily available as public documents.
[para. 9.20]

Management and Personnel

75. The Northern Ireland police leadership team should include specialists in
change management. These may be either civilians or police officers, preferably both. The leadership team should produce a programme for change, to be
presented to the Policing Board and reviewed periodically by the Board. The
efficiency and effectiveness of each chief officer should be judged on the basis
of, among other things, their capacity to introduce and adapt to change. [para.
10.3]

76. District commanders should have fully devolved authority over the deployment of personnel (officer and civilian) within their command, devolved
budgets (including salary budgets), authority to purchase a range of goods and
services, and to finance local policing initiatives. They should reach service
level agreements with all headquarter support departments. [para. 10.7]

77. It should be a high priority of management to ensure that the appraisal system
is fully effective. This system should be used as part of the promotion and
selection process. An officer's capacity for change should be assessed and
should also be taken into account in the promotion and selection process.
[para. 10.10]

78. District commanders should be required regularly to account to their senior officers for the patterns of crime and police activity in their district and to explain how they propose to address their districts' problems. [para. 10.11]
79. An automated trend identification system for complaints should be introduced. [para. 10.12]
80. The use of trend information should be followed up by management, and as appropriate by the department responsible for discipline, and guidance should be drawn up to help managers use this information effectively. [para. 10.13]
81. Police managers should use random checks as a way to monitor the behaviour of their officers in dealings with the public and their integrity. [para. 10.14]
82. Police management should use all the tools at its disposal, including when necessary the administrative dismissal process, to ensure that high professional and ethical standards are consistently met. [para. 10.15]
83. There should be a tenure policy, so that officers do not have inordinately long postings in any specialist area of the police. [para. 10.16]
84. Officers injured on duty should be treated as a separate category for sickness recording purposes. [para. 10.17]
85. A new policy should be formulated for the management of long-term sickness absence, incorporating appropriate arrangements for medical retirement, career counselling and welfare support. A system of rewards, as well as sanctions, should be introduced as part of the sickness management policy. [para. 10.19]
86. There should be a more detailed review of sickness absence, to establish underlying causes and to make recommendations to address them. [para. 10.19]
87. A substantial fund should be set up to help injured police officers, injured retired officers and their families, as well as police widows. [para. 10.20]
88. The Widows Association should be given an office in police premises, free of charge, and a regular source of finance adequate to run their organization. [para. 10.21]
89. The Assistant Chief Constables currently responsible for support services should be replaced by two civilian Assistant Chief Officers, one responsible for personnel issues and one for finance and administration. [para. 10.22]
90. There should be a rigorous programme of civilianisation of jobs which do not require police powers, training or experience, exceptions being made only when it can be demonstrated that there is a good reason for a police officer to occupy the position. [para. 10.23]
91. The Policing Board and the police service should initiate a review of police support services with a view to contracting out those services where this will enhance the efficient management of resources. Consideration should be given to allowing 'management buy-outs' of support services by police officers or civilian employees interested in continuing to provide those services as a private sector company, and in such cases management buy-out contractors should be offered a secure contract for at least three years to enable them to establish themselves before having to tender for renewal. [para. 10.25]
92. The police should commission a comprehensive audit of the whole police estate, to include outside experts, and develop a strategy for achieving an

effective and efficient estate to meet the objectives for policing as outlined in this report. [para. 10.28]

Information Technology

93. There should be an urgent, independent, and in-depth strategic review of the use of information technology (IT) in policing. It should benchmark the Northern Ireland police against police services in the rest of the world and devise a properly resourced strategy that places them at the forefront of law enforcement technology within 3 to 5 years. It should be validated by independent assessment. The strategy should deliver fully integrated technology systems that are readily accessible to all staff, and should take advantage of the best analytical and communications systems currently available. Users of the technology should play a key part in devising the strategy, and in assessing its implementation. [para. 11.13]

Structure of the Police Service

94. There should be one district command for each District Council area. [para. 12.4]

95. In general, each district command should be headed by a Superintendent and resourced sufficiently to be self-contained for day-to-day policing purposes and capable of marshalling strength to cope with most unexpected demands. However, in the districts with small populations the commander should be a Chief Inspector, and the districts should draw on assistance from larger neighbouring district commands for functions in which it is not feasible for a small command to be self-sufficient. [para. 12.5]

96. The divisional layer of management and the regional headquarters should be removed, and there should be a direct reporting line from each district commander to the appropriate Assistant Chief Constable at central police headquarters. District commanders in smaller council areas, whatever their rank, should have such a direct reporting line, reflecting the accountability arrangements we have recommended. There should be much greater delegation of decision-making authority to district commanders than is the case now with sub-divisional commanders, including control over devolved budget and all police resources in their district. [para. 12.6]

97. There should be a slimmer structure at police headquarters – one that reflects the shift of focus towards community policing and the delegation of responsibility to district commanders, and permits a more rigorous and strategic approach to management. There should be no more than one Deputy Chief Constable. The number of Assistant Chief Officers should be reduced to six from the present twelve. The position of 'Deputy Assistant Chief Constable' should be deleted forthwith. The rank of Chief Superintendent should be phased out. [para. 12.9]

98. Special Branch and Crime Branch should be brought together under the command of a single Assistant Chief Constable. [para. 12.12]

99. There should be a substantial reduction in the number of officers engaged in

security work in the new, amalgamated command. [para. 12.13]

100. Security officers should be required to keep their district commanders well briefed on security activities in their districts, and district commanders should be fully consulted before security operations are undertaken in their district. [para. 12.14]

101. The support units of Special Branch should be amalgamated into the wider police service. [para. 12.15]

102. Officers should not spend such long periods in security work as has been common in the past [para. 12.16]

103. The future police service should not include a Full Time Reserve. [para. 12.17]

104. There should be an enlarged Part Time Reserve of up to 2,500 officers, the additional recruits to come from those areas in which there are currently very few reservists or none at all. [para. 12.18]

Size of the Police Service

105. Provided the peace process does not collapse and the security situation does not deteriorate significantly from the situation pertaining at present, the approximate size of the police service over the next ten years should be 7,500 full time officers. [para. 13.9]

106. The early retirement or severance package offered to regular officers and full time reservists aged 50 or above should include a generous lump sum payment according to length of service, pension enhancement of up to five years, early payment of pension commutation entitlement and payment in lieu of pension until pensionable age is reached. Full time reservists should be treated as far as possible in the same way as regular officers. [para. 13.12]

107. Regular officers with more than five years' service and all full time reservists, leaving the police service before the age of 50, should receive a substantial lump sum payment. [para. 13.13]

108. The Training and Employment Agency should develop measures for police officers (and civilians) seeking other employment, in consultation with police management and the staff associations. The Police Retraining and Rehabilitation Trust should have a role in this programme, and should have enhanced staffing and funding to enable it to deal with a substantially larger workload. [para. 13.17]

109. Police recruiting agencies in Great Britain should take full account of the policing experience of former RUC reservists in considering applications for employment in police services in Great Britain. [para. 13.19]

110. The British government should offer former reservists the opportunity to participate in British policing contingents in United Nations peacekeeping operations. [para. 13.19]

Composition and Recruitment of the Police Service

111. The Northern Ireland Civil Service management should facilitate transfers of civilian members of the police service to other Northern Ireland departments

and should cooperate with the Policing Board and the Chief Constable in achieving a balanced and representative civilian workforce. [para. 14.16]

112. Every effort should be made to ensure that the composition of the staff of the Policing Board, the NIO Police Division (or any successor body), and the office of the Police Ombudsman should be broadly reflective of the population of Northern Ireland as a whole, particularly in terms of political/religious tradition and gender. [para. 14.17]

113. All community leaders, including political party leaders and local councillors, bishops and priests, schoolteachers and sports authorities, should take steps to remove all discouragements to members of their communities applying to join the police, and make it a priority to encourage them to apply. [para. 15.2]

114. The Gaelic Athletic Association should repeal its rule 21, which prohibits members of the police in Northern Ireland from being members of the Association. [para. 15.2]

115. Liaison should be established between all schools and universities and the police service in Northern Ireland immediately, and work experience attachments and familiarisation days should be organized with active support and encouragement from community leaders and teachers. [para. 15.4]

116. Provided there is active support and encouragement from local political and community leaders, pilot police cadet schemes should be set up. [para. 15.6]

117. The police should contract out the recruitment of both police officers and civilians into the police service. There should be lay involvement, including community representatives, on recruitment panels. [para. 15.7]

118. The recruitment agency should advertise imaginatively and persistently, particularly in places likely to reach groups who are under-represented in the police. [para. 15.8]

119. The agency should advertise beyond Northern Ireland, in the rest of the United Kingdom and in the Republic of Ireland. [para. 15.8]

120. All candidates for the police service should continue to be required to reach a specified standard of merit in the selection procedure. Candidates reaching this standard should then enter a pool from which the required number of recruits can be drawn. [para. 15.9]

121. An equal number of Protestants and Catholics should be drawn from the pool of qualified candidates. [para. 15.10]

122. Priority should be given to creating opportunities for part time working and job-sharing, both for police officers and police service civilians, and career breaks should be introduced. [para. 15.11]

123. Child care facilities should be introduced where practicable, or child care vouchers and flexible shift arrangements offered. [para. 15.11]

124. The recruitment process should be reduced to no more than six months. [para. 15.12]

125. Young people should not be automatically disqualified from entry into the police service for relatively minor criminal offences, particularly if they have since had a number of years without further transgressions. The criteria on this aspect of eligibility should be the same as those in the rest of the United

Kingdom. There should be a procedure for appeal to the Police Ombudsman against disqualification of candidates. [para. 15.13]

126. All officers – those now in service as well as all future recruits – should be obliged to register their interests and associations. The register should be held both by the police service and by the Police Ombudsman. [para. 15.16]

127. The recruitment agency should seek to identify Northern Ireland Catholic officers in other police services, including the Garda Siochana, contact them and encourage them – particularly those in more senior ranks – to apply for positions in the Northern Ireland police. [para. 15.17]

128. Lateral entry of experienced officers from other police services, and secondments or recruitments from non-police organizations should be actively encouraged. [para. 15.18]

Training, Education and Development

129. A training, education and development strategy should be put in place, both for recruit training and for in-service training, which is linked to the aims of this report and to the objectives and priorities set out in the policing plans. These plans should incorporate training and development requirements. [para. 16.4]

130. A total training and development budget should be established, covering all aspects of training, and this should be safeguarded against transfers to other sub-heads. [para. 16.5]

131. The Northern Ireland police should have a new purpose-built police college and the funding for it should be found in the next public spending round. [para. 16.6]

132. There should be service level agreements between police districts/departments and the police Training Branch setting out what the Branch is expected to deliver to the district or department concerned. [para. 16.8]

133. There should be a high degree of civilian input into the recruit training programme. The director of the training centre (and the new college when this is opened) should have both academic qualifications and management expertise. Civilian instructors should be employed, or brought in as necessary to conduct as many elements of the training programme as possible. Some modules of recruit training should be contracted out to universities and delivered on university premises, ideally together with non-police students. [para. 16.10]

134. Civilian recruits to the police service should also attend the police college, and do some of their training together with police officer recruits. [para. 16.11]

135. Recruits who do not already have degrees should be encouraged to acquire appropriate academic qualifications during the first two years of their career. Encouragement should be given to those officers who wish to go on to study for further relevant qualifications. [para. 16.12]

136. Attestation as a police officer should take place only upon successful completion of the recruit training course. A sufficiently rigorous standard should be

required for success in that course; and completion of the course should be marked by a graduation ceremony. [para. 16.13]

137. The hours spent on drill should be considerably reduced. [para. 16.14]

138. Problem-solving and partnership approaches should be central to the recruit training course, and scenario exercises should be further developed as training tools. [para. 16.16]

139. Community awareness training for police recruits should be developed to include representatives of all the main political and religious traditions in Northern Ireland. Community awareness should not be seen as a stand alone element of recruit training; it should be integrated into all aspects of training. [para. 16.17]

140. The Northern Ireland police should introduce a comprehensive tutor officer scheme. Tutor officers should be carefully selected, according to their commitment and adaptability to the new style of policing, and trained. [para. 16.18]

141. Every member of the police service should have, as soon as possible, a course on the impact on policing of the new constitutional arrangements for Northern Ireland, the new policing arrangements set out in this report, and the reforms of the criminal justice system. [para. 16.20]

142. As a matter of priority, all members of the police service should be instructed in the implications for policing of the Human Rights Act 1998, and the wider context of the European Convention on Human Rights and the Universal Declaration of Human Rights. [para. 16.21]

143. All police managers should have management training, as appropriate, and every manager should at some stage of his/her career do a management course in a non-police environment, such as a business school or university. Use should be made of management workshops, so that managers can discuss and develop with each other how best to reshape the police organization. [para. 16.22]

144. Every officer and civilian in the service should undergo adequate training in information technology. [para. 16.23]

145. Opportunities should be taken for joint training with civilian analysts, and members of other police services. [para. 16.23]

146. The Northern Ireland police should draw on the success of neighbourhood policing in such places as the Markets area of Belfast in developing a neighbourhood policing training programme for all members of the police service. Standard training for neighbourhood officers should include modules on such community problems as domestic violence, child abuse, rape, drugs and youth issues and this training should be updated as necessary. [para. 16.24]

147. The training curricula for the police service should be publicly available, and easily accessible, e.g. on the Internet. [para. 16.25]

148. Some training sessions should be open to members of the public to attend, upon application, priority being given to members of the Policing Board or District Policing Partnership Boards, Lay Visitors, or other bodies, statutory or non-governmental, involved in working with the police. [para. 16.26]

149. The new police college should offer a pilot citizens course, to assess demand in Northern Ireland. [para. 16.26]

Culture, Ethos and Symbols

150. While the Royal Ulster Constabulary should not be disbanded, it should henceforth be named the Northern Ireland Police Service. [para. 17.6]
151. The Northern Ireland Police Service should adopt a new badge and symbols which are entirely free from any association with either the British or Irish states. [para. 17.6]
152. The Union flag should no longer be flown from police buildings. [para. 17.6]
153. On those occasions on which it is appropriate to fly a flag on police buildings, the flag flown should be that of the Northern Ireland Police Service and it, too, should be free from associations with the British or Irish states. [para. 17.6]
154. The colour of the current police uniform should be retained, but a new, more practical style of uniform should be provided to police officers. [para. 17.7]
155. Police memorials in police buildings should remain as they are and where they are. [para. 17.8]
156. The maintenance of a neutral working environment should become an assessed management responsibility at all levels of management. [para. 17.9]

Cooperation with other Police Services

157. The Northern Ireland police and the Garda Siochana should have written protocols covering key aspects of cooperation. [para. 18.7]
158. The present pattern of meetings between the police services in Northern Ireland and the Republic should be enhanced by an annual conference, designed to drive forward cooperation in areas of common concern. [para. 18.8]
159. There should be a programme of long-term personnel exchanges, such as fixed-term secondments, between the Northern Ireland police and the Garda, in specialist fields where cooperation between the two services is most needed, such as drugs, and in areas such as training. [para. 18.10]
160. Consideration should be given to posting liaison officers from each service to the central headquarters and/or border area headquarters of the other. [para. 18.10]
161. There should be structured cooperation between the two police services in training. [para. 18.11]
162. There should be joint disaster planning between the Northern Ireland police and the Garda Siochana and the plans should be tested by regular joint exercises. [para. 18.12]
163. Consideration should be given to establishing a provision for an immediate exchange of officers and pooling of investigative teams after major incidents with a substantial cross-border dimension, akin to the arrangements which exist between Kent and the police services of France and Belgium. [para. 18.13]
164. Every effort should be made to ensure that fast, effective and reliable communications are established between the Garda and the Northern Ireland police

both through improved radio links and through compatible IT systems. [para. 18.14]

165. Joint database development should be pursued as a matter of priority in all the main areas of cross-border criminality, such as drugs, smuggling, vehicle theft and terrorism. [para. 18.15]

166. A determined effort should be made to develop exchanges, and long-term secondments, between the Northern Ireland police and police services in Great Britain. [para. 18.16]

167. There should be training exchanges and some joint training between the Northern Ireland police and police services in Great Britain. [para. 18.17]

168. Consideration should be given to structured links between the four principal police training establishments in the British Isles, namely Bramshill (England), Templemore (Republic of Ireland), Tulliallan (Scotland) and Garnerville or the proposed new police college in Northern Ireland. [para. 18.17]

169. International training exchanges should be further developed, focussing in particular on matters where the police in Northern Ireland need overseas police cooperation and on best practice developments in policing worldwide. There should be cooperation with other police services in the field of research. [para. 18.18]

170. The police should develop opportunities to provide more training for overseas police services in their areas of excellence. [para. 18.19]

171. The Northern Ireland police should be ready to participate in future United Nations peace-keeping operations. [para. 18.20]

172. An eminent person, from a country other than the United Kingdom or Ireland, should be appointed as soon as possible as an oversight commissioner with responsibility for supervising the implementation of our recommendations. [para. 19.4]

173. The government, the police service, and the Policing Board (and DPPBs) should provide the oversight commissioner with objectives (with timetables) covering their own responsibilities, and should report on the progress achieved at the periodic review meetings, and account for any failures to achieve objectives. [para. 19.5]

174. The commissioner should in turn report publicly after each review meeting on the progress achieved, together with his or her observations on the extent to which any failures or delays are the responsibility of the policing institutions themselves or due to matters beyond their control. [para. 19.5]

175. The oversight commissioner should be appointed for a term of five years. [para. 19.6]

Review of the Parades Commission (Sir George Quigley, 2002)

CHAPTER 7

HISTORY ON THE MARCH OR FORWARD MARCH?

'There is no street with mute stones and no house without echoes'
Góngora Y Argote (1561–1627)

History on the March

7.1 Both sides to the parades dispute are conditioned by history. As Dr A. T. Q. Stewart[1] put it so aptly:

> To say we can do without [history] is like saying we can breathe without oxygen. It has made us what we are, and is in our bloodstream, in the language we speak, the culture we proclaim, the homes, streets and cities we live in. The call of the past to us is insistent; we cannot ignore it. It presses irredentist claims upon us, impatient for us to pass under its sway.

7.2 Neither tradition is likely to understand – and may even demonise – the other, if it is not recognised that both contributed to the development of politics within a confessional (or sectarian) framework in the 19th century, with religion as the badge of identity.

7.3 So origins are important, not least when considering the parades issue. Orangeism is distinctive in many respects, and not least in its longevity. It has been part of the warp and woof of Irish history for 207 years and has outlived all its protagonists. But, while Orangeism's old adversaries may be gone, the batallioned ghosts remain to haunt it. There is no statute of limitations on memory. When those who have no affinity with Orangeism see it in procession, many of them see history on the march. And they see Orangeism as having been throughout its long history, as well as today, on the wrong side, certainly on the 'opposite' side.

7.4 It is therefore important (without expressing any view of its opinions) to put the phenomenon of what many still regard as the 'bogeyman' of the last couple of hundred years of Irish history in context. Its rise in 1795 is now seen as a consequence rather than a cause of the tensions of the time, the product of long-standing feuds and economic rivalries which the norms of the period (and of many periods in Irish history) made it acceptable to settle by violence. The alliance between the

Catholic peasantry (the Defenders) and the United Irishmen increased Orange fears of Catholic domination. The Government found it expedient to enrol the Orangemen to help suppress the 1798 rebellion and thereby set them up as a political force. From then on, Orangeism was in and out of favour with Government. It was, as it has been said, a matter of reluctant alliance followed by rapid disengagement.

7.5 Orangeism opposed Catholic emancipation but William Cobbett, writing in 1823, said tellingly that 'the Orangemen have for allies all the unconquerable prejudices of ninety-nine hundredths of the people of England'. Throughout their history, like most popular organisations, their ideas were not peculiar to themselves but were shared by many of their contemporaries.

7.6 The institution's fortunes fluctuated, ebbing when there was no threat and its political raison d'être was removed. It was dissolved and reconstituted and from time to time thought it advisable to refrain, and was sometimes statutorily prohibited, from marching, culminating in a ban which lasted from 1850 to 1872.

7.7 Despite sporadic discouragement from the authorities and sometimes even (for various reasons) from some within the leadership, leading to ups and downs in the number and size of parades, the parading tradition persisted.[2] The Belfast News Letter's suggestion (in 1846) that 'in these days of education and enlightenment, Protestantism and loyalty have discovered better modes of asserting themselves than by wearing sashes and walking to the music of fife and drum' fell on deaf ears so far as the rank and file were concerned.

7.8 The 19th century was punctuated by hundreds of communal disturbances, with the major incidents usually involving death and injury. In the second half of the century it was Orange (or more rarely Nationalist) processions which provided what has been described as the casus belli, 'followed by street fighting, burning of houses and schools, and conflicts with the police ... the residential and social apartheid which [the riots] encouraged in turn fostered prejudices and hostilities which rendered the next riot more likely'.[3] Then, as now, there was interminable debate as to whether the activity which resulted in riot caused (in the sense of necessarily caused) or merely precipitated the disorder.

7.9 Orangeism frequently declared that it considered every loyal subject 'as our brother and friend, let his religion be what it may' but, crucially, that left the definition of loyal subject open to interpretation.

7.10 Neither of the great streams of Irish history which emerged as the century wore on had a vision of an inclusive society. The roles played by those who formed each stream were shaped by circumstances rather than by deliberate choice but they were decisive for the creation of the citadels of intolerance which have dominated the social, cultural and political landscape.

7.11 Given the sectarian response which it elicited, the battle for Catholic emancipation, instead of being (as it should have been) the product of a secular alliance, was inevitably fought under almost exclusively Catholic auspices. It has been well said that, by his victory, O'Connell both opened the way to Catholic domination of

Irish representative politics, as the franchise for local and parliamentary elections was progressively opened up, and also provided a working model for later nationalist activists.

7.12 In the zero-sum game which has constituted so much of our history, it was inevitable that Catholic renascence, particularly when expressed in 'clerical nationalism which so fed Protestant terrors of political Catholicism',[4] would be mirrored in a heightened political consciousness amongst Protestants which was reinforced by the growing force of the evangelical movement. The conservative interests which gradually coalesced and achieved a coherent alliance during the era of Home Rule politics included the Orange Order. Indeed O'Connell dubbed the early manifestation of this emerging movement the Orange Party. But it embraced a disparate range of convictions and Professor Theodore Hoppen[5] makes the point that nationalist opinion later in the century, following O'Connell's lead, sustained the comfortable but mistaken belief that what it saw as intransigence was the exclusive preserve of Orangeism rather than the broad tide of Protestant opinion.

7.13 Professor Marianne Elliott[6] describes the Ancient Order of Hibernians as 'a mirror image (if never as strong) of the Orange Order in its sectarian identity and its mesmerisation with parades'. By 1909 it was the main nationalist organisation, 'firmly constitutionalist in its activities'. It 'looked after its own kind within existing sectarian politics'. Professor Elliott makes the vitally important point that:

> The headlong rush of Catholics and Protestants in apparently opposite directions in these years disguises one very important fact: it brought about a measure of stability. With their separate social, educational, religious and political institutions, both communities could feel a certain kind of security.

7.14 The entrenchment of Unionist power in the Northern Ireland which was created in 1921 and the close alignment of the values of the new entity and those of Orangeism ensured that the sense of exclusion felt by nationalism fuelled a hostility which was directed as much against Orangeism as against Unionism. 'Their self-proclaimed Britishness ... [was] held against them, as it [was] this which denied the legitimacy of the 'indivisible island'.[7]

7.15 The inherent differences between those from the two main traditions were steadily enhanced. Whilst their relationships with each other were in some contexts characterised by (a perhaps only superficial) tolerance, in others their social spheres remained quite distant. On a cynical view, keeping apart – each (in Seamus Deane's words) knowing the other by 'fearful reputation' – kept the latent hostility latent. Thirty years of Troubles further deepened division.

7.16 Even this brief survey makes it easy to understand why many from each tradition view contemporary issues through the prism of that tradition's experience of 'the other'.

7.17 I suggest that *both* traditions need to try harder to see *all* the historical actors as players caught up in the complicated choreography of tragic conflict, which converted difference into the disastrous division which still persists. A history which knows only black and white must sharpen present antagonisms, making it seem 'as if time itself has lost the power to separate the centuries'.[8]

7.18 It is our own choice as a society whether we escape from the enslavement of history. The most effective form of revolt may be a joint attempt by *both* traditions to take ownership of our *entire* history.

7.19 A prominent Republican, speaking recently of the Somme anniversary, said that 'at the end of the day the most important thing is to remember what these people died for. If we can create a situation where no one feels alienated, that has to be a good thing'. Belfast's Lord Mayor Alex Maskey has in the same context said that it was his objective 'to seek to identify common ground for all of us in this generation' and has indicated his intention to 'contribute in a positive way' to the development of a public debate about the use of (inter alia) commemorations.

7.20 It is perhaps not irrelevant to the progress which has been made in Derry between the Apprentice Boys and the Bogside Residents Group that its spokesman Donncha MacNiallais could write[9] that he and the Apprentice Boys 'have a common heritage in saluting the courage of the people of Derry during the siege … We all need to accept that none of us is an island. We are the sum of all our parts and we all contribute to the diversity of the Irish people'. That is close to Thomas Merton's observation that 'every other person is a piece of myself, for I am a part and a member of mankind'.

7.21 This year the service in St Columb's Cathedral which was part of the Apprentice Boys of Derry Maiden City Festival was advertised in a Mass bulletin in St Eugene's, which expressed the hope that it would help move things towards 'a community festival event rather than it pertaining to one section of the community'.

7.22 Derry is still, of course, not free from wider tensions. Even as I write, there is news of additional security fencing being erected along the only interface on the west bank. And, in the context of parading itself, there is still insufficient confidence to allow commercial interests in the city to stay open and take full advantage of the influx of people connected with the parades.

7.23 There are community festivals during the summer on the Garvaghy Road and in Ardoyne. It would no doubt be regarded as risible to suggest that Loyal Order parades and festivals such as these could even be spoken of in the same breath or have any connection with each other. But the events of recent years in Derry would have seemed equally improbable in 1969. One has always to remain open to the possibility of being surprised by progress.

7.24 Particulars apart, however, my fundamental point is that unless *both* traditions make a serious attempt to explore together what they have no choice but to regard as a *shared* heritage – to discover together how to remember without replicating – issues such as parades will continue to fester. Deals may be done but the fault lines will be only half-buried. The problem will only be permanently resolved by those on opposite sides of the debate patiently embarking upon a journey of mutual understanding. On all sides, we may have to cast a more wide-angled –

and even sympathetic – look backward in order to be able to move forward. A challenge for the new era is how to accommodate a phenomenon (Orangeism) which prides itself on its Britishness but is also a variety of Irishness.

Forward March

7.25 It is always difficult for any organisation whose roots go deep and which sees the past as a reminder of present dangers to communicate clearly how it relates to the contemporary world in a way which neither betrays itself nor threatens others.

7.26 It might be argued that it is the business of none other than those who espouse Orangeism how it engages with the wider world. I would disagree. Any major institution (and the trade unions and the Press are other obvious examples) has import for the wider society which transcends its own sectional domain. Very relevantly for this Review, parade disputes will become much easier to resolve if 'history on the march' is replaced by an institution which has drawn on its value system to create a *contemporary* Orangeism.

7.27 To illustrate what I mean I have tried to distil, from a book[10] written 35 years ago by luminaries within Orangeism and bearing the imprimatur of the (then) Imperial Grand Master, the essence of what an institution neither betraying its principles nor threatening others might be saying when seeking understanding from those who see only 'history on the march'. Difference per se need not be threatening. AOH lodges proclaimed their distinctive identity in the Resolutions which (according to Press reports) were moved when they held their traditional 15 August demonstration in Donegal town this year: loyalty to the Roman Catholic faith and the peaceful reunification of Ireland.

7.28 The sentences which follow are all derived from the book. Needless to say, there is much more in the book, some of whose polemic is less apt for my purpose.

> The Order are neither bigots nor extremists. They are pledged not to 'injure or upbraid any man because of his religious beliefs'. They stand for tolerance and compassion towards all men, but they stand also for that underlying principle of the Christian faith, the dignity and rights of the individual, against the tyranny either of a soulless state or of an authoritarian Church. It is the duty of Orangemen to support and maintain the laws and constitution. If we lost our constitutional position within the United Kingdom, 'civil and religious liberty for all' would be endangered. This represents the Orange attitude to politics. Orangemen have always been encouraged to recognise the need for a political awareness as responsible members of a free society. An Orangeman recognises the responsibility of political involvement and community service.

> But the Orange Order is pre-eminently a religious organisation. The whole tenor of the movement is religious: by its conditions of membership; by its ritual; by its church services and spiritual affiliations; by its keen interest in the Protestant and evangelical emphases of the Gospel.

This is no Mafia-like brotherhood, no repulsive secret society. The Orange Order has the utmost respect for the rule of law and the Christian ethic. It never condones violence or bigotry. It stands for great principles in faith and conduct. Whilst it accepts the fact that the Protestant religion must be a self-propagating faith it will not deny the same rights to other religious persuasions. There is an abundance of good will on the Orange side.

No large organisation of whatever kind is so perfect that faults cannot be found in it and in its members. The critic who presumes that the Order is blind to its faults is very wrong.

7.29 If this description of Orangeism is still apt, is it adequately reflected in how Orangeism presents itself to – and is perceived by – contemporary society? If not, what needs to be done?

7.30 I hope I shall not be too severely chided for venturing into such territory. I do so in a helpful and constructive spirit. If Orangeism wishes to be better understood, these are the kinds of questions it may want to address – which is not to suggest that in so doing it should be expected to abandon its core beliefs and values. I have been informed by the Grand Orange Lodge of Ireland of its intention to consider in depth the way forward over the next 10 to 20 years. I very much welcome this and believe that it should be applauded on all sides. It would be consistent with the spirit of mutual openness to new possibilities that, in light of developments within Orangeism, those hostile to it would at least be prepared to revisit their perceptions.

7.31 I refer in Chapter 23 to the issue of 'branding'. Brands that excel are created around excellent products. Until people – particularly those not historically predisposed to any sympathy for the Orange brand and who (to continue the figure of speech) are impacted by what they may regard as intrusive and unwelcome 'advertising' in the shape of parades – develop a better understanding of the Loyal Order 'product', the notion of parading as a 'civic endeavour' (to borrow a phrase from the Parades Commission)[11] which enjoys a degree of consensus with those affected by parading is likely to prove elusive.

CHAPTER 9

A VISION FOR THE FUTURE

'Once the concept of "otherness" takes root, the unimaginable becomes possible'.
Slavenka Drakulić

'There is much to do before our pride can move with mercy in its equal stride'.
John Hewitt

9.1 It is generally accepted by those who work in the field of social science that the frame of reference we bring to any problem may lay it more, or less, open to solution. It encapsulates what we assume is valuable and believe is possible.

9.2 It is difficult to see how for Northern Ireland the frame of reference can be other than the plural society, containing many separate interests with a variety of objectives (often divergent) which have to be maintained in some kind of equilibrium if sufficient common purpose is to be achieved. It is not a matter of integrating the various interests. Instead, it is a question of balancing them in a way which gives each the maximum freedom compatible with the general interest of the society as interpreted and articulated by those responsible for its government, with the support of public opinion.

9.3 Such a model implies a multi-cultural society and, functioning effectively, it would also imply no conflict of cultures, which should be complementary rather than competing. But that *could* involve no more than cultural co-habitation – benign apartheid – without the interaction or exchange (inter-culturalism) which might make difference fruitful. It has been suggested that the stark choice in these two types of plural society is between policies based on the acceptance of separation and policies based on the objective of sharing.

9.4 Present reality is not congruent with the plural frame of reference. We are currently opting – whether voluntarily or involuntarily – for separation and confrontation and this choice continues the trend of the past 150 years, when cultural cleavage has been reflected in territorial segregation. We have been well described as sharing a tremendous capacity for congealing into aggressive or defensive blocks. Since the middle of the 19th century, in urban areas most of all and particularly in Belfast, residential segregation (with loyalty to one locality identifying itself in terms of its opposition to another) has been shown to be both a necessary prerequisite for riot and the most popular mechanism for avoiding the sharper penalties of community conflict.[12] It has, of course, proved to be a faulty mechanism. No decade between 1850 and 1940 lacked at least one summer of serious rioting. Violence and the fear of it determined residence preferences. Since segregation increased more in bad times than it reduced in good times, the trend was steadily upwards. In 1999, 71% of public sector housing estates were segregated. Interestingly, 1935–1968 was the longest period in Belfast's history without major riotous confrontations.

9.5 An analysis of the community relations module of the 2001 *Northern Ireland Life and Times Survey* revealed that whilst Protestants and Catholics were slightly more optimistic about community relations than they were 12 years ago, the trend in positive attitudes between 1999 and 2001 was downward and there was also less optimism about the future. It seems a reasonable assumption that these trends would have been strongly reinforced by events of recent months.

9.6 Between 1999 and 2001 there was a steady increase in the desire for single identity communities and a concurrent decrease in the preference for mixed neighbourhoods and, compared with 1989, both communities are now more likely to prefer own religion neighbourhoods. Both Protestants and Catholics are significantly more likely to prefer own religion workplaces. The increasing support between 1989 and 1999 amongst both Protestants and Catholics for mixed religion schools went into reverse between 1999 and 2001.

9.7 The decline in the preference for mixing was sharper in lower occupational groups and within the Protestant community. The response to a question designed to gauge the extent of respect for diversity suggests that Catholics are more likely than Protestants to tolerate cultural expression normally associated with the 'other' community.

9.8 A report of a survey to provide an insight into the cultural and political awareness of young children aged 3 to 6 showed a rapid rate of increase in the proportions of children beginning to identify themselves with one particular community and to make sectarian comments at the ages of 5 (7%) and 6 (15%).

9.9 It is clear that the enforced fraternity at the top, which is the principle informing current arrangements for Government in Northern Ireland and is itself working only imperfectly, has not led to a softening of the sharp edges at community level. Addressing people's inability to live together (or even, peacefully, apart) is the central challenge for our devolved institutions. Otherwise we risk a situation where Northern Ireland (in Professor Edna Longley's words) becomes infinitely devolved, as territorial boundaries are rigidly enforced. Some would see the contention over routes for parades as another aspect of the issue of territoriality.

9.10 Recent trends are in contrast to the results of a survey in 1996,[13] when hopes for a smoother transition to a post-conflict situation were higher. Inter alia, it tested attitudes on the general issue of separation or sharing. A huge majority of both Protestants (80%) and Catholics (94%) chose greater co-operation and sharing in many aspects of their daily lives, whilst only 7% (Protestant) and 2% (Catholics) wanted more separation. When the stakes were increased by seeking views on sharing even at some cost, the Protestant figure was 50% (with separation going up to 24%) whilst the Catholic figure was 70% (with separation going up to 9%). The study concluded that most people wanted Government policy not only to secure equality of treatment and parity of esteem for the two communities but also to ensure that there is choice for those who prefer sharing to separation.

9.11 It is evident that it will be very difficult to achieve consensus around the emotive issue of parading whilst both communities not only consolidate and reinforce the separation which is evident in current trends but also engage in the communal strife which the separateness purports to prevent. The tensions which are adduced as reasons why parades should not take place along certain routes are often attributed to the pervasive pattern of community violence in the locality. To the extent that those who wish to see such parades take place contribute to those tensions, they reduce the prospect of achieving their objective.

9.12 But the relationship between the wider phenomenon of separateness and the parading issue goes deeper than this. It has been argued by those who find parades unwelcome that the parade is the only interest evinced in their locality by the 'other' tradition which the parade represents. This challenges those who seek the ability to parade in all areas as a symbol of cohesiveness to consider what that principle means on a much wider front for the future shaping of a society in Northern Ireland which seeks diversity in dynamic unity.

9.13 I have already suggested in Chapter 7 that *both* communities need to recognise the mixed parentage (in historical terms) of the current generation and take joint ownership of:

'... a history
so complicated, gashed with violence,
split by belief, by blatant pageantry,
that none can safely stir and still feel free,
to voice his hope with any confidence.'[14]

I have also suggested, in Chapter 8, that *both* communities have to meet each others' need to feel secure and respected in their identity.

9.14 The Community Relations Council summed it up well when it said that civil society 'depends on a shared discourse which requires and affirms differences but also allows these to exist in constructive relationships with each other'. That implies the centrality of the notion of interdependence, which requires a recognition by each of their obligations and commitments to the other, leading to the development of a society that is at once cohesive and diverse. People do not need to have a common value system in order to have a common interest. When people are in the same boat, they share an interest in not tipping the boat.

9.15 There is a growing and welcome recognition that within community relations programmes there must be more emphasis on work with single identity groups so that, when intergroup work takes place, those on all sides can perceive themselves as being on an equal footing with others. This is particularly important for any experiencing the nihilism and fatalism which beset those in psychological retreat. A more direct route to cross-community work may simply engage those already most disposed to interact with the 'other' and bypass those most averse to a cross-community agenda. It has been well said that:

> Only when individuals are comfortable with their own group identity and have some sympathy for the position of others, can contact provide a constructive medium through which prejudice, intolerance, and negative social stereotypes are addressed.[15]

9.16 There are obvious dangers in single identity work. People whose definition of themselves is dependent on their suspicion of, or hostility to, others may be reinforced in that tendency and cultural distinctiveness may become even more key to self-esteem. Single identity work needs to challenge people with the question posed by the Very Reverend Dr John Dunlop:

> If we are not prepared to be enriched by proximity to and interaction with people who are different, have we any future here other than in diminished and frozen isolation?

9.17 Intergroup initiatives which are predicated on the prior existence of trust are likely to be still-born, since trust has an opportunity to develop only in the context of relationship. As trust strengthens, the aim should be to create the ability and the will to act collectively for the common good.

9.18 The task is daunting. It was put to me in evidence that more people are 'finding something deep within them that can't stand the other'. I have no doubt that the fault lines revealed by the parades issue are merely part of a complex network of such lines, reflecting a deeply riven society.

9.19 As this Report suggests, much can be done, even in current circumstances, to ease the tensions around that issue. And, of course, to the extent that this is done, it will contribute to the creation of the inter (rather than multi) cultural society which is an imperative for Northern Ireland's well-being. But equally I have no doubt that significant progress on the wider front would produce a much more benign context in which to tackle not only the parades, but many other, issues.

9.20 All – on both sides or none – whether seeking solutions to contentious parades or to a badly fractured and even dysfunctional society, are unlikely to get far without a vision of an inclusive, open, tolerant, compassionate society whose members have the self-confidence to embrace diversity and thrive on difference.

Notes

1. *The Shape of Irish History* (Belfast: Blackstaff Press, 2001), p. 186.
2. The origins of the Orange parading culture as ritual social behaviour can be traced back to the first birthday of William III after the Battle of the Boyne, celebrated in Dublin on 4 November 1690. Throughout the 18th century (and not least during the period of the Volunteer movement which ante-dated the formation of the Orange Order in 1795) it was the King's role in the Glorious Revolution rather than his military campaign that was commemorated, although it was not long before there were separate celebrations linked to the famous battles. Celebrations in this latter mould soon eclipsed the more inclusive Williamite vision of early Orangeism, although as late as 1805, Dr William Drennan, Ulster Presbyterian progenitor with Wolfe Tone of the United Irishmen, could comment severely when King William's statue was disfigured in Dublin, that 'to make his statue an instigation of bigotry is to disgrace his memory, for he was one of the best of men' (*The Drennan McTier letters*, Vol. III, ed. J. Agnew (1999), p. 388).
3. I. Budge and C. O'Leary, *Belfast Approach to Crisis* (London: St Martin's Press, 1973).
4. Marianne Elliott, *The Catholics of Ulster* (London: Allen Lane, 2000), p. 265.
5. K. T. Hoppen, *Ireland since 1800, Conflict and Conformity*, 2nd edition (London: Longman, 1999), pp. 137–38.
6. *The Catholics of Ulster.*
7. Frank Wright, *Northern Ireland: A Comparative Analysis* (Lanham, MD: Rowman and Littlefield, 1987), p. 158.
8. Hoppen, *Ireland since 1800*, p. 1.
9. *News@the Forum*, Issue 3, Spring.
10. M. W. Dewar, J. Brown and S. E. Long, *Orangeism* (Belfast: Grand Orange Lodge of Ireland, 1967).
11. Third Annual Report, p. 15.
12. A. C. Hepburn, *A Past Apart: Studies in the History of Catholic Belfast, 1850–1950* (Belfast: Ulster Historical Association, 1996).
13. T. Hadden, C. Irwin and F. Boal, *Separation or Sharing* (1996).
14. *The Collected Poems of John Hewitt*, ed. F. Ormsby (Belfast: Blackstaff Press, 1991).
15. J. Hughes, 'Community Relations in Northern Ireland: Lessons from Drumcree', *Journal of Ethnic and Migration Studies*, 24(3), pp. 433–50.

Index

Act of Union 105, 140
Ad Hoc Congressional Committee for Irish
    Affairs 78
Ad Hoc Liaison Committee (AHLC) 62
Adams, Gerry
    ceasefire 37
    Clinton 36, 37, 38
    decommissioning 129, 170
    Good Friday Agreement 107, 131, 172
    Gore talks 39
    Hume talks 35, 102, 103
    IRA scepticism towards 41
    managed IRA disengagement 210
    Mitchell 36
    suspension of Executive 130
    unionists 39
    US visas 36–8, 74, 76–7, 79, 84, 103
Agreement see Good Friday Agreement
Ahern, Bertie 42, 90, 91, 105, 118, 131, 132
AHLC see Ad Hoc Liaison Committee
Ahtisaari, Maarti 42
Ala, Abu 54, 56, 57, 59, 61
American Brands case 82–4
Americans for a New Irish Agenda 72–3,
    74
ANC 45–53
Anderson, Benedict 134
Anglo-Irish Agreement (1985) 124–8
    Anglo-Irish support 70–1
    consent principle 102, 104, 105, 106
    exclusive approach 128
    Good Friday Agreement 8, 90, 105, 117,
        126–7
    Irish government 32, 125
    justice administration 126
    SDLP 114
    Sinn Féin 114
    text 228–33

Thatcher 32–3
three-strand approach 102–3
unionists 102–3, 126
US 70–1, 81, 103
Anglo-Irish conflict, pre 1921 Treaty 167
Anglo-Irish Ministerial Council 102
Anglo-Irish settlement (1920–1) 7, 117
Annesley, Hugh 40–1
anti-Catholic discrimination 35, 79
    see also MacBride Principles
apartheid 46–7, 47–8
Apprentice Boys parades 162
Arafat, Yasser 12–13, 34, 54, 57, 59, 62
armed struggle
    political alternative 65–6, 67, 110, 134,
        162
    see also conflict resolution
arms crisis (1970) 112–13
arms decommissioning see
    decommissioning
Army Council, IRA 113, 131, 168
Arthur, Paul 1, 9–10, 147–56
Asfour, Hassan 56
the Assembly 106, 107, 129, 144
Aughey, Arthur 145

'back channel' approaches 60, 128
Ballymena, parades 162
Barth, Karl 18
Bean, Kevin 8–9, 133–46
Beilin, Yossi 55
Belfast Agreement see Good Friday
    Agreement
Bell, J. Bowyer 136, 149
Bill of Rights, support for 90
Birmingham Six 5, 69
Blair, Tony
    Ahern 118, 131

Good Friday Agreement 42, 90, 91, 104, 105
  Omagh bomb 94
  Unionists 35
Blaney, Neil 112
Bloody Sunday 99, 158
Bloomfield Commission (1998) 276–9
Bogside 158
bomb-making knowledge 166
Botha, P.W. 46, 47–8, 49, 50
Breuilly, John 135
Brink, André 147, 154, 155
British cultural attitudes to Irish 180
British demilitarization 131, 132, 133
British government
  channels of communication 7
  containment strategies 143
  counter-insurgency initiatives 142
  former Yugoslavia 64
  Irish government 131
  on Irish-American/Irish relations 69
  MacBride Campaign 81
  republicans 115, 153
  role in Irish affairs 130, 137
  security forces 101, 112, 125, 142
  Ulster Unionist Party 116
  US relations 73–4, 78–9, 83, 89–90
  see also Good Friday Agreement
British intelligence 35, 113, 142
British security forces 101, 125, 142
British troops, arrival 112
British-Irish Council 8, 127
Britishness 176, 185
Brooke, Peter 35, 102, 115, 153
Bruton, John 38, 39
Buckland, Patrick 3
Burgess, Paul 182
Burke, Edmund 18
Buruma, Ian 150
Bush, George 27, 34, 72, 73–4
Buthelezi, Mangosuthu 52

Canary Wharf *see* Docklands bombing
Carter, Jimmy 32, 34, 113, 153, 193
'Castle Catholics' 84
Catholic Church 176, 180, 184
Catholic Gael 183–6
Catholics
  attitudes towards Protestants 179–81
  emancipation 34

middle class 9, 103, 133, 138, 142–3, 144
  population statistics 99, 178, 179
ceasefires
  Combined Loyalist Military Command 168, 169
  Good Friday Agreement 21, 172
  IRA
    Adams and 37
    breakdown (1996) 42, 116, 130, 169
    first (1994) 74–5, 130, 133, 162, 168–9, 186
    Irish America 68–9, 74–5
    restoration (1997) 104, 169
    as strategy 103
    US facilitation 69, 103
Celtic Tiger 107
census (1991) 183
channels of communication 7, 51–2, 54–66, 151
Chastelain, General John de
  Good Friday Agreement 42, 154
  International Body for Decommissioning 40, 124, 129
  IRA 114, 124
Church of Rome *see* Catholic Church
Civic Forum 105
civic identity 135
civic nationalism 134–5
civic republicanism 133–4
civil order 90
civil rights movement (Northern Ireland) 99, 111–12, 163
civil society 17, 19, 20, 143
civil war, Irish (1922–3) 167
'Clausewitz in reverse' 159, 162
Clinton, Bill
  Adams visa 36–7, 77
  decommissioning 39
  former Yugoslavia 27–8
  Good Friday Agreement 6, 91–2
  involvement in Irish question 5, 34–5, 72, 73–4, 153
  IRA ceasefire 103
  Irish-Americans for Clinton group 72–3
  MacBride Principles 84–5
  Middle East mediation 61
  Omagh bomb 94, 154
  Trimble 39, 77
  visits to Northern Ireland 40, 77, 116

Cochrane, Fergal 162
Collins, Michael 129
Combined Loyalist Military Command
    168, 169
communal identity 150
communist regimes, collapse of 48–9
compromise 18, 93, 96–108, 131, 139–40
concluding negotiations, means of 19
conflict resolution
    clear moral choice 46–7
    communist regimes collapse 48–9
    conducive factors 18–20, 46–9, 92–4
    conflict life span 151
    costs of domination 47–8
    engagement of surrounding countries
        33
    impartial body involvement 40
    international climate 47
    internationalization 25–43
    loneliness of leadership 50–1
    minor parties role 52–3
    negotiators' qualities 41, 51–2
    Norwegian peace facilitations 54–66
    politics of deadlock 49
    reconciliation 147–56
    transformation 147, 150
consent principle 102, 104, 105, 106
consociational democracy 160
constitution
    changes to Irish 105, 120, 125–7, 130–1,
        208–9
    Constitutional Convention 101
    liberal democratic 45
    Royal Commission on 148
Corrigan, Mairead 149
cost-benefit reasoning 22
costs of domination 47–8
Coulter, Colin 207–20
Council, Orange Order 165
Council of Ireland 100, 120
Council of the Isles 8, 127
counter-insurgency 138
Cox, Harvey 1, 9, 157–74
criminal justice system 122, 127
cultural attitudes 135, 180
cultural equality 133
cultural nationalism 135
culture, identity and 176
culture of peace 171
culture of tolerance 155

Darby, John 148–9
Dayton Peace Accords (1995) 26, 28, 29,
    40, 64
De Klerk, Frederick William 45, 46, 48–9,
    50, 53
deadlock 40, 44–5, 49, 66, 101–2
death toll 119, 155, 164, 169, 171
Declaration of Mutual Recognition 54
Declaration of Principles (Middle East
    conflict) 12–13, 54–5, 61
decommissioning
    Adams and 129, 170
    bomb-making knowledge 166
    crucial issue 130–1, 145, 161, 167
    discussion issue (1995) 38–9, 40
    framework 106, 117, 155
    fudge of 129–30
    Good Friday Agreement 130–1
    impossibility of 170
    International Body for
        Decommissioning 5–6, 40–1, 124,
        129, 147–8
    international initiatives 40, 41, 42–3
    international inspection 117
    IRA reluctance 132, 168, 172
    Major and 41
    Mandelson on 7, 119, 122
    Mitchell Report 147–8
    Sinn Féin 9, 39, 42, 130, 170
    Unionists 107
    US 39, 40
    see also Chastelain; Mitchell
Decree on Ecumenism, Vatican Council
    (1964) 193
Defence Forces, Ireland 109
demilitarization, British 131, 132, 133
democracy, consociational 160
Democratic Unionist Party (DUP) 41, 100,
    106, 120, 173, 178, 207, 209, 210
    increase in votes 210–11
demographic 'solution' 99
de Valera, Eamon 34, 97, 111, 209
devolution, Scottish and Welsh 127, 173
dialogue 114, 151–2
diplomacy 60, 65, 109, 110, 153
Direct Rule 99, 98, 99, 104, 105
discrimination, anti-Catholic 35, 79
Docklands bombing (1996) 41, 130, 168,
    169
Doherty, Patrick 80, 81, 83, 85

domination, economic costs 47–8
Donlon, Sean 68, 69
double minority model 98–9, 104
Downing Street Joint Declaration (1993)
  draft 115
  Good Friday Agreement 90, 131, 153
  internationalization prior to 33
  Irish Government 7, 177
  negotiations 7, 36, 126
  text 249–53
  Trimble 39
drugs scene 169
Drumcree 103, 116, 157–9, 162–5, 210,
  211, 216
Duigan, Sean 167–8
Dukakis, George 83
DUP *see* Democratic Unionist Party

Easter Rising (1916) 111, 137, 166
economic assistance, international 61–2, 65
economic development 107
economy
  potential of 20–3
  racketeering 170
education, integration 176
Education Act (1947) 99
Education for Mutual Understanding
  programme 182
Edwards, John 81
Egeland, Jan 3–4, 33, 54–66
Elliott, Marianne 1–10, 175–91, 240–5
employment 94, 179, 183, 186
  see also MacBride Principles
Enniskillen 114
equality
  agenda 10, 162, 168
  cultural 133
Equality Commission, Northern Ireland
  121
Errera, Roger 150
Ervine, David 75
Erwin, Alec 45
ethnic cleansing 26
ethnic conflicts, prevention 29–30
ethnic identity 135
ethnic nationalism 134, 136, 144
EU *see* European Union
Europe, United States of 15–16
European Social Fund 143
European Union (EU) 15–16, 27–9, 40, 154

exclusive approach 68–9, 100, 128, 131
  see also Anglo-Irish Agreement
Executive Council of Ireland 100–1, 107
  see also Joint Executive
expulsions, UDP and Sinn Féin 91, 115–16

Fair Employment Commission 100
Fair Employment (Northern Ireland) Acts
  79, 81, 85
Faulkner, Brian 32, 100, 101
Faulkner, William 16, 118
Feeney, 'Chuck' 36
Fianna Fáil 35, 111, 114, 116, 130
Fisher, Richard 96
Fitt, Gerry 69, 99, 101
Fitzgerald, Dr Garret 8, 32–3, 70, 80,
  124–5, 129
Flannery, Michael 70
Foley, Michael 155
Foley, Thomas 73, 78
former Yugoslavia *see* Yugoslavia
Forum for Peace and Reconciliation
  115–16
fragment societies 98
Framework Document (1995) 19–20, 116,
  153, 254–64
Free Presbyterians 177
Friends of Ireland group, US Congress 69
fundraising, US for IRA 38–9

Gael, Catholic 183–5
Gallagher, Eric 1, 188, 245–8
Galvin, Martin 82
Gardaí 109
Garvaghy road 162, 163
Garvin, Tom 136
Gaza 54, 56, 58, 59, 61
Gellner, Ernest 134, 135, 136
Gibney, Jim 139
Ginifer, Jeremy 13–14
Glencree Conference 193
Glenstal Conference 193
Goldin, Comptroller Harrison J. 79–80,
  82, 85
Good Friday Agreement (1998)
  Adams 107, 131
  ambiguities (deliberate) 158
  Anglo-Irish Agreement 8, 90, 105, 117,
    127–8
  The Assembly 105, 106, 107, 129, 144

British government 7, 42, 90–1, 104,
    105, 119–32
  ceasefires 21
  concessions 105, 167
  decommissioning 130–1
  Democratic Unionist Party 100, 106,
    106
  Downing Street Declaration 90, 131,
    153
  electoral support 42, 92, 95, 171
  Goodall on 8, 124–32
  implementation 21–2, 93, 117–18,
    154–5, 157–74
  Irish government 42, 90, 91, 105, 117–8
  Mandelson on 119–23
  Mitchell on 42, 89–95, 117
  names used for 96, 151
  nationalist middle class benefits 133
  nationality 104–8, 137
  North-South dimension 117–18, 133
  Orange Order 107
  peace *process* 169
  republicanism 137, 144
  RUC 106, 130, 155
  SDLP 105, 106, 107, 127–8
  Shirlow and Coulter on 207–20
  Sinn Féin 105, 107, 128, 131, 139, 172
  steps towards 153
  Sunningdale 107, 114
  suspension of institutions 119, 122, 124,
    129, 130, 145
  text 265–75
  Trimble 106, 107
  unionists 105–7, 132, 159
  US 6, 91–2
  weaknesses 159
Goodall, David 8, 124–32
Gorbachev, President Mikhail 47
Gore, Al 38
Government of Ireland Act (1920) 105,
    120
grass roots 161, 187
grievance mentality 180
Groote Schuur Minute 44
Group of Seven 18, 22
Guildford Four 5, 69
Gulf War (1990–91) 55, 72

Hani, Chris 49, 51
Harnden, Toby 158, 166

Hartley, Tom 139
Haughey, Charles 5, 68, 69, 70–1, 113–14
Hayes, Maurice 6, 10, 96–108, 169
Heaney, Seamus 9, 108, 149, 151–2, 171
Heath, Edward 35, 100, 119
Heathrow airport, mortar bombing 5, 38
Hewitt, John 97–8
Hillsborough Agreement *see* Anglo-Irish
    Agreement
Hirschfeld, Yair 55, 56, 57
Hobsbawm, Eric 134
Holkerri, Harri 40, 42
Holst, Johan 54, 59
Holy Cross dispute 210, 211, 213, 217,
    218
Home Rule 118
Horgan, John 97
Hughes, Brendan 133
Human Rights Commission, Northern
    Ireland 100, 121
Human Rights for Ireland Day (1978) 72
Hume, John
  Adams talks 35, 102, 103
  early involvement 112, 137
  on grievance mentality 180
  hopes for future 154
  IRA talks 114
  Irish government 125
  MacBride Principles 78, 80
  Major government 35
  Nobel peace award 39, 149, 152
  Sinn Féin talks 126
  Sunningdale 100
  US talks 40, 76
hunger strikes 9, 70–1, 102, 113, 137

identity
  civic 135
  communal 150
  culture 176
  ethnic 135
  Irish national 134
  politics of 135, 139–40, 161
  religion and 175–91, 192–206
  shared Northern Irish, little capacity for
    219
identity politics, Orange Order 162
imagined community 134
immigration from Eastern Europe 173
immigration to US (illegal) 71

implementation
  Good Friday Agreement 21–2, 93,
    117–18, 154–5
  Oslo Accords 60–1, 64–5
inclusive approach 68–72, 102, 127–8, 129,
    154
  see also Good Friday Agreement
institutional memory 65
integration
  educational 176
  pluralistic 105
intelligence services
  British 35, 113, 142
  Irish government 109
inter-church groups 192–206
Intergovernmental Conference 8, 126, 127
International Body for Decommissioning
    5–6, 39–40, 124, 129, 147–8
international economic assistance 61–2, 65
International Year for the Culture of Peace
    171
internationalization 25–43
investment, Northern Ireland 20–3
IRA/Provisional IRA 35, 36, 81, 113, 167
  Army Council 113, 131, 168
  'back channel' approach 128
  Border campaign (1956–62) 79
  Chastelain Commission 114, 124
  civil rights movement 99
  cross-border security 125
  de Valera's Irish Republican Army 34
  decommissioning 114, 124, 132, 168,
    170, 172, 173
  direct public approaches to 114
  Docklands bombing 41–2, 116, 130,
    168, 169
  Hume's attempt to meet 114
  Irish government 111
  Irish-America 68–9, 74–5
  Noraid 68, 70, 80, 81, 103
  Real IRA 167
  Sinn Féin 34, 41, 42, 103, 128–30, 140,
    166, 168
  Ulster heartlands 166
  US 38–9, 68–9, 74–5, 103
  see also ceasefires
Ireland, MacBride Principles acceptance
    70
Irish, British cultural attitudes towards
    180–1

Irish America
  Adams visas 76–7
  Clinton 72–3, 73–4
  failures to intervene 78–9
  financial support 130
  hunger-strikes' effects on 70–1
  illegal immigration 71
  IRA ceasefire 68–9, 74–5
  MacBride campaign 5–6, 70, 73, 78–88
  mobilisation factors 84–5
  'outside the box' theory 74–5, 77
  peace process role 67–77, 78–88
  pre-1900s 67–9
  Sinn Féin 68–9, 77
Irish civil war (1922–23) 167
Irish Constitution changes 105, 106, 120,
    125–7, 130–1
the Irish dimension 100, 120, 124, 125–7
Irish Free State 34
Irish government
  British government 131
  constitutional change 105, 106, 120,
    125–7, 130–1
  Downing Street Declaration 7, 177
  economics 21
  hunger-strikes 70
  illegal emigration to US 71
  intelligence services 109
  IRA 111
  'Irish dimension' 100, 120, 124, 125–7
  Northern Ireland relations 19–20, 33,
    100
  Opsahl Commission 177
  peace process role 110–11, 117–18, 120,
    124–5
  Sinn Féin 114
  Sunningdale 100
  Unionists 36, 125
Irish Immigration Reform Movement (US)
    71
Irish Inter-Church Meeting 194–5
Irish National Caucus 78, 79, 81
Irish Republic, discussion on Catholic
    Church 177
Irish Republican Army *see* IRA
Irish School of Ecumenics 195
Irish unity 124
Irish-America
  Anglo-Irish Agreement 103
  initiative (1975) 34

Irish government 70–1
  leaders 36
  pressure on Britain 138
Irish-Americans for Clinton group 72–3
Irishness 176–7, 184, 186–7

Jackson, Harold 98–9
Joint Executive
  inclusive approach 129
  power-sharing 119, 165
  resumption of 131–2
  Sinn Féin participation 144
  suspension 119, 122, 129, 130
  Unionists 107, 165
Jowett, Benjamin 119
Juul, Mona 55, 58–9

Kavanagh, Patrick 148
Keenan, Brian 167
Kennedy, Edward 68, 69, 71, 73, 76
Kingsmill massacre 9, 152
Kinsella, Thomas 96–7
Kissinger, Henry 14, 27, 32
Kostunica, President 29
Kundera, Milan 147
Kyle, Keith 99

Lake, Tony 38
Large, Judith 160–1
Larsen, Terje R. 55, 58–9
leadership 50–1, 160–2, 166
Lijphart, Arend 159–60
Logue, Ken 182
'the long war' strategy 137, 140, 150
Longley, Edna 181
Longley, Michael 108
Lower Ormeau road 162, 163
loyalist paramilitaries 6, 102
loyalist parties 102, 106
  see also Democratic Unionist Party,
    Progressive Unionist Party, Ulster
    Unionist Party

MacBride Principles
  campaign 5–6, 78–88
  governments' responses 70, 73, 80–1
  legality in Northern Ireland 83–4
McCrone, David 135
McGimpsey, Dr Chris 184
McGuinness, Martin 41, 129, 131, 168

McKittrick, David 183
McLaughlin, Michael 139–40
McManus, Father Sean 79, 80, 81–2, 85
McNamara, Kevin 78–88
MacNeice, Louis 147
MacSwiney, Terence 150
Maduna, Penual 46
Maginnis, Ken 35, 39
Maharaj, Mac 46
Major, John
  autobiography 33
  criticisms of 104
  decommissioning 41–2
  Framework Document 116
  Hume relations 35
  Kurdish refugee crisis 25
  US relations 34–5, 39, 72, 73–4, 103
Mallon, Seamus 119, 137, 159, 169
Mandela, Nelson 4, 45–53, 147
Mandelson, Peter 7–8, 117, 119–23, 165
Mansergh, Martin 6–7, 109–18
marriage, mixed 178
Marxism 137
Maryfield Secretariat 102
Mayhew, Patrick 40, 101, 103–4, 115, 116,
    128, 153
Mazen, Abu 57, 62
Mbeki, Thabo 51
Melucci, A. 144
memory 10, 16–17, 65, 107, 147–56, 180
Meyer, Roelf 51–2
Miall, Hugh 159, 166
middle-class Catholics 9, 103, 133, 138,
    142–3, 144
Middle East conflict
  Clinton involvement 61
  Declaration of Principles 12–13, 54–5,
    61
  journalism 60
  peace negotiations 4, 12–14, 54–62
  PLO dual functionality 16
military strategy, British 142
Milosevic, Slobodan 26–7, 29
minor parties, role 52–3
minority, double 98–9
Mitchell, George
  Adams 36
  appointment 85
  Clinton 36
  economic advisor 38, 77

Framework Document 116
Good Friday Agreement 42, 89–95, 117
International Body for
    Decommissioning 5–6, 39–40,
    147–8
Making Peace 33
significance of role 154
Molloy, Francie 139
Molyneaux, Jim 35, 38–9
Monnet, Jean 15–16
moral clarity 46–7, 182
Morrison visas 71
Mowlam, Mo 42

Nairn, Tom 135
nation, origin of modern idea 134–5
nationalism 134–5, 139–40, 183
nationalist movements, 19th and 20th
    century 134
Nationalist Party (NP), South Africa 45, 46,
    47, 52, 53
nationality, overlap model 99, 104
NATO 26–9
negotiators 18–19, 51–2, 60
New Deal 143
New Ireland Forum 114
new nationalism 133, 141–4
New Sinn Féin 141–5
NGOs 62–3, 65, 154
Nixon, Richard 14–15
Nobel awards 50, 149, 152, 170
non-coercion principle 111
Noraid 68, 70, 80, 81, 82, 103
Nordstrom, Carolyn 153
North-South dimension 117–18, 133
North-South Ministerial Council 117–18
Northern Ireland conference, US 76–7
Northern Ireland Economic Council 17
Northern Ireland Growth Challenge 17
Northern Ireland Victims Commission
    (text) 235–9
Norwegian peace facilitations 54–66
    see also Olso Accords
NP *see* Nationalist Party, South Africa
Nye, John 153

O'Brien, Conor Cruise 38, 134
O'Clery, Conor 33, 103
O'Connell, Daniel 34
O'Dowd, Niall 1, 5, 36, 67–77

O'Dwyer, Paul 68, 73
O'Fiaich, Cardinal 114
Omagh bomb (1998) 6, 94, 154, 164, 167,
    170–1, 216
O'Neill, Tip 78
O'Neill, Terence 186
Opsahl Commission (1993) 5, 10, 39,
    175–91, 234–48
Orange Order
    Birmingham Six case 69
    Council 164
    Drumcree marches 103, 116, 157–9,
        162–4
    Good Friday Agreement 107
    identity politics 162
    membership 178
    parades 157–8, 161, 162–5
    Ulster Unionist Party 165
Oslo Accords 153
    'back channel' advantages 60
    Guatemala 63
    international economic assistance 61–2
    Middle East 54–62, 65
    Oslo II 61, 62
'outside the box' theory 74–5, 77
overlap of nationality model 99, 104
Owen, David 1, 3, 4–5, 25–43, 64

Paisley, Ian 41, 42, 172, 178, 209–10
Palestinians
    Ad Hoc Liaison Committee 62
    Oslo Peace Accord 54–5
parades 9, 70, 157–8, 161, 162–5
Parnell, Charles Stewart 34
Partition 34, 97, 105, 139
Patten Report (1999) 6, 118, 127, 132,
    280–95
Patterson, Henry 133
peace-building by inter-church groups
    192–206
Peaceline Ecumenical Communities
    (Belfast) 197–204
the Peace People 149
peace process
    hidden challenges 109–18
    leaders and grassroots 160–1
    research 159
Peace and Reconciliation Fund 143
peace walls, Belfast 6, 93–4, 188, 196–7
Peres, Shimon 13–14, 54, 56–9, 62

PLO 12–14, 16, 54–5
   see also Middle East conflict
pluralistic integration 105
policing reform 100, 106, 117, 121–2, 155,
   208
   see also PSNI; RUC
political alternative to armed struggle
   68–9, 70, 114, 138, 165
politics
   cultural nationalism 135
   of deadlock 49
   healthy 17
   of identity 135, 139–40, 162
   political sub-elites 160
   postmodern 136, 141
   realism 18
   of violence 148–9
population percentages, Catholic and
   Protestant 98–9, 179
Portadown 159, 163
Portadown Orange Order 157–8
post-ideological politics 136, 141
post-republicanism 133–46
postmodern politics 136, 141
Power, Maria 2, 192–206
power-sharing 6, 100–1, 119, 160, 165, 172,
   173, 179, 188
Presbyterian Church in Ireland 83
principle of consent 102, 104, 106, 107
Prior Assembly 114
prisoner release 105, 107, 117, 122, 130,
   155
Progressive Unionist Party 39, 165
proportional representation 100
Propositions Document (1998) 116
Protestants
   attitudes towards Catholics 176–9
   Britishness 176, 185
   Catholic attitudes to 179–81
   population percentage 98–9, 179
   social attitudes 181
   Ulster 185
Provisionalism 133, 136–7, 138
   see also republicanism
PSNI (Police Service of Northern Ireland)
   creation of 208
Pundak, Ron 56
punishment attacks 215
Putin, Vladimir 31

Quigley, George 1, 2, 3, 11–24, 296–305

Rabin, Yitzhak 34, 54, 56–8, 62
race-memory 10
racketeering 169
Ramaphosa, Cyril 42, 45, 51–2
Rambouillet Conference (1999) 27
rapprochement policy 111–12
Reagan, Ronald 47, 72, 81
Real IRA 134, 132, 166–7
reconciliation 12, 29, 108, 139, 147–56
Record of Understanding (South Africa)
   44, 51
referenda 106–7, 127, 165
Reid, Fr Alex 114
religion, identity and 175–91
Renwick, Robin 38
the Republic *see* Irish government
republic, 32-county 137, 184
republicanism 8–9, 69, 133–46, 153, 168
Review of the Parades Commission
   (Quigley)
   text 296–305
Reynolds, Albert 35, 76, 114–16, 167–8
Rhodesia 5, 13–14, 31–2, 37
right-wing parties, South Africa 53
rights-based arguments 19
Rose, Richard 97
Royal Commission on the Constitution 148
RUC (Royal Ulster Constabulary)
   on decommissioning 41
   dissolution of 208
   Good Friday Agreement 106, 130, 155
   Patten Report 6, 118, 127, 132, 240–56
   republicans on 133
   see also policing reform

St Andrews Agreement 85
sanctions 31–2, 47, 64
Sands, Bobby 9, 70, 166
Savir, Uri 54, 57, 59, 61
Scarman, Lord 99
SDLP
   Anglo-Irish Agreement 114
   electoral support 125, 126, 211
   Good Friday Agreement 105, 106, 107,
   127–8, 172, 209
   Sinn Féin 102, 114, 136–7, 144, 153, 172
   Unionists 103
secret societies, 19th century 111

sectarianism 107, 182–3, 207–20
Security Council Resolutions 25, 26, 27, 47, 58
security forces, British 102, 112, 125, 142
segregation (Belfast) 207–20
  increasing 183
self-determination 114, 117
Separate Development, South Africa 46, 47–8
Shankill road 179, 183
  housing intimidation 218
Shirlow, Peter 1, 207–20
shooting and bombing incidents (Belfast) 217–18
Singer, Joel 58
Sinn Féin/Provisional Sinn Féin 81–2, 113, 140–1
  Anglo-Irish Agreement 114
  community focus 140
  decommissioning 9, 39, 42–3, 130, 169, 172
  dialogues with 104
  educational integration 176
  election victory (1918) 111
  electoral strength 126, 129, 137–8, 140–1, 211
  Fianna Fáil 114, 116, 130
  fund raising 38–9
  Good Friday Agreement 105, 107, 128, 139, 172
  Hume 126
  IRA 34, 42, 102–3, 128–30, 166, 168, 172
  Irish government 114
  Irish-America 68–9, 77
  Joint Executive 144
  middle-class constituency 9
  new nationalism 136–7
  New Sinn Féin 141–5
  parades issue 161–2, 165
  as political force 77, 113, 125, 140–1
  SDLP 8, 102, 114, 136–7, 144, 153, 172
  temporary expulsion 91, 116–7
  transformist principles 133
  Trimble relations 117–18
  unionism 103, 139
  US delegation 75
Slabbert, Frederik Van Zyl 3–4, 34, 44–53
Slovo, Joe 51
Smyth, Rev Martyn 69

social attitudes, comparison 181–3
socialist republic, 32-county 137, 184
socio-economic change 142–3
Soderberg, Nancy 73–4, 76–7
Somme, Battle of 164
South Africa
  ANC 45–53
  apartheid 46–7, 47–8
  factors conducive to negotiations 46–9
  free elections (1994) 154
  international acceptance 153
  lessons from 4
  Mont Fleur Project 151
  negotiations 44–53
  Tri-Cameral Parliament 48, 50
  Truth and Reconciliation Commission 12, 108, 155
South African Communist Party 45, 50
South Armagh 158
sovereignty, European pooling of 104
Soviet Union 30, 47, 48–9
Spence, Gusty 75
Spring, Dick 39, 80, 81
stereotypes 10, 182
Stoltenberg, Thorvald 55
Stormont 99, 101, 105, 133
sub-elites, political activists 160
Sullivan Principles 79, 80
Sunningdale Agreement (1973)
  failure 7, 119–21, 124, 126, 159
  Good Friday Agreement 107, 114
  Hume 100
  Irish government 100
  policing reform 100
  power-sharing 6
  sustainability 32
  text 223–7
suspension
  institutions 124, 145
  Joint Executive 119, 122, 129, 130

Taylor, John 35
terrorist attacks (New York, Madrid, Bali, London) 173
Thatcher, Margaret 35, 70, 72, 113–14, 125
third party facilitation 5–6, 45, 54–66
three-strand approach 102–3
Todd, Jennifer 133–4
tolerance 155, 178–9
Tone, Theobald Wolfe 111, 184, 186

Toolis, Kevin 166
tradition 121, 122, 134, 163
transcendence, acts of 151–3
transformational change 9–24, 16, 133, 150
transformist principles, Sinn Féin 133
transitions 140, 145, 170
    see also South Africa, negotiations in
Tri-Cameral Parliament, South Africa 48,
    50
Trimble, David
    Downing Street Declaration 39
    Good Friday Agreement 106, 107
    Joint Executive 165
    Major government 35, 36
    Nobel peace prize 39, 149, 152
    pressure on leadership 131, 132, 165–6,
        170, 172, 210
    Sinn Féin exclusion 117–18
    US 39, 75, 77
troops, arrival of British 112
trust 17, 44, 60, 62, 65, 68
Truth and Reconciliation Commission 12,
    108, 155
Two Track diplomacy 153

UKUP, Good Friday Agreement 106–7
Ulster, IRA heartlands in 166
Ulster Catholics 183–4
Ulster Democratic Party (UDP) 39, 91
Ulster Protestants 185
Ulster Scots 186
Ulster Unionist Party (UUP)
    Adams visa 39
    British government 116, 209
    divisions in 164
    Good Friday Agreement 106, 127–8,
        131, 172
    Irishness 184
    non-coercion principle 111
    Orange Order 164
    political eclipse 172, 173, 211
Ulster Volunteer Force (UVF) 75
UN
    Charter 25
    former Yugoslavia 64
    NATO 27
    Norwegian peace facilitations 62
    Protection Force, Croatia 26
    Security Council Resolutions 25, 26, 27,
        47, 58

unemployment 94, 179, 183, 186
Union, Act of 105, 125, 140
unionism
    divided nature of 160, 162
    legitimacy of 139
Unionist Council 170
Unionists
    Adams visa to US 39
    Anglo-Irish Agreement 102–3, 126
    community endorsement of Agreement
        159
    decommissioning demands 106, 107
    Framework Document 116
    Good Friday Agreement 105–7, 132,
        159
    Irish government 36, 125
    Major government 35–6
    nationalism 139–40
    Pro-agreement 165
    Republicans' attitudes to 139
    SDLP 103
    Sinn Féin 103, 139
    Thatcher government 35
    see also Orange Order
United Ireland 34, 99, 100, 133, 208
United Irishmen 111
United Nations *see* UN
United States Advisory Commission on
    Public Diplomacy 153
United States of America *see* USA
United States of Europe 15–16
USA
    Adams visas 36–8, 74, 76–7, 79, 84–5,
        103
    American South 16
    Anglo-Irish Agreement 70–1, 81, 103
    British government 73–4, 78–9, 83,
        89–90
    ceasefires 69, 103
    conflict resolution involvement 40
    decommissioning 39, 40
    former Yugoslavia 27–8
    Good Friday Agreement 6, 91–2
    Hume talks 40, 76
    immigration to 71
    impeachment debate 89
    IRA 38–9, 103
    Irish-America 67–77
    MacBride Principles 78–88
    Northern Ireland conference 76–7

PLO 55
Rhodesian conflict 32
Sinn Féin 75
Soviet Union 47
state department 55, 78–9
Trimble 39, 75, 77
see also Irish America
UUP *see* Ulster Unionist Party
UVF *see* Ulster Volunteer Force

Vance Plan 26, 29
Vargo, Trina 75
victimhood 147–8, 150
victims 155, 179, 276–9
Viljoen, General Constand 52, 53
violence 93, 101, 118, 148–9, 153, 214–19
visas
    Adams US 36–8, 74, 76–7, 79, 84–5, 103
    Morrison 71

Waldmeier, Patti 50
Welsh, D. 49

warlordism 167, 170
weapons decommissioning *see*
    decommissioning
Whitelaw, William (Willie) 100, 113
Whyte, John 158
Williams, Betty 149
Wilson, Harold 148
Women's Coalition 105
Wright, Billy 91
Wright, Frank 148
Wyschogrod, Edith 151–2

Yeltsin, Boris 30, 31
Young Unionists 107
former Yugoslavia
    British involvement 64
    EU involvement 27–8
    NATO involvement 26–9
    Norwegian peace facilitations 64
    UN involvement 64
    US involvement 27–8